ADMINISTRATIVE LITIGATION SYSTEMS IN GREATER CHINA AND EUROPE

The Rule of Law in China and Comparative Perspectives

Series Editors:
Yuwen Li, Erasmus University Rotterdam, The Netherlands
Fu Hualing, University of Hong Kong, Hong Kong

There is no doctrine more effective than the rule of law in portraying the complex transformation of Chinese society from the rule of men towards the rule of law – a process inaugurated in post-Mao China which is continuing to advance legal reforms to the present day. In other parts of the world, striving for the rule of law is also evident: countries in transition face a similar mission, while the developed democratic countries are forced to tackle new challenges in retaining the high benchmark of the rule of law that has been established.

Research on the legal system in China and in comparison with other countries in the framework of the rule of law covers broad topics of public and private law, substantive law and procedural law, citizens' rights and law enforcement by courts. Based on this broad understanding of the rule of law, the series presents international scholarly work on modern Chinese law including: comparative perspectives, interdisciplinary, and empirical studies.

Other titles in this series

The Judicial System and Reform in Post-Mao China
Stumbling Towards Justice
Yuwen Li
978-1-4724-3605-4

Administrative Litigation Systems in Greater China and Europe

Edited by

YUWEN LI
Erasmus University Rotterdam, The Netherlands

Routledge
Taylor & Francis Group
LONDON AND NEW YORK

First published 2014 by Ashgate Publishing

Published 2016 by Routledge
2 Park Square, Milton Park, Abingdon, Oxfordshire OX14 4RN
711 Third Avenue, New York, NY 10017, USA

First issued in paperback 2016

Routledge is an imprint of the Taylor and Francis Group, an informa business

British Library Cataloguing in Publication Data
A catalogue record for this book is available from the British Library

Library of Congress Cataloging-in-Publication Data
Li, Yuwen, 1962- author.
Administrative litigation systems in greater China and Europe / By Yuwen Li.
p. cm. – (The rule of law in china and comparative perspectives)
Includes bibliographical references and index.
ISBN 978-1-4724-3608-5 (hardback) – ISBN 978-1-4724-3609-2 (ebook) – ISBN 978-1-4724-3610-8 (epub) 1. Government litigation–China. 2. Government litigation–Europe. 3. Administrative procedure–China. 4. Administrative procedure–Europe. I. Title.
K2360.L5 2014
347.51'053–dc23

2014011762

ISBN 13: 978-1-138-63763-4 (pbk)
ISBN 13: 978-1-4724-3608-5 (hbk)

Contents

PART III: ADMINISTRATIVE LITIGATION SYSTEMS IN TRANSITIONAL EASTERN EUROPEAN STATES

List of Figures

List of Tables

List of Abbreviations

ADR	Alternative dispute resolution
ALL	Administrative Litigation Law
ALS	Administrative litigation system
ARL	Administrative Reconsideration Law
BEEA	Bureau of Exit–Entry Administration
BGBl.	Federal Law Gazette (Bundesgesetzblatt)
BGH	German Federal Supreme Court (Bundesgerichtshof)
BGHZ	Collection of Rulings of the German Federal Supreme Court in Civil Matters
BNatSchG	Federal Nature Conservation Act (Bundesnaturschutzgesetz)
BORO	Bill of Rights Ordinance
BPC	Basic People's Court
BVerfG	German Federal Constitutional Court (Bundesverfassungsgericht)
BVerfGE	Collection of Rulings of the German Federal Constitutional Court
BVerwG	German Federal Administrative Court (Bundesverwaltungsgericht)
BVerwGE	Collection of Rulings of the German Federal Administrative Court
CA	Court of Appeal
CCP	Chinese Communist Party
CFA	Court of Final Appeal
CFI	Court of First Instance
CiPL	The Civil Procedure Law
CJ	Chief Justice
CJEU	Court of Justice of the European Union
CPR	Civil Procedure Rules
CrPL	Criminal Procedure Law
DVBl.	Journal for Administrative Law (Deutsches Verwaltungsblatt)
ECHR	European Convention on Human Rights
ECJ	European Court of Justice
ECtHR	European Court of Human Rights
ECR	European Court Reports
EU	European Union
EuGRZ	European Journal for Fundamental Rights (Europäische Grundrechte Zeitschrift)
FGO	Code of Procedure for Fiscal Courts (Finanzgerichtsordnung)
FS	Commemorative Publication (Festschrift)
GCHQ	Government Communications Headquarters
GG	German Constitution (= Basic Law, Grundgesetz)
GmS–OGB	Joint Panel of the Supreme Courts of the Federation (Gemeinsamer Senat der obersten Gerichtshöfe des Bundes)
GVG	Judicial System Act (Gerichtsverfassungsgesetz)
HBV	Hepatitis B virus
HPC	Higher People's Court

IAT	Immigration Appeal Tribunal
ICAC	Independent Commissioner Against Corruption
IPC	Intermediate People's Court
LegCo	Legislative Council
NGO	Non-governmental organization
NPC	National People's Congress
NPCSC	National People's Congress Standing Committee
NTD	New Taiwan Dollar
NVwZ	New Journal for Administrative Law (Neue Zeitschrift für Verwaltungsrecht)
PJ	Permanent Justice
PRC	People's Republic of China
SAC	Supreme Administrative Court
SGG	Social Courts Act (Sozialgerichtsgesetz)
SPC	Supreme People's Court
TEU	EU-Treaty
TFEU	Treaty on the Functioning of the EU
TPB	Town Planning Board
UmwRG	Environmental Appeals Act (Umweltrechtsbehelfsgesetz)
VwGO	Code of Administrative Court Procedure (Verwaltungsgerichtsordnung)
VwVfG	Administrative Proceedings Act (Verwaltungsverfahrensgesetz)
WRV	Weimar Constitution of 1919 (Weimarer Reichsverfassung)
WTO	World Trade Organization
ZPO	Code of Civil Procedure (Zivilprozessordnung)

Notes on Contributors

Mateusz Błachucki is Assistant Professor of the Institute of Legal Studies at the Department of Administrative Law at the Polish Academy of Sciences. He is a member of the Scientific Council of the Institute of Legal Studies. He holds a PhD in Law (thesis on the Polish merger procedure, Polish Academy of Sciences – awarded as second-best PhD thesis defended in Poland in the area of law in 2011), MA (Hons) in Law (University of Warsaw, 2002) and MA in Economics (Warsaw School of Economics, 2003). Furthermore, he gained a fine academic experience during his employment as a lecturer at the University of Cardinal Stefan Wyszyński in Warsaw and Warsaw University. He is the author of two monographs: *System of Polish Merger Procedure* (2012) and *Polish Competition Law: Commentary, Case Law and Texts* (2013). He is editor and co-author of several books: *Recent Issues in Delimitation of Jurisdiction of Civil and Administrative Courts* (2011), *Analysis of Changes in Administrative Procedural Code in 2010–2011* (2012) and *Sources of Administrative Law and Protection of Citizens' Rights and Liberties* (2013). Mateusz has also written various articles in the field of administrative law and procedure, competition law, and state aids.

Wunyu Chang, born in Taiwan, now serves as Professor of Law at National Taipei University, and Adjunct Professor of Law at Fu Jen Catholic University and Soochow University. His main teaching subject is: The Regulations of Administrative Remedy, Code of Civil Procedure. He studied in Fu Jen Catholic University from 1979 to 1987, obtaining the Bachelor of Laws and Master's Degree in Law, and then passed the national examination of the public advocate and the bar exam of attorney in the same year. He was assigned Public Advocate in Taiwan Hualien District Court and Taiwan Taoyuan District Court during 1987 to 1991. In 1991 he went to the University of Munich (Ludwig-Maximilians-Universität München) for PhD research and obtained his doctorate in Law in 1997. He then taught in the Law School of Fu Jen Catholic University till 2008. Currently, he serves additionally as General Secretary of Taiwan Administrative Law Association; Managing Supervisor of the Society of Chinese Constitutional Law; Commissioner of Petitions and Appeals Commission in Presidential Palace; Commissioner of Petitions and Appeals Commission in Executive Yuan; Commissioner of Petitions and Appeals Commission in Council of Agriculture, Executive Yuan; Commissioner of Law and Regulation Commission in Ministry of Examination; Commissioner of Human Rights Protection Advisory Commission in Taipei City Government; Commissioner of Petitions and Appeals Commission in New Taipei City Government; and Commissioner of State Compensation Cases Commission in New Taipei City Government.

Pieter van Dijk was a member of the Netherlands Council of State from 1990 till his retirement in 2013. From 2000 to 2003 and from 2006 to 2010 he was President of its Administrative Jurisdiction Division. From 1996 to 1998 he was also a member of the European Court of Human Rights. From 1999 to 2012 he was a member of the Council of Europe Commission for Democracy through Law ('Venice Commission'). As from 2000 he has been a member of the Netherlands Group of the Permanent Court of Arbitration. From 1976 to 1990 he was Professor of the Law of International Organizations at Utrecht University. Additionally, he is a member of the Royal Netherlands Academy of Arts and Sciences. He holds a LLM from Utrecht University and a PhD (cum laude) from Leiden University. He has published several books, various contributions to books, and numerous articles in the fields of public international law, international human rights law, the law of the European Union and comparative public law.

Yang Feng is a PhD candidate at the Department of Constitutional Law and Administrative Law of the Erasmus School of Law, Erasmus University Rotterdam in the Netherlands. He received his bachelor's degree in Law and master's degree in Constitutional Law and Administrative Law from the Law School of China University of Political Science and Law. From 2010 to 2012, he participated in several research programmes, including 'Research on Institutionalizing China's Administrative Decision-making Procedure', funded by the Legislative Affairs Office of the State Council of China, and 'Research on the Reform of the Structure of Chinese Central Government', funded by the Committee of State Commission Office for Public Sector Reform. He started his PhD programme at the Erasmus School of Law in September 2012. His academic interest lies in relations between the central and local authorities from legal and comparative perspectives. The topic of his PhD research focuses on China's central–local legislative relationship.

Petra Gyöngyi is a PhD candidate at the Department of Jurisprudence of the Erasmus School of Law, Erasmus University Rotterdam in the Netherlands. She obtained her bachelor's degree in Law from the Babes-Bolyai University in Cluj-Napoca, Romania. After graduation, she completed her LLM in Human Rights with Merit at the Central European University in Budapest, Hungary, and she was a trainee at the European Court of Human Rights. In November 2010 she started her PhD research at the Erasmus School of Law with the topic, 'Reconstructing the Liberal-democratic Normative Framework for Judicial Organization in Central and Eastern Europe'. Since 2011 she has been a junior researcher with the School of Human Rights Research in the Netherlands. She has presented her work at international conferences, and in spring 2013 she was a visiting researcher at the Research Institute on Judicial Systems (IRSiG-CNR) in Bologna, Italy.

Chaoyang Jiang is Associate Professor of Administrative Law of Macao and Coordinator of the Master of Law in Chinese Program at the Faculty of Law, University of Macao. He holds a LLB in Law, a Master of Law in Constitutional Law and Administrative Law, and a PhD in Constitutional Law and Administrative Law from Peking University. Since 2006, he has been Associate Professor in the Faculty of Law, Shenzhen Graduate School of Peking University. Currently, he is supervising a number of Chinese and Macao PhD candidates who are writing on public law topics from comparative perspectives. He is also on the panel list of arbitrators on the Shenzhen Court of International Arbitration in China. His recent publications include: *Improvement of the Legal System of Civil Servants in Macao* (2008); *Legal Status of the Basic Law in the National Legal System* (2009); *Deduction or Analogy Method? Comparative Study of Logic of Judicial Interpretations between the Different Legal Traditions* (2009); Judicial Review of Statute of Macao SAR (*Macau Law Review*, 2011); Dualism on Public Law and Private Law and Theoretical Basis of Administrative Law in Macao (*Law Review*, 2012).

Yuwen Li is Professor of Chinese Law and Director of the Erasmus China Law Centre at the Erasmus School of Law, Erasmus University Rotterdam in the Netherlands. She holds a BA in Chinese Law from Peking University, an MA in International Law and International Relations from the Institute of Social Studies, and a PhD in International Law from Utrecht University, the Netherlands. Since 2001, she has acted as Co-director of a number of legal collaborative projects with numerous Chinese institutions, including the Institute of Law of the Chinese Academy of Social Sciences, the National Judges College, the Supreme People's Procuratorate and the Law School of Wuhan University. Currently, she is supervising a number of Chinese PhD candidates who are writing on various legal topics from comparative perspectives. She is also on the panel list of arbitrators of the Shenzhen Court of International Arbitration in the PRC. Her recent publications include: *NGOs in China and Europe: Comparisons and Contrasts* (editor) (2011); *Taking Employment Discrimination Seriously: Chinese and European Perspectives* (editor with Jenny Goldschmidt) (2009). She has published numerous journal articles and book chapters on China law.

Feng Lin is Professor of Law and Director of the Research Centre for Chinese and Comparative Law at the School of Law, City University of Hong Kong. Dr Lin studied Nuclear Physics for three years and then did his LLB at Fudan University in Shanghai, PRC. He obtained his Master of Laws degree in 1992 from the Victoria University of Wellington in New Zealand, and obtained his Doctor of Philosophy degree from Peking University in 1998. Dr Lin was called to the Bar of England and Wales by the Honourable Society of Middle Temple in 1998 and was admitted to practice at the Bar of the High Court of Hong Kong in February 2000. Dr Lin specializes in comparative public law research, including Chinese constitutional law, Hong Kong Basic Law, Chinese and Hong Kong administrative law, and Chinese and comparative environmental law. He has published five books, in addition to more than sixty journal articles and book chapters in those areas. He was a visiting scholar to the East Asian Legal Studies Centre at Harvard Law School in the Fall semester 2010. He is a guest professor at the Research Institute of Constitutionalism and Rule of Law at the Faculty of Law of Renmin University. Dr Lin is a practising barrister in Hong Kong. He currently serves as a Council member of the Hong Kong Bar Association and also as a member of the Special Committee on Constitutional and Human Rights Law.

Yun Ma is a PhD candidate at the Department of Constitutional and Administrative Law of the Erasmus School of Law, Erasmus University Rotterdam in the Netherlands. She graduated with cum laude from the Law School of China University of Political Science and Law (CUPL) with the bachelor's degree in Law. She obtained her master's degree in constitutional and administrative law from CUPL in 2011. Funded by the China Scholarship Council, she has worked as a PhD candidate at the Erasmus School of Law since September 2011 on the topic of comparative legal studies of national parks and other protected areas between the United States of America and China. Her research interests include administrative law, natural resources law and environmental regulation. She has been working as a visiting PhD researcher at Maurer School of Law of Indiana University in the United States since Fall 2013.

Arno Scherzberg holds the Chair of Public Law and Administrative Sciences at the University of Erfurt. After passing his first and second state examinations in Law in 1981 and 1984, he joined the University of Münster as a research assistant at the Institute of Administrative Law and Administrative Sciences. After completing his habilitation (postdoctoral lecturing qualification) in 1998, he joined the universities of Bremen and Erfurt. In 2001 he was elected Deputy Dean of the Faculty of Economics, Law and Social Sciences in Erfurt and served as Dean of this faculty from 2003 to 2006. He has published more than ninety books and articles on German and European constitutional, administrative and procedural law. In 2010 he was awarded a prize for excellent research by the German Association for Law and Society. At present, his main fields of research are information law, German and European risk law in areas of modern technology, as well as Turkey's compliance with European human rights standards. Recent publications include: US/EU-Trade Disputes About Risk Regulation (*Cambridge Review of International Affairs* 19, 2006);

Individualverfassungsbeschwerde, in Dirk Ehlers and Friedrich Schoch (editors), *Rechtsschutz im öffentlichen Recht* (2009); *Risikoabschätzung unter Ungewissheit – Preliminary Risk Assessment im Kontext der Nanotechnologie* (ZUR, 2010); Ökonomische Innovationen unter Einfluss von Politik und Recht – eine staatswissenschaftliche Betrachtung, in Arno Scherzberg (editor), *10 Jahre Staatswissenschaftliche Fakultät* (2012).

Josephine Seidl works as a research assistant at the Chair of Public Law and Administrative Sciences of Prof. Scherzberg. Holding a scholarship from the German National Merit Foundation, she studied German, European and International Law at the University of Giessen. In February 2012 she passed her first state examination as one of the best graduates of the year. At present she is writing her dissertation on the question of how to protect the values of the European Union (Art. 2 TEU) during the entry process into the Union and through sanctions against its current members, especially focusing on the situation in Hungary.

Andrew Le Sueur is Professor of Constitutional Justice at the School of Law, University of Essex, United Kingdom. He graduated with an LLB from the London School of Economics in 1986 and went on to hold academic posts at UCL, the University of Birmingham, and Queen Mary, University of London before joining Essex in August 2013. His research interests are in the broad fields of constitutional and administrative law. He is a co-author of *De Smith's Judicial Review* (2013), a comprehensive analysis of principles applied by the courts in judicial review claims. With Varda Bondy, in 2012 he completed a study of how in the English system redress mechanisms are designed and modified: Designing Redress: A Study about Grievances against Public Bodies. Outside academia, he is a barrister and regularly serves as an adviser to committees of the UK Parliament. He is co-convener of the UK Constitutional Law Group and a member of the Executive Committee of the International Association of Constitutional Law.

Acknowledgements

This book results from a three-year research project on theory and good practice concerning the reform of the administrative litigation system in China. The project is sponsored by the Royal Dutch Embassy in Beijing, and implemented by the Centre for Protection of the Rights of Disadvantaged Citizens at the Law School of Wuhan University and the China Law Centre of the Erasmus School of Law at Erasmus University Rotterdam in the Netherlands. In designing the project we recognised that many Chinese legal scholars were interested in gaining a greater insight into the administrative litigation systems of other jurisdictions. Consequently an international conference was held in Wuhan, China, in October 2012. The chapters in this volume were originally presented as papers at the conference.

It would have been impossible to produce this book without the generous input of all the contributors. It has been such a pleasure to collaborate with this group of international scholars who have been exceptionally efficient in submitting their chapters and commenting on each other's work. The common interest in administrative litigation systems in different legal regimes has drawn us together to share our opinions and concerns, and to inspire each other to critically examine laws and judicial practice in this particular field. I very much hope that our joint effort in producing this book is only the first result of our teamwork, and that our professional cooperation will continue for many years to come.

Upon completing this book, I would like to thank former Dutch Ambassador to China, Rudolf Bekink, for his consistent support and trust in me and my Chinese colleagues in initiating the project. I vividly remember that he candidly reminded me that no government in the world wants citizens to bring lawsuits against them. Yet he conceded that, in the name of the rule of law, judicial review of acts of governmental agencies and officials can be advanced as the last resort for citizens to uphold their rights, as well as to facilitate the exercise of administrative power according to law. My thanks also go to current Dutch ambassador Aart Jacobi in Beijing for his continuous backing of the project. The Embassy has retained its practice of allotting full independence to project partners in implementing project activities. This has been demonstrated by our cooperation with Remy Christini and Joeri Vos, to whom I also owe my sincere gratitude.

My considerable appreciation is owed to Professor Lin Lihong and her team at the Law School of Wuhan University, who hosted the international conference in China. Without the conference, this publication would have been inconceivable. Professor Lin has dedicated her time to advancing the administrative litigation system in China by both teaching and running legal aid centres to assist citizens to litigate in courts. Her courage and wisdom have influenced many Chinese legal scholars, lawyers, judges and law students.

Moreover, I am particularly grateful to Yun Ma for her hard work and persistence in assisting me from the outset to the completion of the project. She has skilfully organised the European experts to participate in the international conference, jointly written two chapters with me, and translated the chapter by Wunyu Chang from Chinese into English. My gratitude is also owed to Kate Elliott for her assistance in editing most of the chapters.

Finally, my sincere appreciation goes to Alison Kirk, Tricia Craggs and Philip Stirups at Ashgate, with whom I have experienced a publication process as pleasant as it was efficient.

YUWEN LI
November 2013

Chapter 1

Introduction

Battling in the Courts: Dynamics of Administrative Litigation Systems across Jurisdictions

Yuwen Li and Yun Ma

Administrative litigation commonly refers to lawsuits filed by individuals and/or companies against decisions of governments and governmental officials who allegedly infringe the rights and interests of the individuals and/or companies involved. In the common law system, the term judicial review is used instead; this generally refers to the review of governmental actions by the judiciary. Despite the differences between administrative litigation and judicial review, these two terms will be used interchangeably hereinafter. As one of the three pillars of the modern litigation system (composed of civil, criminal and administrative litigation systems), the administrative litigation system (ALS) shares the function of resolving disputes with civil litigation, and protecting the members of society, that is akin to the criminal system; however, it also distinguishes itself from the other two due to its unique litigant structure and its inherent constitutional concern, which is to supervise one kind of State power (administrative power) by exercising another kind of State power (judicial power).

In this regard, the birth of administrative litigation is deeply rooted and underpinned by the doctrine of the separation of powers and systems of checks and balances. Moreover, its development cannot be isolated from the developments of the rule of law and constitutionalism. Though embodied with various elements, both terms have overarching concerns about the protection of fundamental human rights and control of State powers. These concerns are at the crux of the fundamental purposes and functions of administrative litigation. From a historical perspective, the realisation of the rule of law and constitutionalism was a driving force for the development of administrative litigation; in England, for example, the ALS was born out of the struggle against the power of the King. On the other hand, the development of administrative litigation can also be a decisive factor in promoting the realisation of the rule of law and constitutionalism.

Bearing this interdependence between the ALS and the realisation of the rule of law and constitutionalism in mind, our research started with examining the development of the ALS in China. Since the Administrative Litigation Law (ALL) was promulgated in 1989, the ALS in mainland China has stumbled forward in the past two decades. Marking an abrupt departure from the long history of judicial practices, the achievements that administrative litigation has attained in China are visible. However, both the ALS and the judicial system as a whole in China are rather nascent. Obstacles remain disappointingly daunting, such as the weakness of judicial independence, a system trapped within the confines of ideology and traditional culture, an overly mighty and unbridled government, and vulnerability to political climate change. These obstacles are also the ones against which China is now struggling in its overarching path towards the rule of law and constitutionalism.

We echo scholars' opinions that administrative litigation aligns itself well as a breakthrough for the attainment of the rule of law and constitutionalism in China.[1] Therefore, strengthened attention needs to be paid to the ALS in China, from both retrospective and prospective perspectives. Based on the introspection of the evolution of ALS in mainland China and with the intent of improving China's legislation and practices, we introduce a comparative perspective by exploring the practices and experiences abroad. The present publication aims at firstly enriching the knowledge about ALSs in different jurisdictions and thus facilitating further comparative studies in this field, and secondly exploring the common factors and divergences among the ALSs across different jurisdictions, and in the process contributing to the overall development of the ALS in China.

Structure of the Book

The present collection of papers selectively covers three regions of the world. Part I mainly focuses on the ALSs in the Greater China region, comprising four chapters addressing the ALSs in the People's Republic of China (PRC), Hong Kong, Macao and Taiwan, respectively. Part II looks into the legislation and practices of administrative litigation in three selected Western jurisdictions: the Netherlands, Germany, and England and Wales. Part III directs the discussion towards the ALSs in two transitional Eastern European countries, namely Poland and Romania.

All of these chapters follow a designed analytical structure and cover several major issues, as follows. Starting from a historical survey of the ALS in the respective countries, a discussion on the institutional structure of handling administrative cases will ensue, drawing upon issues of whether there is an independent system of administrative courts, the relationship between administrative courts and 'ordinary' courts, the qualifications for judges sitting in administrative courts, etc. Subsequently, the core issue of the scope of administrative litigation will be addressed by analysing both the law in the books and the law in practice. Current and in-depth analysis of the jurisdiction of courts and grounds of judicial review will be provided in turn. Then the most controversial issues in the operation of ALS will be investigated, such as tensions between judicial and political forces, mediation in administrative litigation, limits on the access to justice, and efficiency problems of administrative trials. A prospective view of the development of the ALS in the future will be developed, with a particular discussion of the proposed amendments to legislation and new norms in judicial practices.

Main Findings

The jurisdictions we have chosen range from common law to civil law countries. Principal differences with regard to the development of the ALS and, broadly speaking, administrative law as a whole, are observed, such as the sources of law for administrative adjudication, institutional structures, the role of courts, etc. The current status of ALS in a given country is deeply embedded in its domestic historical, cultural and political contexts. Consequently they all retain their own distinctive characteristics. However, modern ALSs illustrate some common features. A converging

---

1 See Yu Zhong, 'Xingzheng Susong de Chonggou: Dangdai Zhongguo Xianzheng Jianshe de Tupokou' (The re-construction of administrative litigation: breakthrough for construction of constitutionalism in current China), 22–1 (2007) *Faxue Luntan (Legal Forum)*, pp. 59–64; Wang Zhuojun, 'Democracy, rule of law and human rights protection under gradually developed constitutionalism: by the clue of administrative law', 2–3 (2007) *Frontiers of Law in China*, pp. 335–352.

process has been occurring, which continually mitigates those differences. This is extensively reflected in the common recognition of the values and significance of administrative litigation in strengthening the rule of law, and the predominant purpose of administrative litigation to review administrative power and protect individuals' rights. This converging process takes place, on an international scale, due to the tendency of internationalisation and the continual exportation of Western legal ideas, such as the separation of powers, constitutionalism and democracy; and, on a regional scale, due to the integration process (such as the European Union (EU)) and the conclusion of regional treaties (such as the European Convention on Human Rights (ECHR)). Our findings on the common features and differences of ALSs across jurisdictions are displayed below.

Historical Review

One of the main issues that each scholar has addressed is a brief historical review of the development of the ALS in domestic countries.

Dating back to the seventeenth century, the English ALS has witnessed an incremental development. Basic principles and grounds of judicial review have been gradually formed and crystallised since that time. During the 1960s, administrative law went through a considerable transformation due to social and political changes. Approaching the new millennium, with the historical enactment of the Human Rights Act of 1998, judicial review in England and Wales has made another stride forward. Recent legislation, such as the Tribunals, Courts and Enforcement Act of 2007, further shapes the judicial review landscape in a new direction.

In Germany, the ALS in its modern form emerged in the second half of the nineteenth century with the first independent administrative courts established in 1863. Suffering from the national–socialist period, the revived form of the ALS was fixed in 1960 when the Federal Code of Administrative Court Procedure was enacted; this serves as the main legal basis for the present day.

In the Netherlands, the current model of the ALS was formulated after 1976, when the Council of State was bestowed with independent administrative jurisdiction.

In Poland, along with the flux of the political regime, the ALS has also gone through its own series of ups and downs. Dating back to the 1920s, the ALS has been gradually shaped and several fundamental acts of the ALS were enacted in 2002.

Romania undertook a similar period of transition to Poland. Though dating back as early as 1864, the modern administrative litigation system was not established in Romania until 1990, when the law on judicial review of administrative acts was enacted. The amendment to the Romanian Constitution in 2003 and the accession to the EU in 2007 further moulded the current framework of ALS.

The ALS in China could be traced back to the judicial practices of *Pingzhengyuan* since 1914. However, due to the instability of the political regime, the modern ALS was not shaped until the late twentieth century. In mainland China, the first and up to now only ALL, was enacted in 1989, which marked the formal establishment of the ALS. To this day, the ALL has not been revised, though proposals have been made since the early millennium. In Taiwan, the modernisation of the ALS that commenced in 1998 was symbolised by the amendments to the Administrative Litigation Law (the Taiwan ALL). Since then, the Taiwan ALL has been further amended on numerous occasions.

The year 1997, when the PRC resumed its sovereignty over Hong Kong, was marked as a watershed in terms of the development of the judicial review system in Hong Kong. Empowered with a high degree of autonomy, Hong Kong retains its original judicial system, which was transplanted from the British one, while at the same time it has developed its own characteristics under its unique constitutional setting of the Basic Law.

From the late 1980s, a 'localisation of the legal system' was initiated in Macao. Since then, Macao's authorities began to translate the legal documents written in Portuguese into Chinese and enact laws both in Portuguese and Chinese so as to provide legal information to local residents, 95 per cent of whom do not know Portuguese. Since Macao's return to China in 1999, the trend of localisation has been accelerated in various circles of judicial work, including administrative litigation.

Through the discussions concerning the history of the development of ALSs by each author, several general findings could be identified, as follows.

Firstly, the modern ALS is relatively new in all jurisdictions, though the German and English systems are deeply rooted in their earlier histories. Furthermore, the ALS has been going through constant changes until the present day. The modernisation of ALS may be deducted from parliamentary legislation on court procedures, institutionalisation of administrative adjudication, the establishment of basic principles, etc. Moreover, by probing into the differences in terms of the historical development of the ALSs in different jurisdictions, one can also see that historical factors, such as a State's political regime and ideology, separation of powers among different State organs, the perception of the judiciary's role etc., have a decisive influence in shaping the ALS in a given jurisdiction. For example, in Hong Kong, it is said that people have more confidence in the judiciary than in the other two branches of government. This explains partially why people would prefer to bring lawsuits before the courts for judicial review. In contrast, in mainland China, confined by traditional culture and ideology, the government possesses a position superior to the judiciary, which makes the nascent ALS suffer from an improper and intensive administrative interference.

Secondly, the development of administrative litigation is closely linked to the development of public administration. On the one hand, apart from traditional taxing and spending, the realm of the State has largely expanded nowadays. The emergence of the welfare state and the regulatory state has intensively expanded the scope of administrative powers. This comes along with intensified friction between the public and private spheres, and the proliferation of disputes between administrative bodies and private individuals. For example, in Hong Kong, in the period of the 1970s to the 1990s, the government's interference with the economy reached its peak, resulting in a rocketing of the number of judicial review cases. On the other hand, the transformation and innovation in public administration has imposed requirements on the quality of administration, such as good governance. This calls for an adaptive response in administrative law. In the UK, due to the New Public Management reform since the 1970s, many public services were delivered by the private sector rather than by public bodies. This has raised questions of identifying the defendants of administrative litigation and extending public law norms to private entities. Furthermore, administrative litigation has also cast significant influence on governmental decision-making and public administration. Judicial review has become the Sword of Damocles for the government and its officials in terms of how to behave in pursuit of the improved performance of the government. For example, in the UK, legal awareness training has been provided since the mid-1980s to help officials spot the risks of judicial review challenges.

Thirdly, for the European countries, explicit influences on their domestic ALSs have been brought about through EU integration and the adoption of the ECHR. Firstly, legal protection of citizens against the actions of the EU institutions is provided by national courts and the European Court of Justice; secondly, the conformity of national legal acts with EU law needs to be guaranteed, which makes the national litigation system subject to EU requirements, either in substantive or in procedural aspects; and thirdly, in accordance with the ECHR, the extent of judicial review by domestic courts is expanded, such as the review of parliamentary legislation and the application of the principle of proportionality.

Institutional Structure

A main distinctive feature in terms of the institutional arrangements of administrative adjudication concerns the issue whether there exists a separate system of administrative courts aside from the ordinary court structure for administrative disputes. Moreover, a relevant issue concerns whether there are special qualification requirements for judges who handle administrative cases.

Generally, there are three models of institutional arrangement: (1) no distinction between administrative adjudication and adjudication on other types of cases; (2) a separate administrative court system; and (3) no separate administrative court system, but a distinction between administrative adjudication and adjudication on other types of cases.

China and Romania fit into the first type. There are no specialised administrative courts in China and administrative cases are dealt with by administrative chambers in the 'ordinary' courts. Specialised administrative courts are similarly not established in Romania. Different to the PRC, Romania retains a specialised section for administrative law at the level of tribunals. For practical organisational matters they might function as joint civil, commercial and administrative law sections. The High Court of Cassation and Justice has a specialised section for administrative law.

Germany, Poland and Taiwan specifically feature in the second type of arrangement with a separate administrative court system. In Germany, the administrative court system is vertically divided into three tiers, which are the (Lower) Administrative Courts, the Higher Administrative Courts and the Federal Administrative Courts. In Poland, the administrative court system comprises two levels of courts, which are the Regional Administrative Court and the Supreme Administrative Court. In Taiwan, the administrative court system consists of two tiers, namely the High Administrative Court and the Supreme Administrative Court. In the 2011 reform, the administrative division was established within the local court setting to handle simple administrative cases. However, the division is still affiliated to the ordinary court system rather than the administrative court system.

In Macao, an administrative court was created as the court of first instance to handle administrative cases and the Intermediate Court serves as the court of appeal for such cases. The Court of Final Appeal is the Supreme Court handling administrative cases in Macao. More noticeably, the Intermediate Court and the Court of Final Appeal will adjudicate not only the administrative cases of appeal from lower-level courts, but also certain cases of first instance.

In England and Wales, and Hong Kong, there is no separate system of administrative courts; however, the handling of administrative cases is distinguished from ordinary cases. Both feature a mixed characteristic of institutional arrangement. In England and Wales, the 'administrative court' is not a freestanding institution. Rather, a part of the Queen's Bench Division within the High Court, designated the Administrative Court since 2000, it has historically been responsible for managing judicial review claims. Reforms in 2007 established a two-tiered system of tribunals to handle cases where there are rights of appeal expressly created by Acts of Parliament. The Upper Tribunal is also empowered to carry out 'judicial review' under certain circumstances. The division of jurisdiction between the administrative court and the tribunals is increasingly more flexible nowadays. Hong Kong naturally follows the English tradition. The power of judicial review is inherently vested in its High Court and this tradition was maintained even after the change of sovereignty in 1997, with the exception of renaming the High Court, the Court of First Instance.

In the Netherlands, the administrative cases at the first instance are handled by the administrative sectors within the 'ordinary' district courts. The institutions receiving the appeal of administrative cases differ in accordance with their subject matter. The Court of Appeal, which handles appeals of civil and criminal cases, also deals with the appeal of tax-related administrative cases. The

Administrative Jurisdiction Division of the Council of State is the highest administrative court with general jurisdiction of administrative appeals. Besides this, there are two separate supreme administrative courts in the Netherlands, which are the Central Appeals Tribunal, dealing with social security and civil service cases, and the Trade and Industry Appeals Tribunal, which receives administrative appeals in the area of socio-economic administrative law.

Concerning the qualification for judges who handle administrative cases, in Taiwan and Poland, it is required by law that the qualifications for judges working in administrative courts are higher than those stipulated for judges working in ordinary courts. In China, qualifications for judges are provided in the Judges Law, which makes no distinction between judges working at an administrative chamber and judges working at other chambers of courts. In Germany there is no difference in qualification between administrative and 'ordinary' judges. The same holds good for the Netherlands; in the district courts, the judges will regularly circulate among the civil, criminal and administrative sectors. In Romania, the lack of expertise of the administrative judges in handling administrative cases and the deficiency in providing continuous training for them raises concerns over the effectiveness of the administrative case judgments.

In England and Wales, High Court justices are nominated by the Lord Chief Justice to hear judicial review claims; they do so in addition to dealing with ordinary civil and some criminal cases. Judges appointed to the First-tier Tribunal are less highly qualified (and some are lay people with no legal qualification) but develop expertise in particular areas of law, such as immigration and social security. Judges of the Upper Tribunal are generally promoted from the First-tier Tribunal or transferred from the High Court.

Scope of Administrative Litigation (Judicial Review)

With regard to the scope of administrative litigation, we approach it from two perspectives, i.e. the scope of jurisdiction of the courts and the grounds of administrative litigation. The former refers specifically to the types of administrative actions or decisions that are amenable to judicial review, the types of rights or legitimate interests that are justiciable, etc. The latter refers to the extent of judicial control over administrative bodies, which is commonly known as the grounds of judicial review in English law. It covers questions such as whether the judiciary reviews also the factual or only the legal questions of a case, and whether the judiciary reviews only the legality or also the reasonableness of the challenged administrative action. Several controversial issues are discussed by the various authors, such as judicial review of primary and secondary legislation, the justiciability of actions taken by delegated non-State bodies, review of discretionary actions taken by administrative authorities, and applications for the principle of proportionality as a ground of judicial review.

In Germany, generally speaking, there are no non-justiciable rights and no executive actions affecting individual rights that are exempt from the jurisdiction of the courts. However, matters of policy and their execution as well as the expedience of the administrative action fall outside the scope of judicial review. Administrative courts are empowered to fully examine the legality of administrative actions as well as the constitutionality and legal conformity of laws and other regulations, on which the administrative action is based. This includes their conformity with EU law. Also the illegality of a discretionary action – if authorities fail to use, abuse or exceed their discretion – falls within the scope of judicial review. However, if the court concludes that a parliamentary law, which was enacted after the ratification of the constitution and on whose validity its decision depends, is unconstitutional, a decision of the Federal Constitutional Court needs to be obtained.

In the Netherlands, the overarching requirement for judicial review is that there must be a written administrative decision. Judicial review is restricted to legality review. The intricacy of the extent of judicial review is reflected in the review of the exercise of discretionary powers by authorities in the form of the adoption of policies. The courts may review whether the policy is reasonable, and in conformity with the law and the principles of proper administration. Such policy rules are distinguished from generally binding regulations that are not under judicial review. According to the Constitution, the Dutch courts are empowered and obliged to review applicable acts of parliament for their conformity with treaties and binding decisions of international organisations, although they may not review their constitutionality.

In England and Wales, courts have creatively used common law methods to create and develop legal principles for judicial control over the legality of administration. The kinds of decisions and the bodies who make the decisions that are amenable to judicial review have been gradually expanded, such as through the exercise of 'prerogative powers'. Moreover, the grounds of judicial review are also expanding and now cover procedural fairness, irrationality, proportionality and legitimate expectations. With regard to the review of parliamentary legislation, under the Human Rights Act 1998, which was enacted to incorporate the ECHR into domestic law, the English courts may make 'declarations of incompatibility' of the parliamentary legislation; this has had the subsidiary effect of undermining the traditional notion of parliamentary supremacy.

Hong Kong follows the British common law. The grounds for judicial review mainly include illegality, procedural impropriety, irrationality and controversially, proportionality. It should be noted that illegality in HK is a much wider concept than in the UK in the sense that HK has a written constitution, i.e. the Basic Law, which not only states its supremacy but also contains provisions on different sectors of the society in addition to fundamental rights. As a result, constitutional review cases constitute a major part of judicial review cases in Hong Kong.

In Poland, the jurisdiction of the administrative courts is explicitly limited by law, and the exceptions are likewise provided for in the law. Administrative decisions are the most important type of administrative acts that fall within the jurisdiction. It is also explicitly provided that 'local law and normative acts adopted by local governments and territorial government administration' are under judicial review by administrative courts. Administrative courts review challenged administrative acts in accordance with the principle of legality. Only cassatory rulings, i.e. rulings to either uphold or set aside the contested actions, could be issued by the courts.

In Romania, the scope of judicial review has evolved through different phases of legislation. The most recent legislation of 2004 defines several standards to demarcate the scope of judicial review, i.e. an administrative act made by a public authority that violates a right or a legitimate interest. The new legislation also expands the scope of review to generally binding administrative acts. Romania adopts a traditional way that deems the principle of legality the core of its judicial review. EU law has embraced the principle of legal proportionality, and the ECHR has elaborated the principle of legal certainty. Influenced by EU law and the ECHR, Romanian judges also apply the principles of legal certainty and proportionality in judicial practice.

In China, the scope of accepted cases by courts, as prescribed in the ALL, is rather limited. It is generally based on two criteria, which are the concrete administrative action, and personal and property rights. This indicates that both statutes and other generally binding rules are excluded from judicial review. However, through judicial practices, courts have carefully and gradually expanded this scope to encompass more areas. This is illustrated in the courts' handling of complaints concerning the right to education. Administrative cases are mainly adjudicated in accordance with the principle of legality. The review on the reasonableness of administrative action is severely restricted.

In Taiwan, the expansion of judicial review is reflected in its gradual expansion of the forms of actions available, from the sole action for rescission to the action of affirmative relief and the declaratory action. Such a process has been promoted by judicial interpretation and amendments to its ALL.

In Macao, the scope of accepting cases has been shaped by a combination of the summarising provision and the enumerative exclusion. First of all, in Macao, the goal of administrative litigation is to effectively protect individual rights and legitimate interests. Access to courts is guaranteed by law. As provided by Article 6(1) of the Law on the Outline of Judicial Organisation in Macao, everyone has the right to bring cases to courts in order to maintain his rights and interests, which are protected by law; courts must not reject those cases on the grounds of a party's lack of economic capacity. Other matters beyond this scope are excluded in an enumerative way. According to relevant laws, courts in Macao do not have jurisdiction over the following cases: acts of the State, political acts, cases concerning the Macao Garrison etc.

From the evolution of the scope of administrative litigation, several findings could be identified as follows. Firstly, a common tendency could be observed across jurisdictions to expand the scope of administrative litigation in terms of both depth and breadth. It could be seen from Romania's gradual expansion of the scope from individual administrative acts to generally binding administrative acts, and from the violation of citizens' rights to legitimate interests. Through this expanding process, administrative litigation is now providing a more comprehensive protection to citizens and control of authorities, although some legislative changes remain contested.

Secondly, the grounds of judicial review have evolved to become a complicated system. In some jurisdictions, a distinction is made between the different types of activities and different degrees of reviewing standards applied to them. For instance, in England and Wales, different standards of review may apply according to whether the case is 'purely domestic' (relating only to national law), whether EU rights are in issue, or whether Convention rights (now protected by the Human Rights Act 1998) are at stake. For example, proportionality is used as a ground for review for EU and Convention rights but not in purely domestic cases. In this way, judicial review of administration becomes a flexible and well-crafted mechanism rather than a rigid one. In the Netherlands system, although judicial review is restricted to legality review, through the principles of good administration grounds such as proportionality and well-founded reasoning have also been introduced. To contrast, China has adopted a 'one-size-fits-all' approach that fails to adapt itself to the complexities of the administration. In Germany the courts have the last word in defining the relevant legal provisions, ascertaining the facts and applying the law to the respective case. This includes the application of the principle of proportionality. The applicable law may, however, leave a margin of discretion to the administrative authorities or consist of vague legal terms meant to implicitly grant them a margin of judgment. In these cases the courts are confined to examining whether this margin has been crossed. By constitution, though, administrative margins of judgment are limited to cases in which a full legal review appears unfeasible or unreasonable, mostly because of specific administrative expertise in the matter.

Thirdly, in most jurisdictions, courts have played a significant role in expanding the scope of administrative litigation. Courts have creatively interpreted statutory legislation or created and developed grounds of judicial review. Even in China where the judicial system is underdeveloped, courts still make a difference in gradually expanding the scope of judicial review.

Judicial Remedies and Alternative Mechanisms

The function of the administrative litigation as a mechanism to resolve disputes besides the traditional perception of controlling the State power and protecting individual's rights is increasingly recognised. Taking this as the point of departure, the unique role of administrative litigation as a dispute-resolving mechanism is changing. More and more alternative mechanisms are available to resolve disputes between public bodies and citizens. In England and Wales, the courts have in reality played a limited role in solving administrative disputes. Other alternatives to courts, such as the use of tribunals, ombudsmen and alternative dispute resolution (ADR) have been proliferating. The figures show that the number of judicial review claims received by the Administrative Court is much smaller than the caseload of tribunals. The system of the Ombudsman is also adopted in the Netherlands, Poland and Romania to resolve administrative disputes and to exert control and supervision of administrative bodies.

The adoption of mediation, as one form of an ADR mechanism, in administrative litigation is controversial and has been singled out for special discussion. Attitudes towards mediation in administrative litigation are different in distinct jurisdictions. For example, in Germany, England and Wales, the Netherlands, Taiwan, and Poland, mediation in administrative litigation is allowed and even encouraged to speed up trial proceedings. In Germany, the Federal Mediation Law was adopted in 2012 to specifically address the issue of mediation.

The practice of mediation in those countries in which it is allowed differs on the ground. For example, in Poland, though mediation in administrative litigation is prescribed by law, it faces the dilemma of under-usage, and thus becomes artificial and empty. Mediation is encouraged and promoted in civil cases in the UK; however, the adoption of mediation in judicial review claims is still controversial. Research shows that there is little room for mediation as an alternative to judicial review and there has been relatively little use in administrative law cases.

The case in China is much more complex. Mediation is expressly prohibited by the ALL. However, the necessity of mediation arises from the practices and the terms of 'cooperation' and 'reconciliation' are purposely used to avoid the explicit illegality of judicial practices. The excessive use of mediation or even compulsory mediation in judicial practices has been harshly criticised.

Challenges

Having achieved great accomplishments, ALS in each jurisdiction also faces considerable challenges. The challenges are deeply embedded in domestic circumstances; therefore, some of them are explicitly context specific in a given jurisdiction, though some common challenges across jurisdictions can also be identified.

The first challenge with ALSs is the unavoidable tension between the judiciary and politics. This intensively reflects on the governmental interference into judicial affairs. In different countries, the form and degree of such intervention can be different. In England and Wales, politicians and judges have gone through periods of tension since the mid-1990s due to the increasing phenomenon that ministers commented on particular judgments and judges. Such tensions were intensified when the Ministry of Justice publicly published proposals to restrict judicial review in 2012. In England and Wales, though the rule of law is generally respected by governmental bodies, the increasing hostility of politicians towards judicial review also entails further and repeating assertion of the value and significance of judicial review in a mature democracy. In China, governmental interference of administrative adjudication can be deemed as the most extensive and serious of them all. It is commonly observed that judicial independence in China is severely jeopardised due to interference by the State organs, such as the Party, the People's Congress, and government. This situation has deteriorated further with regard to administrative litigation due to its specific nature. In addition, China's traditional culture and ideology means that the governments possess a superior position to the judiciary and this has in turn placed the courts and judges in a considerable predicament. The peripheralisation and marginalisation of the administrative chamber in the court system also makes administrative litigation vulnerable.

The second challenge concerns the limits on access to justice. Such limits are reflected in the following aspects:

1. Courts may decide whether or not to accept a case. In this regard, China represents an extreme case in which *li'an nan* (difficulty in having one's case filed by court) is the most serious problem in enabling citizens and private parties to use the ALL to protect their rights and interests. It is commonly complained in China that courts simply refuse to accept cases without providing any reasons. In England and Wales, in terms of the claimants' application for permission to the courts, it is said that the vast majority of permission applications are refused. In addition to the cases that are withdrawn, there are in reality a relatively small number of claims that progress to a full hearing. In Hong Kong, with a change from the 'potential arguability test' to the 'arguability test' with regard to the test for granting leave (permission), courts have actually increased the threshold for judicial review.
2. The high costs of administrative litigation *de facto* preclude citizens from bringing a lawsuit to courts. In England and Wales, it is asserted that judicial review has become unaffordable except for the very poor, the very rich, or claimants who are able to obtain free legal advice. In the Netherlands, in light of the economic crisis and the cash-strapped government, proposals to raise court fees have been made, aiming at making the judicial system self-financing. Concerns arise among scholars that such proposals may jeopardise citizens' access to courts.
3. Preliminary proceedings and other pre-trial requirements may also hamper the realisation of citizens' access to justice. For example, in Germany and the Netherlands, the exhaustion of administrative remedies is deemed to be a prerequisite of administrative litigation. Also, the administrative remedy should not primarily be seen as an instrument to prolong the citizens' way to justice. They are also a cheap tool to make the administration (mostly at higher instance) reconsider the contested act and thus function as an additional instrument of legal review. In England and Wales, limits on access to justice are reflected in the lack of coherence among various remedy mechanisms. The piecemeal nature of its administrative justice system has resulted in dispersed responsibility, and such a complex consequently creates hurdles for citizens to conquer in order to pursue justice.

Thirdly, though an expanding tendency in terms of the scope of judicial review is generally observed, obstacles do indeed remain. The standing requirements have excluded a certain amount of cases from the jurisdiction of courts. The ALL in China distinguishes concrete and abstract administrative actions; only concrete administrative actions may be challenged by private parties whose personal and property rights are infringed. In Germany, it is required that the plaintiff has to prove that his individual right has been infringed upon by the administrative authority. Though with exceptions, the objective infringements of the legal order and the violation of collective interests are generally excluded from judicial review. In contrast, in England and Wales, the standing requirements have been gradually liberalised. Furthermore, deficiencies in reviewing the reasonableness of administrative acts and reviewing the facts resulting from administrative activities may also hamper effective protection of individual rights. In Poland, concerns arise that courts can only review the legal aspects of the case, while an individual's right may be violated by authorities' collection of evidence and fact-finding process.

Lastly, the extensive duration of the court proceedings is mentioned as a considerable challenge to the efficient protection of individuals' rights in many scholars' essays. In the Netherlands, it is submitted that long-lasting administrative procedures create legal uncertainty for private parties involved. In both Germany and the Netherlands, as a response to the requirement of guaranteeing a decision 'within a reasonable time' as prescribed in Article 6 of the ECHR, specific actions have been taken to deal with the prolonged duration problem. Compensation is provided to claimants who suffer from the long duration or delay of court proceedings.

Concluding Remarks

In the latter nineteenth century, the so-called 'droit administratif' (administrative law) became established in France. Featuring the establishment of a separate administrative court system and specifically assigned administrative judges who dealt with administrative cases, the 'droit administratif' distinguished itself from the judicial practices in common law countries. Thus, Dicey critiqued that the 'droit administratif' was totally against the rule of law, and consequently asserted that 'there exists in England no true droit administratif'.[2] This situation has undergone gradual changes over time.[3] Centuries later, in 2000, the 'Administrative Court' was officially created in England. Through this historical prism, we can get a glimpse of the evolution on how administrative law and administrative litigation have been perceived and consequently transformed over time. By referring to the practices of ALS in different jurisdictions, we find that ALSs have undertaken gradual transformations across jurisdictions and such changes have continued to the present day. Nowadays, administrative litigation and judicial review has been commonly adopted by nearly all jurisdictions. It has become an indispensable component of a State's legal system and has been gaining incremental weight.

Different characteristics of domestic ALSs are found across jurisdictions. Meanwhile, some common features of modern ALSs are also identified. They are founded on the same theoretical basis, such as the separation of powers; they share the concerns to review State power and to protect individuals' rights; and they face common challenges to which most jurisdictions have to respond, such as judicial independence.

Situated in this comparative context, China seems to be confronted with more obstacles and hurdles than most, such as the deficiencies in the rule of law, the lack of judicial independence, and the peripheralisation of administrative litigation. Confined by the complex backdrop of China's political and ideological texture, the ALS in China is struggling forward. On the path towards the rule of law and constitutionalism in China, we regard the ALS as the best means of breakthrough considering the interdependence between the ALS and the attainment of the rule of law and constitutionalism. In conducting the comparative study on ALS in various jurisdictions we demonstrate the need for increased academic attention and efforts to be devoted to the field of

2 See generally Albert V. Dicey, *Introduction to the Study of the Law of the Constitution* (Indianapolis: Liberty Fund, 1982), Part II Chapter XII 'Rule of Law Compared with Droit Administratif', pp. 208–239.

3 C. Sumner Lobingier, 'Administrative Law and Droit Administratif: A Comparative Study with an Instructive Model', 91–1 (1942) *University of Pennsylvania Law Review and American Law Register*, pp. 36–58.

administrative litigation, and we sincerely hope that this book will prove fruitful in making some of the first necessary strides in that direction.

PART I
Administrative Litigation Systems in Greater China

Chapter 2
The Hurdle is High: The Administrative Litigation System in the People's Republic of China

Yuwen Li and Yun Ma

Introduction

The administrative litigation system remains nascent in mainland China. Besides the problem that the Administrative Litigation Law (ALL) promulgated in 1989 is out of date as a consequence of rapid economic, social and legal transformation over the past two decades, the implementation of the ALL has also encountered notorious problems, which are dubbed 'three difficulties, one low and one high'. This refers to the difficulty in making one's case accepted in court, difficulties in the trials of administrative cases and difficulties in the execution of administrative judgments, low numbers of administrative cases accepted and handled by the courts, and a high withdrawal rate by plaintiffs.[1] This chapter provides an overview of the history, current legislation and implementation of the law in terms of the administrative litigation system in mainland China. We first provide a concise historical overview of the evolution of the administrative litigation system; then we briefly examine the current legislative framework and other applicable legal rules on the administrative litigation system. In the next section, we discuss the scope and standards of judicial review provided in law, its limitations and expansion in judicial practice; this is followed by an analysis of the most difficult issue of having one's case accepted by courts (*li'an nan*). Next, the predicament of courts and judges in handling administrative cases is discussed, linking this issue closely with the lack of judicial independence in general. We then probe the highly controversial application of reconciliation in the settlement of administrative disputes in courts. Academic proposals on the revision of the ALL are discussed from a prospective view. Lastly, concluding remarks are provided.

A Brief Historical Overview of the Administrative Litigation System in Mainland China

The concept of administrative litigation was first embedded in China in the late Qing dynasty. As a semi-colonial regime, the Qing dynasty was compelled to incorporate the Western ideology and legal systems. The idea of establishing an Administrative Trial Chamber was proposed in 1906, and the Act of Administrative Trial Chamber was drafted in 1909; however, the Qing dynasty collapsed in 1911 even before this Act was promulgated.[2]

In the current scholarly research, the birth of the administrative litigation system is normally traced back to the Provisional Convention of the Republic of China (*linshi yuefa*) issued by the

1 Luo Liping, 'Xingzheng Susong Tiaojie Zhidu Lungang' (Analysis of mediation in administrative cases), 1 (2011) *Dangdai Faxue* (*Modern Jurisprudence*). Full text is available at http://article.chinalawinfo.com/article_print.asp?articleid=68022. Last visited July 2013.

2 Zhang Sheng, 'Zhongguo Jindai Xingzheng Fayuan zhi Yange' (Evolution of the administrative court in modern China), 4 (2002) *Xingzheng Faxue Yanjiu* (*Journal of Administrative Law*), p. 86.

Provisional Nanjing Government in March 1912.[3] It was thereof provided that 'citizens are entitled to bring a lawsuit to the *Pingzhengyuan* against the actions of officials that violate their rights' (Article 10). The establishment of *Pingzhengyuan* is commonly referred to as the rudiment of the administrative court in China. In March 1914, the Organic Act of *Pingzhengyuan* was enacted by the Beijing Government, and two months later, the Convention of the Republic of China (with similar status to the Constitution) further confirmed the authority of *Pingzhengyuan* in handling administrative litigation. The *Pingzhengyuan* started to hear administrative cases in March 1914 and was replaced by the Administrative Court in December 1928 along with the establishment of Nanjing Kuomintang Government. Over nearly 15 years, according to scholarly research, *Pingzhengyuan* heard a total of 407 cases with an average of 28 cases per year.[4] The achievements of legislation and legal practices of *Pingzhengyuan* in this period have contributed to the later legislation and practices of the Administrative Court.[5]

In 1928, the regime of the Nanjing Kuomintang Government was established. Designed by the founder, Sun Yat-sen, of the new regime, the central government was divided into five branches that were the Legislative Yuan, the Executive Yuan, the Judicial Yuan, the Examination Yuan and the Control Yuan. The Judicial Yuan functioned as the supreme judicial organ. Based on the Organic Act of the Judicial Yuan, which was issued in 1928, the Administrative Court was established within the Judicial Yuan to hear administrative cases. The Organic Act of Administrative Court and the Administrative Litigation Law were later issued in November 1932, which established the basic legal framework of the administrative litigation system.

Compared to the *Pingzhengyuan* during the period of the Beijing Government, the administrative court system under the regime of Nanjing Kuomintang Government has evolved in the following three aspects. Firstly, the administrative court was affiliated to the supreme judicial organ, i.e. the Judicial Yuan, while the *Pingzhengyuan* was affiliated to the executive branch of the President. Secondly, the qualifications of judges in the Administrative Court were higher than the ones for the *Pingzhengyuan*. It was required that, before one was nominated as a judge in the Administrative Court, the candidate should have several years' working experience as a senior judge or prosecutor, or have worked as a civil servant for more than four years after graduation of three years' studies in law or finance, etc. Such requirements were not found with regard to the qualification of a judge at *Pingzhengyuan*.[6] Thirdly, the scope of acceptable cases was broader in the Administrative Court than in the *Pingzhengyuan*. Besides the suit brought against administrative actions, which was the only type of case acceptable before the *Pingzhengyuan*, the suits of incidental compensation were also allowed to be brought before the Administrative Court.[7]

Varying statistics on the number of cases that the Administrative Court handled during the period of the Nanjing Kuomintang Government are provided in scholarly research based on

---

3 See Li Xiuqing, 'Cong Pingzhengyuan dao Xingzheng Fayuan: Minguo Shiqi Daluxing Xingzheng Shenpan Zhidu Yanjiu' (From the *Pingzhengyuan* to administrative court: research on the Continent-legal-system-based administrative trial system during the period of the Republic of China), in Wang Limin (ed.), *Zhongguo Falv yu Shehui* (*Law and Society in China*) (Bejing: Peking University Press, 2006). Full text is available at http://article.chinalawinfo.com/Article_Detail.asp?ArticleId=47751. Last visited July 2013. See also Zhang Sheng, *supra* note 2, pp. 84–89.

4 Cai Zhifang, 'Woguo Diyige Xingzheng Susong Shenpan Jigou: Pingzhengyuan' (The first institution of administrative trial in China: the Pingzhengyuan), in Cai Zhifang, *Xingzheng Jiuji yu Xingzheng Faxue* (*Administrative Remedy and Administrative Law*) (Taiwan: Sanmin Shuju, 1993), p. 277.

5 Li Xiuqing, *supra* note 3.

6 See the Administrative Litigation Law of 1932. Citing from Zhang Sheng, *supra* note 2, p. 88.

7 *Ibid.*

different historical documents. According to a scholar from mainland China, Zhang Sheng, during the two-year period from 1933 to 1935, the Administrative Court received 404 complaints, in which 179 were rejected, which accounted for 44 per cent. Within the 225 cases that the Administrative Court handled, the plaintiffs won 43 cases, which accounted for 19 per cent. He states that, during the period from 1933 to 1946, the average number of administrative cases handled by the Administrative Court was around 100 per year, and the rate of conclusion of cases remained at around 50 per cent.[8] Based on these statistics, he concludes that the purpose of the administrative court system to provide remedies to citizens is not fully realised.[9] A survey conducted by Cai Zhifang, a scholar from Taiwan, pointed out that, during the period from 1933 to 1947, the Administrative Court handled 712 cases in total with 48 cases per year. Among these cases, 61.5 per cent of the plaintiffs' complaints were rejected.[10] Despite the differences, these statistics illustrate that the administrative litigation system was undeveloped and limited under the then circumstances of China. The principal reason is that during this period the internal wars and Sino-Japanese war caused an unstable political regime in China, and so the legal system as a whole could not be meaningfully constructed. There were neither internal nor external settings that allowed the administrative litigation system to survive and flourish.

In 1949, the new regime of the People's Republic of China (PRC) was founded. The former legal system was totally abolished by the Chinese Communist Party (CCP) and the construction of the new legal system underwent a sharp shift towards a basis of socialist ideology that was led by the CCP. Discontinuities with the former legislation and practices regarding the administrative litigation system can be witnessed.

In the early stages of the new regime, the administrative litigation system was, in reality, not established. Most of the administrative disputes were settled internally within the administrative body rather than through litigation. The re-establishment of the administrative litigation system only occurred along with the economic reform and social transformation in China in the 1980s.

In the beginning of the 1980s, several laws and regulations provided that citizens could bring a lawsuit to the People's Courts against the decisions made by administrative agencies.[11] With regard to the procedural aspect, in the Civil Procedure Law (for trial implementation) of 1982, it stated that the provisions were applicable to administrative cases that were to be tried by the People's Courts according to the law (Article 3). During this period, the administrative cases were mostly tried at the civil chambers within courts at each level in accordance with civil procedures. From the mid-1980s, initiatives to establish a separate administrative chamber took place at both the central and local levels. According to scholarly research, the first administrative chamber was established by the Intermediate People's Court (IPC) of Wuhan City, Hubei Province in October 1986. In November of the same year, the first administrative chamber at the Basic People's Court (BPC)

---

8 *Ibid.*, p. 89.

9 *Ibid.*, p. 88.

10 Cai Zhifang, *supra* note 4, pp. 306–313. His survey is also used by other scholars: see Li Xiuqing, *supra* note 3.

11 For example, in the Income Tax Law on Chinese–Foreign Equity Joint Ventures of 1980, it was provided that, 'in case of a dispute with the tax authorities over tax payment, a joint venture must pay tax according to the relevant regulations before applying to higher tax authorities for administrative reconsideration. If it does not accept the decision made after the reconsideration, it may bring a lawsuit to the local people's court' (Article 15). See also the Maritime Environmental Protection Law of 1982 (Articles 41&42), the Law on Administration of Entry and Exit of Foreigners Entry of 1986 (Article 29), etc.

was established in Miluo County, Hunan Province.[12] In 1988 the Supreme People's Court (SPC) established its administrative chambers. By 1990 nearly all the local courts at all levels had set up their administrative chamber.[13] At this point, the ALL[14] was promulgated by the National People's Congress (NPC), and became effective in October 1990, which marked the formal establishment of the administrative litigation system in the PRC.

An Overview of the Legislative Framework and Other Applicable Rules in the PRC

Compared to the civil and criminal trial systems, the administrative litigation system is relatively new. The Civil Procedure Law (CiPL) was first promulgated in 1982 for provisional implementation and the Criminal Procedure Law (CrPL) was first issued in 1979, whereas the ALL was promulgated in 1989. With regard to their amendments, the CiPL was substantively amended in 1991 and amended twice in 2007 and 2012; the CrPL was overhauled in 1996 and further amended significantly in 2012; however, the ALL has not been revised once. Despite the NPC deciding to amend the ALL in its five-year legislative plan (2003–2008), it has failed to do so to date. It is quite exceptional in China that a law is not revised after more than 20 years' implementation in view of the rapid proliferation of law-making and law amendments in nearly all legal spheres. It is beyond the intention of this chapter to discuss the pros and cons of the absent amendment to the ALL. However, it clearly proves the lack of consensus among political elites to improve the legislation so as to use it to pursue a higher level of protection of citizens' rights and supervision of governmental institutions to ensure their functioning within the framework of legal constraint. In recent years as a degradation of the overall judicial reform towards independence and professionalisation, many Chinese legal scholars and judges echo the conservative approach of maintaining the ALL in its current form, for fear that alterations may weaken rather than strengthen the nascent system.

The ALL contains 75 articles, with 11 sections covering the general provisions, scope of case acceptance by courts, jurisdiction, parties in proceedings, evidence, initiation of an action and acceptance of cases by courts, trial and judgments, execution, compensation liability for infringement of rights, administrative procedure involving foreign interests, and supplementary provisions. Identical to the normal pattern of the procedural laws in China, the ALL is general and brief. It leaves detailed implementation rules to be made by the SPC. In 1991 the SPC issued the Opinions on Several Issues Concerning the Implementation of Administrative Litigation Law (Trial) with a total of 115 articles,[15] and it was repealed by the Explanations on Several Issues Concerning the Implementation of Administrative Litigation Law in 2000 (hereinafter

12 Liang Fengyun, 'Guanyu Wanshan Xingzheng Shenpan Tizhi De Wenti' (Issues on perfecting the administrative trial system), in Jiang Bixin, et al. (eds), *Zhongguo Xingzheng Susong Zhidu De Wanshan: Xingzheng Susongfa Xiugai Wenti Shiwu Yanjiu* (*Improvement of Administrative Litigation System in China*) (Beijing: Falu chubanshe, 2005), p. 6.

13 Xin Chunying, 'Ershiyi Shiji: Zhongguo Xuyao Shenmeyang De Sifa Quanli?' (Twenty-first century: what kind of judicial power does China need?), in Xin Chunying (ed.), *Gong Fa* (*Public Law*) (Beijing: Falu Chubanshe, 2002), p. 8.

14 The English text of the ALL is available at http://en.chinacourt.org/public/detail.php?id=2695. Last visited July 2013.

15 *Fa (xing) fa* No.19 [1991]. Available at http://www.law-lib.com/law/law_view.asp?id=7697. Last visited July 2013.

the Explanations) with 98 articles.[16] In addition, the SPC also issued the 1997 Rules on Several Issues Concerning Adjudication of Administrative Compensation Cases;[17] the 2002 Rules on Several Issues Concerning Administrative Litigation Evidence;[18] the 2008 Rules on Several Issues Concerning Jurisdiction over Administrative Cases;[19] the 2008 Rules on Several Issues Concerning Withdrawal of Administrative Litigation;[20] the 2009 Rules on Several Issues Concerning Trial of Administrative License Cases;[21] and the 2011 Rules on Several Issues Concerning Trial of Administrative Cases about Disclosure of Government Information.[22] Though the issue on the legal status and hierarchy of judicial interpretations in China is still under debate, in practice, the ALL and these SPC judicial interpretations constitute the main sources of legal rules in guiding judges to handle administrative cases.

These judicial interpretations have not only specified the provisions in the ALL, but also expanded them to some extent. For example, the formats of judgments are expanded through the 2000 Explanations by adding two new types of judgments, which are 'the judgment to reject the plaintiff's claims'[23] and 'the confirmative judgment'[24] to the original four formats, i.e. the judgments to sustain, quash, or modify the original administrative action, and to order the defendant to perform its duties (Article 54 of the ALL).

Relationship between Administrative Reconsideration and Administrative Litigation

Under the current legal framework of China, the administrative reconsideration system and administrative litigation system are the two main administrative remedy mechanisms. The former is

16 *Fashi* No.8 [2000]. Available at http://www.law-lib.com/law/law_view.asp?id=33. Last visited July 2013.

17 *Fashi* No.10 [1997]. Available at http://www.law-lib.com/law/law_view.asp?id=328. Last visited July 2013.

18 *Fashi* No.21 [2002]. Available at http://www.law-lib.com/law/law_view.asp?id=40817. Last visited July 2013.

19 *Fashi* No.1 [2008]. Available at http://www.law-lib.com/law/law_view.asp?id=243717. Last visited July 2013.

20 *Fashi* No.2 [2008]. Available at http://www.law-lib.com/law/law_view.asp?id=243716. Last visited July 2013.

21 *Fashi* No.20 [2009]. Available at http://www.law-lib.com/law/law_view.asp?id=305821. Last visited July 2013.

22 *Fashi* No.17 [2011]. Available at http://www.law-lib.com/law/law_view.asp?id=358265. Last visited July 2013.

23 According to Article 56 of the Explanations, the courts should deliver a judgment to reject the plaintiff's claims under the circumstances that (1) the plaintiffs sue the defendant for its inaction that is not supported by evidence; (2) the administrative action is legal yet questionable in its appropriateness; (3) the administrative action is legal yet needs to be modified or repealed according to the changes of laws and policies; and (4) other circumstances.

24 Article 57 of the Explanations authorises the courts to deliver a judgment to confirm the legality or validity of the administrative action when the courts deem the action to be legal; however, it is not appropriate to deliver a judgment to sustain the administrative action or reject the plaintiff's claims. Under the following circumstances, the courts should deliver a judgment to confirm the illegality or invalidity of the administrative action: (1) the defendant does not perform its duty yet it is already meaningless to order the defendant to perform the duty; (2) the administrative action is illegal yet with nothing to be quashed; and (3) the administrative action is not effectively formed or is invalid.

authoritatively established by the Regulations on the Administrative Reconsideration promulgated by the State Council in 1990, revised in 1994 and replaced by the Administrative Reconsideration Law (ARL) of 1999.

A general principle of the relationship between administrative reconsideration and administrative litigation is provided in Article 37 of the ALL, which states that plaintiffs may choose to apply to the administrative organ at the next higher level for administrative reconsideration or directly bring a lawsuit to the courts. If the plaintiff is not satisfied with the reconsideration decision, they may still be entitled to bring a lawsuit to the courts. In practice, administrative reconsideration is not frequently used. It is roughly calculated that around 70 per cent of administrative cases are not reconsidered before they are brought to the courts.[25] There are three sets of exceptions to the general principle according to relevant laws and regulations.

Firstly, in certain circumstances, administrative reconsideration is a preliminary procedure before the plaintiff can bring a lawsuit. This includes cases relating to confirmation of ownership or usufruct of natural resources (Article 30 (1) of the ARL), cases relating to tax disputes (Article 88 of the Tax Administration Law of 2001), cases relating to decisions made by anti-monopoly authorities on the prohibition or restriction of the concentration of operators (Article 53 of Anti-monopoly Law of 2008), cases relating to the application of trademarks (Article 32 of Trademark Law of 2001), etc.

Secondly, plaintiffs could choose to apply for administrative reconsideration or administrative litigation; however, if the former is chosen, it is not permissible to bring a lawsuit against the reconsideration decision. For example, when the respondent is the government at a provincial level or departments within the State Council, the reconsideration decision made by the State Council will have final and binding force if the applicants choose to apply for administrative reconsideration (Article 14 of the ARL).

Thirdly, the plaintiff can only apply for administrative reconsideration and the reconsideration decision will be final. The most typical case is provided in Article 30 (2) of the ARL, which states that the reconsideration decision made by provincial governments confirming the ownership or usufruct of natural resources, on the basis of the decisions made by the State Council or provincial governments with regard to the survey, delimitation or readjustment of administrative division, or land requisition, is final. In the Law on Administration of Exit and Entry of 2012, it is provided that, if foreigners do not accept the administrative decisions on deportation, restriction on the sphere of their activities, detention or interrogation, they could apply for administrative reconsideration, which would be final (Article 64). Another case is provided in Article 14 of the Regulations on Implementation of the Law on Assemblies, Processions and Demonstrations of 1989, which states that the responsible person may apply for reconsideration to relevant authorities against the decision made by competent authorities not to grant a permission of assembly, procession or demonstration. The reconsideration decision must be enforced without opportunities for further complaints. These provisions in reality deprive citizens of access to courts and are thus criticised by scholars for their legitimacy.[26]

---

25 Li Li, 'Qicheng Xingzheng Susong Anjian Suqian Weijing Xingzheng Fuyi' (70 per cent of administrative cases are not reconsidered before they are brought to courts), *Fazhi Ribao* (*Legal Daily*), 4 December 2006. Full text is available at http://news.sina.com.cn/o/2006-12-04/082310675886s.shtml. Last visited July 2013.

26 Zhang Zhiyuan, 'Lun Xingzheng Fuyi yu Xingzheng Susong zhi Chengxu Xianjie' (Analysis on links between procedures of administrative reconsideration and administrative litigation), 4 (2005) *Xingzheng Faxue Yanjiu* (*Research on Administrative Law*), p. 80.

Though the administrative reconsideration system was legalised by the law, i.e. through the Law on Administrative Reconsideration passed in 1999, later than the administrative litigation system, it has been playing a more and more important role in providing remedies to citizens. In recent years, some scholars even propose that the administrative reconsideration should be the primary mechanism to resolve administrative disputes.[27] Thus, in the proposal to amend the ALL, some scholars argue that administrative reconsideration should be prescribed as a preliminary procedure before all litigation; however, controversy remains. Other scholars stress that the choice should be left to citizens and that it is a necessity to reform the reconsideration system by enhancing its fairness and efficiency.[28]

The Scope of Judicial Review in Law and in Practice

The scope of judicial review is generally provided in Article 2 and concretised in Article 11 of the ALL. These Articles are further explained by Article 12 and 13 of the 2000 Explanations. The ALL also provides the scope of matters that cannot be reviewed, which are detailed in Article 12 and further explained by Articles 1 to 5 of the 2000 Explanations.

With regard to the scope of matters that can be reviewed, it is provided that individuals, companies and social organisations (similar to NGOs) who allege their lawful rights and interests have been infringed by concrete administrative actions of administrative bodies and administrative officials (Article 2 of the ALL), or who have certain legal interests in the concrete administrative actions (Article 12 of the Explanations), can bring lawsuits to courts. The concrete administrative actions are enumerated in Article 11 of the ALL, including:

1. administrative penalties such as detention, fines, revocation of a business licence or permit, order of suspension of production or business activities, or the confiscation of property;
2. compulsory administrative measures such as the restriction of freedom of the person or the sealing up, seizure or freezing of property;
3. infringement by an administrative organ on the managerial autonomy of a business as stipulated by law;
4. refusal to issue or refusal to reply to an application for a permit or licence conforming to the provisions of law;
5. refusal to perform a duty required by law regarding the protection of one's personal and property rights;
6. failing to distribute a pension according to law;
7. demanding administrative organs to perform their duties according to law;
8. infringement upon other personal and property rights.

---

27 Ying Songnian, 'Ba Xingzheng Fuyi Zhidu Jianshe Chengwei Woguo Xingzheng Zhengyi de Zhu Qudao' (To improve the administrative reconsideration system and place it as the main channel to resolve administrative disputes), 5 (2011) *Faxue Luntan* (*Legal Forum*), pp. 5–9.

28 See Yang Weidong, 'Fuyi Qianzhi yihuo Ziyou Xuanze: Woguo Xingzheng Fuyi yu Xingzheng Susong Guanxi de Chuli' (Administrative reconsideration as preliminary or free choice: arrangement of the relationship between administrative reconsideration and administrative litigation in China), 2 (2012) *Xingzheng Faxue Yanjiu* (*Research on Administrative Law*), pp. 71–76.

In order not to be completely limited by the eight types of actions, Article 11 concludes with the general provision that the courts should also accept other administrative cases, which may be initiated in accordance with the provisions of relevant laws and regulations.

In addition, Article 12 of the ALL also provides that courts should not accept suits against administrative actions concerning four types of matters:

1. State acts relating to defence and foreign affairs.
2. Administrative rules and regulations, or decisions and orders with general binding force issued by administrative organs. These are generally referred to as abstract administrative actions.
3. Decisions made by an administrative organ concerning rewards, punishments, appointments, and dismissal of administrative agency personnel. These are considered internal personnel acts.
4. Final decisions made by some administrative organs with the authority to issue final decisions.

Different from the open-ended description on the scope of matters that can be reviewed, this Article exhaustively enumerates the only four matters that cannot be reviewed. However, in the Explanations, besides these four matters, Article 1 adds another four circumstances, namely actions of agencies of public security, national security, etc. that are explicitly authorised by the Criminal Procedure Law; mediation, and arbitration in accordance with law; administrative guidance that is not coercive; repetitive actions to reject the complaints brought by citizens against administrative actions. Moreover, an open-ended clause is provided by referring to actions that do not have substantive effects on the rights and duties of citizens, legal persons and other social organisations.

From these legal provisions, there are generally two criteria in defining the scope of judicial review. The first is concrete administrative action, and the second is personal and property rights.

Concrete vs. Abstract Administrative Actions

The term 'concrete administrative action' is explicitly used in the ALL and the Explanations to exclude 'abstract administrative action' from being subject to judicial review. Abstract administrative action refers to administrative regulations issued by the State Council, administrative rules issued by ministerial-level bodies, administrative decisions, and orders with a general legal binding force. There has been a long debate on whether such distinction should be made. Supporters of ruling out abstract administrative actions from the judicial review mainly contend that the correction of such general administrative actions can be done by legislative bodies through the legislative supervisory system. Moreover, higher-level government has the power to change or withdraw inappropriate decisions or orders made by lower-level government. They also propound that, due to the nature of the general binding force of abstract administrative actions, if any person is allowed to bring a lawsuit against it, courts will not be able to handle the overwhelming number of cases.[29] Proponents of including abstract administrative actions within the scope of judicial review claim that the legislative supervision system lacks a clear procedure and is hardly applied in practice. This is said to have resulted in numerous administrative regulations and rules that violate the legal rights and interests of individuals and business, cannot be challenged.[30] These administrative

29 Discussed in Jiang Mingan (ed.), *Xingzhengfa yu Xingzheng Susongfa* (*Administrative Law and Administrative Litigation Law*) (Beijing: Beijing Daxue Chubanshe, 1999), p. 318.

30 Liu Junxiang, 'Lun Woguo Chouxiang Xingzheng Xingwei de Sifa Shencha' (Analysis on judicial review of abstract administrative action in China), 21–6 (1999) *Xiandai Faxue* (*Modern Law Science*), p. 72; Ma Huaide, 'Xi Chouxiang Xingzheng Xingwei Naru Susong Fanwei Zhi Biyaoxing' (Analysis on the

regulations and rules are dubbed as 'documents headed with red seals' (*hongtou wenjian*).[31] An obvious example of such a violation is the collection of various fees by local governments. It is also argued that under certain circumstances it is difficult or impossible to distinguish between abstract and concrete administrative actions. For judges to review a concrete administrative action, they may have to trace the origin of such an action to the abstract administrative action.

To respond to the debate and dilemma in judicial practice the SPC avoided using the term 'concrete administrative actions' in its 2000 Explanations. Whether this can be deemed to signal the SPC's intention to clarify the issue remains unclear. Accordingly, the final solution to this controversy can only be expected in the future amendment of the ALL. At the same time, the judiciary continues to be blurred by some situations where a distinction between concrete or abstract actions is difficult to determine.

Personal and Property Rights, and other Rights

Another undesirable restriction on the scope of judicial review in Article 11 of the ALL is that the concrete administrative actions are deemed to have infringed the personal or property rights of the plaintiffs. This leaves the question of whether citizens can bring lawsuits if they consider their political rights to have been violated. A reason to explain the limit set up in Article 11 is that in 1989 when the ALL was promulgated there was a lack of substantive laws to protect citizens' other rights. However, this situation changed when a series of new laws was issued, such as the 1989 Law on Assemblies, Processions, and Demonstrations, the 1994 Labor Law and the 1995 Law on Education. The State Council has also issued administrative regulations, such as the 1989 Regulations on Registration and Administration of Social Organisations (later amended in 1998) and the 2001 Regulations on Publishing Administration (later amended in 2011). These laws and regulations provide citizens' rights that go beyond personal and property rights.

Judicial practice over the past two decades demonstrates that courts have gradually expanded their jurisdiction in administrative litigation in a cautious way, which has gone beyond the statutory language of 'personal and property rights'. A typical example of such judicial 'innovation' is the handling of cases relating to the right to education. In the 1990s a growing number of complaints was brought to courts by students concerning universities' decisions to dismiss them, or refusal to issue certificates or diplomas to students who disobeyed university rules. Such complaints concern a student's right to education. In 1998, the BPC in Haidian District in Beijing handled the case of *Tian Yong v. Beijing Science and Technology University*;[32] one year later, the same court concluded the case of *Liu Yanwen v. Peking University*.[33] Both cases are conceived as landmark cases for Chinese courts to accept complaints pertaining to the exercise of the right to education. The Supreme People's Court showed its support to local courts handling such cases by publishing the judgment of the case *Tian Yong v. Beijing Science and Technology University* in the Gazette

---

necessity of including abstract administrative actions to the scope of litigation), 10 (2001) *Renmin Jiancha* (*People's Procuratorate*), pp. 12–15; and Liu Songshan, 'Weifa Xingzheng Guifanxing Wenjian zhi Zeren Zhuijiu' (Responsibility on illegal administrative normative regulations), 4 (2002) *Faxue Yanjiu* (*Legal Studies*), pp. 36–38.

31 See Wang Jingin and Gu Ying, '"Hongtou Wenjian" Weifa zhi Yuanyin ji Duice Lunxi' (Analysis on the reasons for and the resolutions to the illegality of 'documents headed with red seals'), 11 (2005) *Xingzheng yu Fa* (*Administration and Law*), pp. 78–81.

32 The judgment was published in the Gazette of the SPC, No. 4, 1999, pp. 139–142.

33 The judgment can be found at http://www.publiclaw.cn/Comment/Details.asp?NewsId=631&ClassId=&ClassName=典型案例. Last visited March 2013.

of the SPC. Following this, numerous similar cases have been handled by BPCs in places close to universities. Despite China not having the case precedent system, the courts' handling of cases relating to students suing universities proves that some leading cases have been used by courts as references in deciding similar cases.[34]

Another area that shows the courts' expansion of their jurisdiction relates to the right to work. For years, complaints brought by citizens about discrimination in the labour market were not accepted by courts. This situation has gradually changed in recent years. The scope of cases that are accepted by courts relating to employment discrimination covers discrimination based on the height of a person, discrimination based on gender, discrimination of carriers of the hepatitis B virus (HBV), discrimination of HIV carriers, discrimination on the basis of age, and others.[35] Within these cases, some are administrative litigation against personnel bureaus or other administrative agencies, and some are civil litigation against employers, such as companies.

In 2003, the first administrative case relating to employment discrimination of HBV carriers was trialed at the BPC of Wuhu City in Anhui Province. The plaintiff, Zhang Xianzhu, won the first place in the examination of the recruitment of civil servants, which was organised by the Personnel Bureau of Wuhu City. He was later refused by the Personnel Bureau after he was found to be a HBV carrier during the subsequent physical examination. The refusal was finally quashed by the court.[36]

In April 2008 the SPC issued the Announcement on Fully Realising the Role of Administrative Litigation in Providing Forceful Judicial Guarantee for People's Livelihoods.[37] It specifically clarified the scope of the acceptance of administrative cases to include cases concerning citizens' right to education, right to work, distribution of income, medical care, and other areas relevant to people's livelihoods.

Difficulty in Having One's Case Filed by the Courts (*Li'an Nan*)

According to the statistics in 1991 the first year after the ALL became effective, the courts of first instance concluded 25,202 cases; 10 years later the figure rose to 95,984; another decade later the number reached 136,000. This demonstrates that within 20 years the number has increased more than five times. Figure 2.1 shows the number of administrative cases concluded in the first instance by courts all over China from 1998 to 2011.

It should be noted that over the past 30 years the numbers of civil and commercial, criminal, and administrative cases concluded by courts have all increased. This proves that the role of courts in settling disputes has significantly increased. The plausible explanations for this shift are multifold. Firstly, the disputes and conflicts are multiplied and diversified in the transforming society of China. The internal economic reform featured by the 'Reform and Open-up' policy since

34 For a detailed examination of Chinese courts handling cases of students and teachers against universities, see Thomas E. Kellogg, 'Courageous Explorers?: Education Litigation and Judicial Innovation in China', 20 (2007) *Harvard Human Rights Journal*, pp. 141–188.

35 See Research Institute on Human Rights at Sichuan University, 'Zhongguo Fayuan he Zhongcai Jigou Jinzhi Jiuye Qishi Anli Xuan' (Selection of cases on prohibition of employment discrimination by courts and arbitral institutions in China), July 2011. Available at http://www.ilo.org/wcmsp5/groups/public/---asia/---ro-bangkok/---ilo-beijing/documents/publication/wcms_168130.pdf. Last visited July 2013.

36 For more information, see Sina, 'Quanguo Shouli Yigan Qishi An' (The first case of discrimination of HBV carrier). Available at http://news.sina.com.cn/z/ahygqs/index.shtml. Last visited July 2013.

37 *Fa* No.125 [2008]. Available at http://vip.chinalawinfo.com/newlaw2002/slc/slc.asp?db=chl&gid=105575. Last visited July 2013.

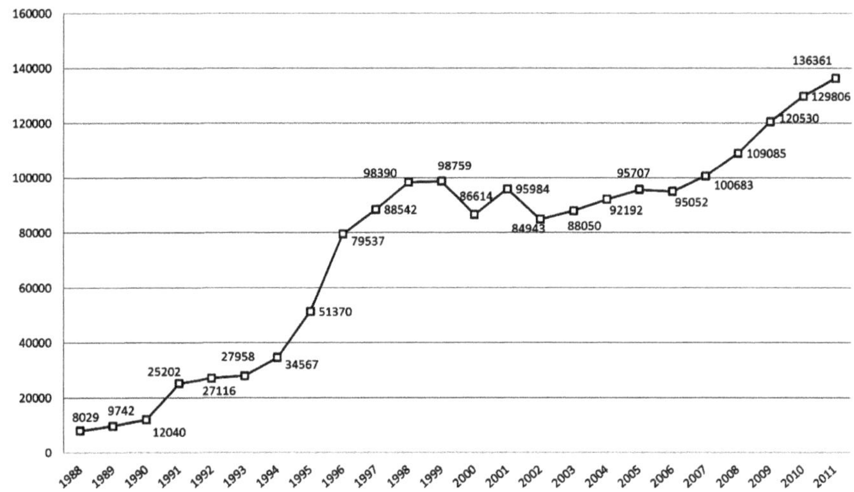

Figure 2.1 The Overall Trend of the Rising Number of Administrative Cases Concluded in the First Instance by All Courts in China, 1988–2011

Source: China Law Yearbooks (1989–2012).

the late 1970s, and the accession to the WTO in 2001 have to a large extent diversified the interests and stakeholders. The accompanying political and social reforms, on the one hand, re-allocate the existing interests pattern, and on the other hand, polarise between the rich and the poor and make the social stratification more explicit than ever. All of these lead to a society replete with conflicts and tensions. Secondly, citizens have a stronger sense of resorting to the courts and relying on the law to have their disputes settled. Bringing litigation to the court is no longer deemed as shameful, which was once the case in earlier times of China; instead, civilisation and modernisation endow legal approaches to conflict-solving with broader social recognition and acceptance. Thirdly, the past 30 years have witnessed a process of enhanced legal education and formation of a team of professional judges. The ability of courts and judges to settle disputes arises. All in all, the disputes are multiplied, the citizens are inclined to resort to the courts, and the ability of judiciary to settle these disputes is enhanced. All of these factors have contributed to the proliferation of cases and the increasing role of courts in settling disputes in China.

Figure 2.2 demonstrates that the most drastic multiplication is civil and commercial cases. For example, in 2011, the figure of civil and commercial cases handled at the first instance was 6,558,621; for criminal cases, 839,973; and for administrative cases, 136,361. This means that civil and commercial cases stand for around 87 per cent of all cases handled at the first instance, criminal cases about 11 per cent and administrative cases approximately 2 per cent.

Despite the increasing trend in general, a common complaint in China is the difficulty to have one's case filed by the courts, which constitutes a major barrier to the exercise of a citizen's right to access the courts. Obviously, we cannot prove such difficulty by statistics simply because there is no record whatsoever. We could get an overall picture of the way the problem was addressed by academic observation. By introducing the indicator of 'rate of administrative litigation' (number of administrative litigations occurring among one million people), Ying Xing points out that, during the period from 1998 to 2008, the average rate of administrative litigation is 73.8 with an average

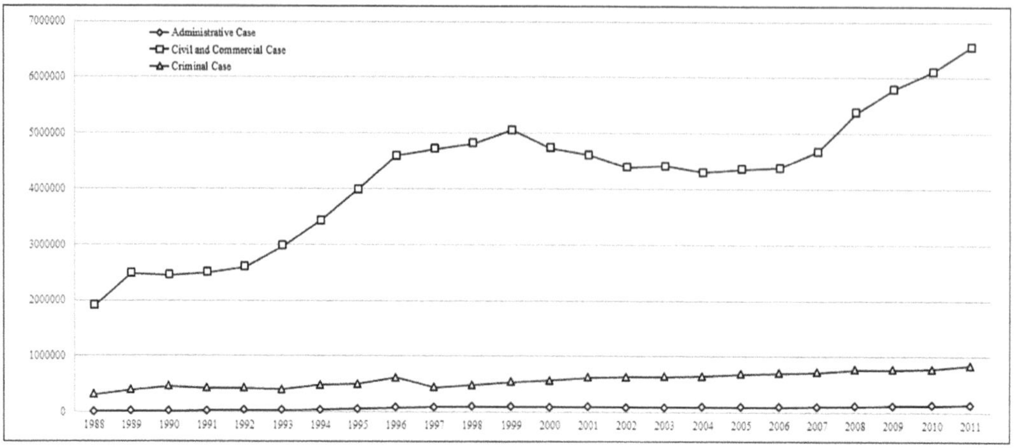

Figure 2.2 Comparison among the Numbers of Administrative, Civil and Commercial, and Criminal Cases Concluded in the First Instance by All Courts in China, 1988–2011

Source: China Law Yearbooks (1989–2012).

increasing rate of 1.45 per cent per year.[38] This means, that among one million people, there are only 73.8 administrative cases brought forward to courts each year. A survey by the Chinese Academy of Social Sciences in 2004 revealed that, among the 632 petitioners who took their cases to the central authority in Beijing, nearly two-thirds of them had at the outset brought their cases to local courts; and 43 per cent reported that the courts did not want to accept their cases, which impelled them to petition administrative officials in Beijing.[39]

According to the ALL (Arts. 37, 39 and 41), there are generally six conditions to be satisfied before a case is admitted and filed, which are:

1. the plaintiff considers that the concrete administrative action has infringed upon their legal rights and interests;
2. the defendant should be specific;
3. there must be a specific claim and a corresponding factual basis;
4. the suit should fall within the scope of acceptance and the jurisdiction of the court;
5. an administrative reconsideration has been applied for where such procedure is the preliminary condition on litigation; and
6. the suit should be brought within the time limit provided by the law.

The difficulties in having one's case filed by courts can take place in various forms. Firstly, the courts refuse to accept the case by providing the reasons that the administrative action does not fall into the scope of cases that are acceptable. For example, it is a final administrative decision,

38 Ying Xing and Xu Yin, 'Li'an Zhengzhixue yu Xingzheng Susonglv de Paihuai: Huabei Liangshi Jiceng Fayuan de Duibi Yanjiu' (Politics of accepting a case by courts and fluctuation of the rate of administrative litigation: comparative analysis of two Basic People's Courts in two cities in north China), 27–6 (2009) *Zhengfa Luntan* (*Tribune of Political Science and Law*), pp. 111–112.

39 Congressional–Executive Commission on China, *Annual Report, 2007*, p. 151. Available at www.cecc.gov/pages/annualRpt/annualRpt07/CECCannRpt2007.pdf. Last visited July 2013.

an abstract administrative action, an action that does not have substantial effects on the rights and duties of citizens, or an internal action. In many cases, the courts do not even give the specific reasons why the case falls outside of the scope. Secondly, the courts may also refuse the cases by arguing that the plaintiff is not qualified to bring a lawsuit as their interests are not directly involved in a particular case. Thirdly, the courts may refuse the case for its lack of clear claims or designated formats of complaints. Lastly, lack of jurisdiction could also be an excuse or disguise for courts to refuse the case.[40] Subsequently, the claimants have to shuttle back and forth among courts at different levels. Failing to obtain satisfactory judicial responses to their claims, they are forced to petition to the central authority for justice.

In practice, some ridiculous excuses have been used by courts to refuse or delay a case. For example, in Cangzhou BPC in Hebei Province, the court delayed filing cases by stating that the judges in handling administrative cases were on an annual leave for holiday at that time.[41] In 2009, 31 judges sued relevant local authorities for demolishing their houses in Nanjing. The judges themselves encountered the same difficulty as ordinary citizens: the case was refused by the IPC of Nanjing city.[42]

To cope with this problem, the SPC has made several judicial explanations in recent years to supervise local courts from arbitrarily refusing the complaints brought by citizens. In 2008 the SPC issued two judicial explanations, which were the Rules on Several Issues Concerning Jurisdiction over Administrative Cases[43] and the Rules on Several Issues Concerning Withdrawal of Administrative Litigation.[44] In the former Rules, the SPC provides that, if the BPC does not file the case nor rule to refuse the case within seven days, the plaintiff can bring the lawsuit to the IPC. The IPC could require the competent BPC to handle the case, designate other BPCs to handle the case or decide to handle the case by itself (Article 3). The later Rules formulate principles and conditions under which withdrawal of claims by plaintiffs is to be allowed by courts, which strengthens the court's review on plaintiffs' withdrawal and to avoid the plaintiffs' withdrawal by intimidation from the defendants. Though these two Rules are not specifically designed to instruct local courts to file cases, they have in effect thwarted local courts' arbitrary refusal to plaintiffs.[45]

In April 2009, the SPC issued the Opinions on Further Strengthening the Work of Communication with Popular Will,[46] which required courts to improve the communication mechanism with netizens

---

40 See Hu Fengyun, 'Qiantan Woguo Xingzheng Susong Li'an Nan de Chengyin ji Duice' (Analysis of the reasons and solutions to the difficulties in having one's case filed by courts in administrative litigations), 25 March 2011. Available at http://old.chinacourt.org/html/article/201103/25/446057.shtml. Last visited July 2013.

41 See blog of lawyer Chen Yanjun. Available at http://hi.baidu.com/aiurcjmbmobbuvd/item/24177972fbc97e215c17895f. Last visited July 2013.

42 See '31 Ming Faguan "Bei Chaiqian", Wenming Weiquan que Nan Li'an' (Houses of 31 judges are demolished. They seek for legal protection of their rights; however it is difficult for their case to be accepted by courts), 17 December 2009, *Dongfang Zaobao* (Oriental Morning Post). Available at http://epaper.dfdaily.com/dfzb/html/2009-12/17/content_177981.htm. Last visited July 2013.

43 *Fashi* No.1 [2008]. Available at http://www.law-lib.com/law/law_view.asp?id=243717. Last visited July 2013.

44 *Fashi* No.2 [2008]. Available at http://www.law-lib.com/law/law_view.asp?id=243716. Last visited July 2013.

45 See 'Xingzheng Susong Ruhe Gaobie Li'an Nan' (How to say goodbye to 'difficulties in having one's cases filed' in administrative litigation), 16 May 2008. Available at http://news.sina.com.cn/c/2008-05-16/114215553631.shtml. Last visited May 2013.

46 *Fafa* No.20 [2009]. Available at http://news.xinhuanet.com/legal/2009-04/14/content_11184305.htm. Last visited July 2013.

through the platform of the internet. In the following June, the SPC disclosed the implementation of this communication mechanism. Among the 13 types of questions raised by netizens, the problem of difficulty in having administrative cases filed by courts ranked second in questions asked most frequently.[47] To address this problem, the SPC issued the Opinions on Protecting the Litigation Rights of Parties in Administrative Litigations According to Law in November 2009.[48] The Opinions specifically address the problem of difficulty in having a case filed by courts and put forward opinions on protecting the litigation rights of citizens from the following six perspectives:

1. to deepen the understanding of the significance of handling administrative litigation;
2. to prohibit shrinking the scope of accepting cases or illegally adding the conditions on the acceptance of cases;
3. to actively accept new types of administrative cases;
4. to improve the working mechanisms and styles;
5. to strengthen the supervision on accepting the administrative cases; and
6. to construct a beneficial external environment of accepting administrative cases by means of guiding the public in exercising their litigation rights properly and cooperating with other government institutions.

The reasons that courts refuse or are reluctant to file administrative cases are multifaceted. Some scholars adopt the concept of the 'politics of accepting a case by courts' to explain this phenomenon. They point out that, when courts make decisions on whether to accept a case or not, they have to review not only the formal conditions prescribed by the ALL, but also the relationship between the concerned dispute and local circumstances, social order and the needs of the CCP, and the relationship between local courts and local governmental and Party authorities.[49] To specify, the reasons could be provided from the following perspectives.

Firstly, due to the intrinsic nature of administrative litigation, defendants of administrative cases are governmental agencies and officials. In this context, judicial independence cannot be guaranteed. Some local governments have issued policy instructions, either to prevent courts from handling certain types of cases, or to order courts to communicate with the governments in advance before accepting certain types of cases.[50] Obviously, courts are largely bridled by such intervention from other authorities.

Secondly, many administrative cases are so politically sensitive that courts are not willing or are unable to deal with them. The political sensitivity can be understood from three dimensions:

1. Some types of administrative cases can be political cases and courts do not take the position that they are capable of handling such cases. The political cases especially touch the issues of freedom of religion, such as Falungong, the freedom of association, such as setting up a

47 Xinhua News Agency, 'Zuigao Fayuan: Minyi Goutong 13 Lei Wenti, 10 Lei yi Tichu Chuli Yijian' (SPC: 13 types of questions raised through communication with populaces, 10 of which are dealt with solutions), 2 June 2009. Available at http://www.gov.cn/jrzg/2009-06/02/content_1330664.htm. Last visited July 2013.

48 *Fafa* No.54 [2009]. Available at http://www.court.gov.cn/qwfb/sfwj/yj/201003/t20100331_3587.htm. Last visited July 2013.

49 Ying Xing and Xu Yin, *supra* note 38, p. 113.

50 Randall Peerenboom, 'A Government of Law: Democracy, Rule of Law and Administrative Law Reform in the PRC', 12–34 (2003) *Journal of Contemporary China*, p. 55.

political party, etc. In practice such cases are few in number. If they occur, they are mainly settled through the channel of political organs rather than adjudication by courts.

2. A considerable amount of administrative cases touch upon local governments and a large group of people whose rights and interests are allegedly infringed. For example, in 2011, most administrative cases are related to resource use (land, forestry, grassland, mineral resources, etc.) and city construction (city planning, demolition, house registration, etc.), which accounts for more than 18 per cent each according to the SPC's report.[51] This is partly due to the process of urbanisation in China. In these types of cases, courts fear that their stepping in would not help to tranquillise the situation. The courts thus find themselves in a dilemma: on the one hand, if the cases are accepted by courts, courts may not have the ability to efficiently solve the conflicts, and moreover, may risk intensifying the tension between the two parties; on the other hand, if the cases are refused, citizens are compelled to resort to other non-judicial complaint avenues, such as 'letter and visit' (*xinfang*). The effectiveness of *xinfang* proves the ineffectiveness of courts, which undermines public trust in the judicial authority.
3. A number of policies or major projects have been issued or approved by a central authority or authority at high level. Examples of the former include the policies of family planning and birth control, re-education through labour, etc. With regard to the latter type, examples include the project of high speed railway. A recent such case occurred in Shanghai. A department building that was still under construction suddenly toppled and fell in June 2009.[52] Affected residents in the community tried to sue relevant administrative agencies for their inaction of supervision at the Minhang BPC in Shanghai, but were refused. The court simply stated to those claimants that 'the district government suggests you calm down, so we would not receive your case'.[53]

Thirdly, traditional Chinese culture and ideology also partly causes this problem. In ancient China, the government officials also act as judges in resolving disputes between two parties. Though gradually being separated from the administrative officials, even today, judges are still treated as 'State cadres'. Conventionally, the Chinese regard government officials as 'bureaucrats shielding one another' (*guan guan xiang hu*), and it is the same case with judges. Under the bureaucratic structure of China, it is deemed that judges, like other officials, serve the State interests and needs of the leading Party. Thus, courts, as a whole, are deemed to have aligned their concerns with the interests of administrative agencies who are defendants of administrative litigation. Moreover, in a '*relations-based*' society like China, judges are personally inclined to keep good contacts with the powerful administrative agencies. Accepting administrative cases and ruling that the defendants lose the cases will probably ruin their personal relationship with administrative officials.

Fourthly, there is a lack of political commitment at the central level to empower courts with formidable capacities to effectively supervise governmental agencies and officials at all levels, making them strictly follow the law when performing their duties. In the 1980s the ALL was designed to be an instrument to use citizens to control grassroots level officials. Thus,

---

51 SPC, *Annual Report of Work of People's Court (2011)* (Beijing: Renmin Fayuan Press, 2012), p. 38.

52 For details of this event, see Netease, 'Shanghai Zaijian Zhuzhailou Zhengti Daota' (A residential building under construction collapses in Shanghai), June 2009. Available at http://news.163.com/special/00013FTN/ShanghaiCollapse.html. Last visited July 2013.

53 See Li Yichuan, 'Falu Jiandu de Neirong, Shouduan yu Chengxu' (Content, method and procedure of legal supervision), in Symposium of the 7th National Conference on Senior Procurators (Dalian, October 2011), p. 761.

a controversial reality is that on the one hand the administrative litigation system is designed to protect citizens' rights from the violation of agencies, and to supervise the government to perform their duties according to law; On the other hand, courts are instructed to report and cooperate with the government in coping with issues that might be harmful to a stable social order and the leadership of governments and the Party.

In order to push forward the use of ALL and to encourage citizens to bring administrative lawsuits to courts, some legal scholars and lawyers have initiated lawsuits to courts themselves. The best known of such scholars who has brought a series of administrative cases to courts is Hao Jinsong.[54] In 2005, he consecutively lodged three suits against the Beijing Railway Bureau within four months. His claims included that the defendant did not provide him with invoices when he had dinner and bought other objects on the train, and when he was charged 2 RMB for getting a refund of a train ticket. Hao lost two cases and only won one in which the court ruled that the defendant should issue an invoice indicating the value equivalent to the objects Hao bought on the train. Moreover, under the pressure from the court and media, the Ministry of Railways finally issued a notice requiring all train bureaus to issue invoices to consumers who have dined or bought commodities on the train. Hao was consequently nominated to quite a number of honorary titles for the success he achieved. In 2006 Hao bought to the court a case against the Ministry of Railways claiming that it was procedurally illegal that the defendant decided to increase the price of train tickets during the Spring Festival without having a public hearing. Actually, as early as 2001, another lawyer, Qiao Zhanxiang, had brought a lawsuit against the Ministry of Railways for its decision to increase the price of train tickets during the Spring Festival. Qiao lost his case, and Hao experienced the same. However, one can claim that Hao actually won, because in January 2007, one month after the court issued its judgment overruling Hao's claim, the Ministry of Railways announced that the price of train tickets would not be increased anymore during the Spring Festival. This was of profound benefits for millions of ordinary Chinese who go to their hometowns for family reunions at this unique period.

In 2001, two law teachers from Southeast University brought a lawsuit against the Planning Bureau of Nanjing City claiming that the construction of viewing decks approved by the defendant ruined the amenities that had been brought to them from the enjoyment of natural beauty. The IPC ruled not to accept the case because it did not fall within its jurisdiction. The HPC did not receive their suit either. However, at last, the government of Nanjing city dismantled the viewing deck in February 2002.[55]

In October 2005, Li Gang, a legal scholar from Tsinghua University, sued the Bureau of Municipal Engineering and Administration in Shanghai for its illegal charging of vehicle tolls for entering Shanghai City. He requested the court to rule that the charging was illegal, the tolls should be refunded, and that the defendant should disclose relevant information relating to the construction and investment of the highway. Li lost this case. He also lost his case in which he sued the Bureau of Municipal Engineering and Administration in Tianjin for similar actions of charging vehicle tolls.[56]

---

54 The cases stated below could be found at the following websites: 'Hao Jinsong Bu Fucong de Gongmin' (Hao Jinsong: a disobedient citizen), available at http://www.infzm.com/content/37096; 'Hao Jinsong Xilie Anjian' (A series of cases brought by Hao Jinsong), available at http://www.dfpilaw.org/show_news.asp?id=846&classid=5&boardid=5. Both last visited March 2013.

55 See 'Huanjing Baohu Xilie Anjian' (A series of cases relating to environmental protection). Available at http://www.dfpilaw.org/show_news.asp?id=847&classid=5&boardid=5. Last visited March 2013.

56 See '"Jinjinfei" Guansi Weiliao, Qinghua Boshi You Gao Shanghai Shou "Jinhufei"' (The case of vehicle tolls in Tianjin is not over yet. The doctor from Tsinghua brings another case suing Shanghai for

The most recent case occurred in 2011, when Professor Lin Lihong, who is well known for her courage in advocating legal aid in administrative cases, brought a lawsuit against the customs authority in Shenzhen. Lin Lihong bought a few books in Hong Kong and the books were taken away by Shenzhen Customs under the excuse that they were 'prohibited books' (*jin shu*). Lin Lihong asked the Customs to provide an official document to prove that the books that she had purchased fell into the catalogue of prohibited books and her request was declined. In December 2011, the judgment was delivered by the IPC of Shenzhen City. Lin's claim was rejected and she subsequently appealed to the HPC in Guangdong Province. The latter court upheld the original judgment in August 2012.[57] It is needless to say that legal scholars have been confronted with various pressures for bringing such cases to courts.

Besides the promotion of the ALL by legal scholars and lawyers, grassroots citizens have also played an important role in promoting the use of the ALL. Zhou Guangli, an ordinary farmer in Shandong Province who is more than 65 years old, has brought more than 100 lawsuits against administrative agencies since 1996. Most of the defendants were governments at village or township level. In the quest for justice Zhou's personal experience is pungent and hard. Reportedly he had won some cases, but he was deemed as a troublemaker in the local governments' eyes. He was retaliated against and beaten several times and was compelled to promise that he would not act as the representative for villagers to bring administrative litigation. Advantageously, as a 'barefoot lawyer' (a person who is not qualified but acts as a lawyer), his bravery and initiatives have gained broad attention from academia and the media.[58] Subsequently, local governments began to treat him seriously and invited him to be a propagandist for administrative litigation at the grassroots level. Zhou Guangli is not the only example of the grassroots individual promoter. Chen Faqing, a disabled farmer from Zhejiang Province, has devoted himself to lodging administrative litigation in environment-related cases for more than 17 years. He has brought numerous administrative litigation against the National Environmental Protection Agency, the Government of Zhejiang Province, the Department of Environmental Protection in Zhejiang Province, the Environmental Protection Bureau of Yuhang District of Hangzhou City in Zhejiang Province, etc. for the reasons of noise, dust, air and water pollution.[59] In 2002, Chen brought a suit at the BPC of Yuhang District

---

charging vehicles tolls). Available at http://news.xinhuanet.com/politics/2005-11/02/content_3717136.htm. Last visited March 2013.

57 See Pil.org.cn, 'Lin Lihong Su Shenzhen Haiguan Shoujiao Qi Jingwai Suogou Tushu Juti Xingzheng Xingwei Weifa An' (Lin Lihong sues the Shenzhen Customs for seizing the books she bought overseas). Available at http://www.pil.org.cn/q_news/q_news_page_3163.html. Last visited May 2013. The judgments are with the authors.

58 See Xie Hui, Guanzhu, '"Zhou Guangli Xianxiang": Da <Fazhi Ribao> Jizhe Wen' (Focus on the Zhou Guangli phenomenon: answers to the journalist from *Legal Daily*), 2001, available at http://article.chinalawinfo.com/Article_Detail.asp?ArticleID=30826; Hao Tiechuan, 'Nongmin 90% Shengsu: Zhou Guangli Xianxiang de Sikao' (A farmer wins for 90 per cent of the suits: thoughts on the Zhou Guangli phenomenon), Jiancha Ribao (The Procuratorate Daily), 11 October 2000, available at http://www.people.com.cn/GB/channel7/498/20001011/266433.html; Zhang Zhiquan, 'Zhou Guangli Xianxiang de Falv Toushi' (Analysis of Zhou Guangli phenomenon from a legal perspective), 3 (2002) *Xingzheng Yu Fa* (*Administration and Law*), pp. 54–55. Both websites last visited July 2013.

59 Chen is broadly reported by the media, not only for his initiation of administrative litigation, but also for his advertising of environmental protection, etc. See Xinhuanet.com, 'Zhejiang Nongmin Chen Faqing Xiang Lianheguo Deng Juankuan 50 Yu Wanyuan Yanjiu Qihou Bianhua' (The farmer, Chen Faqing, from Zhejiang Province donates more than 500,000 RMB to the United Nations and other organisations for research on climate change), 18 November 2010, available at http://news.xinhuanet.com/2010-11/18/c_12787292.htm; People.com, 'Zhongguo Zifei Huanbao Gongyi Guanggao Diyi Ren: Chen Faqing' (The No. 1 figure

against the Environmental Protection Bureau of Yuhang District arguing that the defendant failed to supervise and sanction the polluting enterprises for dust and noise pollution. His claims were rejected by the court. Later in 2003, he brought another suit at the IPC in Hangzhou City against the Zhejiang provincial government and the Department of Environmental Protection in Zhejiang Province arguing that the defendants had nonfeasance in environmental protection. He was again rejected by the courts for the reason that his interest was not directly involved and thus he was not qualified to bring a lawsuit.[60]

On many occasions the plaintiffs lost their cases. The courts' deference to the administrative agencies' actions is evident. Actually, some lawyers and scholars had anticipated that they would not win the cases in courts because powerful actors or complex contexts were involved, but hoped that the cases could pressure governmental agencies to modify their actions or alert them to exercise power within the legal constraints. Occasionally, some administrative agencies made certain changes in responding to the plaintiffs' claims, under the media pressure or intervention from powerful bodies or persons. In this sense, even though the plaintiffs lose the cases in court, they win them in practice.

The Predicament of Courts and Judges

There is no special administrative court in China. Administrative cases are handled by administrative chambers at each court. Compared to civil and criminal chambers and their judges, the administrative chambers and judges face a more troublesome predicament in China. Courts are not incentivised to handle administrative cases due to the unpopular nature of such cases. Within courts administrative cases are treated with less weight than other types of cases. Civil and commercial cases could bring beneficial fees to court, and criminal cases are taken seriously by the Communist Party and governments at every level, for maintaining social safety and order, by providing relatively generous support to courts. In contrast, an overwhelming majority of plaintiffs in administrative cases are poor people, and the litigation fees are considerably low. Unsurprisingly the administrative chamber within courts at each level is considerably small in size, and consequently becomes peripheral and marginalised. In some courts, especially those in remote areas, the number of judges assigned to the chamber is inadequate; in some of the worst situations, the number of judges may not even be enough to form a collegiate panel with a minimum requirement of three judges.[61] Conventionally speaking, working in the administrative chamber is not a preferred choice for judges, either for economic or political reasons. Normally, they receive fewer year-end bonuses, which are partly based on the number of cases handled, than judges working in other chambers. Furthermore, in working as an administrative judge, one has to be sceptical and harsh against the officials working in the agency, which will probably ruin personal contact or '*guanxi*' with these officials.

Citizens are frustrated in bringing cases to courts for solution and there is a growing distrust towards the judiciary and judges as a whole in society. Instead, citizens are more and more inclined

---

of public interests advertising on the topic of environmental protection at his own expense: Chen Faqing), 8 November 2007. Available at http://auto.people.com.cn/GB/25959/107219/107221/6503522.html. Both were last visited in July 2013.

60 For more information on these two cases, see 'Huanjing Baohu Xilie Anjian' (A series of cases relating to environmental protection). Available at http://www.dfpilaw.org/show_news.asp?id=847&classid=5&boardid=5. Last visited July 2013.

61 Liang Fengyun, *supra* note 12, pp. 8–9.

to seek alternative channels to have their disputes settled, such as the 'letter and visit'. This in turn has created the image that the courts' capacity and authority in handling administrative cases is weak, and they have no social legitimacy to strengthen that.

Probing into the reasons of such a predicament faced by courts and judges, the lack of judicial independence stands out. It is widely recognised in China that the executive power has a dominating role in State affairs, and moreover, the judicial power, the executive power and the legislative power are all under the control of one ruling political Party, the CCP.[62] Both internal and external factors exist that interfere with judicial work and thus harm judicial independence.

Internally, in each Chinese court there is an adjudication committee. According to the Organic Law of the People's Courts of 2006, such committees have the functions of assembling trial experiences and discussing major or difficult cases and other issues relevant to the trial of cases (Article 10). Despite the Law using the word to 'discuss' cases, in reality they 'decide' cases. Conventionally the committees work in this way: when a collegiate panel is not sure about the difficult legal issues in a case or feels that the case is politically sensitive or has broad social effects, it reports the case to the head of the chamber; if the head of the chamber is still not sure, he submits the case to an adjudication committee. When the committee holds a meeting to discuss the case, the judge in charge of the case or the head of the chamber will be asked to give an oral introduction of the case. Based on this the members of the committee will give their opinions and decide the judgment of the case. As the adjudication committee decides the case without hearing the case, this is criticised as 'handling a case in camera' (*anxiang caozuo*). There are no accurate statistics on the percentage of administrative cases discussed by the adjudication committees. According to He Haibo's survey completed in 2012, among the 16,139 judgments of administrative cases at the first instance included in the database of 'Beida Fabao', the judgments of administrative cases at the first instance in which the adjudicative committee is mentioned accounts for 4.2 per cent, which is higher than the judgment of civil cases at the first instance (2.0 per cent) and the judgments of criminal cases at the first instance (2.2 per cent).[63] Though the statistics are roughly calculated, it could be generally seen that the adjudication committee has played a considerably important role in deciding administrative cases.

From the external perspective, handling administrative cases is interfered with by other State organs, such as the Party, the People's Congress and governments.[64] Due to the particular nature of the defendants of administrative litigation, and also the fact that some administrative cases relate to sensitive issues that may stir social instability, the interference upon judges in handling administrative cases is higher than in the handling of other cases. It is calculated that approximately 90 per cent of administrative cases are dealt with by BPCs.[65] Therefore, most of the interference on courts' adjudication of administrative cases stems from government organs at the local level. Though the central authority might intend to rectify local governments' misbehaviors, i.e. improper interference on courts' judicial work, it is difficult for such authority to be well

62 For a general discussion on judicial independence in China, see Yuwen Li, *Judicial Independence in China: An Attainable Principle?* (The Hague: Eleven International Publishing, 2013); Margaret Y.K. Woo, 'Adjudication Supervision and Judicial Independence in the P.R.C.', 39 (1991) *The American Journal of Comparative Law*, pp. 95–119.

63 He Haibo, 'Kundun de Xingzheng Susong'. Available at http://law.china.cn/features/2013-04/11/content_5869351_3.htm. Last visited July 2013.

64 Yuwen Li, *supra* note 62, pp. 21–28.

65 Fan Fu, 'Wouguo Xingzheng Shenpan de Lishi Huigu yu Zhanwang' (Historical recall and future prospect of China's administrative litigation system), 10 (2004) *Xingzheng Zhifa yu Xingzheng Shenpan* (Implementation of Administrative Law and Administrative Adjudication), p. 182.

implemented at the local level concerning the problems of local protectionism and local disparity in China. It is normal practice that, during the period when the plenary session of People's Congress is held each year, the judicial work is forced to be suspended. Some 'sensitive cases' are postponed to be tried after the session of People's Congress.

With regard to the administration of courts and judges, the local People's Congresses appoint and remove judges, and the finances of courts are firmly controlled by local governments. This acts as a powerful counter for governments to hold a superior position. In practice, some local courts compromise concerning the aspect of administrative litigation for exchange of benefits of personal and fiscal appropriation with local governments. According to a Chinese expert's study, a government at the township level delayed approving the appropriation of lands for construction of judicial tribunals for three years because it failed an administrative case. A police authority did not show up, on purpose, to the accident site where a court was under siege by mobs, because the police authority lost in an administrative litigation. In some extreme cases, it is explicitly required that filing an administrative case should be based on the approval of government officials in advance, and some courts filed cases, but were forced not to hold open trials.[66]

The pressure exerted on courts is further translated into the pressure on individual judges through internal judicial administration. In practice, judges are evaluated in accordance with indicators such as the rate of appeal, the rate of re-trial through trial supervision procedures, the rate of petition by plaintiffs to higher authorities, etc. Results of such evaluation are closely related to judges' opportunities to be promoted, to receive honours, bonuses, etc. This has resulted in judges being personally reluctant to handle sensitive administrative cases and refusing to accept such cases without giving any justifiable reason to claimants.

Consequences of such a predicament are reflected in the whole process of administrative litigation. As emphasised earlier, the difficulty in having one's case filed by courts is the most explicit consequence. To avoid the risk of being tangled in sensitive cases, and confined by the government's interference, courts and judges selectively choose to handle easier cases and keep those difficult ones out of the court. Moreover, even if the cases are accepted by courts, their results are often disappointing as they are below any reasonable expectation. This is demonstrated by the high rate of withdrawal by plaintiffs, which is closely related to somewhat mandatory usage of reconciliation in administrative litigation.

The Controversy of Coordination and Reconciliation

Article 50 of the ALL explicitly states that courts should not apply mediation in adjudicating administrative cases. However, it is known that courts are forever using the mediation method in handling administrative cases.[67] To avoid the obvious clash with the Law, the word 'reconciliation' (*he jie*) is used instead of mediation (*tiao jie*). However, in reality, reconciliation is *de facto* mediation. Prior to 2003, reconciliation by judges in handling administrative cases was deemed as a practical way to resolve disputes. However, in recent years, as a consequence of popularisation of mediation in courts in dealing with all kind of cases, mediation in administrative cases has been openly highly praised, and, to some extent, 'legitimised' by court practice. In January 2007, the SPC issued Several Opinions on Providing Judicial Guarantee for Construction of Socialist Harmonious

66 Chen Youxi, 'Dui Xingzheng Susong Kunjing de Hongguan Sikao' (Macro analysis of the predicament of administrative litigation), 4 (1993) *Xingzheng Faxue Yanjiu* (*Journal of Administrative Law*), p. 44.

67 See Huang Xuexian, 'Xingzheng Susong Tiaojie Ruogan Redian Wenti Tantao' (Discussion on several debated issued on administrative mediation), 11 (2007) *Faxue* (*Law*), p. 43.

Society, which addressed the issue of proper use of reconciliation in administrative litigation.[68] In March 2007, the SPC issued Several Opinions on Further Displaying the Positive Roles of Litigant Mediation in Constructing Socialist Harmonious Society.[69] The Opinions specified that, depending on the circumstances of the case at hand, courts should promote reconciliation between parties by referring to principles and procedures of civil mediation. In June 2009, the SPC further issued Several Opinions on Doing Well the Work of Administrative Adjudication under Current Circumstances.[70] The Opinions emphasise that the mechanisms of coordination (*xie tiao*) and reconciliation (*he jie*) should be used throughout the whole spectrum of a trial, either before, during or after the session, under the condition that they will not contravene the legal provisions. It is also provided that, where there are difficulties for courts at the lower level to conduct the coordination or reconciliation, they may resort to the courts at the higher level for assistance. In June 2010, the SPC specifically issued Several Opinions on Further Implementing the Working Principle of 'Priority of Mediation, Combination between Mediation and Adjudication'.[71] The usage of coordination and reconciliation is encouraged in administrative cases and even prioritised compared to adjudication. The Opinions specifies that, in administrative compensation (*pei chang*) cases, mediation should be used; it also provides that, under the following circumstances, coordination should be adopted:

1. administrative adjudication (*cai jue*) conducted by administrative agencies to settle civil disputes between private parties with equal status;
2. confirmation of rights (*que quan*) conducted by administrative agencies to confirm the status of ownership and other rights;
3. administrative penalty, administrative expropriation, administrative recuperation (*bu chang*) and administrative contract within the scope of discretion of administrative authorities; and
4. cases in which concrete administrative action is illegal, or legal but not reasonable.

Concerning the last type of case in which coordination mechanism should be used, the court should endeavour to promote the administrative agency to withdraw its illegal actions by itself, or confirm the invalidity of the concrete administrative actions by itself, or re-make a decision.

At the local level, some HPCs have also issued opinions on administrative coordination and reconciliation. For example, in 2006, the HPC in Guangdong Province issued the Opinions on Several Issues Concerning the Coordination and Reconciliation in Administrative Cases.[72] The Opinions specify the principles and process of how the coordination and reconciliation should be conducted. It states that the coordination should be based on the review of the legality of concrete administrative action and conducted on a voluntary basis (Article 4). In 2007, the HPC in Shanghai

68 *Fafa* No.2 [2007]. Available at http://rmfyb.chinacourt.org/public/detail.php?id=105458. Last visited June 2012.

69 *Fafa* No.9 [2007]. Available at http://vip.chinalawinfo.com/newlaw2002/slc/slc.asp?db=chl&gid=89041. Last visited July 2013.

70 *Fafa* No.38 [2009]. Available at http://www.court.gov.cn/qwfb/sfwj/yj/201002/t20100224_1929.htm. Last visited July 2013.

71 *Fafa* No.16 [2010]. Available at http://www.court.gov.cn/qwfb/sfwj/yj/201008/t20100811_8489.htm. Last visited July 2013.

72 *Yuegaofafa* No.42 [2006]. Available at http://www.lawyee.org/Act/Act_Display.asp?RID=589986. Last visited July 2013.

issued the Opinions on Strengthening Coordination and Reconciliation in Administrative Cases, which enumerate eight circumstances where courts should apply coordination.[73]

In addition, some local courts have promoted the so-called model of 'round table trial' in which plaintiffs, defendants and judges sit around a round table instead of the traditional layout of two parties sitting opposite each other during the trial. Invented by Decheng BPC in Dezhou City, Shandong Province, this model is now broadly applied in Henan, Shandong, Jiangsu, Liaoning Provinces, etc.[74] Though some courts use the round-table-trial model just for formal purposes, it could still be seen from the initial aim of this model that coordination and reconciliation are more broadly used in administrative cases at local courts.

Though mediation in administrative cases under the guise of so-called 'coordination and reconciliation' is promoted at both central and local levels, the legitimacy of this 'covert' initiative is still challenged and questioned in academia. Shen Fujun challenges the legality of the Opinions on Several Issues of Coordination and Reconciliation in Administrative Cases issued by the HPC in Guangdong Province. He argues that the HPC in Guangdong Province is not empowered to enact such rules on the basic litigant system that should be enacted by the supreme legislative authority. Furthermore, it is provided in the Opinions that, when the reconciliation is reached at the second instance, the court at second instance may rule to revoke the judgment at the first instance and allow the plaintiff at the first instance to withdraw his claims. This provision contravenes the provision in the ALL that a 'decision on whether to allow the plaintiff to withdraw his claims or not should be made before the judgment or ruling is delivered' (Article 51 of the ALL). Lastly, as the reconciliation agreement is not legally binding, it cannot be executed compulsorily by the courts; therefore, the citizens' rights are still under jeopardy.[75]

Besides the unsolved legitimacy problem of 'coordination and reconciliation' from a theoretical perspective, there are daunting problems in its practical application. Chinese scholars have summarised these problems and dubbed them as 'to promote the mediation by coercion (*yi ya cu tiao*), to compel the mediation by indicating that the result of the judgment will be the same as or even worse than mediation regardless of whether mediation is accepted or not (*yi pan ya tiao*), to compel the mediation by delaying the delivery of a judgment (*yi tuo ya tiao*) and to compel the mediation by temptation (*yi you ya tiao*)'.[76] The deteriorating situation in today's China is that mediation by judges goes through each phase of judicial proceedings. When a case is brought to a court, the division of filing cases will offer mediation to the plaintiff. If this fails mediation will be continued by a judge at the administrative chamber; in case of further failure, the case will enter

73 *Hugaofa* No. 93 (2007). Available at http://gov.eastday.com/renda/gonggao/node2524/node8854/node8855/node8859/u1a1362349.html. Last visited July 2013.

74 See 'Dezhou Fayuan Chuangxin Yuanzhuoshi Xingzheng Shenpan Moshi' (Dezhou court makes innovations on the Round-table-trial model in administrative cases), available at http://old.chinacourt.org/html/article/200807/18/312657.shtml; 'Zhongzhan Fayuan Yuanzhuo Shenpan Xingzheng Anjian' (Zhongzhan Court handles administrative cases in a Round-table-trial model), available at http://old.chinacourt.org/html/article/201104/21/448820.shtml; 'Suzhou Xingzheng Anjian Shouchuang Yuanzhuo Shenpan' (Suzhou initially adopts the Round-table-trial model in administrative cases), available at http://www.js.xinhuanet.com/peace/2009-04/17/content_16304826.htm, etc. All last visited July 2013.

75 Shen Fujun, 'Hexie Tongyi de Xingzheng Susong Xietiao Hejie Jizhi' (Harmonious and unified mechanism of coordination and reconciliation in administrative litigation), 6 (2007) 'Huadong Zhengfa Daxue Xuebao' (*Journal of East China University of Political Science and Law*), pp. 23–24.

76 Wang Jun, 'Dui Fayuan Xingzheng Susong Anjian Xietiao Wenti de Yanjiu' (Research on the coordination of administrative cases used by courts), 2013. Available at http://article.chinalawinfo.com/article_print.asp?articleid=76033. Last visited July 2013.

into the adjudication stage by the same judge or judges. Mediation will be continually offered. Where no mediation agreement is reached during the court hearing and a judgment is about to be made, before the closing of the case the judge(s) will still request parties to consider reaching a mediation agreement rather than the court deliver a judgment.

The current politically dominated mediation in judicial processes has been widely criticised by Chinese scholars who believe and indeed advocate procedural justice as the core of judicial reform. As the unpopular active architect of mediation, the former President of the SPC, Wang Shenjun, has been moved from this position in early 2013, one may expect, or at least wish, that the new President of the SPC could bring the judicial reform onto the right track, including adopting a responsible approach to use judicial mediation in handling administrative disputes.

Chinese Academic Proposals on the Revision of the ALL

Several comprehensive revisions have been published by different research institutes. In 2004, the Project of Judicial Reform and Improvement of the Administrative Litigation System chaired by professor Ma Huaide, published its final report on the *Recommendations of the Revision of the ALL and Explanations of the Reasons*.[77] This version expands the ALL to 201 articles. Another project led by Professor Ying Songnian and sponsored by the China Law Society produced another version in 2011, which expanded the ALL to 181 articles.[78] In February 2012, the Department of Constitutional Law and Administrative Law at Peking University submitted the *Recommendations on the Revision of the ALL* to the NPC, the SPC and the Legislative Affairs Office of the State Council.[79] In March 2012, the *Recommendation on the Revision of the ALL* was also submitted to the relevant authorities by the Institute of Administrative Law at Renmin University.[80]

Besides these publications, a few individual legal experts have contributed to the discussion as well. Liang Fengyun, a judge working at the Administrative Chamber of the SPC, proposes revision of the ALL from eight perspectives:

1. to establish independent administrative courts and re-establish the judicial authority;
2. to emphasise the existing structure of objective litigation (*keguan susong*) (i.e. judicial review on the legality of administrative action, in contrast with subjective litigation (*zhuguan*

77 Ma Huaide (ed.), *Sifa Gaige yu Xingzheng Susong Zhidu de Wanshan: Xingzheng Susongfa Xiugai Jianyi Gao ji Liyou Shuomingshu* (*Judicial Reform and Improvement of the Administrative Litigation System: Recommendations of the Revision of the ALL and Explanations of the Reasons*) (Beijing: China University of Political Science and Law Press, 2004).

78 Recommendations of the Revision of the ALL, presented at the International Seminar on the Revision of the ALL, held in Shanghai, 2011. A brief introduction about the Seminar can be found at http://www.cupl.edu.cn/html/news/col259/2011-12/06/20111206150009663157065_1.html. However, the full text of the draft is currently not publicly available. Last visited July 2013.

79 Full text of the Recommendations is available at http://www.publiclaw.cn/article/Details.asp?NewsId=3688&classid=22&classname=%B9%AB%C3%F1%B2%CE%D3%EB%C1%A2%B7%A8. Last visited July 2013.

80 Mo Yuchuan, et al., 'Woguo Xingzheng Susongfa de Xiugai Luxiang, Xiugai Yaodian he Xiugai Fang'an: Guanyu Xiugai Xingzheng Susongfa de Zhongguo Renmin Daxue Zhuanjia Jianyi Gao' (Tendency, content and scheme of the revision of ALL: about the recommendation version of the revision of ALL from Renmin University), 3 (2012) *Henan Caijing Zhengfa Daxue Xuebao* (*Journal of Henan University of Economics and Political Science*), pp. 17–52.

susong) in which the judiciary reviews the litigant claims of plaintiffs) and strengthen the supervision of the exercise of administrative power;
3. to expand and systematise the formats of actions brought by plaintiffs and protect the citizens' public law rights;
4. to simplify the standing of actions and facilitate citizens to bring lawsuits to the courts;
5. to cautiously design litigant procedures and safeguard the equity and publicity of litigation;
6. to reform the negative nature of judicial power and realise effective judicial supervision;
7. to promote effective implementation of judicial judgments and ensure the realisation of judicial function; and
8. to reform the provision of reference to the Civil Procedure Law and enact the comprehensive code of administrative law.[81]

Yu An, a legal scholar, also proposes the revision of the ALL from three perspectives. He argues that the scope of judicial review should be expanded to include litigation against policies issued by administrative authorities, against normative documents issued by public-service-oriented institutions (public school, public hospital, water service institutions, etc.), against malfeasance or inactions of administrative authorities, against projects invested or approved by the government involving public service infrastructure and mega industrial construction and WTO-related litigation. He also proposes that administrative disputes relating to contracts concluded between the government and individuals should be included in the administrative litigation system, and that reconciliation and mediation should be adopted in dealing with this type of dispute. Lastly, he suggests that local authorities should be empowered with more legislative autonomy relating to administrative litigation to respond to significant local variances.[82]

Yang Weidong, a legal scholar, argues for a shift of paradigm in constructing the whole administrative litigation system from an administrative-action-centred paradigm to a new paradigm focusing on the protection of citizens' rights. Specifically, he proposes that:

1. the principle of review on the legality of administrative action should be confined in the format of rescissory action (*che xiao su song*) and the fundamental principle of the administrative litigation should be the principle of providing a sufficient remedy to citizens;
2. *ad hoc* procedures should be designed to accommodate special types of cases, such as administrative compensation, administrative adjudication, administrative contract, administrative inaction, administrative public interest litigation, etc.; and
3. formats of judgments should be expanded, such as the injunction.[83]

From the scholarly research, it could be summarised that both divergences and convergences of revision of the ALL are found in academia. Controversies remain on whether now is the best time

81 Liang Fengyun, 'Xingzheng Susongfa Xiugai Balun' (Analysis of revision of the Administrative Litigation Law from eight perspectives), 2 (2012) *Huadong Zhengfa Daxue Xuebao* (*Journal of East China University of Political Science and Law*), pp. 102–110.

82 Yu An, 'Fazhan Daoxiang de Xingzheng Susongfa Xiuding Wenti' (Development-oriented revision of the Administrative Litigation Law), 2 (2012) *Huadong Zhengfa Daxue Xuebao* (*Journal of East China University of Political Science and Law*), pp. 96–101.

83 Yang Weidong, 'Xingzheng Susong Jiagou Fenxi: Xingzheng Xingwei Zhongxin Zhuyi Anpai de Fansi' (Analysis of the structure of administrative litigation: rethinking of the administrative-action-centred arrangement), 2 (2012) *Huadong Zhengfa Daxue Xuebao* (*Journal of East China University of Political Science and Law*), pp. 111–117.

to revise the ALL and whether an overhaul of the ALL or tinkering around the edges is desirable.[84] For example, those who argue for an overhaul of the administrative litigation system propose to establish a separate system of administrative courts.[85] Concerning the content of revision, scholars' attention is more or less aligned, such as expansion of the scope of acceptance of administrative cases, strengthening the judicial independence of administrative litigation, expansion of the standing of actions of plaintiffs, and inclusion of administrative public interest litigation, though scholars' opinions vary on the detailed design of the system. Taking the expansion of the scope of case acceptance as an example, though most scholars are in favour of including abstract administrative action into the scope of judicial review, Zou Rong argues that it is not practical to include the abstract administrative action in the scope; as judicial independence cannot be guaranteed for courts to deliver a judgment quashing the government's regulations, there is a risk of abuse of litigant rights by citizens and the realisation and implementation of such judgments cannot be optimistically expected in practice.[86]

Conclusion

Having been in effect for more than 20 years, the ALL has marked itself as a symbol of the formal establishment of the modern administrative litigation system in China. Though such a modern system distinguishes itself from the traditional Chinese perception that 'officials are dignitary and citizens are humble' (*guan gui min jian*) and provides ordinary citizens with the right to sue the government, how far the administrative litigation practices have deviated from the deeply rooted traditional Chinese culture is still questionable. Consequently, the extent to which the Administrative Litigation Law has fulfilled the primary goal of the protection of citizens' rights remains to be continually monitored.

Along with the administrative litigation system stumbling forward, problems are revealed in terms of both the ALL and its implementation. Firstly, the legal texts prescribed in the ALL are oversimplified and obsolete. This is verified by our discussion of the scope of acceptance of administrative cases, and also the controversy of mediation in administrative cases. On the one hand, new types of cases and claims are challenging the restrictive conditions set in the ALL; and on the other hand, the prohibitive provisions in the ALL are trickily dodged due to the necessity arising from judicial practices. Secondly, as to the practices, the difficulty of having one's case accepted and filed by courts has generated overwhelming concerns. This is partially due to arbitrary intervention from local governments, and the unwillingness of courts and judges to handle certain types of cases. The consequences of these phenomena are frustrating and destructive. As many administrative disputes cannot be solved on time, claimants are compelled to seek non-judicial remedies, such as petitions to the central government. In some even worse situations, desperate

84 Zhang Jiansheng argues that the time is ripe for an overhaul of the ALL. See Zhang Jiansheng, 'Xingzheng Susongfa Xiugai de Jiben Lichang' (Basic position on revision of the ALL), 1 (2013) *Guangdong Shehui Kexue* (Guangdong Social Science), pp. 12–19. Full text is available at http://article.chinalawinfo.com/Article_Detail.asp?ArticleId=75872#4. Last visited July 2013.

85 See Liang Fengyun, *supra* note 81. See also Ma Huaide, 'Sifa Gaige yu Xingzheng Susong Zhidu de Wanshan' (Judicial reform and improvement of the administrative litigation system), 8 (2005) *Falv Shiyong* (*Implementation of Law*), pp. 2–5.

86 Zou Rong, 'Xingzheng Guifan Sifa Shencha de Lujing' (Judicial review approach to administrative normative documents), 2 (2012) *Huadong Zhengfa Daxue Xuebao* (*Journal of East China University of Political Science and Law*), pp. 118–124.

claimants resort to violent solutions that result in frequent mass disturbances and social instability. Thirdly, a lack of judicial independence means that the courts and judges are stuck in a predicament. The administrative chamber is peripheral within courts and social trust in the fairness and justice of judges in adjudicating administrative cases is suffering. Under the government-centred structure, courts are inferior to the administrative power both ideologically and practically.

Revision of the ALL to make it adaptable to practical social needs and to strengthen its ability to protect citizens' rights is inevitable. However, consensus is yet to be reached on how to revise the current law. It is foreseeable that the path towards a fully fledged administrative litigation system and effective implementation of the law in practice can be formidable and frustrating. Adolescence of the modern administrative litigation system needs to struggle with various obstacles, such as the superiority of administrative power, lack of judicial independence, weak consciousness on citizens' rights, and nascent formation of civil society. The improvement of the administrative litigation system in China not only needs a mere amendment to the ALL, but also supportive political reforms, education for citizens, contribution of lawyers and civil societies, and promotion and supervision by the public media. From the cases shown in this chapter, it is delightful to find that many courageous ordinary citizens have devoted themselves to promoting administrative litigation. Apart from individuals, it is expected, and seems to be desirable, that more legal persons, either enterprises or NGOs, would also actively participate in using the law to defend their own, as well as public, rights and interests.

Chapter 3
The Administrative Litigation (Judicial Review) System in Hong Kong and its Future

Feng Lin

Introduction

Hong Kong was a British colony from around the middle of the nineteenth century to almost the end of the twentieth century. As a result, the British system of judicial review, which is part of its common law, had been transplanted to Hong Kong during that period. After the People's Republic of China (PRC) resumed its sovereignty over Hong Kong on 1 July 1997, the Basic Law of the PRC for the Hong Kong Special Administrative Region (Basic Law), enacted by the National People's Congress (NPC), became Hong Kong's constitutional document, replacing the former colonial constitutional documents, i.e. the Letters Patent and Royal Instructions. As a result of this shift in sovereignty, British cases no longer have binding effect in Hong Kong. However, Article 84 of the Basic Law provides that courts in Hong Kong may make reference to judicial precedent in other common law jurisdictions. On the one hand, this constitutional development has made it possible for courts in Hong Kong to maintain their common law roots and take the most favourable components of other common law jurisdictions. On the other, it also enables Hong Kong courts to develop common law, including within the administrative litigation system (judicial review),[1] through incorporating characteristics that are unique to Hong Kong.

Since the system of judicial review in Hong Kong is quite similar to that of many other common law jurisdictions, in addition to introducing the system itself, this chapter will focus on how Hong Kong courts have applied as well as developed the system. After this introduction, the second part will first introduce the historical development of judicial review in Hong Kong. The third part will discuss the court structure in Hong Kong and jurisdiction over judicial review cases. The fourth part will discuss the scope of juridical review. Thereafter, the fifth part will discuss the main grounds for judicial review. The discussion will demonstrate that, while most of the grounds for judicial review in Hong Kong are the same as in other common law jurisdictions, Hong Kong courts have developed several of them differently in their specific application. The sixth part of the chapter will highlight some of the questions and challenges facing judicial review in Hong Kong, concluding with the argument that judicial review in Hong Kong will continue to develop alongside its counterparts in other common law jurisdictions and that its unique constitutional setting will enable it to develop its own characteristics in some aspects of judicial review.

1 Since administrative litigation in Hong Kong is called judicial review, this chapter will use the term judicial review instead of administrative litigation.

Historical Development of Judicial Review in Hong Kong

The Transplantation of the English Judicial Review System in Hong Kong

As early as 1841, the United Kingdom started to apply its law to British nationals and foreigners residing in Hong Kong. By 1843, the British Government had appointed a governor for Hong Kong and had given him the authority to legislate on behalf of Hong Kong.[2] According to one of the constitutional documents, the Letters Patent, the Governor was required to consult the Legislative Council, and legislate according to the advice of the latter.[3] The Supreme Court Ordinance was enacted in 1844 by the Governor at that time. S. 3 of the Ordinance provided that all English law would be applied in Hong Kong. That Ordinance was later amended several times and s. 5 of the amended Ordinance provided that English law would apply in Hong Kong from 5 April 1843. In 1966 the Legislature in Hong Kong adopted the Application of English Laws Ordinance, which had amended the relevant provisions in the Supreme Court Ordinance. S. 3 of the Application of English Laws Ordinance provided that the common law and the rules of equity shall be in force in Hong Kong (a) so far as they are applicable to the circumstances of Hong Kong or its inhabitants, or (b) subject to such modifications as such circumstances may require, or (c) subject to any amendment thereof (whenever made) by (i) any Order in Council that applies to Hong Kong; (ii) any Act that applies to Hong Kong; or (iii) any Ordinance. It further provided that the common law and the rules of equity in England would be in force in Hong Kong notwithstanding any amendment thereof as part of the law of England made at any time by an Order in Council or Act that did not apply to Hong Kong.[4]

Since judicial review is an integral component of the common law in England, the above statutory provision in the Application of English Laws Ordinance had the effect of transplanting the whole common law system in England, including the mechanisms of judicial review, to Hong Kong. According to s. 3 of the Application of English Laws Ordinance, all English judicial precedent, including that concerning judicial review, became binding in Hong Kong. Furthermore, since the Letters Patent granted the authority of a final appeal hearing to the Privy Council, final adjudication of all cases in Hong Kong, including judicial review cases, needed to be submitted to the Privy Council located in London. Since the Law Lords sitting in the Privy Council were the same as those sitting in the House of Lords, such an arrangement ensured the consistency of judgments delivered by the Privy Council and House of Lords and accordingly the consistency of the judicial review system in Hong Kong and England before the shift in sovereignty took place.

Development of Judicial Review in Hong Kong

According to Clark and McCoy, there were very few judicial review cases brought forward prior to the 1950s in Hong Kong. Most judicial review cases were heard thereafter. Having collected and read all of the judicial review cases up to 1993, the authors found that over 90 per cent of them

---

2 See Peter Wesley-Smith, *Constitutional & Administrative Law in Hong Kong*, vol. 1, China & Hong Kong Law Studies, Hong Kong, 1987, Chapter 4, pp. 33–82.

3 *Ibid.*, at p. 158.

4 See Peter Wesley-Smith, *An Introduction to the Hong Kong Legal System*, 2nd edn, Oxford University Press, Hong Kong, 1993, pp. 32–37.

were heard after 1950. The total number of cases heard in the 1980s was more than the total figure of all cases heard between 1950 and 1970.[5]

According to information provided by the Hong Kong judiciary, judicial review applications received by the Court of First Instance from 1999 to October 2005 amounted to: 147 (1999), 2752 (2000), 3848 (2001), 204 (2002), 131 (2003), 150 (2004) and 125 (2005).[6] We can see from the above data that there were many more judicial review applications in 2000 and 2001 respectively. This can be mainly attributed to the fact that, after the Court of Final Appeal (CFA) delivered its judgment in the *Ng Ka Ling* case,[7] the National People's Congress Standing Committee (NPCSC) interpreted the Basic Law in 1999 for the first time, and stated explicitly that the interpretation would not have retrospective effect. The NPCSC Interpretation led many potential right of abode applicants to apply for judicial review on the basis of their worries that they might lose their right of abode due to their failure to lodge judicial review applications. It is therefore fair to derive that the sudden increase in judicial review cases in 2000 and 2001 had a specific historical basis. In other years also within this period, the number of judicial review applications had proven relatively stable, varying from 125 to 200. In comparison with the number of judicial review cases in 1990, the number almost doubled during this period.

According to Clark and McCoy,[8] the development of judicial review and the increase in the number of cases is closely related to the development of public administration in Hong Kong since the 1950s. During that period, alongside the 1960s, though the Hong Kong Government regulated the economy, it only regulated limited aspects of the economy. This provides the reasoning for why there were not many judicial review cases. The Government's interference with the economy reached its peak between the 1970s and 1990s, which was reflected through the large number of ordinances enacted by the Hong Kong Government at that time. In 1970 and 1990, the Government enacted 105 and 106 ordinances respectively, which included amendments to already existing ordinances. They argued that, with the increase in the number of ordinances enacted in Hong Kong, it was not surprising that the number of judicial review cases had also increased during that same period. Though not all of the decisions made by governmental organs were in relation to the common law, most of them must be related to the statutes. To put it simply, public administration is based on legislation. Hence, Clark and McCoy have opined that Hong Kong is a society regulated by ordinances.

The enactment of large numbers of ordinances has led to the expansion of the administrative functions of the Government. One of the consequences is that many statutory bodies including boards, tribunals and authorities, have been established since the 1950s.[9] Given that all such statutory bodies exercise public authority, their decisions are all subject to judicial review. However, not only have governmental organs increased, but the relationship between the government and the

5 See David J. Clark and Gerard McCoy, *Hong Kong Administrative Law*, Butterworths, Hong Kong, 1993, at pp. 1–4.

6 Some information was obtained by the writer of this chapter in undertaking another research project and is on file with the writer, while the remaining information is from the Chief Justice's speech at the Ceremonial Opening of the Legal Year 2006.

7 (1999) 2 HKCFAR 4. This is the first right of abode case decided by the Court of Final Appeal.

8 See above n. 5, at pp. 4–18.

9 See Mohan Bharwaney, Administrative Tribunals in Hong Kong, 6 HKLJ, 1976, p. 189–226; see also James O'Neil, An Analysis of Government's Use of Administrative Tribunals, an unpublished Master's thesis written in 1986, on file with the University of Hong Kong Library.

economic system has also changed. It has also been argued that the Government not only regulates the economy, but also tries its best to make the economy more reasonable and centralized.[10]

According to the above discussion, it is not difficult to notice that every major change in the development of judicial review in Hong Kong has been caused by the enactment of a statute, whether local or external. The enactment of large amounts of legislation has led to the expansion of governmental functions and also the increase in statutory bodies and therefore the expansion of the objects subject to judicial review.

Furthermore, constitutional development in Hong Kong is another major impetus behind the development of judicial review in Hong Kong. There are two major constitutional developments worthy of mention. One is the enactment of the Bill of Rights Ordinance in 1991, the other is the application of the new constitutional document, i.e. the Basic Law, in Hong Kong in 1997. Such constitutional developments have enhanced people's awareness of their rights and desire to protect their fundamental rights through judicial means, especially utilizing the procedures of judicial review.

The Court Structure in Hong Kong and Jurisdiction over Judicial Review Cases

Court Structure in Hong Kong

Paragraph 3 of Article 3 of the Sino-British Joint Declaration provides:

> The Hong Kong Special Administrative Region will be vested with executive, legislative and independent judicial power, including that of final adjudication. The laws currently in force in Hong Kong will remain basically unchanged.

Such a provision has been given more detail by Article 81 of the Basic Law, which states:

> The Court of Final Appeal, the High Court, district courts, magistrates' courts and other special courts shall be established in the Hong Kong Special Administrative Region. The High Court shall comprise the Court of Appeal and the Court of First Instance.
>
> The judicial system previously practiced in Hong Kong shall be maintained except for those changes consequent upon the establishment of the Court of Final Appeal of the Hong Kong Special Administrative Region.

Prior to the change of sovereignty in 1997, Hong Kong, as a British colony, did not have the authority of final adjudication. The highest judicial organ for Hong Kong was the judicial committee of the Privy Council in England. With leave of either the Court of Appeal in Hong Kong or the Privy Council, Hong Kong cases could be appealed to the Privy Council. Since 1 July 1997, sovereignty over Hong Kong has been transferred from the United Kingdom to the PRC. Such a constitutional change has made it impossible for the Privy Council to remain the court of final adjudication for Hong Kong; it was then up to the PRC to determine which court should exercise the final adjudicative authority for Hong Kong after 1 July 1997. Through Article 81 of the Basic Law, the

10 See above n. 5, at pp. 4–18.

PRC has decided to set up the Court of Final Appeal (CFA) in Hong Kong, which will exercise the final adjudicative authority.

The establishment of the CFA in Hong Kong has proven to be a major change in Hong Kong's judicial system. This gives the courts in Hong Kong the authority to exercise final adjudicative authority over cases within its jurisdiction. It also means that the Supreme People's Court, the highest court in the PRC, will not exercise the final adjudicative authority over cases within Hong Kong's jurisdiction. Aside from this, the Basic Law has maintained the pre-existing judicial system in Hong Kong by merely changing the names of some of the courts. The original Supreme Court in Hong Kong will no longer act as Supreme Court, but instead be renamed the High Court. The original Court of Appeal of the Supreme Court has since been renamed the Court of Appeal of the High Court. The original High Court of the Supreme Court has been renamed the Court of First Instance of the High Court. The names of district courts and magistrates have remained the same.[11]

All of the courts in Hong Kong include: the CFA, High Court, District Court, and Magistracy. The High Court includes both the Court of Appeal and the Court of First Instance (CFI). In addition to the formal courts, there also exist some tribunals that are treated as judicial organs. This includes the Land Tribunal, Labour Tribunal and Small Claims Tribunal. Though they are not formal courts, they are widely used in daily life and are treated as components of the judiciary.

The relationship between them can be displayed through the following diagram:

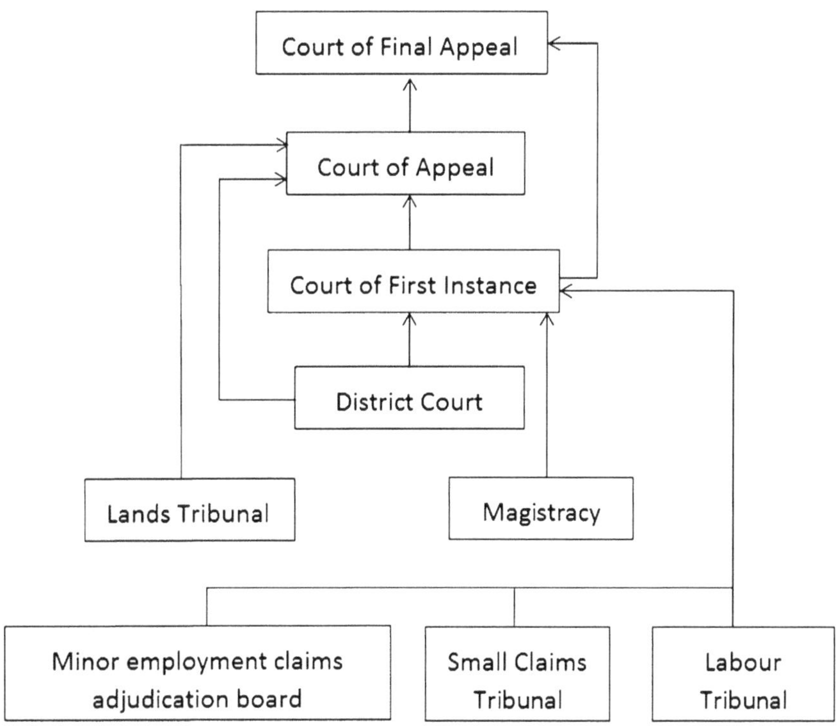

Figure 3.1 The Structure of Courts in Hong Kong

11 But the Chinese name of District Court has been changed from 'difang fayuan' to 'quyu fayuan'.

The jurisdiction over most cases in Hong Kong is stipulated by ordinances enacted by the Legislative Council in Hong Kong. The only exception is the jurisdiction of the Court of First Instance over judicial review cases, which has a combination of common law and statutory law. S. 12 of the High Court Ordinance (Cap. 4) provides that it shall be a superior court of record and its civil jurisdiction shall consist of:

a. original jurisdiction and authority of a like nature and extent as that held and exercised by the Chancery, Family and Queen's Bench Divisions of the High Court of Justice in England; and
b. any other jurisdiction, whether original or appellate jurisdiction, conferred on it by any law.[12]

In England, judicial review is the inherent power of the High Court. This is because, due to its historical basis, the High Court as a judicial organ has the power to review the legality of any organization, including administrative organizations. Such power of review can only be exercised by the High Court, not any other courts. The source of such power derives from the status and function of the High Court, not from any statutes. Before the change of sovereignty in 1997, Hong Kong, as a British colony, had naturally followed British legal traditions. Only the previous High Court could exercise the power of judicial review. After the change of sovereignty, Hong Kong maintained the previous court system and also the common law system. As a result, the inherent power of judicial review of the High Court (current Court of First Instance) has been retained.

After the change of sovereignty in 1997, in addition to the common law source of judicial review, the Basic Law has provided a constitutional source for judicial review for Hong Kong. Article 35 of the Basic Law provides:

> Hong Kong residents shall have the right to confidential legal advice, access to the courts, choice of lawyers for timely protection of their lawful rights and interests or for representation in the courts, and to judicial remedies.
>
> Hong Kong residents shall have the right to institute legal proceedings in the courts against the acts of the executive authorities and their personnel.

Hence, in juxtaposition to England, there are now two avenues for judicial review in Hong Kong: one is through the common law and the other is constitutional.

Scope of Judicial Review

This concerns whether a decision of a particular organ can be reviewed by the judiciary. Hong Kong has followed the British common law in determining the scope of judicial review. Specifically speaking, there exist two approaches in determining whether a body is reviewable. The English courts have often focused upon the legal source of a body's powers, rather than the function it is performing, in order to determine whether a decision is subject to judicial review. In many situations this continues to be a helpful, though limited, approach because most judicial review

12 See s. 12(2) of the Ordinance.

cases are brought to challenge the legality of governmental organizations, or the exercise of discretionary power by them.[13]

Traditional Approach: Source of Power

The traditional approach is to look at the source of power of a body. If the source of power is statutory, whether it is on the basis of the Basic Law, ordinances, or subsidiary legislation promulgated in Hong Kong, that body is judicially reviewable.[14] The body exercising such power may itself be a governmental organ, or a statutory body, or even an autonomous body. For example, the Hong Kong Bar Association is an autonomous body, but its governing body, i.e. the Bar Council, has been granted authority by the Legal Practitioners Ordinance (Cap. 159) to exercise the disciplinary power of all barristers. The exercise of such power is statute-based and therefore capable of being subject to judicial review.

In most cases, by following the traditional approach, we can already determine whether a body is reviewable or not. Most decisions challenged in Hong Kong are made by either governmental organs or statutory bodies.[15]

Modern Approach: Functional Approach

However, in addition to the exercise of statutory power or prerogative power that may impact negatively on the rights and interests of the relevant parties, some other bodies may also make decisions affecting the rights and interests of third parties. Such bodies will not be subject to judicial review under the traditional source of power approach. But there is clearly a necessity to subject them to some degree of judicial scrutiny because their decisions may affect either the interests of the general public or a sector of them. This provides the reasoning behind the development of the functional approach.[16]

In the *Datafin* case,[17] the British Court of Appeal laid down the following criterion to determine whether an organization performs a public function and therefore is judicially reviewable:

> it is possible to find enumerations of factors giving rise to the jurisdiction, but it is a fatal error to regard the presence of all those factors as essential or as being exclusive of other factors. Possibly the only essential elements are what can be described as a public element, which can take many different forms, and the exclusion from the jurisdiction of bodies whose sole source of power is a consensual submission to its jurisdiction.[18]

This criterion has been followed in subsequent cases decided by Hong Kong courts.[19] Thus, the only criterion that has been formally recognized by courts in determining reviewability is the

13 See *De Smith, Woolf & Jowell's Principles of Judicial Review*, Sweet & Maxwell, London, 1999, at pp. 60–64.

14 For detailed discussion, see Swati Jhaveri et al., Hong Kong Administrative Law, LexisNexis Butterworths, 2010, at pp. 134–159.

15 *Ibid.*

16 For more detailed discussion of the development of the public function approach in England, please refer to n. 13, at pp. 65–73.

17 The full citation is: *R v. Panel on Takeovers and Mergers, ex p. Datafin plc.* [1987] Q.B. 815.

18 *Ibid.*

19 See, for example, *Pacific Century Insurance Co Ltd v. Insurance Claims Complaints Bureau* [1999] 3 HKLRD 720 and *Anderson Asphalt Ltd and Others v. The Secretary for Justice* [2009] 3 HKLRD 215.

existence of 'public elements'. Any criteria used by courts in other cases, such as the 'but for' test, and 'governmental acquiescence or encouragement',[20] can only be treated as factors that can be taken into account in determining whether or not 'public elements' exist. Other factors that may also be taken into account by Hong Kong courts include the source of power, the nature of the organization, its means of funding, and so on. The satisfaction or existence of one of these cannot determine conclusively the reviewability of the organization in question. The court must consider all of the relevant factors and take a holistic view in determining whether or not 'public elements' exist and therefore the reviewability of the organization.[21]

There are two advantages to the public function approach. Firstly, it enables the courts to articulate more explicitly the modern constitutional role of judicial review – that is, the judiciary shall control the exercise of public functions through specific cases (the common law control of public functions) and the judiciary shall provide redress for grievances where no other remedies exist. Secondly, the CFI can ensure that organizations, whether nominally public or private, when performing public functions comply with the law and achieve acceptable standards of administration.[22]

In applying the public function approach, it is foreseeable that Hong Kong courts will also follow the exception in the *Datafin* case. That is to say, if the sole source of power of an organization is consensual submission, that organization is not judicially reviewable, despite performing a public function. There are two cases in this regard concerning the decisions made by the Hong Kong Jockey Club where the courts decided the cases on other grounds than the exception in *Datafin*.[23]

After determining the reviewability of an organization, it does not mean that a judicial review application can be lodged against any decisions formed by that organization. In determining whether a specific decision is reviewable, it is still necessary to examine whether the specific decision is made through exercising a public function of a public body. For example, in a series of cases, the Hong Kong courts have held that a statutory body such as the Airport Authority is reviewable, yet its decision on whether or not to enter into a private contract with a private company is not relevant to the exercising of a public function and therefore cannot be scrutinized.[24]

Standing and Leave Requirements

Standing

Standing concerns questions of who can bring a case to the court. Wade and Forsyth have said the following about standing: 'the law starts from the position that remedies are correlative with rights, and that only those whose own rights are at stake are eligible to be awarded remedies. No one else

---

20 See *Pacific Century Insurance Co Ltd v. Insurance Claims Complaints Bureau* [1999] 3 HKLRD 720.

21 *Ibid.*

22 There are two different approaches towards judicial review: one is the doctrine of ultra vires, the other is the common law approach. For detailed discussion of the difference between the two, please refer to: Mark Elliott, *Beatson, Matthews and Elliott's Administrative Law*, 3rd edn, Oxford University Press, Oxford, 2005, at pp. 11–23.

23 The two cases are *Harris Tsang Shing Kung and Another v. The Royal Hong Kong Jockey Club* HCMP1746/1985, and *Kevin Moses v. The Stewards of The Royal Hong Kong Jockey Club* HCMP1450/1981.

24 See for example, *Matteograssi SpA v. The Airport Authority* [1998] 2 HKLRD 213.

will have the necessary standing before the court'.[25] The corollary is that there exist cases in which nobody is qualified to bring a case because nobody's rights or interests are at stake.

However, there is also a need to view standing from a constitutional angle. With judicial review, it is all about who should have access to justice in getting a wrongful public law redressed. As a matter of principle, it cannot be right for a person with a meritorious challenge to a wrongful public law to be turned away by the court on the basis that their rights or interests are not sufficiently affected by that wrongdoing.

Law on standing in Hong Kong has in general followed British legislation and case law. S. 21K(3) of the High Court Ordinance (Cap. 4) provides:

> No application for judicial review shall be made unless the leave of the Court of First Instance has been obtained in accordance with rules of court; and the court shall not grant leave to make such an application unless it considers that the applicant has a sufficient interest in the matter to which the application relates.

That section has been copied by Order 53, Rule 3 of the High Court Rules.[26] These two statutory provisions have set 'sufficient interest' as the standard for determining whether an applicant for judicial review has standing. As to parameters of what does and does not constitute a 'sufficient interest', it is up to the court to decide. In this respect the British leading case of *Inland Revenue Commissioners v. National Federation of Self-employed and Small Businesses Ltd.* is also the authority in Hong Kong.[27] In judicial practice, courts in Hong Kong may use the requirement of standing to screen out some of the cases that lack the personal interest of the applicant.[28] But overall, they are very liberal with regard to standing. They are unwilling to permit technical arguments of standing to infringe upon determining the legal issues on their merits and believe that an issue of illegality should be decided by the courts.[29] With regard to public interest judicial review cases, Hong Kong courts have again proven very liberal. For example, in the case of *Town Planning Board v. Society for the Protection of the Harbour Ltd*, standing was simply not an issue for the court according to its judgment.[30]

Leave

Leave is a unique requirement of judicial review proceedings in contrast to private law litigation. In judicial review, an applicant can only move on to the substantive trial stage if he can obtain leave

25 See William Wade and Christopher Forsyth, *Administrative Law*, 9th edn, Oxford University Press, Oxford, 2014, at p. 679.

26 Order 53, Rule 3 provides: '(1) No application for judicial review shall be made unless the leave of the Court has been obtained in accordance with this rule. ... (7) The Court shall not grant leave unless it considers that the applicant has a sufficient interest in the matter to which the application relates'.

27 [1982] AC 617. It is commonly called 'the National Federation Self-employed Case' or 'Fleet Street Casuals Case'.

28 See *Re Chan Yu Man*, HCAL 77/2005; *Mok Tai Kei v. Constitutional Affairs Bureau of the HKSAR & Ors* [2005] 1 HKLRD 860. For detailed discussion, please also refer to Swati Jhaveri et al., above n. 14, at pp. 182–184.

29 See for example *The Association of Expatriate Civil Servants of Hong Kong v. The Chief Executive of HKSAR* [1998] 1 HKLRD 615.

30 [2004] 1 HKLRD 396. This is a case about a challenge of reclamation of part of Victoria Harbour by the Hong Kong Government and its decision was challenged by a public interest organization, i.e. the Society for the Protection of the Harbour Ltd.

(permission) from the CFI at leave stage. This is specifically provided for by s. 21K(3) of the High Court Ordinance (Cap. 4) and Order 53, Rule 3(1) of the Rules of the High Court. According to these two statutory provisions, standing is a necessary but not sufficient interest for an applicant to obtain leave. The existence of the leave requirement has been argued to serve the interests of not only efficient management, but also that of the applicants and the respondents.[31] This means that the leave requirement aims to achieve an appropriate balance between public and private interests.

The exact test for determining whether an applicant should be granted leave is left to the court to decide. Judicial attitude has evolved over the years. For a long period of time, Hong Kong courts have followed the 'potential arguability test' set down by Lord Diplock in *Inland Revenue Commissioners v. National Federation of Self-employed and Small Businesses Ltd.*[32] The acceptance of the 'potential arguability test' was through the case of *R v. Director of Immigration, ex parte Ho Ming-sai.*[33] This was an appeal by Ho Ming-sai and others against the refusal of Nazareth JA, sitting as an additional judge of the High Court, to grant them leave to apply for judicial review of a decision of the Director of Immigration. The latter referred to a decision refusing to exercise his undisputed discretion under s. 3 of the Immigration Ordinance (Cap. 115) as to authorize Ho Ming-sai and her sister to remain in Hong Kong, where they had landed unlawfully during November 1990. Kempster JA remarked in the judgment:[34]

> He (Nazareth JA) should have asked himself whether the material before him disclosed matters which, on further consideration, might demonstrate an arguable case for the grant of the relief claimed. Put another way, by Lord Donaldson MR in R v Civil Service Appeal Board, ex parte Cunningham [1992] ICR 816 at 823, [1991] 4 All ER 310 at 315: '… leave will only be granted if the applicant makes out a prima facie case that something has gone wrong of a nature and extent which might call for the exercise of the judicial review jurisdiction'.

The problem was that, before this case was decided by the CA in Hong Kong, the case of *R v. Legal Aid Board ex parte Hughes* was already decided in England, in which Lord Donaldson MR voiced the following: 'In an ex parte application, leave to judicial review should only be granted if prima facie there is already an arguable case for granting the relief claimed'.[35] That means a different test, i.e. 'the arguability test', was adopted. So at present in England two different tests co-exist.

In many later cases, the test adopted in *Ho Ming-sai* had been challenged and reviewed by the Hong Kong courts more than once and alternatives such as a flexible approach have been suggested.[36] The debate on which test is preferable was finally put to an end by the CFA's judgment

---

31 See A. Le Sueur and M. Sunkin, Applications for Judicial Review: The Requirement of Leave, PL, 1992, p. 102.

32 In that case, Lord Diplock said the following: 'If, on a quick perusal of the material then available, the court thinks that it discloses what might on further consideration turn out to be an arguable case in favour of granting to the applicant the relief claimed, it ought, in the exercise of a judicial discretion, to give him leave to apply for that relief'.

33 (1993) 3 HKPLR 157.

34 Litton JA put the test slightly differently, as follows: 'It is not intended that in dealing with an application for leave under O. 53, r.3, the court should anticipate the outcome as if all the relevant evidence were already before the court. It is not intended that the court should, at the threshold stage, entertain elaborate arguments on the facts and the law'.

35 (1992) 23 HLR at 702–703.

36 See for example, *Wong Chung Ki v. Chief Executive*, CACV 1/2000; and *Shen Yin Fun v. Director of Legal Aid*, HCAL 183/2002.

in *Winnie Cheung & Anor v. Chan Po Fun Peter*.[37] This case was in relation to whether a certified public accountant who had been removed from the register for six months should be granted leave to challenge the decision of the Hong Kong Society of Accountants for not considering his application for re-admission prior to the expiry of the removal period. His application for leave to apply for judicial review was dismissed by the CFI. But leave was granted to him by the CA to appeal against the decision of the CFI out of time. The case was finally appealed to the CFA. Li Chief Justice (CJ) expressed the following in the judgment about the test for granting leave:[38]

> The requirement for leave to apply for judicial review is an important filter introduced by statute. Section 21K(3) of the High Court Ordinance, Cap. 4 and Order 53 rule 3(1) of the Rules of the High Court. Its purpose is to prevent public authorities from being unduly vexed with unarguable challenges. Whilst in a society governed by the rule of law, it is of fundamental importance for citizens to have access to the courts to challenge decisions made by public authorities on judicial review, the public interest in good public administration requires that public authorities should not have to face uncertainty as to the validity of their decisions as a result of unarguable claims. Nor should third parties affected by their decisions face such uncertainty.
>
> The purpose of the leave requirement would be better served by the adoption of the arguability test instead of the potential arguability test. The granting of leave to apply for judicial review is a matter for the court's discretion to be exercised judicially. The test which should be applied is the arguability test. Under this test, arguability must mean reasonable arguability. A claim for relief which is not reasonably arguable could not be regarded as arguable. A reasonably arguable case is one which enjoys realistic prospects of success. Whilst the test adopted represents a higher threshold than the potential arguability test, claims which are reasonably arguable would be given leave to go forward under it. It is in the public interest that challenges which are not reasonably arguable should not be given leave to proceed.

So now the test for determining leave in Hong Kong has changed from the 'potential arguability test' to the 'arguability test'. It is clear that the threshold for judicial review has been increased by the CFI through the adoption of the new test. It is now more difficult to obtain leave than before. According to Li CJ, the 'arguability test' will better serve the purpose of the leave requirement to balance the interests of good administration and third parties on the one hand and citizens' rights to have access to the courts on the other. But he did not explain why the 'arguability test' will serve the purpose of the leave requirement better than the 'potential arguability test', as both tests are still used in England.

The reason is most likely to be that there have been too many different kinds of applications for judicial review brought before the courts after the change of sovereignty. Though he had sent out his warning that certain disputes should not be brought to the courts and would be better resolved by the executive and legislative branches, his warning has not been well received.[39] There are two choices available to him. One is to tighten the requirement of standing, the other is to tighten the requirement of leave. Since the former will deprive the applicant of the opportunity for his argument on the merits before the courts, the latter choice is obviously a better one. The 'arguability test' will enable the court to refuse to grant leave for an unmeritorious application for judicial review.

37 [2007] 5 HKC 145, FACV 10/2007.

38 *Ibid.*, paras 14 and 15 of the judgment.

39 The Chief Justice's speech at Ceremonial Opening of the Legal Year 2006, available at: http://www.info.gov.hk/gia/general/200601/09/P200601090137.htm [accessed: 21 May 2014].

Grounds for Judicial Review

Hong Kong has its own written constitution, i.e. the Basic Law, which contains provisions on almost every matter that relates to society. Hence, in judicial review in Hong Kong, the scope covered by the doctrine of ultra vires or illegality is much wider than that seen in England. More importantly, the existence of a written constitution has made it possible for the courts in Hong Kong to review the ultra vires acts of not only administrative organs but also the Legislative Council.

Traditionally, all specific grounds of judicial review are deemed to derive from the doctrine of ultra vires and/or a specific manifestation of the doctrine of ultra vires. Lord Diplock suggested, in the case of GCHQ,[40] a new classification of grounds for judicial review, i.e. (i) illegality, (ii) procedural impropriety, and (iii) irrationality. He also stated that, with the development of society, new grounds were bound to arise. He gave the example of proportionality and pointed out that it might develop into a fully fledged ground for judicial review in the future.[41] This section will discuss how each category of grounds for judicial review has been applied and developed by the Hong Kong courts under its unique constitutional setting as a special administrative region within the sovereign state of the PRC, which itself adopts a completely different legal system.

Illegality

As has been argued in the Halsbury's Laws of Hong Kong, if exercising executive power may affect the rights and interests of an individual, there must exist a lawful basis for it.[42] In the case of Hong Kong, the source of power for the executive branch may derive either directly or indirectly from the Basic Law, other statutes including ordinances and subsidiary legislation, or the common law. Whether the exercise of power by the executive branch is within the parameters set down by the various sources of law is up to the court to decide. Illegality is one of the three categories of grounds according to Lord Diplock's classification. It consists of some specific bases upon which an application for judicial review can be formulated. The essence of this ground is to ensure that, in exercising public authority, the executive branch has not exceeded its jurisdiction and has not abused its authority or its discretionary power. Given that Hong Kong has a very detailed written constitution, i.e. the Basic Law, this ground has, in contrast to the situation in Britain, a unique function of ensuring the constitutionality of both legislative and executive acts.

Constitutionality Review

Since the enactment and coming into effect of the Bill of Rights Ordinance (BORO) in 1991, the number of judicial review cases brought on the grounds of a violation of the BORO has constituted a substantial percentage of the total judicial review cases. In addition, the issue of constitutionality of legislative and/or executive acts has also been brought up as a collateral issue in other categories of cases, such as criminal cases. The very first case on the BORO, *Sin Yau-ming*, was brought up in such a way.[43] Another case that was appealed to the Privy Council before the change of sovereignty

40 The full citation of the case is *Council of Civil Service Unions v. Minister for the Civil Service* [1985] AC 374, 410.

41 *Ibid.*

42 See Tim Parker, Administrative Law, in *Halsbury's Laws of Hong Kong*, vol. 1, LexisNexis Butterworths, Hong Kong, 2011 reissue, para. 10.002, at pp. 6–9.

43 *R v. Sin Yau-ming* [1992] 1 HKCLR 127.

was *Mingpao*.[44] This action challenged the constitutionality of a certain section of the Prevention of Bribery Ordinance (Cap. 201).

Following the change of sovereignty on 1 July 1997, Hong Kong has a new constitutional document – the Basic Law. In comparison with the colonial constitutional documents, i.e. the Letters Patent and Royal Instructions, the Basic Law is much more detailed and contains provisions on most aspects of social life in Hong Kong. In addition to the standard provisions on the constitutional structure and fundamental rights, the Basic Law also contains provisions on public finance, monetary affairs, trade, industry and commerce, land leases, shipping, civil aviation,[45] education, science, culture, sports, religion, labour, and social services.[46] With the Basic Law providing such a wide coverage, this gives rise in theory to the possibility of challenging the constitutionality of various legislative and/or administrative acts in those areas. Indeed in reality, judicial practice has borne that possibility. This aligns Hong Kong more closely to those countries with a written constitution.

Retention and Exercise of Discretionary Power

Discretionary power is usually granted by a piece of legislation to a specific agency and decision-making is expected to be carried out by that specific agency. It follows that as a general policy the delegation of such discretionary power to other agencies is prohibited. Its constitutional justification is the legislative intention behind it. If the legislature has specified that a particular agency should take the decision, its will must prevail. In the UK, this can be derived from the constitutional principle of parliamentary sovereignty. In the case of Hong Kong, it is also true in that the Basic Law has granted the legislative authority to the Legislative Council (LegCo), which is a reflection of the NPC's intentions. If the LegCo confers a discretionary power onto a particular agency, that agency has a statutory duty to exercise it.

However, on the other hand, it has been argued that demands of expediency, pragmatism, and good administration may sometimes require the delegation of a statutory discretionary power to other agencies or persons. Otherwise, the efficient conduct of the government may be compromised by rigid application of the non-delegation principle. Hence a proper balance needs to be struck between the retention of discretionary power and delegation. Courts have developed rules to achieve such an objective.

In dealing with issues of both constraining and exercising discretionary power in Hong Kong, Clark and McCoy have noted that the first thing to do is to find out if 'delegation provisions exist in any relevant, specific ordinance'.[47] If the answer is no, one should then proceed to the Interpretation and General Clauses Ordinance (Cap. 1). One specific example is s. 63 of that ordinance, which provides that the Chief Executive may delegate their authority to other governmental officials.[48]

44 The full citation of the case is: *Ming Pao Newspapers Limited v. Attorney-General* [1996] AC 907.

45 See Chapter V of the Basic Law.

46 See Chapter VI of the Basic Law.

47 See above n. 5, at pp. 143–147.

48 '(1) Where any Ordinance confers powers or imposes duties upon the Chief Executive, he may delegate any person by name or the person holding any office designated by him to exercise such powers or perform such duties on his behalf and thereupon, or from the date specified by the Chief Executive, the person so delegated shall have and may exercise such powers and perform such duties. (2) Nothing in subsection (1) shall authorize the Chief Executive to delegate any person to make subsidiary legislation, issue proclamations or to determine any appeal. (Replaced 26 of 1998 s. 22) (3) Where any Ordinance confers powers or imposes duties upon the Chief Executive and such power is exercised or such duty is performed by any public officer,

As to the issue of whether or not a statutory discretionary power has been retained or properly exercised by its statutory holder, one needs guidance from the case law. In *Re Hong Kong Hunter's Association*,[49] the Director of Agriculture and Fisheries, under s. 14 of the Wild Animals Protection Ordinance (Cap. 170), was the licensing authority empowered to issue game licences that were valid for one year. In December 1979 applications were made to him for the renewal of various licences but were all refused without any explanation, although the applicants were informed that a circular letter would be sent to them. Subsequently, such a letter was sent on behalf of the Director advising that the issue of game licences had been discontinued following a decision of the Executive Council that game hunting should be prohibited, and that current licences would remain valid until their expiration or until the law was amended. At the time of the proceedings no amendment to the relevant law had been made. It was argued on behalf of the Director that he had acted appropriately in allowing a policy decision to guide the use of his discretion. The High Court held that (1) the Director had not exercised his discretion independently and/or judicially in accordance with the provisions of the Ordinance in deciding he would not renew any licences, because he felt his discretion was fettered by the policy directive of the Executive Council; (2) as a licensing authority the Director should have dealt with each application for licences on their merits and should not have issued a general blanket refusal to consider any applications once the licences had expired. The essential point of this case is that the Director exercised his authority under 'dictation' and therefore failed to exercise his discretion under s. 14 of the Ordinance.[50]

In the more recent case of *Lai Tak Shing v. Director of Home Affairs*,[51] the Court of Appeal held that discretionary power had not been exercised by the Director of Home Affairs when the Director had refused to add Tsing Yi Hui to the list of indigenous villages in schedule 2 to the Village Representative Election Ordinance (Cap. 576). The CA held that section 67 of the Ordinance conferred discretion to amend the schedule and that it was an unlawful restraint on the exercise of that discretion to permit a question of policy, endorsed by the legislature conclusively to determine the exercise of discretion.

These two cases show that the decision-makers in Hong Kong are required by courts to actually exercise their statutory discretion and should not follow blindly another agency's view in making decisions and furthermore should not allow a policy to constrain their use of their discretionary powers. This is the same in England.

As far as the delegation of authority is concerned, Hong Kong courts have followed the Caltona Principle, which was described by Lord Greene in *Carltona Ltd. v. Commissioners of Works*:[52]

> The duties imposed upon Ministers and the powers given to Ministers are normally exercised under the authority of the Ministers by responsible officials of the department. Public business could not be carried on if that were not the case. Constitutionally, the decision of such an official is, of course, the decision of the Minister. The Minister is responsible. It is he who must answer before Parliament for anything that his official had done under his authority …

The Carltona principle has been applied by Hong Kong courts in a series of cases. It means that, within the Government, any civil servant at a particular rank within a certain department can

the Chief Executive shall, unless the contrary is proved, be deemed to have delegated such public officer under subsection (1) to exercise the power or perform the duty.'

49 [1980] HKLR 179 (HC).

50 *Ibid.*

51 CACV 201/2005.

52 [1943] 2 All E.R. 560.

lawfully exercise the authority granted to the head of that department without the necessity of any explicit delegation of power.

As to the theoretical justification for the Carltona principle, Kaplan J, made the following observation on the principle in *Re Chiu*: 'The principle is not in reality one of delegation at all. Legally the act of the official is the act of the minister. There is no need for prior authorization or subsequent ratification by the minister.'[53]

Abuse of Discretionary Power

There are several specific grounds in Hong Kong in which one can challenge the abuse of discretionary power by the executive branch.

Exercise of discretionary power for an improper purpose

If a discretionary power granted for one purpose is exercised for a different purpose, it has not been validly exercised in law. Such use of the discretionary power can be challenged through judicial review on the grounds of exercising discretionary power for an improper purpose. Hong Kong has followed British practice in this respect. We shall show how this ground has been applied through the ensuing case.

In *Chan Lau-fong v. A-G*,[54] the applicants were the owners of 19 lots of land in Hoi Pa Village, Tsuen Wan, where land was resumed by the Government as part of the implementation of the Tsuen Wan District Outline Zoning Plan. In July 1990 notification of the resumption of the lots was outlined in the Gazette. That notice included in its heading the words, 'resumption of land for development at Hoi Pa Village – remaining engineering works'. The resumption order was made pursuant to section 3 of the Town Planning Ordinance (Cap. 131), which provides that, 'Whenever the Governor in Council decides that the resumption of any land is required for a public purpose, the Governor may order the resumption thereof under this Ordinance'. The definition of public purpose is contained in section 2 of the Ordinance, and includes the '(d) resumption for any purpose of whatsoever description whether *ejusdem generis* with any of the above purposes or not, which the Governor in Council may decide to be a public purpose'.

Before the High Court the applicants advanced two bases to support their argument that the decision of the Governor in Council was ultra vires. The first was that the only element of 'public purpose' that could be relied upon in making the resumption was roadworks, and only a small portion of the lots were affected by those works. The second basis was that, properly construed, the Gazette resumption notice had identified 'remaining engineering works' as the purpose of the resumption and that, since the only engineering works contemplated were those roadworks, the resumption was ultra vires in respect of the remainder of those lots unaffected by the roadworks.

The High Court dismissed the application on the basis that the roadworks formed only part of the whole development, and that civil engineering works would be required for the clearance of the lots, and for the provision of an adequate drainage system. On appeal, the prevailing view was that the crucial question is a matter of construction, i.e. whether the heading of the resumption notice was to be taken into account when construing the body of the notice. The ambit of the general language in the body of the notice should be considered as limited to the specific purpose specified in the heading. However, the applicants needed to show that the effect of the heading, read in conjunction with the body of the notice and the contents of the resumption plan, was that the notice specified only the remaining engineering works as the public purpose of the resumption.

53 *Re Chiu* [1992] 2 HKLR 57.

54 [1992] 2 HKLR 203.

Even assuming that the only engineering works identifiable under the notice were the roadworks, the heading of the notice was, nevertheless, clearly not confined to engineering works. Hence, the CA held that the combined effect of the heading and the body of the notice was that the resumption order was an order for the development at Hoi Pa Village including the remaining engineering works. That was the public purpose for which the Governor had made the order.

This case shows that the essence in the application of this ground for judicial review is the proper interpretation of the purpose permitted under the statute, and then the identification of the actual purpose of the decision-maker. The issue for the court to decide is whether the permitted statutory purpose covers the actual purpose of the decision-maker. But in many cases, improper purpose may also be argued to be an irrelevant consideration that the decision-maker should not take into account; and this is the next ground which the paper will discuss.

Taking into account irrelevant considerations and/or failure to take into account relevant considerations

If a discretionary power that is exercised has been influenced by considerations that cannot lawfully be taken into account, or has disregarded relevant considerations that should be taken into account, such an exercise of the power will normally be regarded as invalid in law. The British case of *Padfield v. Minister of Agriculture, Fisheries and Food* remains a leading case in Hong Kong and is still applied.[55]

In the local case of *Hermes Pacific Ltd v. Commissioner of Customs and Excise*,[56] the issue between the parties was whether the appellant's luxury soap products were 'cosmetics' as defined in s. 76 of the Dutiable Commodities Ordinance (Cap. 109), or whether they came within the proviso to that section whereby soaps and certain other personal care products were excluded from the definition of 'cosmetics', unless they purported to be one of the preparations coming within the definition of 'cosmetics'. The soaps were part of a line of perfumed products produced by the appellant and were promoted as such. Their marketing conveyed the impression of promoting personal attractiveness. The fragrances in the soaps were dissolved in essential oils, unlike the smells of ordinary soaps, which derive from chemical or synthetic ingredients. The packaging of the soaps suggested that they were akin to cosmetics rather than bath or toiletry soaps and they sold for 25 times the price of ordinary soap. After considering all these factors, the Commissioner determined that the soaps purported to be fragrances and to promote good grooming and thus were among the preparations that came within the definition of 'cosmetics' and therefore were dutiable under the Ordinance.

The trial judge upheld the Commissioner's determination.[57] On appeal, the CA was of the view that the Commissioner was not given a decision-making power or an administrative role in determining whether an item was dutiable. The court was bound to interpret the Ordinance against the backdrop of the facts. Since it was clear that the legislature did not intend to render all soap

55 [1968] AC 997.

56 [1988] 2 HKLR 165 CA.

57 The reasons given by the trial judges are as follows. The legislature had intended to make dutiable any preparation or substance the use or application of which contributed more than simple bodily cleanliness. Moreover, the legislature had left it to the Commissioner to determine which soap products were cosmetics and which not; and the Commissioner was justified in looking not only at the soaps but also at the way in which they were packaged, advertised and marketed generally, and was entitled to distinguish these soaps from others whose smells derived from chemical or synthetic ingredients. Accordingly, the trial judge held that the Commissioner's determination was not one to which a reasonable person or tribunal ought not to have come.

products dutiable, the person asserting that a particular soap fulfilled the necessary conditions would need to establish that fact. The packaging and advertising of the soaps were relevant to the question of whether they purported to be 'cosmetics'. However, other factors relied upon by the Commissioner were not relevant: an item could not 'purport to be' a cosmetic by reason of (i) price, (ii) presence in a range of products that were cosmetics, (iii) place, number or type of sales outlet, or (iv) due to its pleasant smell. Under the legislation, soaps were not dutiable simply on account of contributing more than simple bodily cleanliness, nor was it intended that luxury soaps be dutiable and others not. Furthermore, it had not been shown that any of the soaps purported to be fragrances, or that they promoted or purported to promote good grooming any more than any other toilet soap. The CA allowed the appeal by the appellant.

In the case of *Capital Rich Development Ltd & Another v. Town Planning Board*,[58] the Court of Appeal considered the situation where several factors have been considered by the decision-maker, i.e. the Town Planning Board (TPB) in deciding whether to approve the objection raised by the applicants in the case to excise their land from the comprehensive development plan of the Urban Renewable Authority (a statutory body). The court could not say that, without the irrelevant consideration, the TPB would have reached the same conclusion based solely on other relevant considerations. It could not say with confidence that the decision was valid based solely on planning grounds. That means that the irrelevant considerations had material influence. Hence it held that the decision could be quashed.

The aforementioned two cases show that, in relying on the grounds of irrelevant considerations, there are two essential elements: one is to prove that certain irrelevant considerations have been taken into account by the decision-maker; the other is that the irrelevant consideration/s has/have materially influenced the decision-maker in reaching their conclusion.

Procedural Impropriety

In addition to illegality, procedural impropriety is another vast category of grounds for judicial review. This category has developed on the basis of the traditional doctrine of natural justice but has been expanded to cover more specific grounds. The main specific grounds within this category include: (i) failure to comply with specific statutory procedures; (ii) legitimate expectation; and (iii) the doctrine of natural justice.

Failure to Comply with Statutory Procedures

The general rule is that a breach of a mandatory procedural requirement will be subject to judicial review, but a breach of directory requirement will not. Whether or not a statutory procedural requirement is mandatory or directory is a matter of statutory construction. Even if a requirement is indeed mandatory, substantial compliance is sufficient. The British leading case in this area is *R v. Secretary of State for the Home Department, ex parte Jeyeanthan*.[59] In this case, it was held that,

58 [2007] 2 HKLRD 155.

59 [1999] 3 All ER 231. The facts of the case are as follows. Special adjudicators allowed applications for asylum by R and J. In both cases the Secretary of State sought to challenge the decision in the Immigration Appeal Tribunal (the IAT), but failed to submit the application form for leave to appeal prescribed by r 13(3) of Asylum Appeals (Procedure) Rules 1993. Instead, he applied for leave to appeal by letters that contained all the relevant information required by the prescribed form save for the declaration of truth. In J's case, a challenge was made, but was rejected by the IAT. On J's application for judicial review, the judge held that the

in determining the consequences of a failure to comply with a procedural requirement, the court had to assess the intention of the legislator against the factual circumstances of non-compliance, and in most cases it would be of little if any assistance to inquire as to whether the requirement was mandatory or directory. That question was at the most a first step, and normally there were other questions that were likely to be of greater assistance, namely: (i) whether the statutory requirement had been fulfilled if there had been substantial compliance with it and, if so, whether there had been such compliance; (ii) whether the non-compliance was capable of being waived, and if so, whether it had been, could or should be waived; and (iii) what was the consequence of non-compliance if it was not capable of being waived or had not been waived. In the case in question, there had been substantial non-compliance since a form containing a declaration of truth was a very different document from a form without such a declaration. However, that non-compliance was an irregularity that could be cured by the Immigration Appeals Tribunal under the relevant statutory rule, and that rule had to be given a broad interpretation in order to avoid injustice to asylum seekers who were likely to make procedural errors.

In *Nina T. H. Wang v. Commissioner of Inland Revenue*, the Privy Council stated:[60]

> … their Lordships consider that when a question like the present one arises – an alleged failure to comply with a time provision – it is simpler and better to avoid these two words 'mandatory' and 'directory' and to ask two questions. The first is whether the legislature intended the person making the determination to comply with the time provision, whether a fixed time or a reasonable time. Secondly, if so, did the legislature intend that a failure to comply with such a time provision would deprive the decision maker of jurisdiction and render any decision which he purported to make null and void?

The above two cases have been applied in the case of *Commissioner of Inland Revenue v. Loganathan*,[61] where the trial judge held that sending out notices for the payment of additional tax to the taxpayer by two different deputy commissioners, constituted substantial compliance with the statutory notice requirement under section 82A(4).

From the discussion of the above cases, one can observe that, in cases concerning non-compliance with statutory procedures, courts will not focus on the nature of the statutory procedures, i.e. whether they are mandatory or directory. Instead, the court will focus on the intentions of the legislature to see whether the non-compliance would potentially defeat the original intention of the legislature.

Legitimate Expectation

Legitimate expectation is concerned with the extent to which a public authority's powers may be limited by views of how it should act. One can still observe the balancing-act of both protecting administrative autonomy on the one hand and pursuing conflicting policy goals, such as legal certainty, on the other. There exist two sub-categories of legitimate expectation, namely procedural and substantive legitimate expectation.

Secretary of State's application substantially failed to comply with the prescribed form and that accordingly the IAT's decision was a nullity. The Secretary of State appealed, contending that the non-compliance was not substantial and that it was an irregularity that could be cured under r 38 of the Immigration Appeals (Procedure) Rules 1984. J and R contended that r 13(3) of the 1993 rules should be strictly applied.

60 [1994] 4 HKTC 15.

61 [2000] 2 HKC 516.

Procedural legitimate expectation

As far as procedural legitimate expectation is concerned, the leading case in Hong Kong that was appealed to the Privy Council, refers to *Attorney-General of Hong Kong v. Ng Yeun Shiu.*[62] In this case, the applicant who was born in China entered Hong Kong illegally from Macau in 1967. In 1976 he was removed to Macau but re-entered illegally shortly after and subsequently remained in Hong Kong. By 1980 he was the part-owner of a small factory in Hong Kong. In October 1980 the government announced changes in its immigration policy. It abandoned its 'reached base' policy whereby illegal entrants had been allowed to remain once they had reached the urban areas without being arrested and it stated that those who had entered illegally would be repatriated. It gave power to the Director of Immigration to make removal orders against such persons. The announcement created fears among illegal entrants living in Hong Kong who had entered from Macau and who were of Chinese origin that they would be repatriated to mainland China.

On their petitioning the Governor, a senior immigration officer made an announcement with the government policy that each illegal entrant from Macau would be interviewed and their cases treated on their merits. Having undergone questioning by an immigration officer, the applicant was detained and the Director of Immigration then made a removal order against him without giving him an opportunity to make any representation as to why he should not be removed. The applicant applied to the High Court for an order of certiorari to quash the removal order and prohibit the Director from executing it, but failed. On his appeal to the Court of Appeal, he was granted an order that prevented the Director from executing the removal order until he had given the applicant an opportunity to be heard. The Government appealed to the Privy Council.

The Privy Council focused on the specific issue of whether the applicant had a right to a hearing in the particular circumstances of this case. Their Lordships were of the view that the phrase 'legitimate expectation' is an apt one to express the underlying principle, and the word 'legitimate' means 'reasonable', and accordingly 'legitimate expectations' are capable of including expectations that go beyond enforceable legal rights, provided that they have some reasonable basis. Furthermore, their Lordships saw no reason why the principle should not be applicable when the person who will be affected by the decision is an alien.

As for the justification for the principle, their Lordships had described it as follows:[63]

> … when a public authority has promised to follow a certain procedure, it is in the interest of good administration that it should act fairly and should implement its promise, so long as implementation does not interfere with its statutory duty. The principle is also justified by the further consideration that, when the promise was made, the authority must have considered that it would be assisted in discharging its duty fairly by any representations from interested parties and as a general rule that is correct.

In conclusion, their Lordships opined that the principle that a public authority is bound by its undertakings regarding the procedure it will follow, provided that this does not conflict with their duty, is certainly applicable to the undertaking given by the Government of Hong Kong to the applicant in announcing that each case would be considered on its merits.

With the roots cemented in this case, the ground of procedural legitimate expectation has been firmly established in Hong Kong. In the eyes of their Lordships, protection of procedural legitimate expectation is in the interests of good administration. The confirmation of this ground by courts in

62 [1983] 2 AC 629.

63 *Ibid.*

Hong Kong will bring Hong Kong on par with those countries where written constitutions contain a right to good administration.

Substantive legitimate expectation

The substantive protection of legitimate expectation is more controversial in that it impacts upon the range of decisions open to the decision-maker. The enforcement of substantive expectations may ultimately result in the denial of the decision-maker's discretion in cases where the court concludes that the expectation needs to be satisfied.

The leading case in Hong Kong is *Ng Siu Tung & Others v. Director of Immigration*,[64] which is another important right of abode case. After the judgment of the CFA in *Ng Ka Ling*, the NPCSC issued an interpretation in 1999 to in effect overrule that judgment. But Art. 158(3) provides that 'judgments previously rendered shall not be affected'. The applicants in this case, over 5000 in total, did not join the previous proceedings or commence new actions, but they claimed that they were in the same position as the parties in the judgments. At issue was who was to be entitled to the benefit of the judgments in *Ng Ka Ling* and therefore not affected by the NPCSC Interpretation.[65]

The applicants raised two arguments. One was on the basis that, in accordance with Art. 158(3) of the Basic Law, they had an accrued right under the judgments and should therefore not be affected by the Interpretation. The other was that, even if they were affected, they had a legitimate expectation, as a result of various public statements and representations made by the Government during the *Ng Ka Ling* and *Chan Kam Nga* litigation,[66] and in light of how that litigation was conducted, that they would receive the same treatment as the parties in those two cases and effect should be given to such legitimate expectation.

In delivering the judgment for the majority of the CFA, Li CJ confirmed that the doctrine of substantive legitimate expectation (to be referred to as 'the doctrine') formed part of the administrative law of Hong Kong. Under this doctrine, a failure to honour a legitimate expectation of a substantive outcome or benefit might, in the absence of any overriding reason of law or policy excluding its operation, result in such unfairness to individuals as to amount to an abuse of power justifying intervention by the court. He further explained that the doctrine comprised four elements:[67]

1. the legitimate expectation arose from a promise or representation, the expectation being that the promise or representation would be honoured, that it should be properly taken into account in the decision-making process so long as to do so would fall within the power, statutory or otherwise, of the decision-maker;
2. in the absence of reasons recognized by law for not giving effect to legitimate expectation, effect should be given, and if effect is not given, the decision-maker should express their reasons so that they might be tested by a court in the event that the decision is challenged;
3. even if the decision involved the making of a political choice by reference to policy considerations, the decision-maker must make the choice in the light of the legitimate expectation of the parties, the failing of which would usually result in the decision being vitiated by reason of failure to take account of a relevant consideration and thereby constituting an abuse of power; and

64 [2002] 1 HKLRD 561.

65 See above n. 7.

66 Chan Kam Nga was another applicant in the case of *Ng Ka Ling*.

67 [2002] 1 HKLRD 561.

4. it would only be in exceptional cases where the court would be satisfied that the failure to take account of a relevant consideration had not affected the decision. But once the court is satisfied that this is the case, the decision cannot be quashed.

So the highest court in Hong Kong has decided that the doctrine of substantive legitimate expectation is one of the grounds upon which individuals can rely in order to challenge the executive branch for failing to honour their promises of substantive rights/interests. But the CFA was also very cautious in its application of this ground. It has stated clearly that the protection of substantive legitimate expectation should not defeat the purpose of existing legislation. In this specific case, Li CJ was of the view that the number of applicants was limited (though quite a large group) and that the Director of Immigration possessed discretionary power under the relevant ordinance to grant right of abode under the relevant ordinance. These two factors led him to the conclusion that the applicants' claims to substantive legitimate expectation, in this instance the right of abode, should indeed be protected.

Detrimental reliance?

In applying the grounds of both procedural and substantive legitimate expectation, one controversial issue is whether or not the applicants are required to show that they have actually relied on the promise. In other jurisdictions, it is generally considered that detrimental reliance is not necessary.[68] In Hong Kong, the majority of the CFA in the case of *Ng Siu Tung* did not find it necessary to decide whether detrimental reliance was required in order to allow for review on the basis of legitimate expectation because the representations in question were found to be calculated to induce reliance. But Bokhary Permanent Justice (PJ) opined that, 'if a person is in a class to which a representation is directed, the fact that he was unaware of it until after the decision disappointing it was made ought not to deprive him of the benefit of the representation. Legitimate expectation in this context does not depend upon the knowledge and state of mind of the individual concerned. A person is not to be denied enforcement of a legitimate expectation of his class merely because he only learned of it after the decision was made'.[69] Though detrimental reliance is not essential, he suggested that the evidence of detrimental reliance can nevertheless strengthen the applicant's case for enforcing a legitimate expectation where he has altered his position in reliance of that legitimate expectation so that he would suffer detriment if that expectation is not fulfilled.[70] He also mentioned that only in exceptional circumstances would detrimental reliance be required in order to succeed on legitimate expectation grounds.[71]

The above obiter of Bokhary PJ is consistent with the judicial position on this issue in other commonwealth jurisdictions. Hence, it is foreseeable that such obiter will be followed in the future case law.

Doctrine of Nature Justice

Natural justice has achieved something of the status of a fundamental right and applies also to disciplinary bodies. However, it must also be a flexible principle. It has been observed by judges

68 See for example, above n. 25, at pp. 500–509.

69 See above n. 64, para. 355, at pp. 665–666; see also Stanley de Smith, Harry Woolf and Jeffrey Jowell, *Judicial Review of Administrative Action*, 5th edn, Sweet & Maxwell, London, 1995, at p. 426, para. 8–058.

70 *Ibid.*

71 One example he gave was the case of *R v. Secretary for State for Education and Employment, ex p B (A Minor)* [2000] 1 WLR 1115, in which a quick correction by an executive of a misrepresentation of its policy, made inadvertently, was held not to amount to an abuse of power.

that 'it is not possible to lay down rigid rules as to when the principles of natural justice are to apply: nor as to their scope and extent. Everything depends on the subject-matter'.[72] This explains why other more specific grounds have evolved from the original doctrine of natural justice.

The rule against bias

This is a well-established common law ground for judicial review and has been used for centuries in common law jurisdictions. In determining whether prejudice exists, the courts need a test. Since Hong Kong was a colony of the UK, it followed the test that had been established by the House of Lords, prior to the change of sovereignty. In the case of *R v. Gough*,[73] the House of Lords held that, except where a person acting in a judicial capacity had a direct pecuniary interest in the outcome of proceedings, when the court would assume bias and automatically disqualify him from adjudication, the test to be applied in all cases of apparent bias, was whether, having regard to the relevant circumstances, there was a real danger of bias on the part of the relevant member of the tribunal in question, in the sense that he might unfairly regard or have unfairly regarded with favour or disfavour the case of a party to the issue under consideration by him.[74]

Two years later, in the case of *Panel on Takeovers and Mergers v. Cheng Kai Man William*,[75] which was appealed from Hong Kong to the Privy Council, the Privy Council adopted the same test in determining whether or not prejudice existed.

However, the House of Lords revisited the issue of what should be the proper test to be adopted to determine the existence of prejudice in the case of *Porter v. Magill*,[76] believing that the 'fair-minded and informed observer' test is a more preferable one than the 'real danger' test and deciding to adopt the former as the accepted norm.

In 2003, the CFA in Hong Kong had an opportunity to look into this issue in the case of *Deacons v. White & Case Limited Liability Partnership & Others*.[77] Since both parties in the case agreed that the proper test should be 'the fair-minded and informed observer' test, the CFA applied said test without any detailed analysis of the reasoning for doing so, merely accepting the test as the most preferable for Hong Kong. Ribeiro PJ made the following comment on the test in the above case:[78]

> It is unnecessary for us to comment definitively on the applicable test. It suffices for present purposes to note that both the applicants and the respondent agree that the test in Hong Kong is the reasonable apprehension of bias test developed as aforesaid and that the Court of Appeal was of a like mind. There is accordingly no question of great general or public importance dividing the parties or the court below as to what the proper test is.

This case shows that the Hong Kong legal profession and the judiciary are quite willing to follow the latest developments in other common law jurisdictions, including England.

The right to be heard

The courts took their stand several centuries ago on the broad principle that bodies entrusted with legal power could not validly exercise it without first hearing from the person who was potentially

72 *R v. Gaming Board for Great Britain ex p. Benaim and Khaida* [1970] 2 QB 417.
73 [1993] AC 646.
74 *Ibid.*
75 (1995) 3 HKC 517.
76 [2001] UKHL 67, [2002] 2 WLR 37.
77 [2004] 1 HKLRD 291.
78 *Ibid*, para. 30 of the judgment, at pp. 300–301.

going to suffer. This principle was applied very widely to administrative as well as judicial acts. Over the years, in addition to the right to an actual hearing, several specific rights have evolved from it:

The right to know the opposing case

The right to know the opposing case is a notion that developed from the aforementioned right to be heard. Lord Denning once said the following:

> If the right to be heard is to be a real right which is worth anything, it must carry with it a right in the accused man to know the case which is made against him. He must know what evidence has been given and what statements have been made affecting him: and then he must be given a fair opportunity to correct or contradict them.[79]

In the case of *Leung Fok Wah Oil v. Commissioner of Police*,[80] the respondent, a police sergeant, had incurred substantial debts exceeding $700,000 and had been classified as having unmanageable debts. He was charged with a disciplinary offence in that he failed to be prudent in his financial affairs through incurring unmanageable debts, which in turn impaired his efficiency as a police officer, contrary to Police General Orders. He was found guilty of the offence by the disciplinary tribunal that referred the matter of punishment to a Senior Police Officer, who reduced his rank to a constable and dismissed him from the police force. The respondent appealed to the appellant against both the finding of guilt and the penalty imposed. The Deputy Commissioner of Police who was exercising the delegated authority of the appellant, dismissed the appeal. The respondent sought judicial review of the decisions of the tribunal, the Senior Police Officer and the Deputy Commissioner. The trial judge granted the application against the Deputy Commissioner on the grounds that fairness was not observed in the appeal because some materials relied on by the Deputy Commissioner were not disclosed to the respondent. The appellant appealed to the Court of Appeal and the respondent cross-appealed.

The Court of Appeal held unanimously:[81]

> The principle of fairness which was incorporated in the disciplinary procedure required the disclosure of materials so that a person who might be adversely affected by the decision would have an opportunity to make their representations. There was no real distinction between the first instance hearing before the tribunal and the appeal to the Commissioner of Police in terms of the disclosure of documents. Once it was accepted by the Commissioner that he should disclose material which was adverse to the appellant and not previously disclosed by him, the distinction would become meaningless.
>
> The defaulter report which consisted of staffing notes and memos prepared by the responsible officers at various stages of the disciplinary procedure should be disclosed to the respondent as a matter of fairness so they can make a meaningful presentation in the appeal petition. The fact that the Commissioner stated that the memos did not contain new material was irrelevant, as disclosure should not depend on the views of an individual on the nature of the content but instead as a matter of a procedural requirement.

79 *Surinder Singh Kanda v. The Government of the Federation of Malaya* (1962) 28 MLJ 169.

80 [2002] 3 HKC 1.

81 *Ibid.*

This case has confirmed that the right to be heard or the principle of fairness in general includes a requirement that materials in the hands of the decision-maker should be first disclosed to the person whose rights/interests might be adversely affected.

Duty to give reasoning

The principles of natural justice do not, as yet, include any general rule that reasons should be given for decisions made. Nevertheless, there is a strong case to be made for giving reasons as an essential element of administrative justice. Unless a person can discover the reasoning behind a decision, he may be unable to tell whether it is reviewable or not. As a result, he may be deprived of the protection of the law. A right to reasons should therefore be an indispensable element of a sound system of judicial review. This has been acknowledged by the British House of Lords, in a case where it stated, 'No single factor has inhibited the development of English administrative law as seriously as the absence of any general obligation upon public authorities to give reasons for their decisions'.[82]

In Hong Kong, the law does not recognize a general duty to give reasons for administrative decisions. But a leading case does exist that questions whether or not the reasons given are adequate once a statutory duty to provide reasoning is found.

In the case of *Oriental Daily Publisher v. Commissioner for Television and Entertainment Licensing Authority*,[83] the Obscene Articles Tribunal determined that two sets of photographs of semi-naked women published by the appellant were indecent after a magistrate referred them to it during a criminal prosecution. In its decision, the Tribunal said it had considered all of the submissions from the defence counsel and had reminded itself of the standard of criminal cases. It gave three reasons for its conclusion: each photograph exceeded the standard of morality, decency and propriety that was generally accepted by reasonable members of the public; the dominant effect of each photograph was indecent and by reason of indecency it was not suitable to be published to a juvenile. It was agreed that the Tribunal was under a duty to give reasons for its decision. At issue was whether the Tribunal satisfied this duty by merely identifying the criteria that it was obliged to consider under s. 10 of the Control of Obscene and Indecent Articles Ordinance (Cap. 390). The respondent submitted that concepts of indecency and obscenity were abstract and difficult to express and that the reasons given by the Tribunal were adequate. The appellant appealed unsuccessfully to the CFI and then to the CA, on the grounds that the Tribunal had not given adequate reasons for its decision, and they further appealed to the CFA.

In allowing the appeal, the CFA held that, where there was a duty to give reasons, it must be discharged by giving adequate reasons. What amounted to adequate reasons depended on the context in which the decision-maker was operating and the circumstances of each case. The reasons given by the Tribunal should show that the Tribunal had addressed the substantial issues before it, and show why the Tribunal had come to its decision. There might be cases where the contents of the articles in question would virtually speak for themselves. In these cases, the duty to give reasons could be discharged by describing the contents without disclosing much more. Apart from this kind of case, a decision on indecency or obscenity that merely recited the statutory guidelines in the Ordinance would not normally be adequate. Whether reasons were adequate in each case was a matter to be approached sensibly. Where a point of law was raised, the reasons for a decision should usually set out the findings of fact, the point of law at issue, and the process of reasoning leading to the conclusion.[84]

82 *R v. Home Secretary ex p. Doody* [1994] 1 AC 531.

83 [1998] 4 HKC 505.

84 *Ibid.*

Though courts are unwilling to prescribe a common law duty for all decision-makers to give reasons for their decisions, once there is a statutory duty to give reasons, courts in Hong Kong are willing to make sure that the duty has been properly complied with. Hence, the LegCo in Hong Kong has a positive role to play in the supervision of the executive branch by setting down such specific requirements.

Right to professional legal representation

The leading case in Hong Kong on the right to legal representation is *Lam Siu Po v. Commissioner of Police*.[85] In this case, the appellant, Lam Siu Po, was a police officer and was disciplined by the Police Force. Regulation 9(11) and (12) of the Police (Discipline) Regulations, made by the Chief Executive in Council under the regulation-making power conferred by s. 45 of the Police Force Ordinance (Cap. 232), as it was at that time, barred him from having professional legal representation at his disciplinary hearing. He was convicted at the hearing. Thereafter, he challenged, among others, the validity of the statutory bar against professional legal representation on the grounds that the exclusion of professional legal representation by the relevant regulations deprived him of a fair hearing. In particular, he argued that his right under Art. 10 of the BORO had been infringed.[86]

He lost before both the CFI and the CA, but was granted leave by the CA to appeal to the CFA on three legal issues of which two were relevant here, (1) whether Art. 10 is engaged in police disciplinary proceedings; and (2) whether regulations 9(11) and 9(12) are consistent with Art. 10 of the BORO.

Ribeiro PJ is of the view that a specific charge brought before a particular disciplinary tribunal may or may not attract Art. 10 protections, depending on whether it involves the determination of a criminal charge or of the individual's civil rights and obligations, and a line should be drawn between the enforcement of internal discipline on the one hand and disciplinary measures affecting the individual's civil rights and obligations on the other.[87] It is for the court to decide on which side of the line any particular case falls. In his view, Art. 10 is clearly engaged in the present case because the appellant undoubtedly faced a determination of his rights and obligations in a suit of law, meaning his civil rights and obligations.[88] As to the second issue, he is of the view that the Commissioner has not provided sufficient justification for excluding Art. 10 protections in the disciplinary proceedings.[89] He concluded by stating:[90]

---

85 (2009) 12 HKCFAR 237.

86 It provides, 'All persons shall be equal before the courts and tribunals. In the determination of any criminal charge against him, or of his rights and obligations in a suit at law, everyone shall be entitled to a fair and public hearing by a competent, independent and impartial tribunal established by law. The press and the public may be excluded from all or part of a trial for reasons of morals, public order or national security in a democratic society, or when the interest of the private lives of the parties so requires, or to the extent strictly necessary in the opinion of the court in special circumstances where publicity would prejudice the interests of justice; but any judgment rendered in a criminal case or in a suit at law shall be made public except where the interest of juvenile persons otherwise requires or the proceedings concern matrimonial disputes or the guardianship of children.'

87 See above n. 85, para. 92 of the judgment.

88 See above n. 85, para. 93 of the judgment.

89 See above n. 85, para. 96 of the judgment.

90 See above n. 85, para. 103 of the judgment.

> I do not accept that the requirements of the police disciplinary tribunals in Hong Kong justify a total ban on legal representation regardless of the requirements of fairness. There seems to me to be little doubt that the effective functioning of the Police Force as a disciplined service will not be impaired by allowing its disciplinary tribunals a discretion to permit an officer to be legally represented where fairness so dictates. No ground of public necessity has been suggested as a basis for excluding the constitutional protection.

In conclusion, he was of the view that no objective grounds had been established to justify excluding the disciplinary proceedings in the present case from the protection of Article 10.[91]

Bukhary PJ has put the criterion for the application of Art. 10 to disciplinary proceedings somewhat differently:[92]

> The fair hearing clause of Art.10 of the Bill of Rights guarantees the fairness of the hearings to which it applies. Whether it applies to disciplinary proceedings depends on whether such proceedings are determinations of rights and obligations in suits at law within its meaning. If they are, then the fairness of such proceedings is secure. Let it be remembered that fairness does not always carry a right to be legally represented. It only carries a right to be legally represented when denying that right would be unfair. The rights typically involved in disciplinary proceedings are important ones extending to the right to remain in a profession, service or occupation.

So nowadays in Hong Kong, whether a right exists to legal representation in a particular disciplinary hearing depends on the nature of the hearing, in particular, whether the hearing affects the civil rights and interests of the person in question. In the above case, both the appellant and the CFA relied on the right to a fair hearing under Art. 10 of the BORO. This is reasonable because, through the BORO, international jurisprudence on human rights can easily be brought into Hong Kong. But even without such explicit provisions in the BORO, it would still remain likely that the courts would be willing to uphold such a right conditionally.

The right of appeal: curing the failure to observe natural justice

One legal issue that is very important to both parties in a judicial review procedure is whether a failure to comply with procedural requirements such as natural justice will definitely lead to a remedy. In this respect, Hong Kong has followed precedent from the European Court.

In the case of *R v. Lift Contractors' Disciplinary Board, ex parte Otis Elevator Co (Hong Kong) Ltd*,[93] an accident occurred during maintenance work carried out by A, a registered lift contractor. The Director of Electrical and Mechanical Services appointed a disciplinary board under s. 11E(1) of the Lifts and Escalators (Safety) Ordinance (Cap. 618) and brought charges of negligence against A before the board. A objected to the jurisdiction of the board on the grounds that the Director was the prosecutor in proceedings before the disciplinary board, appointed by himself, with himself or his representative forming part of the board and as such the board failed to act as 'an independent and impartial tribunal' as required by Art. 10 of the BORO. The board's ruling that ss. 11E(1), (2) and (3) of the Ordinance admitted of a construction consistent with the BORO was challenged successfully by A in proceedings for judicial review. The trial judge ruled that the provision in s. 11E(2)(d) of the Ordinance that the Director or his representative should be a member of the

91 See above n. 85, para. 106 of the judgment.

92 See above n. 85, para. 23 of the judgment.

93 (1995) 5 HKPLR 78 (CA).

disciplinary board was inconsistent with the BORO and should be repealed.[94] The Government appealed, contending that, having regard to the entire regime for dealing with a suspect's rights and obligations, the statutory scheme as a whole met the minimum requirements of Art. 10 of the BORO. In allowing the appeal, the Court of Appeal held that their primary concern centred upon the constitutional validity of the statutory scheme for dealing with suspected negligence and misconduct on the part of registered contractors under the Ordinance: whether that scheme met the minimum requirements of 'fairness' under Art. 10. If a scheme was flawed operationally, it might go a long way in showing that it was flawed constitutionally. But, at the end of the day, what had to be judged was not how it worked in practice but how the legislature had formulated the scheme. Even if the disciplinary tribunal, established under s. 11E of the Ordinance, failed to meet the requirements of Art. 10 by itself, s. 11I saved the scheme from inconsistency with the BORO. It was because of the fact that the appeal was through a re-hearing and the High Court had ample powers of control of the appeal procedure that Art. 10 requirements were met.

This case is again one based on Art. 10 of the BORO. But the principle coming out of the judgment has a wider influence on the failure to comply with all sorts of procedural rights requirements. The importance of this case rests on the fact that, when the courts examine whether or not procedural requirements have been complied with, they look at the whole dispute resolution scheme, rather than only the administrative part. So long as the requirements are met at the final stage of the dispute resolution mechanism, it will be adequate.

Irrationality/Wednesbury Unreasonableness

This ground was first established by Lord Greene in the case of *Associated Provincial Picture Houses Ltd. v. Wednesbury Corpn*,[95] in which he stated that the court should intervene if a decision-maker makes a decision which is 'so unreasonable that no reasonable authority could ever have come to it'.[96] In the *GCHQ* case,[97] Lord Diplock used 'irrationality' to replace 'Wednesbury unreasonableness' and remarked as follows:[98]

> By 'irrationality' I mean what can now be succinctly referred to as 'Wednesbury unreasonableness'. It applies to a decision which is so outrageous in its defiance of logic or of accepted moral standards that no sensible person who had applied his mind to the question to be decided could have arrived at it.

In Hong Kong, according to Clark and McCoy,[99] the discussion of Wednesbury unreasonableness was first made in the case of *Singway Ltd v. The Attorney General*.[100] In this case, it was argued that failure to grant an opportunity of appeal to the applicant constituted 'Wednesbury unreasonablenss'.[101] Leonard J. rejected the argument because he could not see 'how the absence of a right of appeal of itself constitutes unreasonableness', and in his view there was no 'manifest arbitrariness, injustice

94 [1994] HKLY 10.
95 [1948] 1 KB 223.
96 *Ibid.*
97 See above n. 40.
98 *Ibid.*, at pp. 410–411.
99 See above n. 5, at pp. 305–309.
100 [1974] HKLR 275.
101 *Ibid.*, at pp. 309–320.

or partiality' in the failure to provide for any system of appeal.[102] More detailed discussions were undertaken in the case of *Nguyen Ho and Others v. Director of Immigration and Another*.[103] In this case, nine Vietnamese asylum seekers who had not been determined as refugees were granted leave to apply to the High Court to quash those determinations by way of judicial review. During the course of the hearing, the applicants sought to introduce affidavit evidence relating to conditions of persecution in the Socialist Republic of Vietnam that was not before the Director of Immigration or the Refugee Status Review Board. The respondents objected to the admission of such evidence and the trial judge rejected the application. On appeal, the appellants argued that such evidence was admissible, (a) to show the lacuna that existed in the knowledge of the Immigration Officers or the Board, and (b) to show that the decisions were Wednesbury unreasonable. What the appellant had argued for in essence was the failure to take into account relevant considerations,[104] rather than typical unreasonableness. But with regard to the typical unreasonableness ground, Sir Derek Cons opined that it could 'only be judged with regard to what was known to the inferior tribunal at the time.'[105]

Shortly after the change of sovereignty, in *Lau Kong Yung v. Director of Immigration*,[106] a leading right of abode case, the CFA's attitude towards irrationality remained the same as that of the Hong Kong courts before the change of sovereignty. Litton PJ observed the following regarding the permissible parameters of a challenge based on Wednesbury unreasonableness:[107]

> Where a department head of government is entrusted by the Legislature with administrative responsibilities it is not for the courts to say how those responsibilities should be discharged. It is only where the administrator has acted beyond the range of responses reasonably open to him under the statutory scheme that the court's power of intervention under Section 21 of the High Court Ordinance can properly be invoked.

By 2004, in the case of *Town Planning Board v. Society for the Protection of the Harbour Ltd.*,[108] the trial judge declared that the Board's decisions with regard to the draft plan to reclaim part of the sea from the Victoria Harbour were made in contravention of the Protection of the Harbour Ordinance (Cap. 531) and were therefore Wednesbury unreasonable. But the CFA refused to endorse the view of the trial judge and made the following observations:

> In relation to the proposed reclamation for the waterfront promenade, the Judge's finding that the decisions in question were unreasonable, properly understood, meant that the Board had failed to direct itself properly in law as it had misinterpreted the Ordinance ...[109]
>
> ...
>
> ... the Ordinance does not give rise to any fundamental or constitutional right, what is the appropriate standard of judicial review remains for future consideration: whether the standard should only be the traditional standard of irrationality or whether, having regard to the unique legal status of the harbour, the standard should be a more intensive one.[110]

---

102 *Ibid.*, at pp. 314–316.
103 [1991] 1 HKLR 576.
104 *Ibid.*
105 *Ibid.*
106 (1998) 2 HKCFAR 300.
107 *Ibid.*
108 [2004] 1 HKLRD 396.
109 *Ibid.*, para. 19 of the judgment of the CFA.
110 See above n. 106, para. 68 of the judgment of the CFA.

It is clear that the CFA has taken a conservative approach and refused to state its position on whether the application of the Wednesbury test should be made more liberal. In most cases, the argument based on irrationality/Wednesbury unreasonableness has been unsuccessful in Hong Kong.

However, there are a few cases in which arguments on irrationality grounds have proven successful. One of them is the case of *Ng Wing Hung v. Commissioner of Registration.*[111] The applicant in the case argued that the Tribunal's decision was Wednesbury unreasonable because (a) there was no or insufficient evidence to prove that his One-way Permit was obtained unlawfully by him under the PRC law; (b) the Tribunal had failed to take into account a number of relevant considerations, but accorded manifestly excessive weight to the application form enclosed in the letter from the BEEA. The CFI held that the Tribunal had to address the arguments and issues raised by the applicant on the reliability of the four letters and the documents provided by the Authorities from mainland China and the failure to do so made its conclusion Wednesbury unreasonable.[112]

A detailed study of the judgment shows that the first part of the trial judge's argument in favour of Wednesbury unreasonableness was based on the lack of evidence to prove the essential facts and there exist similar cases in England in which the courts upheld Wednesbury unreasonableness for similar reasons. But the second part of the justification for the existence of Wednesbury unreasonableness was more appropriately to be called, the failure to take into account relevant considerations in making decisions, rather than the typical unreasonableness case.

Hence, it is fair to say that it is very difficult to win a case on the grounds of irrationality/ Wednesbury unreasonableness because the standard is so high in a society governed by the rule of law, as in Hong Kong; it is indeed very rare for a public body to make an irrational decision. This is why it is so rare to find cases succeeding on the grounds of irrationality in Hong Kong.

Proportionality

Proportionality means that a public authority should adopt only those measures that are strictly necessary for the performance of its functions. If the public authority has a choice between several appropriate measures then recourse should be made to the mildest and least restrictive course of action available. As Lord Diplock once explained, 'You must not use a steam hammer to crack a nut, if a nutcracker would do'.[113]

Proportionality is a ground transplanted from civil law jurisdictions, such as Germany. The attitude of the judiciary in common law jurisdiction such as Britain and Hong Kong towards this ground has changed over the years from absolute rejection/denial to partial adoption in some categories of cases.[114] In Hong Kong, the attitude of the judiciary is completely different in two different kinds of cases. In cases not relating to fundamental rights, the courts are very conservative. For example, in the case of *Chu Ping Tak Tim v. Commissioner of Police*,[115] the trial judge said the following on the topic of the principle of proportionality:[116]

111 HCAL 125/2006.

112 *Ibid.*

113 *R v. Goldstein* [1983] 1 All ER 434, 436e.

114 For detailed discussion of proportionality in England, please refer to Elliot, above n. 22, at pp. 256–291.

115 2002–3 HKC 663; 2002 HKC LEXIS 119.

116 See paras 49–50 of the judgment of the above case.

> In my judgment, it is not really essential to determine whether the doctrine of proportionality exists as an independent ground under English and Hong Kong law on judicial review or should be subsumed under the traditional headings.
>
> In either case, the same judicial restraint must be exercised. As I said, the court essentially plays a supervisory role over the decision of the tribunal below. It does not exercise an appellate role as such. This is true in relation to a decision on liability as well as a decision on punishment or sentencing. Unless the sentence or punishment is so out of proportion to the offence in question, as to be perverse or unduly oppressive, I see no ground for intervention.

This shows that Hong Kong courts are not enthusiastic in applying proportionality in ordinary judicial review cases. Even in applying proportionality, it would require a higher degree of proportionality between the punishment and offence, which is almost equal to the requirement under the ground of Wednesbury unreasonableness.

In cases relating to fundamental human rights, however, Hong Kong courts are quite comfortable in applying the proportionality principle and in fact have applied the principle since the 1990s consistently. In the *Mingpao case*,[117] there was no dispute with regard to the application of the proportionality principle between the parties. The dispute was over whether a statutory provision to criminalize the leaking of information by Mingpao Daily and its reporters of investigation by the Independent Commissioner Against Corruption (ICAC) of some land developers in Hong Kong was necessary in order to fight against the evil of corruption in Hong Kong. In applying the principle, the Privy Council deviated from the standard applied by the European Court and held that in determining whether the relevant statutory provision was necessary to preserve the integrity of investigations into corruption in Hong Kong, 'Hong Kong courts were entitled to construe the word 'necessary' in its normal meaning rather than equating it with "pressing social need"'.[118]

After the change of sovereignty, in a leading case on flag desecration, *Ng Kung siu*,[119] the CFA continued to apply the proportionality principle. A few years later in 2005, the CFA further fine-tuned the principle of proportionality in its application in Hong Kong in the case of *Leung Kwok Hung & Others v. HKSAR*.[120] In addition to confirming that the word 'necessary' should be given its ordinary meaning, the majority of the CFA has observed the following about the formulation of the proportionality test in Hong Kong:[121]

> The legitimate purposes for restriction of the right of peaceful assembly were set out in the relevant constitutional text. Article 21 of the ICCPR specified the only legitimate purposes. This list was exhaustive. Therefore, the proportionality test should be formulated in these terms: (a) the restriction must be rationally connected with one or more of the legitimate purposes; and (b) the means used to impair the right of peaceful assembly must be no more than was necessary to accomplish the legitimate purpose in question.

117 [1996] 6 HKPLR 103.

118 *Ibid.*

119 The full citation of the case is: *HKSAR v. Ng Kung Siu & Another* (1999) 2 HKCFAR 442.

120 [2005] 3 HKLRD 164.

121 *Ibid.*

This is an adaption of the tripartite test adopted by the Privy Council in the *De Freitas* case[122] and later confirmed by the House of Lords in the *Daly* case[123] where the first element of the test was that 'the legislative objective is sufficiently important to justify limiting a fundamental right'.[124] For this adaption, the CFA has the following explanation:[125]

> Compared to the proportionality test formulated above for Hong Kong, the De Freitas test has incorporated an extra requirement, namely whether the legislative objective is sufficiently important to justify limiting a fundamental right. The Privy Council considered this extra requirement appropriate in De Freitas as the relevant constitutional instrument prescribed only the general formula of what is reasonably justifiable in a democratic society without specifying the permissible purposes for which a restriction could be imposed. In contrast, in the Hong Kong context, in relation to the right of peaceful assembly, the legitimate purposes for which a restriction may be imposed on the right are constitutionally set out in a comprehensive manner. That being so, the extra requirement, whatever its relevance may be in other situations, is unnecessary in the present context.

This explanation indicates clearly that the adaption is justified by the unique constitutional setting in Hong Kong. The BORO in Hong Kong has copied verbatim all of the provisions in the ICCPR and Art. 39 of the Basic Law has confirmed that the ICCPR as it applied to Hong Kong, shall continue to be applied. This unique way of incorporating the ICCPR into Hong Kong's domestic law is different from the incorporation of the European Convention on Human Rights by the UK through the enactment of the Human Rights Act in 1998. Such a difference in constitutional setting has led to the difference in the specific application of the principle of proportionality.

Conclusion

It is not difficult to see that the judicial review system in Hong Kong has maintained the fundamentals of the British judicial review system after the change of sovereignty and in many aspects they are the same. But over the years, courts in Hong Kong have developed some aspects of the system differently from England due to its unique constitutional as well as social and economic settings. Such unique characteristics are worthy of highlighting. The first is the legal justification for the CFI to exercise the power of judicial review. The change of sovereignty and its new constitutional document has added another constitutional authorization for the courts to exercise its supervision over the executive branch.

The second is the test for granting leave. As discussed above, the CFA has now decided to adopt the arguability test among three possible alternative tests for determining whether leave should be granted. This is again due to the unique constitutional setting in Hong Kong. It is a widely recognized rule of law society, just short of fully fledged democracy. As a result, people have more confidence in the judiciary than in the other two branches of the government, i.e. the executive and the legislature. That is one of the essential reasons why people bring all sorts of disputes before the courts through the means of judicial review. But as argued by Li CJ, the courts' role and expertise is

122 [1999] 1 AC 69. In this case, the Privy Council held that the first element of the tripartite test is 'the legislative objective is sufficiently important to justify limiting a fundamental right'.

123 *R (Daly)* [2001] 2 AC 532.

124 *Ibid.*

125 See above n. 120.

only limited to legality. The CFA finally chose to increase the threshold for judicial review in order to screen out certain cases that were unsuitable for judicial decision-making.

The third is about the organs subject to judicial review. Since Hong Kong has a written constitution, courts in Hong Kong can conduct constitutional review and review the constitutionality of legislative acts quite frequently. This authority is believed by the courts, the legal professions, as well as scholars to have existed even before the change of sovereignty. After this change, the courts have continued to exercise such power even though scholars from mainland China are dubious of the existence of such constitutional review authority under the Basic Law. Despite such challenges from some mainland scholars, it is well established and accepted in Hong Kong that courts can review the constitutionality of legislative acts.

The fourth is closely related to the third and concerns the scope of illegality as being much broader in Hong Kong than in England, due to the richness of the Basic Law. The broadness of the coverage of the Basic Law has led the ground of illegality to cover constitutionality. As a result, the courts in Hong Kong face a new challenge that was not there before the change of the sovereignty (because the colonial constitutional documents contained much less detail than the Basic Law). They are essentially required to perform the role of constitutional courts in civil law jurisdictions.

The fifth is in relation to the test for the application of proportionality. The CFA has modified the tripartite test established by the Privy Council and the House of Lords to a two-step test again, due to Hong Kong's unique constitutional setting and method of incorporation of the ICCPR into its local legislation. Furthermore, the standard for determining 'necessity' has been held to be different from that used in Europe by the European Court. This standard was already determined by the Privy Council before the change of sovereignty, on their awareness that Hong Kong was different from England and other European countries.

As to the future of the judicial review system in Hong Kong, it is foreseeable that it will continue to develop together with other common law jurisdictions, especially those in the Commonwealth, and will learn from these jurisdictions. While most areas of the system are already developed and will only face fine-tuning, there are two major areas that may need further development. One concerns the duty to give reasoning for a decision. In this regard, it is possible for the courts in Hong Kong to give their support and endorsement of a common law duty to give reasons if the legislature will not take appropriate actions to address this problem and/or the executive branch refuses to given reasons for their decisions. Second, is the future of irrationality and proportionality as two separate grounds for review? Hong Kong courts are still reluctant to use the criterion under irrationality in cases not relating to fundamental rights, while certain signs are already emerging in other jurisdictions. With developments in other jurisdictions, there are two possible trends. One is for the courts to lower the criterion under irrationality to bring it to the level of proportionality. The other is to use proportionality to replace irrationality. In this respect, it is predictable that courts in Hong Kong will be heavily influenced by courts in other Commonwealth jurisdictions and it is not hard to predict which trend will be followed by the courts in Hong Kong.

Chapter 4
The Administrative Litigation System in Macao

Chaoyang Jiang and Yang Feng

Introduction

In the early sixteenth century, under the temporary permission of the local government of the Ming Dynasty (1368–1644 AD), the Portuguese came to the region known as present-day Macao, and in the ensuing years, they were permitted to carry out trading activities. In the middle of the seventeenth century, a permanent settlement was established by the Portuguese in Macao. Nevertheless, at least in the seventeenth century and the early eighteenth century those activities were under the strict supervision of the Chinese authorities, and the administrative and judicial authorities remained under the ultimate control of China.[1] Since the middle of the nineteenth century, China's sovereignty to Macao was gradually eroded by the Portuguese and in 1887, the Qing government (1644–1911) and Portuguese government signed the Sino-Portuguese Treaty of Amity and Commerce, in which Portugal obtained administrative authority over Macao.[2] From that time Macao was officially under the jurisdiction of Portugal, and correspondingly Portuguese laws became the most important, if not solitary, legal norms in Macao.[3] As such, Macao's judicial system to this day retains an evident Portuguese characteristic.

Since the 1960s, the most visible trend of Macao's legal system has been its localization. In 1976, the Portuguese Constitution recognized that the Macao region was Chinese territory under Portuguese administration and subsequently Macao obtained legislative autonomy.[4] Consistent with this trend, Macao's administrative litigation system has evolved rapidly. The current setup of Macao's administrative litigation system was institutionalized by a stream of laws in the 1990s, the most important of which are the Basic Law of the Macao Special Administrative Region of the PRC promulgated in 1990 and the Law of Outline of Macao Judicial Structure promulgated in 1991. It is justified to say that Macao's administrative litigation system at present, to a great extent, is shaped by the Portuguese legal system and its local needs.

This chapter discusses the administrative litigation system in Macao, with the focus predominantly on the current system in place, set against the backdrop of historical influences and the subsequent developments in the law. The chapter comprises six parts. Introductory remarks

---

1 For the effort of Chinese government to maintain the control over Macao before the middle nineteenth century, see Zhou Wei, 'Falv Zhimin yu Wenmin Zhixu De Zhuanhuan yi Shijiu Shiji Zhongqi Aomen Falv Wenhua de Bianqian Weili' (Legal colonization and the shift of the civilization order, taking the evolution of the legal culture in Macao in the middle nineteenth century as an example), 2 (2011) *Bijiaofa Yanjiu (Research on Comparative Law)*, pp. 145–146; Liu Haiou, 'Lun Putaoyafa dui Aomen Diqu de Yingxiang Licheng' (The influence of the Portuguese law on the region of Macao), 20 (2006) *Xiandai Faxue (Contemporary Law Review)*, pp. 52–54.

2 Zhi Liangwu, Faqin Lin and Zhihui He (eds), *Aomen Renwen Shehui Kexue Yanjiu Wenxuan-Lishi* (Selection of Studies in Humanities and Social Sciences of Macao: History) (Beijing: Zhongguo Shehui Kexue Chubanshe, 2009), pp. 993–1002.

3 Liu Haiou, supra note 1, pp. 54–55.

4 Ibid., 55.

are given in the first part. The second part provides a brief overview of the history of Macao's administrative litigation system, which can be divided into three influential periods. The third part analyzes the current legislation relating to the administrative litigation system. The fourth part constitutes the categorization of cases brought before the courts, an in-depth examination of the system, and the jurisdiction for accepting cases. Following this is the fifth part, which examines the significance and role played by judicial opinions in cases, concerning both the administrative litigation system as a whole and also subsequent cases. The final part of this chapter draws upon the deficiencies that can be witnessed in the law itself and what effects this has on the administrative litigation system in practice, alongside closing observations.

Historical Overview

The Period of Portuguese Rule

After the establishment of the Portuguese colonial rule over Macao in the middle nineteenth century, Portuguese legal system was applied in Macao. During this period, the litigation system in Macao became a component of Portugal's overseas judicial system. Consistent with the emergence of the system of separate administrative courts in Portugal, the Court of Audit and Administration was established in Macao in 1927. This court served as the first instance court for administrative, tax and audit cases.[5] The Organic Principle of Macao (*aomen zuzhi zhangcheng*), passed in 1976, further defined the functions and powers of the Court of Audit and Administration.[6] According to this law, the Court of Audit and Administration had jurisdiction over the following matters:

1. examining the annual accounts of the government's finances and submitting reports to the Legislative Council for further investigation;
2. scrutinizing all of the accounts associated with administrative institutions and public enterprises (hospitals, universities, schools etc.);
3. assessing the actions performed by Macao's administrative institutions;
4. evaluating the yearly account and corresponding report produced by Macao's department of finance.

Generally speaking, during this colonial period, Portuguese courts were the courts of appeal for those cases in Macao. The Court of Audit of Portugal was the court of appeal for audit cases in Macao; and the Supreme Administrative Court of Portugal had jurisdiction over appeal cases of administration and tax in Macao.[7] In practice, given various reasons such as long distance between Macao and Lisbon, language barrier, high financial and time costs, the appellant administrative cases during this period was scarce.[8]

---

5 Jiang Enci, 'Aomen Guodu Shijqi Sifa Gaige zhi Guigu yu Qianzhan' (Macao judicial reform in transitional period: review and prospects), 23 (1994) *Xingzheng (Administration)*, p. 189.

6 The Organic Principle of Macao served as the constitutional document until 20 December 1999, when it was replaced by the Basic Law of the Macao Special Administrative Region of the People's Republic of China.

7 Mi Wanying and He Weining, Aomen Diqu Xingzheng Susong: Zhidu, Lifa yu Anli (Administrative Litigation in Macao: System, Legislation and Cases) (Hangzhou: Zhejiang Daxue Chubanshe, 2011), p. 4.

8 Xie Gengliang, 'Falv Yizhi Falv Wenhua yu Falv Fazhan Aomenfa Xianzhuang de Pipan (Legal transplantation, legal culture and the development of the law, critiques on the present Macao law), 5 (2009) *Bijiaofa Yanjiu (Research on Comparative Law)*, p. 7.

Prior to 1982, the Court of Audit and Administration did not have its own full-time judges. Instead, it comprised three part-time members: a judge from the Common Jurisdiction Court, who served as President of the Court of Audit and Administration, and two administrative officials, who were in charge of civil administration (*minzheng shiwu*) and registration (*dengji*) respectively. The two officials in the Court of Audit and Administration were appointed by the governor of Macao. Because two out of the total three members in the Court of Audit and Administration were not judges, this court in effect was not a judicial organ.[9] This situation changed in 1989 when the Macao government decided that all three members should be judges. Consequently, the three judges in the Court of Audit and Administration came from the Common Jurisdiction Court, the president of which served as President of the Court of Audit and Administration.

It is particularly noteworthy that during the period of Portuguese rule, like civil and criminal litigations, administrative litigation operated in a purely Portuguese way. Portuguese Laws and Portuguese judicial proceedings were directly applied in Macao. Prior to 1991, all the laws applied in Macao were in Portuguese and these legal texts did not have corresponding Chinese translation.[10] All the judges originated from Portugal. As a matter of fact, until 1996 neither Chinese nor native Portuguese who were born in Macao were appointed as Judges in Macao[11] and all Portuguese judges and procuratorates in Macao at that time did not know Chinese.[12] Despite the fact that most Macao residents were Chinese who do not know Portuguese, Portuguese was the only language used in the administrative litigation and the other two types of litigations.

The Transitional Period (1987–1999)

The transitional period lasted from 1987, when the Sino-Portuguese Joint Declaration was signed, to 20 December 1999, when Macao was returned to China. This period witnessed the trend of 'the localization of legal system', which generally includes the following elements: bilingual legislation (in both Portuguese and Chinese), localization of judicial personnel, localization of judicial organs, legal translation and compilation of cases.[13] This section will focus on the evolution of the administrative courts in Macao and their jurisdictions. In 1990, the Portuguese Parliament revised the Organic Principle of Macao, for the first time, recognizing the judicial autonomy of Macao. Article 51 of the revised Organic Principle of Macao provided that 'the region of Macao has its own judicial organs, which enjoy autonomy and the judicial organs and autonomous authority should adapt to local specific needs.' However, in this transitional period, judge selection was still under the authority of Portugal.

During this period, the most important law was the Law of Bases of Macao's Judicial System (*sifa zuzhi gangyao fa*), which was passed in August 1991.[14] This law greatly reshaped the administrative court system, the most noticeable change of which was dividing the Court of Audit and Administration into the Administrative Court and the Court of Audit. The organization and

9 Ibid., p. 9.

10 Ma Jinbao, 'Aomen Tequ de Sifa Bendihua' (Judicial localization in the Macao Special Administrative Region), 2 (2009) *Guojia Jianchaguan Xueyuan Xuebao (Journal of National Prosecutors College)*, p. 86.

11 In 1996, only one lawyer in Macao was Chinese. See ibid.

12 Xie Gengliang, supra note 8, p. 4.

13 Localization concerning judiciary is deemed as the key of the localization of legal system in Macao. For more discussion on the judicial localization and legal localization and their necessity see Zhouwei and Liu Haiou, supra note 1; Shu Yaozhi. 'The Process of Macao Legal Localization in Post-Return Times'. 12 (2011) *Zhejiang Social Sciences*, p. 29; Ma Jinbao, supra note 10; Xie Gengliang, supra note 8.

14 The text of this law is available in Mi Wanying and He Weining, supra note 6, pp. 135–158.

function of the Administrative Court in Macao was further defined in two laws enacted in 1992: 'the New Rules of Judicial Organization in Macao' and 'the Regulation of the Court of Audit in Macao'.

In the transitional period, the Administrative Court served as the court of first instance handling administrative, tax and customs cases, with the High Court taking on the role of the court of second instance of those cases. There was one judge in the Administrative Court. Unlike the judges in the Court of Audit and Administration in colonial period, which were part-time judges, the judge working in the Administrative Court was full-time. The High Court consisted of two tribunals. The first tribunal with four judges had jurisdiction over ordinary cases. The second tribunal with three judges had jurisdiction over appellant cases concerning administrative, tax and customs and it also accepted cases of first instance under certain conditions. At that time, although substantial changes were made by the Macao government to reshape its administrative litigation system, the proceedings of administrative litigation continued to apply Portuguese laws, such as 'The General Principles on the Court of Administration' and the 'The Tax and Administrative Court Procedure Law'.

In terms of the scope of jurisdiction, the Administrative Court had authority for cases concerning administration, tax and customs, whilst the ambit of the Court of Audit featured cases concerning conducting audits of governmental operations. According to the Law of Bases of Macao's Judicial System, the jurisdiction of Macao's Administrative Court included:

1. cases brought against administrative acts performed by the secretaries (*sizhang*) or other administrative authorities;
2. cases brought against administrative acts performed by the public sector with legal personality and autonomy;
3. cases brought against administrative acts performed by administrative institutions and administrative public enterprises (hospitals, universities, etc.);
4. cases brought against administrative acts performed by franchisees;
5. cases brought against other unlawful acts performed by the abovementioned institutions;
6. cases brought concerning the realization of rights or interests protected by the law;
7. cases concerning administrative contracts;
8. cases brought forward concerning administrative compensation;
9. cases involving the election of a public corporation;
10. other cases brought under the jurisdiction of the Administrative Court;
11. cases of suspending the effect of administrative acts;
12. cases requesting administrative authority to provide certain files or certificates;
13. cases requiring the execution of verdicts;
14. cases requesting individuals or franchises to act in a certain way;
15. cases brought concerning the investigation of evidence.

The Administrative Court at that time had jurisdiction over tax cases, including:

1. cases brought concerning tax settlements;
2. cases involving tax benefits;
3. cases brought concerning unlawful (but not criminal) tax actions;
4. cases concerning compulsory levies of tax fines and the costs of tax litigation;
5. cases against unlawful tax provisions;
6. cases for the request of evidence in an investigation;

7. cases brought for requesting the execution of a verdict arrived at by the Administrative Court.

Aside from this, the Administrative Court also had jurisdiction over customs cases, which covered:

1. cases brought concerning customs settlement;
2. cases involving customs benefits;
3. cases of unlawful (but not criminal) tax acts;
4. cases brought for the request of evidence in investigations;
5. cases brought for requesting the execution of a verdict made by the Administrative Court.

At that time, the Macao High Court not only served as the court of second instance, but also had jurisdiction over certain cases in the first instance, which included:

1. cases brought against administrative acts performed by the Legislative Council, its President, its presidium and its members;
2. cases involving administrative acts performed by the Assistant Prosecutor General and the High Commissioner Against Corruption and Against the Violation of Administrative Laws;
3. cases brought against unlawful provisions or administrative acts made by the above entities;
4. cases brought concerning a jurisdiction conflict between administrative institutions, which are not affiliated with the same higher authorities;
5. cases of jurisdictional conflicts amongst both courts and the administrative authority.

Consistent with the trends of the localization of legal system, Macao courts obtained the power of final adjudication on most of the administrative cases. Nevertheless, some cases would be brought to Portuguese courts. These mainly referred to cases concerning administrative acts performed by the Governor or the Administrative Secretary, and cases concerning the constitutionality and legality of legal norms. These two categories of cases were under the jurisdiction of the Portuguese Supreme Administrative Court of Portugal and the Portuguese Constitutional Court respectively. The ultimate power of final adjudication was not conferred upon Macao until June 1999, when the President of Portugal issued a decree, conferring complete judicial power to the courts in Macao. Thus, the judicial power that had been previously exercised by the Portuguese Supreme Administrative Court and the Portuguese Constitutional Court was handed down to the Macao High Court.

The Special Administrative Region: A Return to Chinese Rule

After Macao's return to China in 1999, the trend of localization of legal system is accelerated. A stream of laws governing Macao's administrative litigation was passed by the Chinese national legislature as well as the legislature in Macao, and subsequently, a new administrative litigation system was established. The Basic Law of the Macao Special Administrative Region of the People's Republic of China enacted by the National People's Congress serves as the constitutional document in Macao. According to Article 36(2) of the Basic Law, Macao residents have the right to institute legal proceedings in the courts against the acts of the executive authorities and their personnel. This provision is widely regarded as forming the founding source and groundwork for the administrative litigation system in Macao, which stands as a Special Administrative Region in China. In the meantime, according to Article 84 of the Basic Law, the Primary Court, the Intermediate Court and the Court of Final Appeal were to be established in the Macao Special Administrative Region; and in accordance with Article 86, the Administrative Court was established, which would have jurisdiction over administrative cases and tax cases. Importantly, if certain parties refuse to accept judgments by the Administrative Court, they would have the right to file appeal claims to the Intermediate Court.

The delineation of functions and powers of the Macao courts was first defined by 'Detailed Measures for the Creation of Judicial Organizations of the Macao Special Administrative Region', which were passed by the Ninth plenary session of the Preparatory Committee of the Macao Special Administrative Region of the National People's Congress in July 1999. According to these Detailed Measures, the allocation of judicial power was provided for: the Intermediate Court would not merely be the appellate court of the Court of First Instance, but also the first instance court for cases of a more serious nature. The Court of Final Appeal would adjudicate not only the appeal cases resulting from the decisions of the lower-level courts, but also more serious first-instance cases. In this way, the Intermediate Court and the Court of Final Appeal are also the first instance courts for certain administrative cases.

According to Article 87 of the Basic Law, judges of the courts of the Macao Special Administrative Region at all levels shall be appointed by the Chief Executive on the recommendation of an independent commission composed of judges, lawyers and luminaries in Macao. Judges would be chosen on the basis of their professional qualifications, and persons with foreign nationality are also capable of being employed as judges. However, the president of the Court of Final Appeal should be a Chinese citizen who is a permanent resident of Macao. Until recently, there have been one judge in the Administrative Court, 10 judges in the Intermediate Court and three judges in the Court of Final Appeal.[15]

Current Administrative Litigation System in Macao

The Current Law

Laws relating to Macao's administrative litigation system can be distinctly separated into two branches of promulgated laws. Firstly, there are pre-existing Macao laws, the most important of which include: No. 110/99/M Decree 'Administrative Litigation Code', No. 55/99/M Decree 'Civil Litigation Code', No. 57/99/M Decree 'Approving the Administrative Procedure Code' and No. 28/91/M Decree 'Civil Liability System of Making Contracts with Administrative Authorities, Public Corporations and Their Right Holders', and No. 28/91/M Decree 'Administrative Compensation System'. The second branch is the Law of Bases of Macao's Judicial System, which entered into force in December 1999.

Categorization of Cases

In accordance with the Macao Administrative Procedure Code, copies of the judgments, issued by the collegial panel of the Intermediate Court and the Court of the Final Appeal, should be submitted to the Printing Department of the Macao Government for publishing on a quarterly basis. It should be noted that the working language of courts in Macao is Portuguese and Chinese. Given the fact that the nature of translating Chinese/Portuguese judgments is lengthy and time consuming, publications of the copies of judgments are commonly delayed for several years. The

15 The list of judges in the courts of Macao is available at the official website of the Macao court, see http://www.court.gov.mo/zh/subpage/ta#. Last visited June 2013.

judgments issued by the Intermediate Court and the Court of Final Appeal can be found on their court websites. Some of the judgments are written both in Portuguese and Chinese, whilst others are merely in Portuguese. Judgments delivered by the Administrative Court are neither published nor uploaded onto the website.

Judgments issued by the Court of Final Appeal are of great significance, due to the fact that the Court of Final Appeal is the highest-level court in Macao, exercising final adjudicative power. Between 20 December 1999 and 30 December 2012, the number of judgments concerning administrative litigation issued by the Court of Final Appeal stood at 192, which is approximately 14 cases per year on average. They are categorized in Table 4.1:[16]

Table 4.1 Judgments concerning Administrative Litigation Issued by the Court of Final Appeal in Macao between 20 December 1999 and 30 December 2012

Category	Number
Customs cases of appeal	0
Tax cases of appeal	3
Administrative cases of appeal	170
Election of officials cases of appeal	3
Cases of appeal concerning the rights of assembly and demonstration	11
Cases of appeal based on conflicting verdicts issued by different collegial panels	1
Jurisdiction conflicts (administrative court)	1
Unifying judicial opinions (administrative litigation and administrative law and tax law)[17]	3
Total	192

As shown in Table 4.1, there were 170 administrative appeal cases set against the 192 total cases during that period of time; 152 of these judgments were written in Chinese. In terms of their content, those 152 cases can be divided into the following sub-categories:

16 For more details of the number of administrative cases in Macao, see Macao court website: http://www.court.gov.mo/. Last visited March 2013.

17 The cases concerning unifying judicial opinions shall meet the following conditions. Firstly, in terms of the same basic legal issue, the measures taken by the respective two collegial panels from either the Intermediate Court or the Court of Final Appeal to deal with the issue are contradictory. Secondly, interested parties refute these judgments and appeal to the Court of Final Appeal for unifying judicial opinions.

Table 4.2 Judgments Written in Chinese Issued by the Court of Final Appeal in Macao between 20 December 1999 and 30 December 2012

Category	Number
Issuing permit or licence	6
Housing demolition and land expropriation	9
Land grant	3
Public grant (open tendering)	11
Residency permit	28
Deportation and prohibition of entry	12
Disciplinary acts for public officials	28
Payment, welfare, evaluation, retirement of public officials	29
Administrative penalties	12
Administrative compensation and administrative payment	5
Administrative contracts	3
The legality of the provisions issued by administrative organs	2
Other	4
Total	152

The Three Levels of Court Structure

In accordance with the Basic Law, Macao's administrative lawsuits are under the jurisdiction of the Administrative Court, the Intermediate Court and the Court of Final Appeal. Only the Administrative Court, the lowest among the three, is established specially for administrative litigation. The Administrative Court is the court of first instance for administrative cases, consisting of one judge. Unlike the Primary Court, the Administrative Court does not establish any tribunals. In most cases, a single judge is used to deal with administrative cases in the Administrative Court. In case that a collegial panel is needed, the administrative cases would be heard by two judges appointed by the Judge Committee and one judge who is in charge of files. The Intermediate Court comprises two tribunals with ten judges: criminal litigation tribunal and other litigation tribunal. The Intermediate Court deals with cases in the form of collegial panels. The formation of the tribunals is determined by the Judge Committee, with the following factors taken into consideration: the need for the trial, the expertise of the judges and the personal preference of judges. In terms of the Court of Final Appeal, a collegial panel is used to handle cases and there are three judges in the Court of the Final Appeal. As mentioned before, the President of the Court of Final Appeal is chosen amongst judges and appointed by the Chief Executive; and he or she must be a Chinese citizen, who is a permanent resident of Macao. There is no judicial assessor system in Macao. The Macao court structure is provided in Figure 4.1:

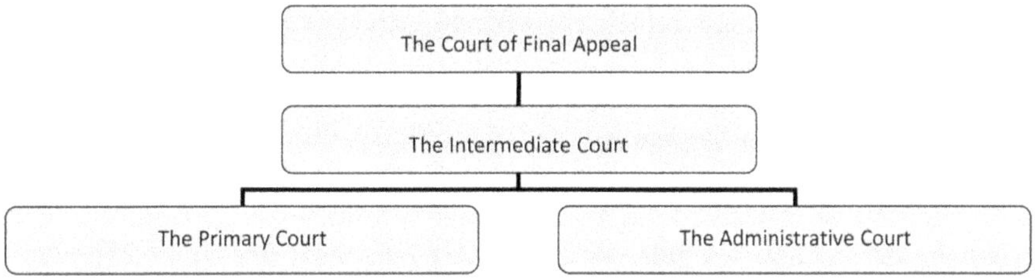

Figure 4.1 The Macao Court Structure

The Trial Mechanism: The Court of Second Instance as the Final Instance

The independence of the Courts is outlined by the Basic Law and the Law of Bases of Macao's Judicial System. Article 83 of the Basic Law stipulates that the Courts in Macao shall exercise judicial power independently and are subordinate to nothing other than the law and must not be subject to any interference. Article 6(1) of the Law of Bases of Macao's Judicial System also provides that courts are independent and they shall make judgments in accordance with the jurisdiction conferred by the law and shall not be interfered with by other powers, nor show compliance to any instructions or orders.

Importantly, in terms of administrative litigation, the second instance of the court is the final instance. Generally speaking, parties who refute the judgments of the Administrative Court can appeal to the Intermediate Court. If in turn these parties then wish to contest the judgment of the Intermediate Court as the Court of First Instance, they may appeal to the Court of Final Appeal. The judgments issued by the Court of Final Appeal are the final judgments, even if those cases are of the first instance and are subsequently of a final and binding nature.

In accordance with the Administrative Litigation Code, an appeal may be filed to a higher court, if the parties in question refute the judgment of a lower court. The classification of appeal claims include: common appeals, appeals filed for mutually contradictory judgments issued by respective collegial panels, and appeals for the retrial of a case. The common appeals are filed for judgments that do not take effect. The latter two appeals are filed for judgments that are effective.

Appeals filed for mutually contradictory judgments issued by respective collegial panels include situations where:

1. the two judgments issued by two collegial panels of the Court of Final Appeal are contradictory;
2. the two judgments issued by two collegial panels of the Intermediate Court (as the court of second instance) are contradictory or the judgments issued by the Intermediate Court and that of the Court of Final Appeal are contradictory;
3. judgments issued by a lower court and that of a higher court are contradictory.

The appeal for retrial refers to the fact that under certain conditions appeals may be filed for judgments that are already effective. Those appeals should be filed within 90 days (180 days if filed by the Procuratorates) from the effective date of the judgments. The Intermediate Court will hear both the facts and legal application of the case, whereas the Court of Final Appeal would only vet the elements of legal application.[18]

Classification of Administrative Litigation

In Macao, administrative appeals to the administrative institutions and administrative litigation are the two main means through which one can protect individual rights and legitimate interests from wayward administrative institutions. Administrative appeals to the administrative institutions are not a precondition for bringing administrative litigation. Judicial mediation between parties and administrative institutions, which is applied in mainland China, is neither provided by law nor applied in practice in Macao. In accordance with the Administrative Litigation Code, Macao administrative litigation can be divided into six categories:

1. judicial litigation (*sifa shangsu*);
2. litigation of administration (*xingzheng zhisu*);
3. cases concerning disputes concerning administrative regulations (*dui guifan zhi zhengyi*);
4. cases concerning disputes arising from elections (*dui xuanju zhi sifa zhengsong*);
5. cases concerning jurisdiction conflicts (*guanxiaquan chongtu*);
6. cases concerning preventative and preserving procedure (*yufang ji baoquan chengxu*).

Judicial Litigation

Judicial litigation refers to cases brought forward that request the courts to repeal or nullify administrative acts, on the basis that those acts violate the law or legal principles. Judicial litigation is the most common type of administrative litigation in Macao, and its importance is highlighted by the legislation. For example, 69 provisions of the Administrative Litigation Code concern judicial litigation, which accounts for more than one third of its total 187 provisions.

Generally speaking, the courts in Macao only evaluate the legality of administrative acts. This has been specified in the Macao Administrative Litigation Code, Article 20 of which decrees: '(the courts) only evaluate the legality of administrative acts in judicial litigation, the purposes of which are to annul alleged acts or claim them inexistence or invalidity; except as otherwise provided by law'. In this sense, the courts in Macao do not take the rationality into consideration while deciding whether certain administrative acts should be annulled or not. Some critics stated that it was too narrow that the courts only vet the legality of administrative acts, which weakened the judicial supervision on the executive branch; the solution was to take the rationality into consideration and except annulment and invalidation of administrative acts, the judgments should incorporate other kinds of results.[19]

---

18 Su Zhexian, 'Aomen Tebie Xingzhengqu Xingzheng Susong de Zhidu' (Administrative litigation system in the Macao Special Administrative Region), 55 (2002) *Xingzheng (Administration)*, p. 35.

19 Yu Zuohe, Xingzheng Sifa Shangsu Cunzai de Wenti jiqi Gaijin – Jiyu Aomen Tebie Xingzhengqu Xingzheng Suzong Fadian de Shijiao (The problems and solutions of the judicial litigation – based on the analysis of the Administrative Litigation Code in the Macao Special Administrative Region) 5 (2011) *Xingzheng Luntan (Administrative Tribune)*, p. 75.

Litigation of Administration

Cases of administration are parallel to interpleader litigation in civil law. The difference between cases of administration and interpleader litigation is that the former is based on administrative legal relations.[20] The characteristics of litigation of administration can be summarized as follows: (1) courts can make judgments on prestation; (2) unless otherwise stipulated by the law, this type of litigation can apply civil procedures concerning interpleader litigation. The cases of administration can be further divided into five categories.

The first category relates to cases for claiming the protection of rights, the goal of which is to identify rights enjoyed by individuals with the involvement of the courts. Those rights should, according to laws, be protected or provided by government institutions. According to Article 100 of the Administrative Litigation Code, cases for claiming rights may be filed when no administrative acts were taken and the objective of the claim is to identify rights or interests that are under dispute. Those rights and interests may include:

1. basic rights;
2. rights requesting a certain amount of money;
3. rights requesting a certain object;
4. rights requesting certain conduct.

The court with jurisdiction in this respect is the Administrative Court.

The second category is cases for requesting administrative acts. Such cases are filed, aiming to request the administrative institutions to perform certain acts according to the law. According to Article 11 of the Administrative Litigation Code, if administrative institutions do not or refuse to perform certain acts that they are obliged to perform in accordance with the law, parties can file either cases concerning judicial litigation or cases for requesting administrative acts. The following conditions can apply to these two types of litigation: (1) the requests are expressly rejected by administrative institutions; (2) tacit rejection; (3) requests are rejected and the rejections are implied by other administrative acts.

It is noticeable that, in this type of litigation, if cases concern the exercise of administrative discretionary power, courts can only ask relevant administrative institutions to perform certain acts, other than giving specific content of acts. Nevertheless, it is permissible for courts to give proper legal instructions concerning the content of acts based on actual needs. The courts with jurisdiction are the Administrative Court and the Intermediate Court. If the administrative ranking of defendants is not higher than Director of Bureau (*juzhang*), the Administrative Court would be the court of first instance; if the administrative ranking of defendants is higher than Director of Bureau, the court of first instance is the Intermediate Court.

The third category concerns cases brought for obtaining information. In accordance with the principle of transparency of public administration and the right of obtaining information, residents of Macao have the right to ask administrative authority to provide unclassified information. If Macao's administrative authority does not satisfy this request, relevant parties can bring lawsuits in order to protect their rights. Article 108(1) of the Administrative Litigation Code provides that, in accordance with Articles 63 to 67 of the Administrative Procedure Code, individuals have the following rights: to obtain information and files, and to receive certificates. The jurisdiction in these cases is vested in the Administrative Court.

20 Mi Wanying and He Weining, supra note 6, p. 28.

The fourth category is cases brought for administrative contracts. In accordance with Article 165(1) of the Administrative Procedure Code, administrative contracts are the agreements concerning the establishment, change or extinction of certain administrative legal relationships. According to this definition, administrative contracts are different to administrative acts, which only reflect the unilateral intent of the administrative institutions.

According to the Administrative Procedure Code, administrative contracts can be categorized as the following:

1. contracts of public construction projects;
2. franchise contracts for public projects;
3. franchise contracts of public projects and public services;
4. franchise contracts of lottery industry;
5. contracts for continuing supplies;
6. contracts of providing labour directly for the public interest.

According to Article 113 of the Administrative Procedure Code, the purpose of the litigation of administrative contracts is to address disputes concerning these issues:

1. cases brought concerning the validity of the contract, namely, requesting the court to nullify the contract;
2. cases brought concerning the interpretation of contracts;
3. cases brought concerning the implementation of contracts, namely requesting counterparts to fulfil their contractual obligations;
4. cases brought for civil contractual liability, including liability for breaching contracts, liability for refusing to fulfill contractual obligations, the liability of delayed performance and the liability of defective performance.

The court with jurisdiction is the Administrative Court in these instances.

The fifth category is cases brought for non-contractual civil liability. Non-contractual civil liability refers to the civil liability 'outside of contracts' in the sphere of public law. In accordance with No.28/91/M Decree, those liabilities include liability of unlawful acts, objective civil liability (risk liability) and liability of lawful infringement. The administrative officials do not bear non-contractual civil liability unless their unlawful acts exceed their administrative mandates or those unlawful acts are intentionally conducted. Under these two conditions, the administrative authority would give compensation in advance and then ask concerned officials to pay this back.

Cases Concerning Disputes with Regard to Administrative Regulations

If administrative regulations issued by the Chief Executive violate laws and infringe individuals' rights, the concerned individuals can file lawsuits to courts to annul those unlawful administrative regulations. It shall be noticed that courts in Macao only assess whether administrative regulations are in accordance with ordinary laws and constitutional laws; national laws (promulgated by the National People's Congress of China) applied in Macao, international treaties and agreement are excluded. With respect to those cases, the Intermediate Court and the Court of Final Appeal serve as the court of first instance and the court of second instance respectively.

Cases Concerning Disputes Arising from Elections

The disputes arising from election affairs can be resolved by judicial organs. This type of case belongs to emergency litigation proceedings, which can proceed during holidays, and its trial is given priority over other types of cases. Both the Administrative Court and the Court of Final Appeal have jurisdiction over cases concerning disputes arising from elections. More specifically, the disputes arising from the election of the Chief Executive and the election of the members of the Legislative Council are within the jurisdiction of the Court of Final Appeal. Other cases concerning election disputes, for example, the cases concerning disputes arising from elections of members of the Judge Committee are vested in the Intermediate Court.

Cases Concerning Jurisdiction Conflicts

The Administrative Court has the authority to deal with cases concerning the delineation of the functions between administrative institutions. The jurisdiction conflicts amongst courts should be dealt with by a court at the next level. The content of the judgments in this type of case should: (1) point out the administrative institutions that possess concerned jurisdiction; (2) adjudicate the invalidity of administrative acts exercised by other administrative institutions.

Cases Concerning Unlawful Administrative Penalty

Cases brought for administrative penalties refer to the cases filed by parties who refuse to pay the fine, or other penalties imposed by the administrative institutions. There are three possibilities concerning the result of this type of case. First, judges consider that the reasons for filing cases are not justified and therefore applications are rejected. Second, judges consider that the reasons for filing cases are justified and the plaintiffs are innocent, and therefore the concerned administrative acts would be annulled. Third, judges consider that the reasons for filing the cases are justified but the penalties imposed upon the parties should be readjusted, and therefore new penalties would need to be set down in the judgments. This type of case would be under the jurisdiction of the Administrative Court.

Cases Concerning Preventative and Preserving Procedures

In principle, all litigation should be completed within an appropriate period. However, due to various reasons, some litigation is lengthy. In this sense, the preventative and preserving procedures are necessary for protecting individual interests and rights more effectively. More specifically, under certain conditions, parties can request courts to suspend the execution of administrative acts, to ask counterparts to perform certain acts, and to examine evidence in advance.

Scope for the Acceptance of Cases

The Summarizing Provision and the Enumerative Exclusion

According to the Law of Bases of Macao's Judicial System, administrative litigation refers to the activities of courts in dealing with legal disputes deriving from affairs within the areas of administration, tax and customs. The goal of administrative litigation is to effectively protect individual rights and legitimate interests. A guarantee is provided for in the law to ensure accessibility to courts. As provided by Article 6(1) of the Law of Bases of Macao's Judicial System, everyone has the right to bring cases to courts in order to maintain his or her rights and interests, which are protected by the law; courts must not reject those cases on the grounds that the parties lack economic capacity.

The scope of accepting cases is shaped by the combination of the summarizing provision and the enumerative exclusion. First of all, the scope for accepting cases within Macao's administrative litigation system is shaped by the summarizing provision. Article 36(2) of the Basic Law provides that Macao residents should have the right to institute legal proceedings in courts against the acts of executive authorities and their personnel. According to Article 2 of the Administrative Litigation Code in Macao, which concerns the principle of effective judicial protection, in administrative litigation all of the public rights and interests protected by law should have corresponding effective judicial measures and the necessary preventative and protective procedures to guarantee the effectiveness of those measures.

In the meantime, other matters beyond this scope are excluded in an enumerative way. According to the Basic Law, courts in Macao do not have jurisdiction over the acts of the State, which comprise acts in the domain of defence and foreign affairs, and acts exercised by central government (for example, the decisions issued by the Standing Committee of the National People's Congress and the State Council). According to Article 19 of the Law of Bases of Macao's Judicial System, political acts performed by the Chief Executive and the Legislative Council are excluded from the jurisdiction of courts in Macao. Those acts refer to laying out government policies, dissolving the Legislative Council, and impeaching the Chief Executive, etc.

In accordance with Articles 20 to 27 of the Law on Garrisoning the Macao Special Administrative Region, criminal offences committed by members of the Macao Garrison shall be under the jurisdiction of the military judicial courts and cases of tort arising from acts committed by members of the Macao Garrison when performing their official duties should be subject to the jurisdiction of the Supreme People's Court of the People's Republic of China. And Macao courts should not enforce judgments or orders on any weapon, equipment, material or other property of the Garrison in Macao.

Criteria in Dividing the Jurisdiction amongst Courts

There are three main elements that in turn influence to which court cases are brought: the amount of money in question or sought, the significance of cases, and the urgency of the cases.

Amount

Administrative cases where the amount in dispute is less than 50,000 Macao Pataca and cases of tax and customs where the disputed amount is less than 15,000 Macao Pataca would be tried by the Administrative Court. The Intermediate Court has jurisdiction over administrative cases and cases of tax and customs where the amount does not exceed 1 million Macao Pataca. Administrative, tax and customs cases with the amount in dispute exceeding 1 million Macao Pataca would be tried by the Court of Final Appeal.

Generally speaking, the principle of 'amount' is applicable only where the amount in dispute can be ascertained. Thus, the following lawsuits cannot apply the principle of 'amount':

1. cases in which the disputed amount cannot be ascertained;
2. cases concerning disputes arising from administrative regulations;
3. cases concerning disputes arising from elections;

4. cases brought for unlawful administrative acts;
5. cases concerning preventative and preserving procedures.

Significance

In accordance with Articles 7 and 8 of the Detailed Measures for the Creation of Judicial Organizations of Macao, passed by the Preparatory Committee for the Macao Special Administrative Region under the National People's Congress in December 1999, the Intermediate Court and the Court of Final Appeal are not only the appeal judgment courts, but also serve as the courts of first instance for certain major cases.

On the other hand, the Law of Bases of Macao's Judicial System also reflects the division of jurisdiction amongst courts based on the significance of the defendants in question. Article 30 of this law stipulates that the Administrative Court has jurisdiction over the administrative actions performed by the following entities:

1. Director of Bureau or other administrative institutions whose rankings are no higher than that of the Director of Bureau;
2. public corporations;
3. franchises;
4. institutions of public groups;
5. public interest enterprises;
6. municipal institutions or public sectors.

According to the Law of Bases of Macao's Judicial System, as the court of first instance, the Intermediate Court has jurisdiction for cases filed for the acts conducted by the following officials or institutions:

1. the Chief Executive, the President of the Legislative Council, and the President of the Court of the Final Appeal;
2. Secretaries of the departments, Commissioner against Corruption, Director of Audit, Director of Police, and Director of Customers;
3. members of the Executive Council and members of the Legislative Council, Procurator General, the leading members of the Police and Customs;
4. the Executive Committee of the Legislative Counsel;
5. the Independent Commission and its president for recommending judges, Judge's Committee and its President, the President of the Intermediate Court, the President of the Court for the First Instance, and the judges of the Supervision Bureau;
6. Procurator Committee and its President, Assistant Procurator General, and Procurators;
7. other administrative institutions, which outrank the Director of Bureau.

Urgency

In accordance with the law on the 'Right of Assembly and Right of Demonstration', any protester can file a lawsuit for a decision made by an authority that prohibits or limits this assembly or demonstration. This litigation should be filed within eight days from the date of receiving the decision. Those cases can be brought directly and neither party is required to pay the court fees in advance nor to submit all of the evidence. The Court of Final Appeal should deliver the verdict in the ensuing five days. This type of litigation, relevant to the citizen's political rights and freedom of speech, has a certain nature of emergency and would be within the jurisdiction of the Court of Final Appeal.

Categorizing Cases in Macao's Administrative Litigation System: The Role of Judicial Opinion

According to the Civil Code in Macao, there are two sources of law in Macao: direct and indirect. Direct sources include: laws, general rules issued by Macao institutions with authority, general rules issued by national institutions within their jurisdiction and international treaties. Indirect sources include customary rules and the principle of equity. Courts take the customary rules into consideration only when those rules do not violate the principle of good faith and are provided by law. Courts may deal with cases with reference to the principle of equity when the following conditions exist: (1) it is allowed by law; (2) it is agreed by parties and accepted by laws; (3) it is agreed by parties in accordance with the provisions of arbitration. In this sense, the judicial interpretation, judgments and judicial opinions are within the confines of indirect sources of law in Macao. It should be noticed that, compared to indirect sources, direct source are preferential for courts.

It is axiomatic that courts need to interpret laws by applying certain interpretative measures in order to make judgments. When courts in Macao interpret laws, they explore the literal meaning of legal texts and seek the intention of the legislatures. In accordance with the Civil Code in Macao, interpreting laws should take into consideration not only the literal meaning but also the entire legal system and the specific conditions when the laws were drafted and implemented.

Administrative institutions should abide by judgments delivered by the courts. According to Article 8 of the Law of Bases of Macao's Judicial System, the judgments delivered by courts have binding force on all public and private entities and are preferential to the decisions issued by other authorities. In this sense, administrative institutions should take judicial opinion into consideration, when they are performing their functions, in order to minimize the possibility of losing administrative lawsuits.

Major Problems in the Administrative Litigation System in Macao

First, although 'the localization of legal system' was initiated in Macao in the late 1980s, its process has not yet been completed. Since the late 1980s, Macao's authorities began to translate legal documents written in Portuguese into Chinese and enact laws both in Portuguese and Chinese so as to provide legal information to local residents. Nevertheless, Portuguese was the only language used in court trials and judgments were made in Portuguese. After Macao's return in 1999, the localization of legal sytem has been accelerated in various circles of judicial work. Chinese is more frequently used in the Administrative Court. However, before 2007, the Intermediate Court and the Court of Final Appeal retained their Portuguese-style court trials. For example, three of the ten judges in the Intermediate Court originated from Portugal.

More noticeably, the judgments issued by the Intermediate Court and the Court of Final Appeal can be found on the official court website of Macao. Some of those judgments are written both in Portuguese and Chinese, and the rest are only in Portuguese. In accordance with the Administrative Procedure Code in Macao, the copies of the judgments, issued by the collegial panel of the Intermediate Court and the Court of the Final Appeal, shall be submitted to the Printing Department of the Macao Government and the latter shall publish these copies of the judgments every quarter. Because the translation speed of Chinese/Portuguese judgments is slow, publications of the copies of the judgments are delayed for several years.

The second problem materializes within the administrative litigation system in Macao is its low trial efficiency. The low trial efficiency of the courts in Macao is a long-standing phenomenon.

According to the report on the judicial works in 1999, the courts at various levels in Macao had 89,810 unsolved cases by the end of 1999, which posed a huge burden for the courts in Macao after Macao's return.[21] A more recent and precise data was provided in the judicial annual report of the courts in Macao issued by the Court of Final Appeal in Macao in the 2009. According to this report, by the end of 2008 the Administrative Court had 100 unsolved administrative cases, accounting for 52.6 per cent of the total administrative cases that was received by the Administrative Court; as the courts of appeal for various kinds of cases including administrative cases, the Intermediate Court and the Court of final Appeal had 628 and 17 unsolved cases, accounting for 52.8 per cent and 18.9 per cent of the total cases respectively.[22]

The low trial efficiency of the courts in Macao largely results from the excessive complexity of the judicial proceeding as a whole.[23] Some downsides of the low trial efficiency are observable, such as the delay of trials, the increase of litigation costs and the increase of legislative workload. How to improve trial efficiency has drawn the attention of the legal circle in Macao. As He Chaoming, the Procurator-General of the Macao Special Administrative Region, suggested in 2007, the judicial reform in Macao should be guided by the principle of the improvement of efficiency.[24]

The third problem that challenges the administrative litigation in Macao is the rampancy of the 'independent administrative regulation' (duli guizhang). Independent administrative regulation refers to the regulation, which is formulated by the Executive Branch, governs certain social life that has not been governed by law.[25] The Basic Law grants a wide range of powers and functions to the Chief Executive and the Macao government.[26] Concerning the regulation on the matters within its functions and powers, the Macao government under the leadership of the Chief Executive has the discretion to decide whether submit these matters to the legislative council for lawmaking or formulate independent administrative regulations to regulate them. At present, the executive branch is the principal organ to submit legislative proposals to the Legislative Council and it is also active in making independent administrative regulations. For example, all the twenty-four laws passed by the Legislative Council from October 2009 to early 2010 were proposed by the Macao government and during this period, it enacted 35 independent administrative regulations.[27]

---

21 Ma Jinbao, supra note 10, p. 86.

22 More remarkable is the number of the unsolved cases by the Primary Court, which totaled 12810, accounting for 54.9 per cent of the total cases received by the end of 2008. The data is cited from Xie Gengliang, supra note 8, p. 1.

23 One scholar pointed out that the severely lacking of personnel for Chinese–Portuguese legal translation also delayed the trial efficiency of the courts in Macao. See Hu Xuexiang, 'Guanyu Aomen Fazhijianshe Wenti de Sikao' (Problems on the development of the legal system in Macao), 12 (1999) *Jingji Qianyan (Forward Position in Economics)*, p. 16.

24 He Chaoming, 'Aomen Tebie Xingzhengqu Sifa Zhidu de Zhuyao Tezheng Jiqi Yunzuo' (The main features and operation of the judicial system in the Macao Special Administrative Region), 1 (2007) *Renmin Jiancha Renmin Jiancha (People's Procuratorial Semimonthly)*, pp. 55–57.

25 The concept of 'independent administrative regulation' was first incepted in the 13/2009 law, namely, Guanyu Dingli Neibu Guifan de Falv Zhidu (legislative system concerning the making of internal regulations). The text of this law is available at the website of the Printing Bureau of Macao Government http://bo.io.gov.mo/bo/i/2009/30/lei13_cn.asp, last visited June 2013.

26 The articles of the Basic Law concerning the functions and powers of the Executive Chief and Macao government include Article 50, 64, 118, 116, 119, 123 and 125.

27 Xu Chang. Zailun Aomen Tebie Xingzhengqu Xingzheng Fagui Xingzhi he Diwei Wenti (The nature and status of the administrative regulation in the Macao Special Administrative Region), 1 (2011) *Dangdai Gangao Yanjiu (Study on Hong Kong and Macao)*, pp. 17–18.

The issue that arises is: choosing which way to regulate the matters is under the discretion of the Macao government and Macao Legislative Council has no power to intervene the choice of the Macao government. The only way to vet the independent administrative regulation is through administrative litigation. As discussed earlier, the courts in Macao has the jurisdiction to vet the legality of the administrative regulations. However, the effect of this judicial approach on vetting independent administrative regulations is highly restricted, The reason is that there is only one condition to annul administrative regulations, that is, they contravene laws. Given the fact that no laws exist governing the same matters as governed by the independent administrative regulations, there are no criteria to vet and annul independent administrative regulations. One feasible solution to strengthen the judicial supervision on independent administrative regulation is that the Macao Legislative Council can set some principles and standards for the making of the independent administrative regulation, which not only enable the legislative council to supervise the exercise of the administrative powers by the government, but also provides certain criteria for the courts to vet the independent administrative regulation.

The fourth problem is that the courts in Macao cannot rely on the Basic Law to vet the administrative regulations. As decreed by Article 88(2) of the Macao Administrative Litigation Code, the administrative litigation concerning disputes against administrative regulations does not include administrative regulations that 'contravening provisions of the fundamental law or the principles revealed by the fundamental law'. 'Fundamental law' in the Macao Administrative Litigation Code refers to the Basic Law. As the constitutional document in Macao, the Basic Law not only regulates the operation of public organs but also sets standards on the protection of the basic rights of citizens. Undoubtedly, recognizing the Basic Law as the criteria to vet the validity of administrative regulations can better protect citizens' rights and interests in Macao.

Chapter 5
The Past, Present and Future of the Administrative Litigation System in Taiwan

Wunyu Chang
(translated by Yun Ma)

Introduction

In Taiwan, the central government comprises five branches: the Legislative Yuan, the Executive Yuan, the Judicial Yuan, the Examination Yuan and the Control Yuan. The Legislative Yuan is the supreme legislative authority, the Executive Yuan is the executive branch of the government, the Judicial Yuan is the highest judicial organ,[1] the Examination Yuan is the highest organ presiding over matters relating to examination, employment, registration, and so on, and the Control Yuan is the highest organ exercising powers over consent, impeachment, censure and auditing. The idea of the first three branches is equivalent to the doctrine of the separation of powers, i.e., the legislative, executive and judicial powers, in the Western context.

The system of the administrative courts is separated from the system of the ordinary courts in Taiwan. The administrative court system consists of a two-tiered arrangement, namely, the High Administrative Court and the Supreme Administrative Court. According to the amendments to the Administrative Litigation Law in 2011, the administrative division was set within the local court to handle simple administrative cases. Thus, the administrative division is still affiliated to the ordinary court system rather than the administrative court.

According to the Organic Law of the Administrative Courts in Taiwan, the qualification of judges in administrative courts is higher than those in ordinary courts. The qualified candidates need firstly to be reviewed by the Reviewing Committee established by the Judicial Yuan, and later to pass the pre-service training before they are nominated to be a judge in the administrative courts (Articles 17 and 18). As guaranteed by the Constitution (Article 80 and 81), the administrative courts are highly independent in Taiwan. There are rarely factors that will interfere with the judicial independence of administrative trials.

Currently, there is no jury system established within Taiwan. The administrative cases are tried by a collegial panel consisting of three judges at the High Administrative Court or five judges at the Supreme Administrative Court. Simple cases are tried by a single judge at the administrative division within the local courts.[2]

1 To be concise, under the institutional structure of the separation of five powers, the Judicial Yuan is in charge of adjudication upon civil, criminal and administrative cases, hearing cases with regard to disciplinary measures against civil servants, interpreting the Constitution and unifying the interpretations of laws and orders. The Justices of the Constitutional Court (also known as the Grand Justices) are set within the Judicial Yuan to interpret the Constitution and render uniform interpretations of laws and orders. For details, see the official website of the Judicial Yuan, available at http://www.judicial.gov.tw/. Last visited March 2013.

2 See Articles 10 and 15 of Organic Law of Administrative Court (2011), and Article 232 of Administrative Litigation Law (2013).

The modernization of the administrative litigation system in Taiwan commenced in 1998. Since then, the Administrative Litigation Law has been amended on numerous occasions. These amendments have outlined the process of development and evolution of the administrative litigation system. In this chapter, I shall firstly trace back the evolution of Administrative Litigation Law, and then address specifically several important issues in the administrative litigation system: for example, the format of the actions brought by the plaintiffs, the participation of third parties in administrative proceedings, the disposing right of parties, the reference to the Civil Procedure Law. Lastly, I shall give my concluding remarks in suggesting how to further improve the legislation of administrative litigation in Taiwan.

The Evolution of Administrative Litigation Law in Taiwan

At the very outset of the development of the administrative litigation system in Taiwan, a separation of the administrative courts from the civil (ordinary) courts was adopted. With regard to the reference to the foreign legal system, the system in Taiwan has witnessed a gradual shift from a pro-Austrian approach to a pro-Germanic approach; and the internal administrative appeal system (*suyuan*) within the administrative institutions and the external judicial review (administrative litigation) have both been adopted. The year of 1998 is deemed to be the watershed period of the administrative litigation system, as the provisions on administrative litigation before 1998 were, to some extent, too simple to be applied. Modernization of the administrative litigation system has evolved with a series of vital amendments to the law.

Since 1998, the Administrative Litigation Law has been amended several times, for example in 2007, 2010, 2011. The main reasoning for such continual amendment is due to the evolution and transformation of the legal system, social structure, economic environment and the people's attitude towards administrative litigation. The purpose for such amendments is to more effectively 'protect the rights and interests of citizens and ensure the legal exercise of State's administrative power', as prescribed in Article 1 of the Administrative Litigation Law. Through all of these amendments, one can observe that the Administrative Litigation Law in Taiwan has advanced from a simple law to a fully fledged one.

The First Period: Prior to 1998

As early as 1914, the Regulations on the Administrative Litigation Law were enacted by the Beijing Government and the *Pinngzhengyuan* was established to handle administrative litigation cases. The *Pinngzhengyuan* was affiliated to the President; such a model resembled its French counterpart, i.e., the nature of the power that the *Pinngzhengyuan* held was not a judicial power.[3] However, the *Pinngzhengyuan* conducted its adjudication independently from the intervention of the executive power, which was similar to the situation in the states of Southern Germany, Austria and Japan before the Second World War.[4] Though the Regulations, compared with the current law of administrative litigation, could not be viewed as advanced, they adopted several modern principles in litigation, such as oral examination and public hearing. They also resembled

3 Weng Yuesheng, *Xingzhengfa yu Xiandai Fazhi Guojia (Administrative Law and Modern Country Governed by Rule of Law)(4th edition)*, symposium of articles, National Taiwan University, Taipei, June 1982, p. 387.

4 Wu Geng, *Xingzheng Zhengsong Fa Lun (Research on Administrative Disputes and Litigation) (5th edition)* (Taipei: Angel Publishing Co. Ltd., 2011), p. 26.

the current law in force, with regard to several aspects. For example, a plaintiff was not allowed to withdraw their claim at their own free will, and the execution of the administration action could not be suspended during the duration of the legal proceedings.[5] Moreover, with the system of *Suzhengshi*, the matter of which persons were entitled to independently bring a lawsuit against the administrative agency over its action of the violation of private rights before the lawsuit would have been brought by the private party, was established by the Regulations.[6] Though this system was later abolished, concerning the system of 'public interest representative' (*Vertreter des öffentlichen Interesses*) provided in Article 36 of the Law of Germany on Administrative Court (§ 36 VwGO), with regard to which persons were entitled to act as a participant in proceedings independent from the plaintiff and defendant[7] for the purpose of safeguarding the public interest,[8] the system of *Suzhengshi* provided in the Regulations still had its merits.

After the establishment of the national government of the Republic of China, the Administrative Litigation Law was released in 1932 and subsequently amended in 1935, 1936 and 1937. The 1937 version of the act remained the most important one until the further amendment was passed in 1998, though between this period the legislation went through a degree of further alteration. The pace of development of the administrative litigation system slowed due to inadequate attention to the construction of the administrative law system and a weak sense of administration according to the law (*yifa xingzheng*).[9] There was only one format of administrative litigation, which was through the rescissory action (*chexiao susong*), though a claim for damages could also be made incidentally together with the rescissory action.[10] The action for affirmative relief, which is commonly observed now due to the emerging ideas of active administration (*jifu xingzheng*) and the development of a welfare state, was not explicitly included at that time. Some reasons could be provided to explain such deficiencies. Firstly, it was assumed that the format of rescissory action would suffice because the main threats to the citizens' fundamental rights arose from an illegal violation through the exercise of the State's public power. Secondly, taking the theory of the separation of powers into consideration, the administrative remedy mechanism was designed on the idea that the judiciary should restrain itself from intervening in matters pertaining to administration. To contrast, as there was only one administrative court nationwide then, the internal review mechanism within the administrative organ was strengthened at that time. The administrative appeal (*suyuan*) and re-appeal (*zaisuyuan*) systems were established as preliminary procedures before lodging an administrative litigation claim. If a citizen was not content with the re-appeal decision, they could bring a rescissory action to the administrative court in applying for the rescission of the administrative action, administrative appeal decision and re-appeal decision.

With regard to the use of the various methods through which the parties can attack or defend their legal positions,[11] in the administrative litigation proceedings, the adversary system

---

5 *Supra* note 3, Weng Yuesheng, pp. 387–388.

6 Lin Jidong, *Xingzheng Fa (Administrative Law) (5th edition)* (Taipei: San Min Book Co., Ltd., 1983), p. 521.

7 Cf. § 63 VwGO.

8 The difference between a 'public interest representative' and a *Suzhengshi* is that the public interest representative can only participate in the proceedings, rather than bring a lawsuit.

9 *Supra* note 6, Lin Jidong, p. 522.

10 Article 2(1) of Administrative Litigation Law (1937).

11 The means of attack or defence refers to the conduct of the parties in litigation, such as using methods of cross examination, for the purpose of convincing the judges that what one party has argued is justifiable, and what the other party has argued is not justifiable. Presentation of evidences is one of the means of attack or defence.

(*Beibringungsgrundsatz* or *Verhandlungsmaxime*) was adopted during this period, which was similar to the civil litigation system. Though the presiding judge was obliged to clarify and interpret, they were not allowed to initiate investigations *ex officio* into the means of the attack or defence that the parties had not claimed, and the evidence collected therein could not be employed as the basis for a judgment. This provision clashed with the nature of public interest considerations and the principle of 'equality of arms' in litigation, because there was a discrepancy between the competences to propose the means of attack or defence between normal citizens and professional administrative agencies. Judicial justice could not be safeguarded if the court retreated from filling in such gaps.

The administrative court was in charge of handling ordinary administrative litigation cases; by comparison, *ad hoc* administrative courts were also created, for example, the Disciplinary Commission on Civil Servants was established within the Judicial Yuan to handle those cases relating particularly to disciplinary proceedings for civil servants;[12] and the Disciplinary Commission on Lawyers and Disciplinary Review Commission on Lawyers was formed in accordance with the Law of Lawyers.[13]

The Second Period: Since 1998

Considering the fact that there was only one format of administrative action prior to 1998, the safeguarding of citizens' legal rights and interests was insufficient. The claim to relief would be rejected by the administrative court due to the lack of an appropriate choice of actions, and the rights could thus not be effectively protected and remedied ('Where there is no remedy, there is no right'), which went against the principles of democracy and the rule of law. In order to fill in this gap, it was declared by the Council of Grand Justices of the Constitutional Court of Judicial Yuan in a judicial explanation of *Shizi* No.466:

> The access to courts as prescribed in Article 16 of the Constitution aims at guaranteeing that all citizens are entitled to bring a law suit and receive a fair hearing in accordance with legal procedures. With regard to the issue of which procedure – ordinary litigation procedure or administrative litigation procedure – is to be adopted, it is up to the legislature who will make a decision after deliberating over the nature of the lawsuit and functions of the existing litigation systems. According to the law in force, the dual system of courts respectively receiving civil and administrative litigations has been adopted in Taiwan. Disputes arising from civil law relationships would be subjected to the jurisdiction of ordinary courts and disputes arising from public law relationships would be subjected to the jurisdiction of administrative courts, unless the law provides otherwise. The State provides living security to the civil servants and enacts the Insurance Law of Civil Servants. The Central Trust Bureau affiliated to the Ministry of Finance under the Administrative Yuan is delegated by the Ministry of Civil Servants (*quanxubu*) under the Examination Yuan to provide insurance to the civil servants and pay by cash after the occurrence of the insurance accidents. As the insurance to the civil servants is one type of social insurance which falls within the jurisdiction of public law, the disputes arising from payment related to the insurance of civil servants should be subjected to administrative litigation procedures. However, under the current legal framework, there is no action of affirmative relief (*jifu susong*) except for the only one type of 'incidental damage and compensation litigation' which results in the payment related to the insurance of civil

12 After the Judge Law came into force in 2012, the Division on Disciplines of Judges within the Judicial Yuan was also an *ad hoc* administrative court.

13 *Shizi*, No.378.

> servants not as a matter of course though the disputes arising therefrom should be subjected to administrative remedy. The administrative litigation system needs to be comprehensively amended by relevant authorities as soon as possible and before reaching that end, effective judicial remedies should be provided to citizens. With regard to relief, the citizen should be heard by the ordinary court for claims of remedy if they fail to do so via the administrative remedy mechanism, in order to accord with the original intention of the Constitution.

In this interpretation, the Grand Justices pointed out that, on the one hand, the ordinary court should hear the cases over which the special courts lack jurisdiction. Hence, if the administrative court decided to reject the plaintiff's claim on the basis of the vacancy of the specific type of action of affirmative relief, the ordinary court should hear the case to avoid the citizens' rights not being remedied. This argument might find its backdrop in the provision of Article 19(1) of the Basic Law of the Federal Republic of Germany.[14] On the other hand, the Grand Justices further required that the Administrative Litigation Law should be amended as soon as possible in order to provide a sufficient remedy for the citizens. Actually, as early as around 1975, there have been scholars who have appealed to amend the Administrative Litigation Law.[15] The Commission for the Amendment of the Administrative Litigation System was established in July 1981 by the Judicial Yuan. As the amendments related to the adjustment of the boundaries of the powers of the Administrative Yuan and its affiliated agencies, a compromise was made by the Commission by adopting a 'dual-track' solution, when it submitted the drafts to the Legislative Yuan for approval. In this way, for example, a choice could be made by the citizen, after the procedures of administrative appeal (*suyuan*), whether to re-appeal (*zaisuyuan*) (internal review within the administrative system), or to directly lodge an administrative litigation claim to the High Administrative Court (external judicial review). Fortunately, the provision for 're-appeal' was finally abolished due to the opposing opinions brought forward during the legislative process within the Legislative Yuan.[16] Since that time, the current administrative litigation system has been cultivated and moulded into a sustainable and efficient system of recourse for administrative justice.

Major Revisions in 1998[17]

The establishment of the High Administrative Court

Historically, there was only one administrative court nationwide; the judgment made at the first instance was also the final one. The scope of its judicial review covered the facts of the case and the law, and a written review was adopted in principle. To facilitate the citizens bringing lawsuits, the legislature established three additional High Administrative Courts as the courts of first instance. A collegiate panel consisting of three judges was adopted in principle and a summary procedure with one judge presiding over the case was also adopted to deal with simple matters. The scope of review was limited to the relevant facts at the first instance. If a party refused to accept such a judgment, they could appeal or raise a petition (*kanggao*) to the Supreme Administrative Court on

14 Art. 19 Abs. 4 GG: 'Wird jemand durch die öffentliche Gewalt in seinen Rechten verletzt, so steht ihm der Rechtsweg offen. Soweit eine andere Zuständigkeit nicht begründet ist, ist der ordentliche Rechtsweg gegeben. Artikel 10 Abs. 2 Satz 2 bleibt unberührt.'

15 Mr Sun Tiqian has appealed many times to amend the Administrative Litigation Law. See *supra* note 3, Weng Yuesheng, footnote 38 at p. 396.

16 Wu Geng, *Xingzheng Zhengsong Fa Lun (Research on Administrative Disputes and Litigations) (6th edition)* (Taipei: Angel Publishing Co. Ltd., 2012), p. 16.

17 The amendments were released in 1998 and became effective as of 2000.

the basis that there was a violation of the law in the judgment at the first instance. In this sense, the Supreme Administrative Court could only review the application of the law instead of the facts of the case.

The increase in the variety of actions

In response to the interpretation of *Shizi* No.466, the Legislative Yuan increased the variety of actions available to parties through adding the action of affirmative relief (*jifu susong*) and declaratory action (*queren susong*) together with the former action for rescission (*chexiao susong*). This was a pivotal part of the 1998 amendments. The legal confirmation of the action of affirmative relief enabled citizens to request the court to impose duties of action or inaction upon the administrative agencies. The specific format of the action to impose an obligation (*keyi yiwu susong*) enabled the plaintiffs to request for a beneficial action, i.e., an administrative action that would confer interests to the private individuals (*shouyi xingzheng chufen*). This new modification was of great importance as it strengthened the principle of the welfare state (*Sozialstaatsprinzip*). Furthermore, the format of the declaratory action also broadened the available channels open to citizens for remedying injustice. Once an administrative action (that violated private rights) was withdrawn by the agency, a plaintiff's claim on the basis of a rescissory action or an action of affirmative relief might be rejected by the ruling of the court. The format of declaratory litigation enabled citizens to proceed with the remedying process upon the withdrawn administrative action.

However, for the purpose of reducing the workload of the courts, it was provided that, in principle, the administrative appeal was the preliminary procedure before bringing forward a rescissory action or an action to impose an obligation. According to the relevant statistics, around 20 per cent of appealers brought a lawsuit to the administrative court upon the decision of an administrative appeal made by central agencies;[18] the percentage decreased to around 10 with regard to the decisions made by local agencies,[19] which indicated that the aforementioned requirement was in fact a success.

The shift to oral hearings

There was only one administrative court at that time with a limited number of judges, so the format of review was of a written nature. However, without oral statement and cross-examination between the parties, the fact-finding and authenticity of the evidence provided by the court were adversely affected. Therefore, it was decided that oral hearings should be adopted in order to facilitate the court's effective adjudication and safeguard the parties' litigation rights.

Jurisdiction over decisions on the illegality and invalidity of an administrative action

The controversy remained on the issue of which court should have the jurisdiction to decide whether the relevant administrative action was illegal or invalid during the proceedings of civil or criminal litigation. According to Article 12(1) of the Administrative Litigation Law, 'whereas the adjudication of civil or criminal litigation needs to be made on the basis of whether an administrative action is illegal or invalid, the administrative litigation procedure shall be adopted. The trial process in civil or criminal courts shall be suspended before the judgment of administrative litigation is

18 See Statistics Table of Administrative Appeal Cases of the Administrative Yuan and Its Affiliated Agencies (2011.01.01–2011.12.31), available at http://www.ey.gov.tw/Upload/RelFile/7/690983/7cd69b83-62a5-40be-b151-8aad255cf4e9.pdf. Last visited May 2014.

19 See Statistics Table of Administrative Appeal Cases of Local Agencies (2011.01.01–2011.12.31), available at http://www.ey.gov.tw/Upload/RelFile/7/690983/f6a54245-8dac-4c0d-82c6-ef285efa34d1.pdf. Last visited May 2014.

issued.' The ordinary courts are not entitled to make a decision on whether an administrative action was illegal or invalid by claiming the judicial independence they have possessed; be that as it may, the decision they should have made was not binding on the administrative court.

Joint actions

As there may likely be more than one person who jointly holds a right or undertakes a duty in administrative law, the system of 'indispensable joint action' (*biyao canjia*) was provided in the law to solve the problem of when the parties in an 'indispensable joint action' were not suing or sued together, as the co-plaintiffs or co-defendants.

Furthermore, the legal relationship in administrative law is different from the one in civil law: the latter is configured in a 'one party vs. one party' structure, while the former features a 'multi-party vs. multi-party' structure. For example, a specific private party might be affected adversely by an administrative action, while a third party might benefit from it, and vice versa. In addition, it is not always the case that an administrative agency is responsible for a specific private individual when it performs its duties; even if it is the case as stated above, the consideration of the protection of the public interest is always included with regard to the performance of duties by an administrative agency. Hence, the third party who will be affected by the administrative judgment should be notified to participate in the administrative litigation; this system is named 'independent joint action' (*duli canjia*). According to Article 23 of the Administrative Litigation Law, 'the parties in an administrative litigation include plaintiffs, defendants and those who participate in the litigation according to Articles 41 and 42'. This is different from civil litigation, i.e., the parties in an administrative litigation include the ones in an 'indispensable joint action' and 'independent joint action'. Moreover, an administrative agency that has a 'legally identified stake' (*falv shang lihai guanxi*) is also allowed to participate in the litigation for the purpose of assisting the parties; this is named 'auxiliary joint action' (*fuzhu canjia*).

Public interest litigation

The legal relationship in administrative law always relates to public interests, and directly or indirectly relates to citizens' legal rights and interests. If the administrative agency failed to adequately perform its duties and responsibilities that in turn impeded upon public welfare, citizens who were not directly interested were, when statutory conditions were satisfied, entitled to lodge an administrative litigation applying to the court for ordering the administrative agency to fulfil its duties. This format of litigation was called public interest litigation or *actions populares*.

According to Article 9 of the Administrative Litigation Law, 'citizens are entitled to lodge an administrative action against the illegal actions made by the administrative agency for the purpose of safeguarding the public interests, regardless of whether his or her rights or legal interests are related therein, except as otherwise stipulated by law'. Generally speaking, the provisions of public interest litigation could be commonly found in the field of environmental protection: for example, the Waste Disposal Act, the Air Pollution Control Act, the Water Pollution Control Act, the Soil Pollution Control Act, and so on. It could also be found in the area of intellectual property protection: for example, the Patent Law (Article 67).

As written notice had already been issued by citizens to the administrative agency before such litigation was instigated, and the agency had clearly expressed its attitude that it refused to perform its duties, preliminary procedures, such as administrative appeal, were thus not necessary.

The suspension of the execution of administrative actions and the provisional protection of rights
Though the principle of 'non-suspension of execution' was adopted, according to Article 116 of the Administrative Litigation Law, application to suspend the execution could be made by the parties when specific legal conditions were satisfied. In addition, applications to preserve measures (*baoquan cuoshi*) could be made to the court before the judgment was issued, in cases where it would be impossible or extremely difficult to satisfy a claim by compulsory execution in the future. These measures include provisional appropriation (*jia kouya*) provided in Article 293 and provisional disposition (*jia chufen*) provided in Article 298.

*Circumstantial judgments (*qingkuang panjue*)*
Concerning the principle of 'no-suspension of execution', the original administrative action might be executed partially or completely during the proceedings of litigation, and more parties and interests might be involved due to the execution of this action. Public interest might be harmed more seriously if the original administrative action was held to be illegal and about to be rescinded by the administrative court. Hence, it was provided in Article 198 that,

> (1) Upon receiving a revocation litigation, the administrative court could reject the plaintiff's claim after considering the damage that the plaintiff has suffered, the compensation, the preventive measures and all other considerations, if it finds that revocation or modification of the former administrative action or decision explicitly contradicts the public interest, though the action or decision stated above is found to be illegal; (2) It shall be indicated in the judgment that the former action or decision is illegal.

This provision stemmed from Article 31 of the Administrative Event Litigation Law of Japan. It was severely criticized by scholars who stated that it contradicted the principle of the rule of law and failed to protect the rights of citizens. However, the legislators insisted that the provision of circumstantial judgments and exceptional circumstances was of necessity for the purpose of avoiding serious violations of the public interest in case of revocation of illegal administrative actions.

Meanwhile, considerable compensation should be given to the plaintiff if the administrative court held that the validity of an illegal administrative action needed to be sustained at the cost of violation of legal rights and interests of private individuals. It was provided in Article 199 of the Administrative Litigation Law that,

> (1) When a judgment is issued in accordance with the previous Article, the court shall, upon the claims of the plaintiff, order the administrative agency to compensate the damages that the plaintiff has suffered due to the agency's illegal action or decision; (2) A compensation claim shall be made to the High Administrative Court within one year after the judgment aforesaid shall be made, under the circumstance that the claim is not made by the plaintiff according to the previous provision.

Re-trial
It was stated in Article 284 that,

> (1) A third party shall claim for a re-trial against a valid administrative judgment, in the case that his or her rights are damaged by this judgment that rescinds or modifies the original action or decision and is made in a proceeding he or she did not participate in due to reasons that he or she cannot be blamed for, which makes it impossible for him or her to bring forward an attack or defence method that will suffice to affect the result of the judgment; (2) The aforesaid claim shall

be made within the fixed 30 days from the date when he or she should know the judgment. The right to claim is disfranchised after one year since the judgment is issued.

Moreover, it was provided in Article 290 that, '(1) The original litigation procedures shall be resumed according to the level of trial once a ruling of re-trial is made. The claimer shall automatically be a participant of the litigation once the original procedure is resumed'.

Major Amendments of 2007

After the Administrative Litigation Law was amended in 1998, the Civil Procedure Law was amended several times since this period. As the Civil Procedure Law could be applied *mutatis mutandis* in the field of administrative litigation, provisions in the Administrative Litigation Law also needed updating. Moreover, the sharp increase in the number of administrative litigation cases during this period, partly because of the *pro bono* nature of administrative litigation prescribed in the 1998 Law, has imposed a huge burden on the High Administrative Court and also on the Supreme Administrative Court. Within this context, the Administrative Litigation Law was systematically amended in 2007. The main amendments this time included: the division of jurisdiction, the agent *ad litem*, and the litigation costs.

The division of jurisdiction

One of the most important amendments concerned the division of jurisdiction, which included the determination of jurisdiction, solution of (negative) conflicts, and the measures to be taken in the case of an absence of jurisdiction. The amendment was embodied in the added Article 12(1) to Article 12(4) after the original Article 12, of which the most important was Article 12(2), which stated that,

> (1) When the administrative court deems itself eligible with the jurisdiction over a case and has issued a judgment, other courts shall be bound by the judgment; (2) If the administrative court deems that it does not have the jurisdiction, it should, *ex officio*, refer the case to the courts that have the jurisdiction. In the case of numerousness of courts that have the jurisdiction and that designation of courts has been made by the plaintiff, the case shall be referred to the court that the plaintiff has designated; (3) If the referee deems that it does not have the jurisdiction either after a ruling of referral is made, it shall make a decision to suspend the litigation procedures and request the Grand Justices in the Judicial Yuan to make an interpretation; (4) If the referee is deemed to be without jurisdiction after the interpretation is made by the Grand Justices, it shall re-refer the case to the court with jurisdiction; (5) If there is a dispute between parties with regard to whether the administrative court has the jurisdiction or not, the administrative court shall make a ruling first; (6) The administrative court shall consult the opinions of the parties before it makes the decision in accordance with the terms (2) and (4).

This Article is predominantly in reference to Article 17(1) of the Organic Law of the Courts in Germany.[20] It was previously provided in the former Article 17(1) of the Organic Law that ordinary courts should decide which court shall have the jurisdiction in case of a dispute arising therein.

20 For further discussion on the legislative history of this Article, see Zhang Wenyu, *Quanli yu Jiuji: yi Xingzheng Susong wei Zhongxin (Rights and Remedies: With a Focus on Administrative Litigation)* (Taipei: Angel Publishing Co. Ltd., 2005), p. 372; Carl-Hermann Ule, Verwaltungsprozeßrecht *(Administrative Procedural Law) (9th edition)* (München: C.H. Beck, 1987), section 57.

Though the administrative court might deem itself empowered with jurisdiction, its decision was not binding to ordinary courts. This provision was later amended. It was provided that, if the administrative court ruled that it had jurisdiction over a particular case and had already made a judgment, such decision or judgment would be binding to other courts and other courts were not allowed to question this or to make a countervailing decision.

Item (2) of this Article referred to the disposition by an administrative court when it deemed that it did not have the jurisdiction over a particular case. According to Item 1(1) of Article 107 of the former Administrative Litigation Law,[21] if the plaintiff wrongly identified the division of jurisdiction and brought a law suit to the administrative court, the court should dismiss their application. This provision was explicitly in defiance of the purpose of safeguarding citizens' litigation rights prescribed in the Constitution. Thus it was further provided by the Grand Justices of the Constitutional Court in *Shizi* No.540 that,

> if it is held, by the Grand Justices' interpretation, that a particular event is a sort of civil event and the administrative court has no jurisdiction over such a case, the administrative court shall, besides dismissing the plaintiff's application, refer the case *ex officio* to the ordinary courts who have jurisdiction over this particular case. The referee shall hear the case and proceed with the litigation in accordance with the Grand Justices' interpretation on the division of jurisdiction to protect the constitutional litigation rights of citizens.

Article 107 was amended accordingly in 2007.

As professional knowledge is needed in dividing jurisdiction, it is sometimes even difficult for experts to make an accurate decision. In order to prevent parties (citizens) from suffering any harm or detriment to their interests due to the difficulty in identifying the division of jurisdiction,[22] when the administrative court deems that it does not have jurisdiction over a case, it should refer the case to the court that has the relevant jurisdiction. The plaintiff's option should be respected if they have designated a court from the numerous ones that have jurisdiction in this regard.

Proper identification of jurisdiction is a prerequisite of the legality of litigation. The division of jurisdiction is prescribed in the law and could not be substantially determined by referral between the courts. Therefore, even if a decision of referral has been made, when the referee deems that it does not have the jurisdiction either, it should make a decision to suspend the litigation procedures and request the Grand Justices in the Judicial Yuan to make an interpretation. After the interpretation is made, if the referee is deemed to be without jurisdiction, then it should re-refer the case to the court with jurisdiction.

In order to protect the litigation rights of citizens (right of due process) and ensure the correctness of the court's decision on whether it has jurisdiction or not, when the parties have disputes over whether the administrative court has jurisdiction or not, the administrative court should make a preliminary ruling with regard to this issue. Furthermore, the court should consult the parties in advance in order to provide them with the opportunity to express their opinions.

The agent ad litem

Considering the fact that professional knowledge is needed in administrative litigation, it was provided in the Administrative Litigation Law that, in principle, only a certified attorney was

21 A similar provision is provided in Item 1(1) of Article 249 of the Civil Litigation Law.

22 This especially in cases where it was related to issues such as obedience to the time limit of administrative litigation, suspension of the time limit, and so on.

qualified to be the agent *ad litem* for an administrative litigation and permission from the presiding judge was needed for any exceptional cases. A ruling needed to be issued by the presiding judge to make such permission; the permission would be presumed to have been obtained in the case where the ruling thereof was not made and an agent *ad litem* who was not a certified attorney had actually participated in the proceedings.

Though a person who was not a certified attorney was allowed to be the agent *ad litem* upon the permission from the presiding judge, the permission could be revoked by the presiding judge at any time during the proceedings if it was found that they were not qualified or it was not appropriate for them to participate in the litigation (Article 49).

The litigation fees

Administrative litigation was formerly free of charge. However, due to the overburdened judiciary, the charging of litigation fees was provided in the amendment. It was prescribed in Article 98 that,

> (1) the litigation fee refers to the cost of trial and other necessary costs for the litigation that shall be borne by the party who loses. However, the defendant shall bear the fee with regard to litigation lodged in accordance with Article 198; (2) the fee of a trial is 4,000 New Taiwan Dollar (NTD) per case; it shall be reduced to 2,000 NTD when a summary procedure would be used.

The standard by which one can decide the litigation fees in a case is not based on the quantity or price of the subject matter, but, formally speaking, on the number of claims. No extra fee would be charged if numerous objects were claimed once, or a modification or a supplement of the original claim or a counterclaim were made (Article 98(1)).

The cost of a trial should be pre-paid before the plaintiff lodged a suit unless otherwise provided by the law. Other litigation costs should be pre-paid before a party appealed, petitioned, applied for a re-trial or made other claims; the administrative court should order the relevant obligators to pay the costs if they failed to do so and the court should dismiss the claims aforesaid if the costs were still not paid after its ordering. With regard to the necessary costs for the proceedings of litigation, these should also be pre-paid by the parties; the administrative court could not proceed with the litigation if the costs were not paid. If the administrative court deemed that it was of necessity to proceed with the litigation, the relevant costs could be covered by State finances in advance, which should be levied upon the onerous parties after the judgment was made or the litigation ended up without a judgment.

Concerning the level of income of the Taiwanese, the charging of litigation fees as prescribed in the Law is not beyond their affordability. Citizens' right of access to the courts is safeguarded by the Constitution (Article 16); hence, the charging of litigation fees should not be so high that citizens cannot exercise their rights *de facto*. Furthermore, the legal aid system is prescribed in the Administrative Litigation Law (Articles 101–103), which provides further guarantees for citizens to exercise their rights of access to the courts.

Major Amendments of 2010

The amendments of the Administrative Litigation Law, 66 articles in total, were passed by the Legislative Yuan on 22 December 2009 and released by the Presidential Order on 13 January 2010. As in recent years, the Civil Procedure Law has been amended several times and the Administrative Litigation Law was amended in 2010 in order for it to be harmonized with the new provisions and development tendencies in the field of Civil Procedure Law. The major revisions are briefly discussed below.[23]

Adding a time limit to a lawsuit

According to Article 5 of the amended Law, it was provided that citizens could directly bring a lawsuit typed as 'obligation-imposing litigation' if the authority of appeal delayed in making a decision thereof. Moreover, the time limit was not formerly provided in the event of: (1) an 'obligation imposing litigation' (Article 4); (2) a 'revocation litigation' or 'obligation imposing litigation', in which case the administrative appeal was not preliminary (Article 5). The amendment this time filled in this vacuum by providing explicit time limits (Article 106).

Adding exceptional cases to territorial jurisdiction

According to Article 15, an administrative case with regard to a dispute over a right or legal relationship in public law, except for the ones relating to the acquisition, expropriation or appropriation of real estate should be under the jurisdiction of the administrative court where the real estate is located. According to Article 15(1), an administrative case with regard to the duties of civil servants should be under the jurisdiction of the administrative court where the civil servant performs their duty. According to Article 15(2), a case relating to the insurance concluded according to public law should be under the jurisdiction of the administrative court where the domicile of the plaintiff is located or where the insured conducts their occupational activities.

The situations stated above are the exceptions to the principle of territorial jurisdiction, i.e., 'where the defendant is located'. Especially in the case of insurance concluded according to public law, the principle has shifted to 'where the plaintiff is located'. These provisions aim to facilitate the citizens, who are comparatively subordinated to the administrative agency, to bring a lawsuit and facilitate the court in investigating the facts and collecting the necessary evidence.

Delivery to the legal representative

It was provided in Article 64 that delivery to a person who had no capacity of action should be done to all their legal representatives to protect their interests, unless the domiciles or residences of one or more of the legal representatives were unknown. This amendment was to be harmonized with the provisions in the Civil Procedure Law.

Increasing the amount of money of the object below which the summary procedure could be applied

With the purpose of reducing the workload of the High Administrative Court and expanding the scope of cases in which the summary procedure could be applied, Article 229 of the Administrative Litigation Law was amended, and the amount of money was thus increased from 200,000 NTD in the former Act to 400,000 NTD in the replacing one.

Amending the provisions for re-trial

To avoid the abuse of the right of action by the parties, it was provided in Article 274(1) that, with regard to re-trial proceedings, when the administrative court ruled that there was no just cause for a re-trial and rejected the application, the parties would not be allowed to re-file a suit for re-trial against the former binding judgment or the judgment rejecting the application for the re-trial.

23 The explanation that follows is cited from the Announcement of the Judicial Yuan on the Explanation of the Draft of the Amendments to the Administrative Litigation Law.

Amending the general principle of applying the Civil Procedure Law mutatis mutandis
Formerly, the circumstances in which the Civil Procedure Law would be applied *mutatis mutandis* were enumerated; however, considering the continuous amendments to the Civil Procedure Law, a blanket principle of applying the Civil Procedure Law *mutatis mutandis* in administrative litigation cases was added providing that, besides the specific circumstances formulated in separate sections of the Administrative Litigation Law, the provisions in the Civil Procedure Law would be totally applied to the administrative litigation so long as there was no contradiction with the nature of administrative litigation (Article 307(1)).

Major Amendments of 2011

In the former Law, there are only three administrative courts presiding over administrative litigation cases at the first instance: the High Administrative Court in Taipei, Taizhong and Gaoxiong. This situation brought quite an inconvenience for the citizens who wished to lodge a lawsuit. Furthermore, in the earlier times, considering that there was only one administrative court in Taiwan, the cases relating to administrative adjudication on cases of traffic accidents were tried by ordinary courts. Nowadays, since the Administrative Litigation Law has been effective for more than ten years, it is time to expand the scope of the cases to be handled by the administrative courts. Under this context, the Administrative Litigation Law was amended twice in both May and November 2011. The amendments in May added one article and amended two articles, which mainly related to the delivery of litigant documents, the summary procedure and agent *ad litem*. The amendments in November related to 67 articles, the main content of which referred to the establishment of the administrative division within the local courts and the trial proceedings about cases of traffic accidents.

The delivery of litigant documents by mail to the location of the competent autonomous organizations or police authorities (jicun songda)
As there was a difference between administrative litigation law and civil procedure law with regard to the effective date of delivery of the litigant documents by mail to the location of the competent autonomous organizations or police authorities (*jicun songda*), it was standardized that the delivery would become effective after 10 days of the mailing to the competent organization or authority.

Only the attorney is, in principle, qualified to be an agent of the appellate trial before the Supreme Administrative Court
Article 241(1) was added to the Administrative Litigation Law, providing that,

> (1) The appellant shall appoint an attorney to be the agent in case of an appeal with regard to the judgment made by the High Administrative Court, unless one of the following circumstances shall be met: 1. The appellant or their legal representative is qualified to practise as an attorney; or is a professor or associate professor of public law working at a university or institute that is examined and approved by the Department of Education; 2. With regard to tax administrative cases, the appellant or their legal representative is qualified to practise as an accountant; 3. With regard to patent administrative cases, the appellant or their legal representative is qualified to practise as a patent attorney or a patent agent in accordance with the law; (2) A person who is not qualified to practise as an attorney could also be the agent *ad litem* if one of the following circumstances is met and the Supreme Administrative Court deems it appropriate: 1. the spouse of, a person who has a blood relationship within three generations, or relationship in law within two generations with the

> appellant who is qualified for practices as an attorney; 2. a person who is qualified to practise as an accountant in tax administrative cases; 3. a person who is qualified to practise as a patent attorney or a patent agent in accordance with the law; and 4. the working staff who practise in the field of the legal system, legal practice, administrative appeals or litigation-related work in the legal person of public law (*gong faren*), central or local administrative agencies or unincorporated society in public law (*gongfa shang fei faren tuanti*); (3) The third and fourth items in Article 466(1), Article 466(2) and 466(3) in the Civil Procedure Law are applied under the two circumstances stated above, *mutatis mutandis*.

According to this provision, the appellant should, in principle, appoint an attorney as their agent *ad litem* in the appellate case before the Supreme Administrative Court. This provision has its reference to Article 466(1) of the Civil Procedure Law.

To establish the administrative division within local courts

The administrative division was set within the local courts, in accordance with the amended Administrative Litigation Law, and it was provided that those divisions were affiliated to the system of administrative courts. The two-tiered system of administrative litigation was thus changed to a three-tiered one. This has facilitated citizens to bring a lawsuit, because local courts have already been broadly established at the county or city levels. The tendency towards development in the future is shifting in the direction of establishing local administrative courts.

Amending the trial proceedings of simple cases

With regard to simple cases, the administrative division within the local courts should have the jurisdiction over the first instance; the party could appeal or petition (*kanggao*) to the High Administrative Court if they were not content with the judgment at the first instance. However, the condition on such an appeal or petition was that there was a violation of the law in the judgment at the first instance, which meant that the trial at the first instance by the administrative divisions within the local courts was a trial based on the facts (*shishi shen*), while the trial at the second instance by the High Administrative Court was a trial based on the law (*falv shen*), which was, moreover, final. Exceptions were made when the court at the second instance saw a necessity to assure the unification of adjudicative opinions; it could refer the case to the Supreme Administrative Court for a trial as the second instance.

Provisions on adjudication of administrative decisions on traffic accidents

The cases relating to traffic decisions were formerly adjudicated by the ordinary courts; however, as the administrative decisions and punishments on the traffic accidents fell into the domain of administrative law, it was more appropriate to be tried by the administrative court. The Act was thus amended, providing that disputes arising from administrative decisions on traffic accidents should be under the jurisdiction of the administrative divisions within the local courts.

According to Article 237(3), the first instance of a trial on an administrative decision on a traffic accident should be under the jurisdiction of the administrative divisions within the local courts, except for the case where other causes of actions were brought together. Furthermore, to facilitate the plaintiff bringing the lawsuit, the aforesaid trial shall be under the jurisdiction of the courts where the plaintiff's domicile, residence or dwelling was located or where the illegal behaviour occurred (Article 237(2)).

Moreover, the charging of litigation costs with regard to the traffic decisions differed between ordinary cases and simple cases: the cost of the first instance proceedings was 300 NTD and the appeal case was 750 NTD (Article 237(5)), which was lower than the ordinary or simple ones due to its more trivial nature.

Other matters under the jurisdiction of administrative divisions within local courts

Along with the establishment of the administrative divisions within the local courts, a number of functions were transferred to the local level. It was provided that applications for preserving evidence (*baoquan*), provisional appropriation (*jia kouya*), provisional disposition (*jia chufen*), and compulsory enforcement and the objection of debtors were allowed to be proposed to the administrative divisions within the local courts.

Trial of ordinary cases

With regard to ordinary cases, the jurisdiction of the first instance was still reserved for the High Administrative Court. The party could appeal or petition (*kanggao*) to the Supreme Administrative Court if they were not content with the judgment issued at the first instance. However, such an appeal or petition had the prerequisite that there was a violation of the law in the former judgment, which meant that the trial at the first instance was one based on the facts (*shishi shen*), while the trial at the second instance was one based on the law (*falv shen*), which was, moreover, final.

Expansion of the Formats of Actions brought by Plaintiffs

It should be highlighted that the amendments of the Administrative Litigation Law in Taiwan since 1998 illustrate a significant improvement in expanding the formats of actions, which offers a stronger and more comprehensive protection of citizens' rights. When the Administrative Litigation Law was amended in 1998, the variety of the formats of actions was increased, from the sole format of an action for rescission, to the action of affirmative relief (including an action to impose an obligation and an ordinary action of affirmative relief) and the declaratory action. In this section, I shall firstly elaborate on these four forms of actions, and then analyze the combination of actions in a lawsuit.

An Action for Rescission

This action was the original format of administrative litigation.

According to Article 4 of the current Administrative Litigation Law, it was provided that,

> (1) When a citizen considers that his or her right or legal interests are harmed by the illegal administrative action by central or local agencies, he or she shall bring an action of revocation to the High Administrative Court if he or she brings an administrative review in accordance with the Administrative Review Act and is still not content with the review decision, the decision is not issued three months after the date when the application was made, or the decision is not issued two months after the date when the time limit to make a review decision was extended; (2) An administrative action ultra vires or with an abuse of power shall be deemed as illegal; (3) The interested party rather than the applicant of administrative review could bring an action of revocation to the High Administrative Court when he or she thinks that the decision of administrative review, as stated above in the first item, violates his or her interests or legal interests.

An Action to Impose an Obligation (keyi yiwu susong)

There were two circumstances with regard to the action to impose an obligation on the relevant agency, the first of which was that the agency delayed to formulate an action and the second that the agency refused to make an action.

According to Article 5 of the Administrative Litigation Law, it was stated that,

> (1) A citizen shall bring an action to the High Administrative Court, after going through the procedures of an administrative review, requesting a specific agency to make an administrative action or make an administrative action with specific contents, if he or she thinks that the central or local agency violates his or her rights or legal interests after he or she makes an application to the agency thereof and the agency does not take actions to which it is onerous within a prescribed period according to the law; (2) A citizen shall bring an action to the High Administrative Court, after going through the procedures of an administrative review, requesting a specific agency to make an administrative action or make an administrative action with specific contents, if he or she thinks that the central or local agency violates his or her rights or legal interests after he or she makes an application to but is rejected by the agency thereof.

This form of action applies in cases where the affirmative relief made by the administrative agency needs to be based on the prerequisite of an administrative action to be made by the agency to determine the citizens' rights and duties.[24] If an administrative action is not a prerequisite for the affirmative relief, or an administrative action has already been made for the relief, the action of affirmative relief should be lodged by citizens, instead of the action to impose an obligation. For example, in the case where a civil servant applies for their pension, the existence of an approval for the retirement is a prerequisite for such relief. Therefore, if the administrative agency does not approve the retirement, an action to impose litigation should be lodged. However, if the retirement has already been approved, but the civil servant does not receive the pension, the plaintiff should lodge an action of affirmative relief.[25]

An Ordinary Action of Affirmative Relief (yiban jifu susong)

It was stated in Article 8 that,

> (1) A citizen shall bring an action of affirmative relief when a property-related relief occurs, or an application to deliver a non-property-related relief in a form rather than an administrative action is made between a citizen and central or local agencies due to reasons in public law. It is the same case with regard to a relief related to a contract in public law; (2) When the judgment of an action of affirmative relief aforesaid needs to be made based on whether an administrative action should be rescinded, the application for the relief shall be made together with a rescissory action brought in accordance with item (1) or (3) of Article 4. If the plaintiff fails to make such an application, the presiding judge shall inform him or her that he or she could make such an application; (3) The High Administrative Court shall have first instance jurisdiction over an action of affirmative relief unless it is otherwise specified.

24 See the judgment made by the Supreme Administrative Court (*Panzi*, No.1447) in 1993.
25 See the judgment made by the Supreme Administrative Court (*Panzi*, No.147) in 1998.

The form of an administrative action is a typical form of how public power is exercised, the characteristic of which is that the administrative agency determines the rights and duties of citizens *ex parte*; the citizen is just the recipient (counterpart) (*xiangdui ren*) of the administrative action rather than a co-decision-maker on their rights or duties. With regard to the rescissory action and the action to impose an obligation, as both of them relate to reviewing the declaration of will by the administrative agency (*gaoquan yisi biaoshi/Willenserklaerung*), it was required that an exhaustion of proceedings of administrative review within the administrative system was, in principle, preliminary before a lawsuit could be brought by the plaintiff. In contrast, if the subject matter in administrative litigation, between citizens and agencies or between different agencies, was not an administrative action, it would not be imperative to supply the administrative system with a chance to self-review. The procedure of an administrative review was hence not preliminary in the case of an action of affirmative relief.

A Declaratory Action (queren susong)

According to Article 6 of the Administrative Litigation Law, it was stated that,

> (1) With regard to a litigation that aims at declaring the nullity of an administrative action, or determining the existence or non-existence of a legal relationship, the plaintiff shall have a legitimate interest in the declaratory judgment, or else he or she is not entitled to bring such a suit; it is also the same case with regard to the litigation aims at declaring the illegality of an administrative action that has already been executed and there is no possibility that it could be re-instated, or an administrative action that has ceased to exist; (2) The plaintiff shall lodge a litigation that aims at declaring the nullity of an administrative action only if he or she has already applied to the original agency who made the action for declaring the nullity of the action and been refused, or has not received a reply after 30 days of his or her application; (3) An action of declaration should not be brought if there is availability of other forms of actions, such as a rescissory action, an action to impose litigation or an action of affirmative relief, except the case of an action aiming at declaring the nullity of an administrative action; (4) When the plaintiff wrongly brings a declaratory action in which case he or she should bring a rescissory action or an action to impose an obligation, and he or she does not go through the procedures of administrative appeal, the High Administrative Court should refer the case to the competent administrative appeal authority in the form of a ruling; the date when the administrative court receives the suit is deemed to be the date when the plaintiff brings an administrative appeal.

According to this Article, an action of declaration could be divided into the following three types:

1. an action to declare the nullity of an administrative action;
2. an action to determine the existence or non-existence of a public law relationship; and
3. an action to declare the illegality of an administrative action.

A Combination of Actions

According to Article 115 of the Administrative Litigation Law, 'Articles 245, 246, 248, 252, 253, 257, 261, 263 and 264 prescribed in the Civil Procedure Act are applied *mutatis mutandis* in this section'. It was provided in Article 248 of the Civil Procedure Act that, 'with regard to the several actions against the same defendant, except for the exclusive jurisdiction, the plaintiff shall bring a combined law suit to one of the courts who has jurisdiction over one of the actions. However, when different litigation procedures shall be applied to the actions aforesaid, the provision above shall not be applicable.' The proviso stated in Article 248 referred to the restriction of a combined action between actions related to properties and actions related to persons (*renshi susong*), while the latter form of action did not exist in administrative litigation, hence there was no additional restriction to the combination of actions except for cases of exclusive jurisdiction, and the combination applied to all formats of actions.

A controversial Article is referred to in Article 7 of the Administrative Litigation Law, which stated, 'The claims for compensation and other property-related relief shall be brought together with an administrative litigation'. The original provision was item (1) of Article 2 of the Administrative Litigation Law before its amendment in 1998, which stated, 'the plaintiff can bring incidental claims for compensation before the completion of the proceedings of an administrative litigation'. There was only one format of action then, which was the rescissory action. In order to facilitate the plaintiff's claim for compensation, it was provided in the law that an incidental claim for compensation was allowed to be brought with a rescissory action. However, after the amendments in 1998, the formats of actions had been expanded to the action of affirmative relief, hence the plaintiff could bring an action of affirmative relief based on the provision of a combination of actions under Article 115. In this sense, Article 7 seemed to be made redundant. However, a misunderstanding of Article 7 was still prevalent either in practice or in the literature, claiming that a specific format of action was provided in Article 7. According to the Item 2 of Article 8 of Administrative Litigation Law, 'when the action of affirmative relief should be conditioned on whether the administrative action should be rescinded or not, the claim of affirmative relief should be brought together with the rescissory action in accordance with Item 1 or 3 of Article 4. The presiding judge should inform the plaintiff that they are entitled to such a claim if they fail to do so.' It could be seen that an action for affirmative relief could be combined with a rescissory action; such a combination accorded with the provision in Article 115. Thus, as far as the author is concerned, Article 7 should be deleted in order to avoid unnecessary misunderstanding within the amendment in the future.

The System of Third Parties in Administrative Litigation

The legal relationship in administrative law is always multilateral and sometimes directly relates to the rights and interests of third parties. In order to provide the opportunity to all of the interested parties to participate in the litigation and protect their rights and interests, and to settle the disputes at one time in pursuing legal stability and litigation efficiency,[26] the system of joint action was substantially amended in the amendments to the Administrative Litigation Law in 1998. The parties of an administrative litigation claim included not only the plaintiff and the defendant, but also 'the party in an indispensable joint action' (*biyao canjia ren*) (Article 41) and 'the party in an independent joint action' (*duli canjia* ren) (Article 42). The judgment was binding to the parties in an indispensable joint action and independent joint action (Article 47). Furthermore, when the administrative agency or interested party deemed it necessary, they might claim for an 'auxiliary

26 Cf. Erich Eyermann, *Verwaltungsgerichtsordnung (Administrative Court Procedure) (11th edition)* (München: C.H. Beck, 2000), § 65 Rn. 1; Ferdinand O. Kopp and Wolf-Rüdiger Schenke, *Verwaltungsgerichtsordnung (Administrative Court Procedure) (11th edition)* (München: C.H. Beck, 1998), § 65 Rn. 1; Friedrich Schoch, Eberhard Schmidt-Aßmann and Rainer Pietzner, *Verwaltungsgerichtsordnung (Administrative Court Procedere) (11th edition)* (München: C.H. Beck, 2001), § 65 Rn. 3.

joint action' (*fuzhu canjia*), and the court could also rule the agency to participate in an 'auxiliary joint action' (Article 44).

The Indispensable Joint Action

It was stated in Article 41 of Administrative Litigation Law that, 'when the object of the litigation (*susong biaodi*) needs to be co-determined (*einheitlich festgestellt werden*) by the third party and one of the two parties in the litigation, the administrative court should rule that the third party should participate in the litigation.' This format of joint action was named an 'indispensable joint action'.

The Independent Joint Action

It was stated in Article 42 of the Administrative Litigation Law that,

> when the administrative court deems that the outcome of a rescissory action might cause harm to the rights and legal interests of a third party, it shall order him or her to independently participate in the litigation proceedings, or it shall order to approve his or her participation based on his or her application. The Item 3 of Article 39 is applicable *mutatis mutandis* with regard to the circumstance aforesaid. The independent party shall bring forward independent attack–defend methods. The provisions in the former two items are applied *mutatis mutandis* in other formats of actions. If the party who brought an administrative appeal has already lodged a rescissory action to the High Administrative Court, and the interested party lodges another suit with regard to the same issue, it shall be deemed to the joint action as stated in item (1) of this Article.

This format of joint action was named an 'independent joint action'.

The Auxiliary Joint Action

It was stated in Article 44 of the Administrative Litigation Law that, 'when the administrative court deems it necessary for other administrative agencies to assist one of the parties, it shall order other agencies to participate in the litigation. The agencies aforesaid or a third party who is interested could also apply for participating in the litigation.' This provision resembled the provision in Article 58 of the Civil Procedure Act and was named an 'auxiliary joint action'.

Ordinary Procedures and Summary Procedures

The litigation procedure was divided into ordinary and summary procedures in accordance with the nature of the case at hand. The two-tiered trial system was adopted in both procedures. With regard to the simple cases in which the summary procedure is applied, it was formerly provided that such a case would be tried by a single judge in the High Administrative Court; since September 2012, it was amended that the administrative division within the local courts would have the jurisdiction over the first instance. The lodging of a suit or other declaration or statement in a simple case could be made in an oral way (Article 231(1)) and it would be tried by a single judge (Article 232).

It was formerly provided that a judgment could be made without oral debate with regard to a simple case. However, the amendment in 2012 provided that the oral debate should be conducted before a judgment would be issued, in principle, to adequately protect the rights of citizens.

The party could appeal or petition (*kanggao*) to the High Administrative Court if they were not content with the judgment at the first instance. However, the condition on such an appeal or petition was that there was a violation of the law in the judgment at the first instance, which meant that the trial at the first instance by the administrative divisions within the local courts was a trial based on the facts (*shishi shen*), while the trial at the second instance by the High Administrative Court was a trial based on the law (*falv shen*), which was, moreover, final. If the court at the second instance deemed it necessary to assure the unification of adjudicative opinions, it could refer the case to the Supreme Administrative Court (Article 235(1)).

If the summary procedure was wrongly applied by the court in a case where the ordinary procedure should have been applied, and the party was not content with the wrongly applied procedure and appealed to the High Administrative Court, the High Administrative Court should invalidate the original judgment and make a judgment of the first instance instead, in accordance with ordinary procedures. However, if the party had already expressed no objection to the wrongly applied procedure during the proceedings of the first instance, or had a declaration or statement to the litigation, the procedural flaw was deemed to have been mended and the party was not allowed to appeal for an application of invalidating the original judgment for the reason of its procedural flaw (Article 236(1)). The High Administrative Court should thus go on with the trial at the second instance in accordance with summary procedures.

With regard to the ordinary cases, the High Administrative Court should have the jurisdiction over the first instance cases and would be tried by a collegial panel consisting of three judges (with reference to Item 1 of Article 3 of the Organic Act of Administrative Court). The party could appeal or raise a petition (*kanggao*) to the Supreme Administrative Court if they were not content with the judgment at the first instance on the basis that there was a violation of the law in the judgment at the first instance (Article 242), which meant that the trial at the first instance by the High Administrative Court was a trial based on the facts (*shishi shen*), while the trial at the second instance by the Supreme Administrative Court was a trial based on the law (*falv shen*), which was, moreover, final. The trial before the Supreme Administrative Court should be conducted by a collegial panel consisting of five judges (with reference to Item 2 of Article 3 of the Organic Act of Administrative Court).

The Disposing Right of Parties in Administrative Litigation

The disposing right (*chufen quan*/*Verfügungsfreiheit*) referred to the freedom of parties to dispose of the matters related to the object of the litigation (*susong biaodi*) or proceedings of the litigation (*susong xishu*); such disposition should be binding to the court.

Withdrawal

It was stated in Article 113 that, '(1) the plaintiff shall withdraw part or all of his or her claims before the judgment is made. However, it is not applicable to the case when the withdrawal impedes safeguarding of public interests; (2) the defendant's consent with the withdrawal made by the plaintiff aforesaid shall be obtained in advance if he or she has already participated in the oral debate.'

As far as the legislators were concerned, the purpose of the administrative litigation was not only to protect the rights and interests of the citizens, but also to safeguard the exercise of the State's administrative power. Hence, the disposing rights of the citizens to the proceedings should be restricted when it impeded upon the legal order. When a withdrawal impeded the safeguarding of public interests, the court should order to dismiss such a withdrawal, and the plaintiff should not petition against such an order (Article 114).

As far as the author is concerned, the application of this provision may be confronted with practical obstacles. The system of *Suzhengshi* was established in the Administrative Litigation Law of 1914, concerning which persons were entitled to participate in the proceedings for the purpose of safeguarding public interests, and the system of the 'public interest representative' was also provided in the Administrative Court Act of Germany, concerning which persons could participate in the proceedings independent from the plaintiff or defendant. However, no similar systems were provided for in this Act. If the plaintiff wished to withdraw the litigation, yet their withdrawal was not approved by the court, the plaintiff and defendant might not be active in participating in the proceedings. Under this circumstance, the court needed to actively intervene in accordance with the provision in Article 184 of Administrative Litigation Law, which stated that, 'with regard to the protection of the public interests in an administrative litigation, if the parties are not present in the session on the day of oral debate without due causes, the administrative court shall investigate the fact *ex officio* and issue a judgment without going through oral debate.' Though public interests might be protected in this way, the courts might also be over-burdened. Furthermore, a judgment without oral debate between the parties might impede the neutrality of the judiciary. As there was no unanimous criterion on deciding whether an action went against public interests or not, the application of this Article was largely based on the personal judgments of the judges. These obstacles still need to be overcome in the future.

Renouncement and Admission

It was stated in Article 202 that, 'the parties can renounce or admit the object of litigation during the oral debates conditioning that the parties have disposing right over the object and such disposition does not relate to the public interests. The administrative court could issue a judgment ruling that the party who renounce or admit loses the suit'. It was required that the parties could renounce or admit only when it did not relate to the public interest. However, if one looked back to the legislative interpretation of the 1998 Administrative Litigation Law, it could be found that most of the administrative litigation related to the public interest. In particular, when Article 113 was amended in 2011, it was provided in the legislative interpretation that,

> Item (1) of Article 114 in the original Act, which provides that 'a withdrawal of litigation is not allowed when it impedes public interests', is endemic to Taiwan. Because of this provision, the former part of Item 1 in Article 114 that entitles the party's disposing right shall exist in name only. As nearly none of the administrative litigations is not related to public interests, if the party is not allowed to withdraw a litigation that relates to public interest, the former part of item (1) of this Article that entitles the citizen to decide, based on his or her own responsibilities, whether or not to apply to the administrative court for protecting his or her rights would be useless, thus there is a necessity to amend this Article ...

Concerning the interpretation of this amendment, the restrictions of 'not relating to public interests' prescribed in Article 202 would block all possibilities for the parties to renounce or admit. As far as the author is concerned, as the legislators amended Article 113 to further facilitate the plaintiff's withdrawal, Article 202 should also be amended to 'not impeding public interests' if there is such a necessity of amendment in the future.

In practice, when the defendant admitted, the administrative court ruled that it lost the suit immediately without investigating whether it had the disposing right on the object of litigation or not.[27] Attention should be paid to this situation and further discussion is required in this area.

Reconciliation[28]

It was stated in Article 219 that,

> (1) the administrative court could reconciliate between the parties no matter how far the trial proceeds under the conditions that the parties have the right to dispose of the subject matter of the action and such disposition doesn't contradict the public interests. It is equally applied to an appointed judge (*shouming faguan*) or an entrusted judge (*shoutuo faguan*); (2) A third party could participate in the reconciliation upon the permission from the administrative court. The administrative court could notify the third party to participate when it deems necessary.

The conditions upon reconciliation could be divided into both the procedural aspect and the substantive aspect.

Procedural conditions
From a procedural aspect, the parties need to meet the following conditions to engage in the process of reconciliation:

1. the parties qualify with standing, i.e., they have identifiable legal stakes in the litigation;
2. the parties have the capacity to bring a lawsuit;
3. the reconciliation should be concluded before the court in proceedings, the appointed judge who is in charge of trying the case (*shouming faguan*), or the judge who is entrusted by the court to assist in the trial or investigation of the case (*shoutuo faguan*);
4. the parties have the disposing right on the object of the reconciliation and compromise with each other mutually;
5. the reconciliation should not impede the safeguarding of public interests; and
6. a record of reconciliation should be made.

Substantive conditions
According to Article 136 of the Administrative Litigation Law,

> if the fact or legal relationship which provides the basis for an administrative action cannot be determined even if the administrative agency conducts an investigation into it *ex officio*, for the purpose of effective realization of administrative purpose and settlement of disputes, the administrative agency shall reconciliate with and conclude an administrative contract with citizens to substitute an administrative action.

Firstly, the parties should have the capacity to bring an action in administrative law (with reference to Articles 21 and 22 of the Administrative Procedure Act). Furthermore, the general conditions

27 See the judgment by the Administrative Court in 1976 (*Panzi*, No.1273).

28 For a detailed discussion on reconciliation, see Zhang Wenyu, 'Xingzheng susong zhi susong hejie' (Reconciliation in administrative litigation), 108 (2008) *Taiwan Faxue Zazhi (Taiwan Legal Review)*, pp. 116–134.

of concluding a private contract provided in the civil law are also required herein, such as the declaration of a will that they are willing to enter into a contract and be bound by their will.[29]

Secondly, a specific condition of the administrative law should also be satisfied. If the administrative agency cannot, in line with reasonable expectations, find out the factual or legal relationship that serves the basis of an administrative action in accordance with its own reasonable judgment or discretion, especially concerning the time and money needed for the investigation and whether it is proportional to the expected result, it can conclude a reconciliation contract with citizens, according to Article 136 of the Administrative Procedure Act, without exhausting all possible means of investigation. However, the provision of reconciliation is not an exemption of the administrative agency's duty to investigate *ex officio*. The agency should not be lazy in the investigation from the beginning; instead, it should firstly conduct the investigation until the conditions of concluding a reconciliation contract are satisfied, then it can cease its investigation.[30]

The legal effects of reconciliation: procedural aspect

The main effect of reconciliation is to cease the litigant's proceedings. If a final judgment was made by the court before, it will become invalid after reconciliation is made between the parties.

According to Article 222 of the Administrative Litigation Law, when reconciliation is concluded, with regard to its effects, Articles 213, 214 and 216 of the Administrative Litigation Law are applicable *mutatis mutandis*. The legal finality (*Rechtskraft/res judicata*) is formulated, formally and substantially speaking, between the parties (unless otherwise provided for in the law, or a third party participates or consents) who conclude a reconciliation, i.e., the parties should not bring a suit any more upon the object determined by the reconciliation (with reference to Item 9 of Article 107 of the Administrative Litigation Law); only when the conditions prescribed in the law are satisfied, can an application to resume the trial be made (with reference to Article 223 of the Administrative Litigation Law), and furthermore, the rights and duties created by reconciliation are binding on the parties and the court, which means that the court should not make a judgment that is inconsistent with this.

This provision with regard to administrative reconciliation was different from the one in the Civil Procedure Law (Article 380). The legal effect of reconciliation 'referred to' the one of a determined judgment, rather than possessing the one of a determined judgment, hence differences between the effects of reconciliation and a judgment existed. In detail, the effect of reconciliation is binding to the parties instead of a third party. Even though in the case of an action of affirmative relief or a declaratory action, the parties could claim for the binding effects of a judgment on a third party, the reconciliation concluded by the parties, instead of a judgment made by the competent judiciary, should not have the binding effect to others, i.e., the third party would still be entitled to bring a law suit and make different claims. This explained why it was provided in Article 222 that, when a reconciliation was concluded, with regard to its effects, Articles 213, 214 and 216 of the Administrative Litigation Law were applicable *mutatis mutandis*, while Article 215 was not included herein, which stated, 'the judgment that rescinds or changes original administrative action or decision is binding to the third party' was not included.

29 Cf. Paul Stelkens, Heinz Bonk and Michael Sachs, *Verwaltungsverfahrensgesetz (Administrative Procedere Act) (6th edition)* (München: C.H. Beck, 2001), § 55 Rn. 35.

30 Cf. *supra* note 29, Paul Stelkens, Heinz Bonk and Michael Sachs, aaO., § 55 Rn. 42.

The legal effects of reconciliation: substantial aspect

The substantial effects of reconciliation were two-fold, i.e., positive and negative. The former referred to the effect that the new legal relationship brought about between the parties by the reconciliation substituted the former one, i.e., the former relationship did not exist anymore to the parties after a reconciliation contract was concluded. The latter referred to the effect that the parties should not claim the former state before the conclusion of reconciliation after the reconciliation contract took its effect.

As the reconciliation possessed the status of a quasi-determined judgment, as prescribed in the Administrative Litigation Law, its effect extended to the successors of the parties who participated in the litigation proceedings, or the ones who possessed the claimed objects for the interests of the parties or their successors (with reference to Article 214).

The Applicability of Reconciliation to the Various Actions

An action of affirmative relief and a declaratory action

Reconciliation could be established against an object of litigation. The object of litigation in an action of affirmative relief was that 'the plaintiff applies to the court for issuing a judgment ordering the defendant to fulfill specific duties based on the plaintiff's claims with regard to specific facts and specific laws and regulations', while the object of litigation of a declaratory action was that 'the plaintiff applies to the court for issuing a judgment affirming the specific legal relationship or fact between the defendant and him or her based on the plaintiff's claims with regard to specific facts and specific laws and regulations'. In principle, the action for affirmative relief and the declaratory action only relate to the rights and duties between the parties. Hence, if the parties had disposing rights over the litigation object, and the content of the reconciliation did not interfere with others, the rights and duties between the parties could be determined either by the judgment issued by the court, or by the parties themselves, the two options of which should not be differentiated. However, when the parties did not have the disposing rights, were not allowed to conclude an administrative contract, or the reconciliation impeded upon the public interest, the reconciliation should not be concluded; though the claims for appointment to be a civil servant or affirming the invalidity of an election or dismissal fell into the types of an action of affirmative relief or a declaratory action, the reconciliation was not allowed in such cases.

An action for rescission

In a 'structuring litigation' (*xingcheng susong*), the court creates, alters or eliminates a legal relationship by issuing a judgment. A rescissory action is one of such structuring litigations. Once the structuring judgment is made, even before it is actually executed, creation, alternation or elimination of the legal relationship already occurs. Considering its intensive effect in this regard, a structuring judgment should, in principle, be exclusively made by the court, rather than being affected by the parties' will.

When reconciliation is concluded between the parties, such reconciliation possesses the effect equivalent to one of a structuring judgment, which means the reconciliation could, to some degree, replace the judgment issued by the court. However, considering the effect of a structuring judgment stated above, whether the reconciliation should be allowed in a structuring litigation is controversial.

Theoretically speaking, some scholars point out that reconciliation is based on the doctrine of disposition (*chufenquan zhuyi*), and the free will of the parties to conclude reconciliation should be respected in this regard. However, the claim in a rescissory action is an application to the court to issue a structuring judgment and rescind the administrative action that was made by the administrative agency. If reconciliation is allowed in a rescissory action, the parties' choices shall intervene in judging whether an administrative action should be rescinded or not.

Hence, in practice, it is rarely considered that, in a structuring litigation, the reconciliation that has been conducted only has its effects in the substantive aspect rather than the litigant aspect. It is not accepted that reconciliation could be concluded in a structuring litigation. Thus, with regard to a rescissory action, the parties could not conclude reconciliation.

Reference to the Civil Procedure Law

The fundamental purposes of administrative litigation and civil litigation are to protect the rights and interests of the parties. Compared to the Administrative Litigation Law, the Civil Procedure Law has a long history of development and is more advanced. Therefore, since the theories or practices of the Civil Procedure Law have developed over time, the Administrative Litigation Law has been amended in order to reflect the latest developments in the former field. The provisions in the Civil Procedure Law could be applied *mutatis mutandis* in the field of administrative litigation where a specific provision was missing in the Administrative Litigation Law and no qualitative difference was found between the two circumstances.

With regard to the way in which the Civil Procedure Law may be applied, a general method of enumeration was formerly provided, i.e., the circumstances that the Civil Procedure Law would be applied *mutatis mutandis* were enumerated in separate chapters and sections of the Administrative Litigation Law. However, this means of enumeration triggers a controversy: should all of the Articles that are not enumerated be excluded from application to the field of administrative litigation? With regard to the enumerated ones, are there any Articles that should not be applied due to the intrinsic differences in their nature? The fact that continuous amendments were made to the Civil Procedure Law also poses risks for this enumeration method, thus a blanket principle of applying the Civil Procedure Law *mutatis mutandis* in the administrative litigation cases was added, providing that the provisions in the Civil Procedure Law would be totally applied to the administrative litigation so long as there was no contradiction with the nature of administrative litigation (Article 307(1)). The particularities of administrative litigation that might cause such a contradiction include that the court may investigate and collect evidence *ex officio*, the disposing rights (*chufen quan*) of parties are restricted, and so on. Articles that were enumerated in the former Act are still valid under the amended Act, which exemplifies the blanket principle.[31]

Prospects for Development in the Future

Though quite a few amendments have been made to the Administrative Litigation Law and the Law has been gradually modernized, improvements in certain aspects still require attention. Firstly, the provisions that impose a co-operative duty (*xieli yiwu*) on the parties need to be explicitly stated, and these provisions need to be integrated with the provisions that the court should investigate and collect evidence initiatively. With a clear statutory statement of the party's co-operative duty, the court could thus order a party to provide means of attack or defence within a specific period and dismiss those means that are provided in a delay. This would relieve the burden of the court to investigate and collect evidence itself.

31 See Item 1 of Article 307 in the Legislative Explanations.

Secondly, the jurisdiction of the administrative courts needs to be expanded. The cases that are under the jurisdiction of ordinary courts now, such as the election, dismissal, State compensation and security of social orders, should be tried by the administrative courts. The judges in civil courts who are without expertise are not qualified to try such administrative litigation.

Thirdly, the administrative divisions within the local courts should be systemized into part of the administrative court system. They are now subordinated to the system of local courts and the trial of administrative litigation is only a working affair allocated to the judges in ordinary courts. The local administrative courts should be established as soon as possible. The trial system of administrative litigation would then be changed to become three-tiered, and the third instance would be the last instance. This would definitely facilitate the protection of citizens' fundamental rights and would remain in keeping with the principle of running and promoting a country under the rule of law (*Rechtsstaat*).

PART II
Administrative Litigation Systems in Western Democracies

Chapter 6
Judicial Review of Administrative Decisions in the Netherlands

Pieter van Dijk

Introduction

It is only since 1976 that a general system of administrative jurisdiction has existed in the Netherlands. Before that time there were certain special administrative courts for specific matters, such as the Central Appeals Board for Social Security, while the civil courts were, and still are, competent to deal with the lawfulness of governmental acts or failures to act in tort actions. However, in general, appeal against administrative action laid with the Crown, in which system a decision was taken by the King/Queen under the responsibility of the Government and on the advice of the Council of State.

In 1976 a special division of the Council of State was invested with independent administrative jurisdiction. For a large category of administrative disputes, such as those concerning urban and rural planning, and concerning the environment, access to Crown appeal remained open. However, after the European Court of Human Rights had decided that this remedy was not in conformity with the right of access to an independent and impartial court,[1] the Administrative Jurisdiction Division of the Council of State became the judicial body with general jurisdiction to review administrative decisions for their lawfulness.

In the present contribution this general system of administrative jurisdiction will be described, leaving out specificities concerning the jurisdiction and procedures of special administrative courts that are still in existence in the Netherlands.

Scope of Jurisdiction

Categories of Administrative Decisions Eligible for Review

An interested party may apply to the competent administrative court for judicial review of administrative decisions.

The object of an application for judicial review by an administrative court has to be a decision as defined in section 1:3, subsection 1, of the General Administrative Law Act:[2] *viz*. (1) a written decision (2) of an administrative authority (3) constituting a legal act under public law. These various elements of the concept of 'decision' will be explained hereafter.

---

1 European Court of Human Rights, judgment of 23 October 1985, *Benthem v. the Netherlands*.

2 The General Administrative Law Act entered into force on 1 January 1994. Unless otherwise stated, use has been made here of the English translation of the General Administrative Law Act as found at www.justitie.nl/onderwerpen/wetgeving/awb/Wettekst_awb/. Last visited December 2013.

A written decision
The challenged administrative decision must be in writing, but there are no other requirements governing its external features.

An administrative authority
The term 'administrative authority' is broadly defined in section 1:1 of the General Administrative Law Act. There are two main categories of administrative authorities: (a) organs of legal persons established under public law (e.g. the State, a province or a municipality), and (b) other persons or bodies invested with public authority. However, various authorities, persons and bodies are expressly indicated as not being administrative authorities in that sense, since they do not constitutionally belong to the public administration (in the sense of the executive). These include the legislature, Parliament, the judiciary and corporate bodies or offices charged with a scrutinising or advisory role independently of the public administration.

A legal act
The term 'legal act' means an act intended to have one or more external legal consequences for the relationship between the administrative authority and one or more other persons or entities. Decisions of a purely internal character such as instructions are not decisions in the sense referred to above. The term 'legal consequence' is generally understood to mean the creation, modification or termination of a legal relationship. A 'legal relationship' may be a right, entitlement, obligation, competence or legal status *vis-à-vis* the administrative authority concerned. Even where the administrative authority concerned lacks the competence to bring about the intended legal consequence, it will be sufficient for the administrative act to be eligible for review, if the authority concerned acted with the intention to bring about a legal consequence. In such a case, the presumption of competence is sufficient to assume the existence of an administrative decision that is open to review. A legal act comes under public law if the administrative authority derives the competence to perform the act from a legal power created especially for the public administration by or pursuant to the law. In certain circumstances an implicit statutory power or even an unwritten public law power is sufficient for this purpose. And as said above: even the mere presumption of a public law power is sufficient to assume the existence of an administrative decision. Such a decision may then be annulled for lack of competence.

While only decisions in the above sense are eligible for review by administrative courts, an interested party may also raise before the administrative court the issue of whether an act constitutes a decision in that sense and whether an administrative authority has wrongly failed to make such a decision.

As a rule, an application to the administrative court for review is preceded by an objection to the administrative authority concerned (*bezwaarschriftprocedure*). According to settled case law, a decision taken on such an objection is, by definition, a legal act under public law and, therefore, always constitutes a decision within the meaning of the General Administrative Law Act. Such a decision is therefore always eligible for judicial review.

Section 6:2 of the General Administrative Law Act provides that a written refusal to make a decision and a failure to make a decision in due time are equated with a decision for the purposes of statutory regulations governing administrative objection and judicial review.

Jurisdiction and Exclusions

Criteria for determining the competence of administrative courts

In determining which court is competent, a distinction is made between hierarchical and geographic competence. The former concept relates to the question as to which type and instance of court is competent to hear a case at any given stage of the proceedings. The latter concept relates to the question as to where in the Netherlands the application for judicial review has to be lodged.

Which type and instance of court is competent to hear an application for judicial review is regulated in sections 8:1, 8:6 and 8:7 of the General Administrative Law Act. The basic rule is that, once the preliminary administrative procedure of objection or administrative review has been completed, an application for judicial review may be made to the administrative court. The administrative law divisions of the 19 district courts function as the general administrative courts of first instance. However, statutes other than the General Administrative Law Act may provide that application for review of certain decisions or acts lies to a special administrative court. The main special administrative courts are the Administrative Jurisdiction Division of the Council of State as a court of first instance, the Central Appeals Board for Social Security (*Centrale Raad van Beroep*) and the Industrial Appeals Tribunal (*College van Beroep voor het bedrijfsleven*).

In principle, the Administrative Jurisdiction Division of the Council of State is the competent appeal court against decisions of the district courts, unless the Social Security Appeals Act, the Administrative Jurisdiction (Trade and Industry) Act or the Taxation Act provides that appeal be brought to, respectively, the Central Appeals Board for Social Security, the Industrial Appeals Tribunal or a taxation chamber of a court of appeal. The Central Appeals Board for Social Security hears appeals in cases involving social security law, public service law, pensions, and student grants and loans. Appeals against decisions made under certain statutes in the socio-economic field, in particular in the field of competition law, are brought to the Industrial Appeals Tribunal. The taxation chambers of the courts of appeal have jurisdiction to hear appeals in tax cases. Only in the latter cases, appeal for cassation lies to the Court of Cassation (*Hoge Raad*).

Several statutes make exceptions to the principle of judicial review in two instances by providing for cases to be heard by a court of first and final instance. For example, until recently the Administrative Jurisdiction Division of the Council of State heard appeals concerning urban and rural planning and in environmental cases at first and final instance, and for a certain category of appeals that still is the case. Under a small number of statutes, mainly concerning benefits and special pensions for war victims and special categories of pension cases, the Central Appeals Board for Social Security hears applications for review as court of first and final instance. Applications for review of decisions made in cases concerning socio-economic or agricultural issues are brought to the Industrial Appeals Tribunal as court of first and final instance.

As regards the geographic jurisdiction of the 19 district courts, the place in which the administrative body concerned has its seat determines where applications involving judicial review of decisions of regional or local authorities such as the provinces, municipalities and water authorities have to be filed. Applications for review of other decisions, for example those made by the central government, are examined by the district court within whose geographic jurisdiction the person lodging the application lives or – in the case of legal persons – has its seat. If the latter is not a resident in the Netherlands or has its seat outside the Netherlands, respectively, the application is examined by the district court within whose geographic jurisdiction the administrative authority concerned has its seat. If applications for review of a decision have been lodged to more than one competent district court, the cases must be heard by the district court that was the first to receive an application. If the applications were lodged simultaneously, they must be examined by the competent district court mentioned first in the Judiciary (Organisation) Act.

Administrative decisions that cannot be submitted to the administrative court for review by reason of the nature or substance of such decisions

no application for review lies against a decision connected with the preparation of a decision, unless the preparatory decision directly affects the interests of the applicant independently of the decision to be prepared (section 6:3 General Administrative Law Act). An example is a decision not to hear an interested party in advance when preparing a decision. Such a decision cannot be submitted for review but may be reviewed by the court together with the ultimate decision.

In addition, applications for judicial review may not be made in respect of certain categories of decision such as: (a) decisions containing a generally binding regulation or a policy rule,[3] as well as decisions cancelling, introducing or approving a generally binding regulation or policy rule (section 8:2 General Administrative Law Act); (b) decisions preparing a legal act under private law (section 8:3 General Administrative Law Act); (c) decisions belonging to one of the categories referred to in section 8:4 of the General Administrative Law Act;[4] in general, these are decisions that are unsuitable or less suitable for judicial review and decisions involving matters relating to legislation that provides for remedies before other courts; (d) decisions made pursuant to a statutory regulation listed in the schedule to which reference is made in section 8:5 of the General

3 A 'generally binding regulation' is a rule issued by a competent public body that has external effect and is binding on those to whom it relates. Generally binding regulations differ from other decisions in that they contain general, abstract rules that are suitable for repeated application in practice without further specification. A 'policy rule' is a general rule, not being a generally binding regulation, that lays down a general rule for the exercise of a power of an administrative authority when weighing different interests, determining facts or interpreting statutory regulations, and has been adopted by means of an decision. Policy rules regulate the exercise of existing powers; they do not create new powers.

4 Section 8:4 General Administrative Law Act. No application for judicial review may be instituted against a decision: (a) staying or quashing a decision of another administrative authority; (b) made in extraordinary circumstances pursuant to a power granted or obligation imposed in any statutory regulation for application in such circumstances; (c) made pursuant to a statutory regulation for the protection of the military interests of the Kingdom of the Netherlands or its allies; (d) for an appointment, unless the appeal is instituted by a public servant as referred to in section 1 of the Central and Local Government Personnel Act or a conscript as referred to in section 1 (b) of the Conscripts (Legal Status) Act, their surviving relatives or their successors-in-title; (e) involving an assessment of the knowledge and ability of a candidate or pupil who has been examined in this respect or has been tested in some other way, or establishing assignments or assessment criteria, or containing further rules for such assessment or testing; (f) involving a technical assessment of a vehicle or aircraft or of a measuring device, a part thereof or an auxiliary device; (g) concerning the numbering of lists of candidates, the validity of combinations of lists, the voting procedure, the counting of votes, the determination of vote values and the determination of the result of elections of members of representative assemblies, the declaration of appointment to vacant seats, the appointment of new members of a provincial or municipal council or of the general management of a water authority and the granting of temporary termination of membership of a representative assembly on account of pregnancy and childbirth or sickness; (h) made under a statutory regulation concerning compulsory military service, in so far as it relates to medical examination or re-examination, call-up of reservists, long-term leave or discharge, unless the decision concerns extension of a reservist's call-up or breadwinner's allowance, or the decision has been made under the Armed Forces (Reserve Personnel) Act 1985; (i) consisting of an official act by a court bailiff or notary; (j) as referred to in section 7:1a, subsection 4; (k) containing a refusal under section 2:15; (l) as referred to in section 3:21, subsection 1 (b); (m) containing a demand for payment as referred to section 4:112 or a distress warrant.

Administrative Law Act.[5] This schedule lists decisions that are excluded from judicial review for one or more of the following reasons: they are unsuitable or less suitable for judicial review on account of their nature; they have been made under an arrangement that provides for a remedy before another court (mainly the civil courts); they are mainly of an indicative nature; the decision-making procedure of which the decision forms part includes other decisions that are subject to judicial review; the circumstances are such that the decision-making process as a whole may not be burdened with procedures that will slow down the process and offer little real legal protection.

In addition, special statutes may exclude judicial review in respect of certain decisions. If that is the case, the civil courts have a residual jurisdiction.

Procedure

General Description of Applicable Procedural Rules

Rules of procedure
The General Administrative Law Act contains legal rules governing administrative decision-making and legal rules concerning judicial remedies against administrative decisions and the procedures to be followed.

Chapter 8 of the General Administrative Law Act contains uniform provisions concerning the procedure of judicial review by the administrative law divisions of the district courts. Rules governing judicial review in appeal are contained in special statutes that regulate the organisation of the appeal court concerned, namely the Council of State Act (Administrative Jurisdiction Division of the Council of State), the Social Security Appeals Act (Central Appeals Board for Social Security) and the Administrative Jurisdiction (Trade and Industry) Act (Industrial Appeals Tribunal). These special statutes provide that chapter 8 of the General Administrative Law Act is applicable *mutatis mutandis*.

The provisions of chapter 8 leave the courts a certain margin of discretion at some points as to procedural rules to be applied. To ensure the uniform application of the procedural rules, the district courts have adopted joint guidelines in the 2008 Administrative Law Rules of Procedure. In the same way, the three special administrative courts – the Administrative Jurisdiction Division of the Council of State, the Central Appeals Board for Social Security and the Industrial Appeals Tribunal – have adopted the 2006 Rules of Procedure, while the taxation chambers of the courts of appeal have adopted the 2005 Rules of Procedure. Although these rules of procedure do not qualify as generally binding regulations, they are binding on the courts concerned by virtue of general principles of the proper administration of justice.

Unwritten procedural law plays a supplementary role. Mention could be made of the principles of the proper administration of justice, including the right of access to the courts and that of due process, the right to a decision within a reasonable time and by an independent and impartial court, the right of publicity of procedures and documents and equality of arms, and the right to a properly reasoned judgment. These principles and rights are not all expressly guaranteed under domestic law. However, they have (also) been laid down in international law provisions that are binding on the Netherlands, *inter alia* in the European Convention on Human Rights. The law of the European

5 Section 8:5. No application for judicial review may be lodged against a decision made under a statutory regulation listed in the schedule to this Act.

Union too, including its Charter for Fundamental Rights, contains several guarantees for proper administrative and judicial procedures.

Procedural steps

Under administrative procedural law, the court has a leading role in the conduct of proceedings. This role is, in principle, performed within the limits of the dispute as referred by the parties.

After an application has been lodged with the court for judicial review, the court determines within the limits of the law and the principles of due process how the examination in preparation for the hearing should be organised, how much time the parties will have to perform the procedural acts, what additional documents and information are needed, whether documents introduced in a late stage of the proceedings can still be taken into account, and whether witnesses and/or experts called by the parties may give evidence. In addition, the court has a number of powers that enable it to play an active role. For example, the court may decide that an application for judicial review should be expedited, request information from the parties and appoint experts to examine certain facts underlying the decision. In general, the administrative courts make restrained use of these powers.

The parties are entitled to a number of procedural rights, such as the right to receive or to be informed of documents relating to the case as quickly as possible, to give a written explanation, to be consulted about the appointment of an expert and to comment on his report, to attend any on-the-spot examination, and to address the court orally at the hearing. In addition, the parties may attempt to induce the court to exercise any of the powers just mentioned. The court must give notice of its decision on any such request by separate letter, in the official record of the proceedings at the hearing or in the judgment. Although the parties may not contest procedural (interim) decisions of this kind independently, they may raise them in any appeal lodged against the ultimate decision. Sometimes the court may exercise a power only with the consent of the parties, for instance the power to decide not to hold a second hearing after new information has been provided by one of the parties at the court's request after the first hearing.

Written or oral proceedings

The preliminary examination that starts after receipt of an application is based mainly on written submissions. The administrative authority whose decision has been challenged in a written application sends the documents relating to the case to the court and submits a statement of defence. After the application and statement of defence have been lodged, the court can arrange for the applicant and defendant to lodge further written submissions in the form of a reply and rejoinder. This can sometimes result in the parties reaching agreement, thereby obviating the need for a court decision. Other parties with a direct interest in the case are given the opportunity to state their view of the case in writing. During the preliminary examination the judge can summon the parties to provide evidence or additional data. The court may also decide to hold a site visit.

The preliminary examination is generally concluded by the notification of the parties that a hearing will take place (section 8:56 General Administrative Law Act). The oral hearing gives implementation to the principle that both parties should be heard (*audi et alteram partem*).[6] There are two exceptions to this general rule.

First, the court may decide to close the proceedings at the preliminary examination stage on the grounds that there can be no reasonable doubt about the outcome of the application (section 8:54 of the General Administrative Law Act). No appeal lies against that decision. However, any of the parties may lodge a notice of objection to such a decision with the court concerned (section 8:55

6 However, cases concerning aliens are usually dealt with in a written procedure.

General Administrative Law Act). The sole issue considered in such objection proceedings is whether the court was right to give judgment without holding a hearing. Second, the hearing may be omitted if the parties and the court mutually agree on this in view of the fact that a public hearing would add little to the proceedings.

Single-judge or full-bench chamber

The basic rule is that cases brought before the administrative division of a district court are heard by a single-judge chamber. The justification for this is that, on the one hand, this is the only way in which to deal with the load of cases, while, on the other hand, in principle there is a right of appeal against the judgment where the reverse applies: i.e. as a rule cases are heard on appeal by a full-bench chamber. In cases in which appeal does not lie and judgment is given by the court at first and final instance, the case is generally heard by a full-bench chamber.

Cases may be referred from a single-judge chamber to a full-bench chamber and *vice versa* at any stage of the proceedings. The General Administrative Law Act provides no criteria for referral. Factors that can play a role in referring a case to a full-bench chamber are the complexity of either the legal issues or the facts involved, expected differences of opinion, deviation from previous case law, or the general importance of the case. A full-bench chamber consists of three judges. However, a recent amendment makes it possible for the Supreme Administrative Courts to sit in chambers of five members as a special tool to guarantee uniformity of their case law.

Admissibility Requirements for Lodging an Application for Judicial Review

The person lodging an application for judicial review of an administrative decision must be an interested party and must have lodged the application within the prescribed period and paid the registry fee.[7] The application must also comply with a number of procedural and substantive requirements. For example, it must specify the decision against which the application is directed and a copy of the decision must, where possible, be annexed. The application must state the grounds on which the decision is challenged and must be dated and signed.

If the requirements that the application must be lodged in time and that the registry fee must have been paid are not met, there is no opportunity for rectification. In such cases, the application is declared inadmissible unless the applicant can give good reasons for the failure to comply with the requirements or, with the approval of the court, a payment arrangement has been made for the registry fee.

If the requirements for the contents of the application itself are not met, the applicant is given the opportunity to rectify the default.[8] If the default is not rectified within the prescribed period, the court will declare the application inadmissible. Whether the admissibility requirements have been met is assessed by the court *ex proprio motu*.

The possibility of applying for judicial review is limited to the person who is an 'interested party' in relation to the decision concerned. An interested party is a person whose interest is directly affected by the decision concerned (section 1:2 General Administrative Law Act). The addressee of a decision is, by definition, an interested party. Third parties too may be interested parties.

Apart from natural persons and legal persons under private law such as associations, foundations, limited liability companies (*NVs*) and private companies (*BVs*), legal persons under public law

7 Applications for judicial review of decisions on asylum applications and detention of aliens are excepted from the duty to pay a registry fee.

8 The possibility of rectification can be excluded by specific Act, as occurred in the Aliens Act 2000.

such as the state, provinces and municipalities may be interested parties in relation to a decision made by an administrative authority. A requirement is that the interests of the natural or legal person concerned are directly affected as an actual consequence of the disputed decision. If this requirement is met, the person concerned is, in principle, free to challenge any part of the decision on the basis of any relevant ground, irrespective of whether the part of the decision challenged or the ground relied upon affects his own interests. In certain cases, defined by law, the interest invoked has to be a legal interest. And if his interests are affected by a particular part of a decision, he may act as an interested party in relation to the entire decision.

The applicant's interest must be directly affected by the decision. In other words, there must be a sufficient causal connection between his interest and the disputed decision. A mere derivative interest is not sufficient, for instance in a situation where the decision affects the interest concerned only through a contractual relationship. If, however, the interests of the two parties in such a contractual relationship are diametrically opposed to one another, they are not considered to be derivative only. This was held to be the case where a general practitioner opposed an order made by the Health Care Insurance Supervisory Board exempting a health insurance fund from the obligation to conclude contracts for the provision of GP care. This exemption greatly reduced the chance that the health insurance fund would conclude a contract with the GP concerned for the provision of services for the following year on more favourable terms than in the past. As his business and financial interests were at stake, the family doctor was therefore deemed to be directly affected by the order.[9] And in certain cases the courts have held that a person who has an interest coinciding with that of the person primarily affected, should nonetheless be treated as an interested party. Thus, in a case in which the landlord and the tenant of a property opposed a traffic measure relating to the street in which the property concerned was situated, both were treated as interested parties.[10]

Another category of cases in which an interest is no longer held to be derivative only, comprises cases in which a decision affects an interest resulting from a fundamental right of the person. Thus, when permission is refused and this refusal has, for a person who did not apply for the permission, an impact on his right to respect of his private life, the latter is also an interested party.[11]

The rationale behind the relaxation of this rule is that the person primarily affected by a disputed decision is often not the person most seriously affected, and it cannot automatically be assumed that he or she will be willing to take action.

In addition, the interest must exist at the time of the application and be capable of being determined objectively. A purely subjective feeling of being affected by a certain decision is not sufficient, no matter how strong that feeling may be. Nor are subjective feelings of dissatisfaction or uncertain expectations sufficient. And the interest must be a personal interest, in other words it must be capable of being sufficiently distinguished from the interests of other persons.

The rationale of the requirement that a person who lodges an objection or applies for judicial review must have a direct and personal interest, is to limit to some extent the possibility for taking such action. This is deemed to be especially important in the case of decisions of general scope that

9 Judgment of the Administrative Jurisdiction Division of the Council of State of 29 March 2006, case no. 200505363/1, at www.raadvanstate.nl. Last visited December 2013.

10 Judgment of the Administrative Jurisdiction Division of the Council of State of 14 September 2005, case no. 200410527/1, at www. raadvanstate.nl. Last visited December 2013.

11 Judgment of the Administrative Jurisdiction Division of the Council of State of 21 November 2007, case no. 200702439/1, at www.raadvanstate.nl. Last visited December 2013.

can affect the interests of very many people. In connection with traffic decisions, for example, it is necessary to determine from case to case whose interests are directly affected by such a decision.[12]

The interests of legal persons with a non-commercial objective are deemed to include the general and collective interests that they specifically represent according to their objective as stated in their statutes, and as evidenced by their actual activities (section 1:2, subsection 3, General Administrative Law Act). In the case of collective actions by interest groups, it is therefore important from the point of view of their right to apply for judicial review that collectivities can be treated as legal persons, represent a general and collective interest and do so pursuant to their objectives under their statutes and as evidenced by their actual activities, and that they specifically represent these interests. The interest represented by them must concern the supra-individual interests of the group as a whole, not the interests of one or more clearly identifiable members. Thus, following the granting of a construction permit for a block of flats, a flat owners' association applied for judicial review of the decision and was held to be an interested party since representing the joint interests of its members was part of its object under its statutes. In view of the possible impact of the building plan on the area where its members lived, the interests of the association were directly affected by the decision.[13]

A legal person's objectives according to its articles of association or statutes must not be formulated too widely. If an objective is worded in such a way as to virtually coincide with the public interest, the legal person concerned might claim practically any interest involved. For example, a foundation was held not to be an interested party in relation to a decision refusing a building permit for a brasserie-style restaurant or granting an exemption from a local land-use plan for two pavement cafés. Under its statutes the objective of the foundation was defined as, 'Doing everything that is or may be in the interests of the Oud Verlaat village centre'. This was held to be insufficiently specific and worded in such general terms that it could not be assumed that the interests specifically represented by the foundation were affected by the disputed decision.[14]

Legal Assistance or Representation

Administrative procedural law does not require parties to obtain legal assistance or representation. The only exception is where a party appeals in a tax dispute for cassation to the Court of Cassation and the cassation appeal is heard orally. In such circumstances, the parties must arrange for their case to be argued by counsel.

However, the parties are entitled to be assisted or represented in proceedings (section 8:24, subsection 1, General Administrative Law Act). In practice, frequent use is made of representatives or assistants. No special requirements are made of representatives. However, representatives who are not practising lawyers may be required by the court to produce a written authorisation proving that they are entitled to act for the person, institution or organisation they claim to be representing. In addition, whether or not legal assistance is provided on a professional basis may affect the court's decision for costs. The expense and risk of any acts performed by an authorised representative in the proceedings are borne by the party concerned. If a party explicitly notifies the court that

12 Judgment of the Administrative Jurisdiction Division of the Council of State of 3 July 1998, case no. H01.97.0795, at www.raadvanstate.nl. Last visited December 2013.

13 Judgment of the Administrative Jurisdiction Division of the Council of State of 14 March 2007, case no. 200603493/1, at www.raadvanstate.nl. Last visited December 2013.

14 Judgment of the Administrative Jurisdiction Division of the Council of State of 22 August 2007, case no. 200700414/1, at www.raadvanstate.nl. Last visited December 2013.

he is represented, the court will send any documents relating to the case to the representative (section 6:17 General Administrative Law Act).

Legal Aid

Parties who have insufficient financial means to bear the costs of legal assistance may obtain legal aid under the Legal Aid Act. An application for legal aid is submitted to the Legal Aid Council through the party's representative or lawyer. The Council determines on the basis of the information about income and capital, and the nature of the case, whether the party concerned is eligible for legal aid. The decision of the Legal Aid Council may be appealed.

Use of Electronic Technology (Internet)

Judicial review by an administrative court is instituted by lodging an application for review with the court concerned (section 6:4, subsection 3, General Administrative Law Act). The application can be lodged by mail or by fax (with signature). Originally, the General Administrative Law Act did not provide for the possibility of using electronic technology to lodge an application.[15] Recently, however, part 2.3 of the General Administrative Law Act, which deals with electronic communications in relation to administrative matters, was declared applicable to communications with the administrative courts. This allows litigants to communicate digitally with the administrative courts in proceedings. Case documents and notices of appeal can then be sent electronically.

Suspensive Effect; Emergency or Interim Procedures

The basic rule in administrative law is that an objection or application for review does not suspend the operation of the decision against which it lies (section 6:16 General Administrative Law Act). Nor does an appeal to a court have suspensive effect. This safeguards legal certainty and ensures the proper functioning of the public administration. If an interested party wishes to have the operation of a decision pending an objection or review suspended, he must apply for provisional relief. A special legal regulation may, however, provide for the suspension of the operation of a decision in case of an objection of appeal.

Suspension of a disputed decision may be obtained by means of a request for a provisional remedy. A provisional remedy may provide not only for complete or partial suspension of the decision but also for other measures such as the granting of a provisional licence.

A request for suspension or a provisional remedy is heard by an interim relief judge of the district court or by the President of the higher administrative court, depending on the stage of the procedure in which the request is made. The interim relief judge or the President, as the case may be, may also alter or cancel a previously granted provisional remedy. This may occur where circumstances have changed to such an extent as to warrant alteration or termination of the remedy. The court that deals with the merits of the case may also decide, either of its own motion or on application, to grant a provisional remedy for a limited period to safeguard certain rights

15 However, section 2:15 of the General Administrative Law Act does provide that an objection or application for review may be lodged electronically (by email) with an administrative authority (administrative review), provided that the authority concerned has indicated that this possibility exists.

in case the challenged administrative decision is annulled and the court decision does not bring about a final solution.

A provisional remedy may be requested only if proceedings on the merits of the case are pending before the court at the same time. An application for judicial review must have been lodged (procedural connection) and must concern the decision in relation to which the provisional remedy is requested (substantive connection). A request for a provisional remedy may be made only by a party to the principal procedure. The interim relief judge of the district court or, as the case may be, the President of the higher administrative court that is the competent court to hear the merits may, on request, grant a provisional remedy if urgency and the interests involved require so. As a rule, the purpose of a provisional remedy is to ensure that the provisional implementation of the challenged decision does not have irreversible consequences. Grounds for a provisional remedy will exist in particular if the judge or the President, as the case may be, is provisionally of the opinion that the challenged decision is unlawful and may be annulled in the proceedings on the merits. In reaching his decision, the judge or the President will balance the different interests of the parties concerned.

Judgment on an application for a provisional remedy will be given as promptly as possible. If a provisional remedy is granted, this will take effect immediately after the decision is given. No appeal lies against a decision of the interim relief judge or the President. The provisional remedy does not decide the proceedings on the merits. In practice, however, it may in certain cases be tantamount to a final solution of the dispute. Moreover, the interim relief judge or the President, as the case may be, may decide that he can decide on the merits, if he considers that further consideration of the case could not reasonably be expected to contribute to an assessment on the merits. This is known as 'short-circuiting'. It may benefit legal protection, legal certainty and legal economy, if the parties do not have to wait for judgment longer than is strictly necessary. The case law of the Administrative Jurisdiction Division of the Council of State shows that the deciding factor is whether the information provided in writing and at the hearing is of such a nature that it may be assumed that further inquiries would not yield any relevant new data. It is not necessary for the parties to have given consent for the immediate disposal of the case by the interim relief judge of the district court or by the President of a special administrative court hearing the case at first and final instance. The possibility of short-circuiting also exists on appeal to the Administrative Jurisdiction Division of the Council of State, the Central Appeals Board for Social Security, and the Appeals Tribunal for Trade and Industry, but only if the application for judicial review was heard by a single-judge chamber of the district court or by the interim relief judge of the district court. The possibility of short-circuiting exists only if a hearing is held.[16]

Production of Documents by Administrative Authorities

It is a fundamental principle of proper administration of justice that a party should have access to all documents in the possession of the administrative authority relating to his case. For example, the Central Appeals Board for Social Security has held that the court is obliged to obtain any missing documents from the administrative authority.[17]

Section 8:28 of the General Administrative Law Act provides that, if an administrative court requests the parties to provide written information, they have a duty to comply. During the preliminary examination the court has the power to request not only the parties but also third

16 This condition does not apply in appeal proceedings in immigration cases.

17 Judgment of 30 July 1999, case no. 97/1770-72 AAW/WAO, at www.rechtspraak.nl. Last visited December 2013.

persons to supply written information and documents. Administrative authorities are obliged to comply with such a request from the court, even if they are not a party to the proceedings (section 8:45, subsection 2, General Administrative Law Act). No such obligation exists for private persons who are not a party to the proceedings. If a defendant administrative authority fails to supply the court with documents relating to the case within the prescribed period, the court may apply section 8:44 of the General Administrative Law Act by summoning the administrative authority to appear before the court within two weeks of the expiry of the period for submission of documents. Although administrative authorities who are not a party to the proceedings, are also obliged to comply with a request for information, there are no sanctions for non-compliance. In such cases the court may summon a recalcitrant authority to testify in court and can compel its attendance, if necessary with the help of the police. Witnesses who are summoned by the court must comply with the summons and give evidence. Failure to comply with these obligations is a criminal offence.

If a party does not comply with the obligation to provide information, the court may draw such conclusions from this as it sees fit (section 8:31 General Administrative Law Act). For example, the court may hold that any alleged facts that remain uncertain will be assumed to have been proven or not proven, as the case may be, to the detriment of that party. Where a defendant administrative authority fails to comply with such obligation to provide information, the most far-reaching consequence is that the application for judicial review is declared well founded, possibly accompanied by a decision for compensation or a decision for costs.[18]

The obligation to provide documents is not unconditional. If they have justified reasons, any of the parties may refuse to provide information or documents, or may inform the court that the documents are for its eyes only and may not be disclosed to the other parties involved in the action (section 8:29 General Administrative Law Act). Mere protection of the private life of those concerned is generally not a sufficient reason for holding that limitation of disclosure is warranted. It is necessary to show that disclosure might possibly constitute a serious disadvantage for those concerned.[19] The public authority may also advance the protection of public interests, for example the security of the State.

It is for the court to decide whether the request of an administrative authority to be allowed not to provide certain documents or to limit their disclosure is justified. If the court agrees to limited disclosure, it may take the documents concerned into account only if the parties who have not been shown the documents have no objection to this. The Administrative Jurisdiction Division of the Council of State has held that a party who withholds consent must, in principle, bear any consequences thereof.[20] If the court deems it justified for the information or documents to be kept completely secret (i.e. from the court as well), the obligation to provide information or documents ceases to apply. If one of the other parties withholds consent for judgment to be given on the basis of documents disclosed only to the court, or if the court agrees that documents may be kept completely secret, the case has to be judged by judges who have not seen the documents. For that reason courts usually have a special chamber for examining whether a request for secrecy is justified.

In keeping with the principle of equality of arms and the right to a public hearing, which are also at the basis of article 6 of the European Convention for the Protection of Human Rights and

18 See, for example, the judgment of the Administrative Jurisdiction Division of the Council of State of 9 October 1997, case no. H01.95.0378, at www.raadvanstate.nl. Last visited December 2013.

19 See, for example, the judgment of the Central Appeals Board for Social Security of 10 October 2001, case no. 00/1590, at www.rechtspraak.nl. Last visited December 2013.

20 See, for example, the judgment of the Administrative Jurisdiction Division of the Council of State of 27 July 2005, case no. 200407247/1, at www.raadvanstate.nl. Last visited December 2013.

Fundamental Freedoms, a request for limited disclosure or complete secrecy is granted by the court only in very exceptional circumstances. According to the case law of the Administrative Jurisdiction Division of the Council of State, the possibility of limited disclosure is hedged around by such safeguards that the right to a fair trial is not essentially compromised.[21] The fact that there are good grounds for limited disclosure or secrecy is not decisive. If the documents are of great importance to the proper assessment of the disputed decision, the court may reject the request for this reason.

The administrative authority cannot invoke the need for secrecy in a situation where in virtue of the Government Information (Public Access) Act publication of the information is obligatory, unless a possible exception to this obligation is precisely at issue (section 8:29, subsection 2, General Administrative Law Act).

The Scope of Review by Administrative Courts

Hierarchy of Legal Norms

It is the task of the administrative court to solve the dispute referred to it on the basis of reviewing the challenged administrative decision – and in appeal, the court decision against which appeal has been lodged – for its conformity with the applicable law. Within the limits of the dispute the administrative court must, of its own motion, discover and apply all law relevant to the arguments submitted to it by the parties ('*curia novit jus*'). The parties themselves need not invoke the specific provisions of the law. It is up to the court to *ex officio* translate the parties' arguments into legally correct arguments by supplementing the legal grounds (section 8:69 General Administrative Law Act).

Decisions that are subject to judicial review are reviewed by the administrative court in the light of both written and unwritten law. The court is also competent to determine whether a legal basis on which the challenged decision is grounded, is compatible with higher law or unwritten principles of law. The law by reference to which administrative courts review administrative decisions have the following hierarchy:

1. treaties and binding decisions of international governmental organisations;
2. the Constitution;
3. acts of parliament;
4. decisions in council and royal decrees;
5. ministerial decisions;
6. provincial regulations; and
7. municipal regulations.

Under article 93 of the Constitution, the courts may and must directly apply provisions of treaties and of decisions by international governmental organisations that are 'binding on everyone' (i.e. self-executing). Under article 94 such provisions take precedence over conflicting national law, including the Constitution. An important example of such self-executing treaty provisions are the substantive provisions of the European Convention for the Protection of Human Rights and Fundamental Freedoms. An important example of self-executing provisions of decisions of an

21 Judgment of the Administrative Jurisdiction Division of the Council of State of 13 June 2001, case no. 200003274/1, at www.raadvanstate.nl. Last visited December 2013.

international governmental organisation are the regulations and, to a certain extent, the directives of the European Union.

According to the prevailing doctrine in the Netherlands, precedence of the law of the European Union issues from the character of this law itself; it applies irrespective of what the domestic (constitutional) law of the Member States provides in that respect. Under standing case law of the Court of Justice of the European Union, the Union has its own legal order that has been incorporated into the domestic law of the Member States and that the national courts have to take into account and give precedence. It follows from the autonomous nature of European Union law and the transferral of powers by the Member States that this law takes precedence over any conflicting law of the Member States.[22] The principle of precedence applies to European Union law as a whole, in other words to both primary and secondary law, and to both written and unwritten law. In addition, the principle operates in relation both to the past (i.e. to national rules predating Union law) and to the future (i.e. to national rules of a later date). As regards the legal consequences of this precedence, the Court of Justice of the European Union has held that national rules that are incompatible with Union law shall not be applied. This doctrine implies that European Union law also takes precedence over the Constitution.[23] Whether the same applies in case of a conflict between European Union law and another treaty is still a matter of dispute in legal doctrine.

Under article 120 of the Constitution the courts in the Netherlands are barred from reviewing the constitutionality of Acts of Parliament and of treaties; the express or implied *ex ante* review by the legislator is considered to be the final assessment. However, this system is in practice eroded (or rather 'circumvented') by the obligation for the courts to review Acts of Parliament for their conformity with treaties, since the most important substantive provisions of the Constitution, especially those relating to fundamental rights, have also been incorporated into treaties. The prohibition of judicial constitutional review does not apply to lower legislation and administrative acts.

If the court holds a lower legal provision to be incompatible with a higher legal provision – or with an unwritten principle of law – it will leave all or part of the lower provision out of application.

Interpretation of Statutory Law

As noted above, the administrative courts decide on their own motion what legal rules are applicable, whether they are in force at the relevant time and what they mean. They must also assess whether a statutory regulation should not be applied, either under article 94 of the Constitution (incompatible with a treaty or decision of an international organisation) or because it is incompatible with European Union law. The court hearing the case is not bound in this respect by the legal views expressed by the administrative authority whose decision has been challenged, not even if the latter's views are shared by all other parties to the proceedings. Legal rules that are in force and applicable may not be disregarded by the court; they have to be applied and, if necessary, interpreted.

However, the administrative courts do observe a degree of restraint in interpreting legal rules whose scope cannot be determined *in abstracto* because they have been deliberately formulated by the legislator in such a way as to leave the administrative authority concerned a margin of discretion. In applying a statutory rule in respect of which it has a margin of discretion, the administrative authority can therefore adopt a standing policy that is designed to ensure a uniform application of the rule concerned. In such cases the court reviews whether the statutory purposes underlying

22 Judgment of the European Court of Justice, Case 106/77, Simmenthal, *Jur.* 1978, p. 629.

23 In some Member States, however, like Germany and Italy, the constitutional jurisprudence makes a reservation for the fundamental elements of the domestic democratic constitutional order (the '*Solange*' doctrine).

these open rules, are adequately and reasonably implemented by the policy concerned. Where the scope or meaning of the adopted policy is in dispute, the court will rule on whether or not there are grounds for holding that the policy gives an incorrect interpretation to the rule concerned, or is for other reasons to be deemed unreasonable.

Interpretation of Treaty Law

The interpretation of treaty law is governed by the same principles as the interpretation of statutory law (see above). However, the authority that ultimately rules on the interpretation of the European Union Treaties and other applicable European Union law is the Court of Justice of the European Union. Dutch courts may and, if their judgment will be a final one, must refer a question of interpretation or validity to the Court of Justice for a preliminary ruling, if they need an answer in order to give judgment.

Review of the Exercise of Discretionary Powers

In reviewing administrative decisions challenged before it, the administrative court examines whether and to what extent the applicable law allows the administrative authority discretion to exercise the relevant power in such a way and to such an extent as it has done. Where the legislator allows the administrative authority a margin of discretion, the administrative authority may adopt a policy for the exercise of this discretion in the case at hand and for future cases. Such a policy may take the form of either policy rules or standard courses of conduct. Policy rules define in broad outline how a discretionary power concerned will be exercised. Although a standard course of conduct fulfils the same function as a policy rule in terms of its scope, it is not – unlike a policy rule – laid down in a formal decision. Often, it is simply the product of a series of decisions in individual cases.

The administrative court examines, first of all, whether the applicable law allows any scope for weighing the different interests and whether the limits indicated in the law were respected when the decision was made. The courts observe, however, restraint in reviewing how the administrative authority has exercised its discretion.

If the administrative authority does not have a policy, the court reviews how the interests have been weighed or balanced in the case in question. In view of the political accountability of the administrative authority and the position of the independent judiciary in the Dutch constitutional system, it is not up to the court to decide what would be the most balanced weighing of the competing interests. The scope of judicial review is limited to deciding whether there is such an imbalance in the weighing of the competing interests that the discretionary power has been exercised in a manifestly unreasonable manner.[24]

The applicable policy is not reviewed by the courts of their own motion, and it is not possible to apply to the administrative courts for judicial review of such a policy *in abstracto*. The policy may be reviewed only in the context of an application for review of a decision involving the exercise of the administrative power in a specific case.

If the administrative authority has established a standard course of conduct in relation to the exercise of discretionary powers granted to it, this course of conduct as a rule has to be followed. This ensues not from a particular law but from principles of proper administration, in particular the

24 Judgment of the Central Appeals Tribunal of 14 July 2006, case no. 05/3589 NAWB, at www.rechtspraak.nl. Last visited December 2013.

principle of equality of treatment and the principle of legitimate expectations. If the administrative authority departs from such a standard course of conduct in view of special circumstances, the administrative court assesses whether this departure was indeed grounded on such special circumstances and is reasonable.

Where the administrative authority has drawn up a policy rule to exercise a discretionary power, the policy rule is binding in the sense that the administrative authority is obliged to act in accordance with the adopted policy, unless the consequences for one or more interested parties would, owing to special circumstances, be disproportionate to the purposes of the policy rule (section 4:84 General Administrative Law Act).

In general, the review by the administrative courts to assess compliance with policy rules takes the following form.

First, the court reviews whether, at the abstract level, the policy remains within the framework of the law governing the administrative power. This involves deciding not only whether the policy implements the purpose of the law in an acceptable way, but also whether it remains within the scope of the administrative power (no abuse of power) and the margin of discretion. The judicial review is to this extent a comprehensive one.

The court then goes on to assess whether the manner in which the policy has been established, is in conformity with the law and the principles of proper administration. This involves deciding in particular whether the policy has been formulated with due care in view of the legal interests that may be involved, and whether this has been made sufficiently known to the interested parties. This too involves a comprehensive review by the court.

Finally, as part of the review of the policy at the abstract level, the court determines whether the policy is not unreasonable and not incompatible with the principles of proper administration. The constitutional relationship between the administrative authority and the administrative court implies that the latter must observe restraint in reviewing the manner in which the administrative authority has balanced the various interests in the case at hand and in view of possible future cases. It is sufficient if the policy elaborates in a standard case in a transparent and well-reasoned way what the administrative authority envisaged. If the administrative court concludes that this is not the case, the policy is unlawful and may not form the basis for an administrative decision.

If the administrative court concludes that the policy is acceptable and reasonable at the abstract level, it goes on to examine whether the disputed decision has been made in keeping with that policy, provided that the case in question is of the standard type covered by the policy. In normal cases a policy rule should not be departed from. Repeated departures in normal cases covered by the policy rule amount in effect to a change in the policy rule. Any such change should be made, from the point of view of legal certainty, by means of an amendment that is announced publicly. A one-off departure in a normal case will normally be held in breach of the principle of equality of treatment. In a particular case, however, special circumstances may necessitate an exception to the policy. A departure may be warranted if strict compliance with the policy rule is not necessary or not desirable in view of the scope of the rule and the underlying statutory scheme in the specific case and would cause disproportionate harm to the interested parties. But there should then be special circumstances of which no account was taken when the policy rules were formulated.[25] The question as to whether such special circumstances occur in a given case, is a question of fact that is reviewed by the court in full. As a rule, the authority claiming that departing from the policy was justified, or the private party advocating that the policy should have been departed from, will have

25 Judgment of the Administrative Jurisdiction Division of the Council of State of 13 August 2003, case no. 200206852/1, at www.raadvanstate.nl. Last visited December 2013.

to specify the special circumstances concerned. Whether these circumstances are relevant or, to put it another way, whether it is objectively plausible that these circumstances, if taken into account at the moment the policy was fixed, would have made a difference to the content of the policy, is another question that the court reviews in full. However, the court should observe restraint in reviewing the exercise of the power, if departing from the policy rule has been held justified. The criterion is whether or not the administrative authority acted reasonably in balancing all the different interests involved.

If application is made for judicial review of a decision imposing punitive sanctions (i.e. sanctions that are intended not only to end a situation inconsistent with a particular rule but also to punish the person concerned), the proportionality of imposing the sanction must be reviewed in full by the administrative court in all circumstances. This is because the Dutch administrative courts treat punitive sanctions as 'criminal charges' within the meaning of article 6 of the European Convention for the Protection of Human Rights and Fundamental Freedoms. It follows that the criminal law safeguards are applicable to such sanctions. The restraint that the administrative courts must observe in reviewing decisions made pursuant to a discretionary power does not apply in this case.

It should also be noted that a decision must comply with the principles of due care and reasoning. A decision may be annulled if the principle of due care has been breached because the facts were not properly examined or the authority wrongly failed to seek advice. In addition, a sound reasoning of the decision should be given. This will, for instance, not be deemed to have been given if the decision is based on incorrect facts.

Powers of Administrative Courts Other than Quashing the Decision

When an administrative court quashes a disputed decision, under specific circumstances it may decide that the legal consequences of the annulled decision will stand, or it may settle the dispute itself rather than refer it back to the administrative authority.

In those cases in which annulling the disputed decision would have an unnecessary or undesirable impact, the administrative court may decide to allow the legal consequences of the annulled decision to stand (section 8:72, subsection 3, General Administrative Law Act). This is possible only if the legal position created by the annulled decision is in conformity with the law. The court may exercise this power for reasons of 'procedural economy', namely in situations where the applicant would not benefit from annulment of the decision, or where the annulment is based on certain formal defects in the decision while it is certain that after annulment the administrative authority would reintroduce what is in substance the same decision. Allowing the legal consequences to stand is also desirable if the decision has already had consequences in practice that cannot be undone by the annulment. In such cases, annulment of the disputed decision may nonetheless be a ground for awarding compensation for any damage suffered.

If the annulled decision must be replaced by a different decision, the administrative court may consider it appropriate in specific cases to resolve the dispute itself. For this purpose the court may decide that its judgment will replace the decision (or part of the decision) that has been annulled (section 8:72, subsection 5, General Administrative Law Act).

If the administrative court settles the dispute itself, it may do no more than the administrative authority could and should have done. It is apparent from the history of the legislation concerned that the court may, in principle, exercise the power to settle the dispute itself only if there is just one decision possible in law after the annulment. Until recently it was considered that, if the administrative authority would still have a margin of discretion after annulment of the decision, the administrative court should not settle the case itself. The basic assumption was that the court should not usurp the discretion of the administrative authority in cases where a margin of discretion still exists, but that it may settle the case where the law to be applied is formulated in such peremptory terms as to leave no margin of discretion. However, in recent case law more emphasis is put on the court's conviction, often based on what was put forward at the hearing, that the result of the outcome of the dispute would be no different if it were to be referred back to the administrative authority and that the decision is in keeping with the requirements of the law.

A decision by the administrative court to finally settle the matter may especially be the appropriate solution in cases in which the proceedings have already dragged on for many years (e.g. owing to the slowness of the decision-making procedure or the frequency of the lawsuits brought by the parties) and there is a danger that they will not be completed within a reasonable time (as required by article 6 of the European Convention for the Protection of Human Rights and Fundamental Freedoms). The court may also dispose of the case itself if the parties wish to obtain a final judgment and such disposal is a relatively simple matter for the court, because during the proceedings it has become clear what new decision the administrative authority would make. In case the dispute concerns an amount to be paid or to be paid back, after annulment of the decision the court will as a rule fix the amount itself. A final judgment by the court is also the logical course of action in cases in which it is clear that the objection must be declared inadmissible or in which it has been established that the administrative authority concerned lacked the jurisdiction to make the decision.

The administrative court will as a rule only decide to dispose of the case itself after the parties have been given the opportunity to comment on any further documents, reports and recommendations. Account should also be taken as far as possible of any interests of third parties to the dispute that may be affected by the outcome of the case.

Consequences of Quashing a Challenged Decision

A decision generally has the force of law once it has been made and entered into effect. The system of legal protection under the General Administrative Law Act is based on the possibility of quashing unlawful decisions. An administrative court can deprive a decision of the force of law only by quashing the decision or by suspending it by way of provisional remedy.

If the administrative court considers the decision to be unlawful, it holds that the application for review is well founded and quashes all or part of the challenged decision. Quashing the decision or part of the decision generally leads to the annulment of the legal consequences of that decision or the part of the decision concerned (section 8:72, subsection 2, General Administrative Law Act). In such a case the decision is treated in legal terms as if it had never existed. Quashing of the decision takes effect, in principle, retroactively (*ex tunc*): the legal consequences of the decision or the annulled part of the decision are deemed never to have taken effect. This is a direct and automatic effect of the annulment. The annulment applies *erga omnes* (in relation to everyone).

As a rule, applications for judicial review relate to decisions made by an administrative authority after an objection has been lodged. If the primary decision is not affected by the annulment of the decision on objection, it revives as a consequence of the annulment and the administrative authority has to reconsider the objection lodged against the original decision. If the court decides that the primary decision is also quashed, the administrative authority has to take a new primary decision.

The *de facto* consequences of the challenged decision must be distinguished from the legal consequences. The *de facto* consequences of the decision are not directly affected by the annulment. However, they are placed in a different legal position by the annulment, mainly because it undermines their legal basis. This may necessitate further steps on the part of the administrative authority. For example, the authority may have to undo all or part of that which has been performed in pursuance of the decision and/or take further measures (e.g. the provision of compensation).[26]

Contracts concluded under civil law for the implementation of the decision are also treated as *de facto* and not as legal consequences of the decision. This applies even if the annulled decision was made specifically with a view to the conclusion of the contract: the contract does not cease to be valid simply by virtue of the annulment of the underlying intention of the competent organ of the legal person under public law. Annulment of the decision in question will therefore not always necessarily mean that the administrative authority is no longer bound by the contract.

Sometimes further legal acts are performed under public law in pursuance of a decision. Often these acts are known as secondary decisions. These decisions too are treated as *de facto* consequences in the event of annulment of the underlying decision. When the underlying decision is annulled, the legal basis for the secondary decision also generally ceases to exist. Although this does not directly affect the existence of the secondary decision, it makes the secondary decision susceptible to annulment by the court if challenged in law. If the secondary decision has become irreversible in law, it can no longer be annulled (in any event not by the court). The secondary decision then has formal legal force and is, in principle, a given fact. If a secondary decision has been made for the benefit of a public body, this body is in certain circumstances no longer free to make use of it after the underlying decision has been annulled, even though the secondary decision still has formal legal force.

The annulled decision continues to exist as a historical given – and in certain aspects a legal fact. Such a decision can still have legal consequences, albeit different from those originally intended. Once a decision has been annulled by an administrative court, the making of the decision is deemed to have been a tort that, in principle, entails an obligation to pay compensation. The fault of the administrative authority is thus taken to be an established fact. However, this concerns only the relationship between the administrative authority and the applicant at whose request the decision has been annulled. The annulment does not establish that the annulled decision was also unlawful in relation to third parties (i.e. persons who did not exercise the right to challenge the decision in law).

Means of Ensuring that Administrative Authorities Comply with Judgments

The judgment of the court takes effect as soon as it has been pronounced in public. The purpose of the decision is to achieve a binding resolution of the dispute and ensure legal certainty for the parties. No special judicial procedure is necessary to enforce a judgment. If the judgment provides for the payment of compensation, court registry fees or other charges, it constitutes a writ of execution (section 8:76 General Administrative Law Act). Administrative authorities that are directed by an administrative court to make a fresh decision in keeping with the findings of the judgment almost invariably comply. The court may set a time limit for the fresh decision (section 8:72, subsection 5, General Administrative Law Act). If necessary and either at the request of a party or otherwise, the court may rule that, if and in so far as the administrative authority does not comply with the judgment within a certain period of time, it will owe a daily penalty to the interested party designated by the court (section 8:72, subsection 7, General Administrative Law Act). A penalty of this kind is usually imposed only as *ultimum remedium*, namely once it becomes

---

26 An example of such a measure would be a decision by an administrative authority giving a licence for the demolition of a building erected in accordance with a planning permission that was subsequently annulled; this was the case in the judgment of the Supreme Court of 28 February 1975, Woerden Parish Hall.

apparent that the administrative authority has failed to make a fresh decision or has failed to do so in time or in the correct manner, and the interested party applies for review of the failure to make the decision in time.

As a failure to make a decision in good time is equated with a decision (section 6:2 General Administrative Law Act), an objection and thereafter an application for review is possible where a decision is not given in good time by an administrative authority, whether of its own motion or otherwise.

The General Administrative Law Act was supplemented by the Penalty Payments and Judicial Review (Failure to give Timely Decisions) Act on 1 October 2009. The purpose of this legislation is to provide a more effective remedy for private parties in cases where an administrative authority is slow to make decisions. Subject to certain conditions the Act provides for the administrative authority to owe a penalty in the event of a failure to make the requested decision in good time. This penalty is owed by the authority from two weeks after the day on which the term for making the decision applied for expires, provided that the authority has received a written notice of default from the applicant. The administrative authority owes the applicant a penalty for each day that it remains in default, subject to a maximum of 42 days. The penalty is €20 a day for the first 14 days, €30 a day for the next 14 days, and €40 a day for the remaining days.

Failure to make a decision in time may result not only in the imposition of a penalty but also in an application for judicial review. Since the entry into force of the Penalty Payments and Judicial Review (Failure to give Timely Decisions) Act, there is the possibility to apply directly to the court in the event of a failure to make a decision in time. An applicant is therefore no longer required to first lodge an objection with the administrative authority against its failure to make the decision in time. The application for review can be lodged as soon as the administrative authority is in default and two weeks have expired since the date on which the interested party has given written notice of default to the administrative authority. The court decides on this application within 8 weeks (or 13 weeks if the court considers a hearing to be necessary) of receipt of the application and fulfilment of the requirements of admissibility. If the application is well founded and the authority has still not announced a decision, the court will hold that the administrative authority should make a decision within two weeks of the date on which the judgment is communicated. It will also impose an incremental penalty on the authority for every day that it fails to comply with the judgment.

Some of the Present Challenges to Administrative Jurisdiction in the Netherlands

Although, as indicated above, the Administrative Jurisdiction Division of the Council of State gives judgment in almost all cases within one year, the total administrative procedure usually takes rather long. This hampers efficient and effective administration, also in urgent cases such as construction permits in relation to regulation of traffic or protection of the water; it also creates long-lasting legal uncertainty for the private parties involved, for instance in cases concerning construction permits or alleged violations of environmental regulations. The efforts by the legislature and executive to shorten administrative procedures show an inclination to make regulations for the courts to shorten their proceedings rather than to put pressure on the administrative bodies to take their decisions within a shorter period and avoid as much as possible that the private parties involved feel the need to challenge these decisions in administrative objection and court proceedings. As a consequence, the principles of good administration of justice may come under pressure.

On the other hand, the administrative courts are becoming more and more aware of the fact that the judicial phase of the administrative procedure should bring the dispute, and consequently the total procedure, to an end as often as possible. Therefore, they try to avoid as much as possible that their finding an administrative decision to be in violation of the law, leads to sending the case back to the administrative body concerned ordering it to take a new decision, which may then lead to a second round of administrative objection proceedings and court proceedings in one or two instances. This has led the courts to find ways to give a broad interpretation and application to their power to settle the dispute concerned by taking a final decision. It may do so in those cases where it is evident which new decision the administrative body would have to take. In that way the court will end the procedure without appropriating powers that belong to the executive.

A third recent issue is that of judicial costs. In the light of the economic crisis and the necessity to cut government expenditures, efforts are made to also make the judicial system self-financing. This has led to a substantial rise of court fees for civil and administrative court proceedings. Especially, but not only, for administrative proceedings this may jeopardise certain principles of the rule of law, since judicial supervision of governmental action is not primarily in the interest of private parties who may be specifically affected, but in the interest of the legality of government. Putting up barriers that may prohibit or discourage private parties to challenge administrative decisions before the court will lead to a situation in which the system of judicial control of the legality of government becomes defective. Article 6 of the European Convention for the Protection of Human Rights and Fundamental Freedoms, which guarantees access to court for the determination of civil rights and obligations – the category that also covers most administrative proceedings – comes into play here too. At this moment, the proposals to raise the court fees are still pending before Parliament.

Chapter 7
Administrative Litigation in Germany

Arno Scherzberg and Josephine Seidl

Historical Overview

The German administrative litigation system in its modern form emerged in the second half of the nineteenth century in Baden and Prussia, alongside the establishment of the first independent administrative courts in 1863.[1] Before this period, a clear differentiation between private and public disputes did not exist and no separate review of administrative matters by courts was provided.[2] In its early stages, this 'modern form' was characterized by the separation between adjudication and administration,[3] an extended but still enumerated jurisdiction of the courts, and the guaranteeing of the equal procedural rights of citizens.[4] This shift was due to the emergence of the rule of law in the state–citizen relationship, the increasing recognition of human rights, and a growing demand to protect and legally enforce them.[5]

During the Weimar Republic, the administrative litigation law was incorporated into the Weimar Constitution of 1919 (WRV). Art. 107 WRV,[6] required the independence of judges in order to provide effective protection to citizens and effectively enforce the rule of law.[7] There was, however, an inconsistency between the legal requirement and the legal reality. The young Republic faced many hurdles with regard to the diversity of laws in the different federal states, economic and other post-war problems, and an absent consensus on views of how best to design and realize an effective administrative litigation system.[8] Thus, the judicial system in public law remained incomplete.

After 1933, the republican system was replaced by the Nazi dictatorship and the administrative litigation law became subject to their doctrine. Politically critical issues were exempt from the

1 Bundesverwaltungsgericht (BVerwG), Information and Decision – The Federal Administrative Court of Germany. URL: http://www.bverwg.de/enid/2a15c44a33b911ef4a0fc497c18b8879,0/Information_and_Decisions__EN_/The_Federal_Administrative_Court_g3.html, last visited 09.07.2012.

2 Friedhelm Hufen, *Verwaltungsprozessrecht*, 8th edn (München: Beck, 2011), § 1, para. 1 et seq.

3 At first there was only a separation on the highest court level; cf. Joachim Kronisch, in: Helge Sodan/Jan Ziekow, *Verwaltungsgerichtsordnung, Kommentar*, 3rd edn (Baden-Baden: Nomos, 2010), § 1 VwGO, Rn. 5.

4 Georg-Christoph von Unruh, Die verfassungsrechtliche Bedeutung der preußischen Verwaltungsrechtspflege, in: Hans-Uwe Erichsen/Werner Hoppe/Albert von Mutius (eds), *System des verwaltungsgerichtlichen Rechtsschutzes: FS für Christian-Friedrich Menger* (Köln: Carl Heymanns, 1985), pp. 21–34 at 23; Mahendra P. Singh, *German Administrative Law in Common Law Perspective*, 2nd edn (Berlin: Springer, 2001), p. 24.

5 Hartmut Maurer, *Allgemeines Verwaltungsrecht*, 18th edn (München: Beck, 2011), § 2, para. 5 et seq.; Singh, *supra*, n. 4 at p. 22.

6 Art. 107 WRV: 'In the Empire and in its federal states administrative courts have to be established, according to the laws, to protect the individual against bureaucratic decrees.'

7 Rolf Grawert, Verwaltungsrechtsschutz in der Weimarer Republik, in: Erichsen/Hoppe/von Mutius (eds), *supra*, n. 4 at pp. 35–55, 45.

8 Grawert, *supra*, n. 7 at p. 55.

jurisdiction of the administrative courts and the focus of their review shifted from the protection of individual rights to the enforcement of the (Nazi) laws. Evaluating the role of the administrative courts during this undemocratic period would require a detailed and differentiated analysis and cannot be provided here. The national–socialist period, however, taught Germany the lesson that a functioning litigation system can be abused and will lose its value in society if it is not based on the rule of law, the protection of individual human rights and the independence of the judiciary. It became clear that two legal elements were needed in order to secure the welfare and inner peace of society: a balance between individual rights and public interests, established by the elected representatives of the people, and a functioning and fair judicial system that ensured the realization of individual rights in practice.

In the post-war period some federal states of the new Federal Republic[9] made use of their competency to pass laws on administrative jurisdiction and re-established the principle of the separation of powers, in which the courts were made independent from any public authority.[10] On 21 January 1960 the Federal Code of Administrative Court Procedure (VwGO)[11] was passed, which unified the legal provisions for the procedure of administrative courts in all of the federal states. It still serves as the main legal basis for the present-day administrative litigation system. The VwGO established, amongst other things, a three-stage court system that regulated the composition of the courts and introduced preliminary proceedings and new legal remedies, including the enforcement action.

Contemporary Legal Embedding: Impact of European Union Law

EU law has become an indispensable component of the German legal system and it exerts an enormous influence on substantive as well as procedural law. Upon entry into the EU, all of the member states surrendered a degree of sovereignty and delegated limited legal powers to the EU in the field of legislation and administration. Consequently legal protection against acts of the EU institutions requires some attention.[12]

In the relatively few areas in which EU law is implemented by EU institutions directly, legal protection is provided by the European Courts. Their jurisdiction covers actions or omissions by the organs and legal subjects of the EU. In the case that this legal protection on the EU level should prove to be ineffective or incomplete, national courts would then possibly have to provide subsidiary protection. At the very least, this is the case in Germany, where the Federal Constitutional Court argued in its Maastricht judgment,[13] that every exercise of sovereign power within the area of the application of the German Constitution, including acts originated by the EU, is subject to the guarantees of efficient legal protection in Art. 19 para. 4 GG.[14]

---

9 Rhineland-Palatinate, Saarland, Baden-Württemberg and Berlin.

10 Kronisch, *supra*, n. 3 at § 1 VwGO, Rn. 14.

11 English translation by Neil Musset available under URL: http://www.gesetze-im-internet.de/Teilliste_translations.html, last visited 10.07.2012.

12 Friedrich Schoch, Gerichtliche Verwaltungskontrolle, in: Eberhard Schmidt-Aßmann/Wolfgang Hoffmann-Riem/Andreas Voßkuhle (eds), *Grundlagen des Verwaltungsrechts*, vol. 3 (München: Beck, 2013), § 50 para. 18.

13 BVerfGE 89, 155, 174–175.

14 The German Constitution is called Grundgesetz (GG), meaning 'Basic Law'. It is available in English under URL: http://www.gesetze-im-internet.de/Teilliste_translations.html, last visited 07.08.2012.

Mostly EU law is implemented by institutions of the member states and legal protection is provided for by the national courts. To ensure the conformity of the national legal acts with EU law in these cases, the national litigation systems are, according to the ECJ, subject to two EU requirements.[15] They are applicable as soon as the acts of national authorities serve to implement EU law or national laws, which either transpose EU legislation to the domestic level or are only influenced by it.[16]

Firstly, the national judge considering EU law has to ensure the principle of effectiveness is upheld. This means that national procedural rules applied must not render virtually impossible or excessively difficult the exercising of rights originating from EU law.[17] Secondly, the principle of equivalence demands the same level of protection for rights originating from EU law as is given to cases with a national context.[18] In case of a conflict between national law and EU law, the primacy of EU law has to be observed and national law must be secondary to this.[19] If administrative judges are uncertain about the interpretation of EU law, they are entitled – and in the case of the courts of last instance, even obliged – to initiate a preliminary ruling by the ECJ according to Art. 267 of the Treaty on the Functioning of the EU (TFEU).

As far as EU law is executed, national law, substantive as well as procedural law, must adhere to these requirements. This affects, for example, the conditions for interim relief measures ordered by the courts, the conditions of legal protection in the area of public procurement, and the requirement of standing as a condition for judicial relief, particularly in the area of environmental claims, as will be discussed later. Consequently EU law has a continually increasing influence on the national administrative litigation system, although formally administrative litigation is still under national legislative autonomy.

Fundamental Principles of Administrative Litigation Law

The judicial review of administrative actions is the most common and effective way to exercise control over the executive and establish the rule of law. However, other instruments of control are also in place: political control through the media and the public, financial and political control by parliament and the courts of auditors, as well as the supervision of the EU commission when EU law is applied.[20]

Judicial review in Germany is through the means of constitutional provisions[21] based on four main principles: the rule of law, the separation of powers, the concept of individual rights, and the guarantee of effective judicial protection.

15 ECJ judgment of 16.12.1976, Case C-33/67 (Rewe), ECR 1976, 1989, and judgment of 16.12.1976, Case C-45/76 (Comet), ECR 1976, 2043.

16 Dirk Ehlers, in: Hans-Uwe Erichsen/Dirk Ehlers (eds), *Allgemeines Verwaltungsrecht*, 14th edn (Berlin: De Gruyter, 2010), § 5 VI 1, para. 43 et seq.

17 ECJ judgment of 09.02.1999, Case C-343/96 (Dilexport), ECR 1999, I-579, para. 25.

18 Dirk Ehlers, Die Europäisierung des Verwaltungsprozessrechts, DVBl. 2004, pp. 1441–1450, at 1441.

19 ECJ judgment of 15.07.1964, Case C-6/64 (Costa/ENEL), ECR 1964, 585, at 614.

20 Gunnar Folke Schuppert, *Verwaltungswissenschaft* (Baden-Baden: Nomos, 2000), pp. 891 et seq.

21 Art. 19 para. 4, Art. 20 para. 3, Art. 28 para. 1, Art. 92 and Art. 97 GG.

The Rule of Law

The rule of law as stated in Art. 28 para. 1 (1)[22] and Art. 20 para. 3 GG[23] requires that the German State is organized, bound, and limited by law. It includes the principle of legality or the primacy of law[24] and thus is directly linked to the democratic principle, as it defines the constitution and the Acts of Parliament as the most prominent binding rules for any exercise of public power. It ensures that legal acts subordinate to the primary legislation (including federal statutory orders and by-laws[25] on the federal level as well as on the federal states' level) are authorized by primary legislation and correspond with it, and that the constitution, including the fundamental human rights stated therein and the principle of proportionality, are observed by all three powers of the state.[26] Art. 20 para. 3 GG expressly subordinates the executive to legislation and to the constitution. Art. 1 para. 3 GG defines the fundamental human rights as laid down in Art. 2–19 GG as directly enforceable law.[27] The rule of law further establishes the requirement of law for the exercise of any administrative powers; no executive act may interfere with an individual right without prior authorization by the law that not only defines the respective administrative activity but also makes it foreseeable.[28]

The hierarchy of laws in the German legal order can be illustrated by the following pyramid:

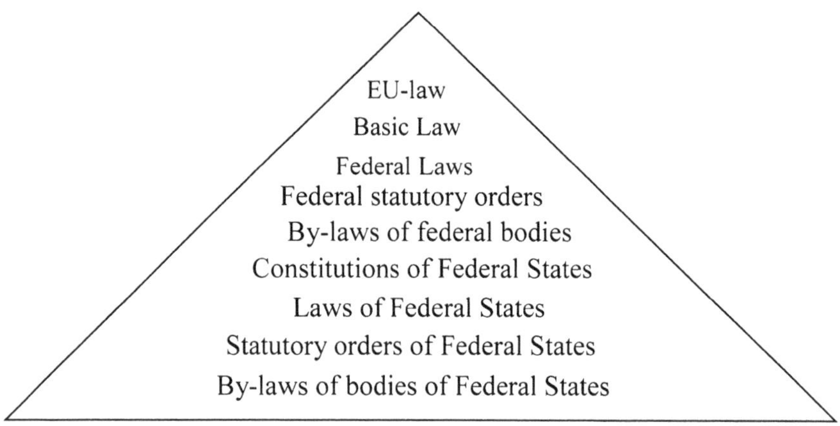

Figure 7.1 Hierarchy of Laws in the German Legal Order

22 Art. 28 para. 1 (1) GG: 'The constitutional order in the federal states (Länder) must conform to the principles of a republican, democratic and social state governed by the rule of law, within the meaning of this Basic Law.'

23 Art 20 para. 3 GG: 'The legislature shall be bound by the constitutional order, the executive and the judiciary by law and justice.'

24 Roman Herzog/Bernd Grzeszick, in: Theodor Maunz/Günter Dürig (eds), *Grundgesetz-Kommentar* (München: Beck, 2012), Art. 20, Part. VI, para. 23, 37.

25 Statutory orders are acts of delegated legislation made by the Government as a whole or by a Government Minister; by-laws are acts of delegated legislation made by autonomous administrative bodies.

26 Helmuth Schulze-Fielitz, in: Horst Dreier (ed.), *Grundgesetz Kommentar*, vol. 2, 2nd edn (Tübingen: Mohr Siebeck, 2006), Art. 20, para. 38.

27 Art. 1 para. 3 GG: 'The following basic rights shall bind the legislature, the executive and the judiciary as directly applicable law.'

28 Singh, *supra*, n. 4 at pp. 129–130.

The Separation of Powers

The separation of the three powers of the state as laid down in Art. 20 para. 2 (2) GG is an essential expression of the rule of law and requires that the legislature, executive and judiciary are separated from, and independent of each other.[29] This serves firstly to secure the rationality of the execution of powers as described in the Pershing decision of the Federal Constitutional Court.[30] The Court argued that the separation of powers supports effective and just state decisions by distributing power according to the capacities, organization and composition of the respective state organs. Secondly, it installs a system of checks and balances in order to prevent the abuse of power. Mainly the independence of the judiciary from political interference (stated in Art. 97 GG) guarantees an effective review of the executive's compliance with the law and the protection of individual freedoms.[31] The separation of powers doctrine also implies that all matters of a judicial nature, whether arising between private citizens or between the citizen and the state, or even within the public sphere, are assigned to the judiciary. Also, no judge may be a member of the executive or the legislature or take up any legislative or executive work or even act as an advisor in the legislative or administrative process.[32]

Open (but Limited) Access to the Courts

For initiating legal control through judicial litigation, unrestricted access to the courts is essential. Art. 19 para. 4 (1) GG guarantees this access to every individual and legal person in case of an alleged or potential infringement of an individual right. Thus, there are no non-justiciable rights and no executive action affecting individual rights may be exempt from jurisdiction. This is meant to secure the notion that citizens are treated as subjects and not as objects to the legal order.

As with most other instruments of legal review within administrative litigation law, the system is designed to protect individual rights.[33] Legal review, therefore, cannot be initiated on the basis of an alleged infringement of 'objective law', i.e. law that does not grant individual rights. Thus, the present concept in principle excludes associational redress, as will be shown below.

Guaranteeing Effective Judicial Protection

Art. 19 para. 4 GG finally demands the effectiveness of judicial protection. Judicial relief, including interim relief measures, cannot be refused if the legal requirements are fulfilled. The administrative court reviews questions of law as well as questions of facts and, since the inquisitorial principle is applied, is neither bound by the executive's perspective nor dependent on the evidence offered by the parties.[34] The parties have the right to a hearing and to use all legal instruments to support or defend their plea concerning both legal and factual issues. All questions relating to the legality of

29 The separation of power, however, does not imply a strict division. There are exemptions, like the convergence in the membership of the government and parliament, cf. Klaus Stern, *Staatsrecht*, vol. 2 (München: Beck, 2001), § 36, pp. 538 f.

30 BVerfGE 68, 1, 86 et seq.

31 BVerfGE 9, 268, 279–280.

32 Singh, *supra*, n. 4 at p. 190.

33 For more details, Arno Scherzberg, Individual Rights in German Public Law, p. 1, http://www.uni-erfurt.de/fileadmin/user-docs/Oeffentliches_Recht/Internetpubli/indrights_germanpubliclaw08.pdf, last visited 23.01.2013.

34 BVerfGE 15, 275, 282.

the administrative action under scrutiny, including its conformity with constitutional provisions, are within the courts' jurisdiction.[35] Legal review, however, is itself bound by the law and limited to its correct application; therefore it does not include suitability, as we shall discuss later.

Complementing the guarantee of effective judicial protection, two other constitutional provisions grant an appellant's right to be heard before a lawful judge, as laid down in Art. 101 para 1 (2) and Art. 103 para 1 GG. This right is specified amongst others in § 21e, 21f GVG, which allows for the allocation of judicial responsibilities within the courts. The schedule of responsibilities is adopted each year in advance, and is based on abstract characteristics so that there is no room for deviation within an individual case. Additional protection derives from Art. 6 ECHR, which guarantees the right to a fair trial.

The Judicial System and Composition of the Courts

The Constitutional Jurisdiction of the Federal Constitutional Court				
The 'ordinary jurisdiction' of the civil and criminal courts	The administrative jurisdiction of the administrative courts	The fiscal jurisdiction of the fiscal courts	The labour jurisdiction of the labour courts	The social jurisdiction of the social courts

Figure 7.2 The Constitutional Jurisdiction of the Federal Constitutional Court[36]

Distribution of Court Competences Between Civil and Administrative Courts

The German judicial system consists of five specialized and independent branches of the judiciary cf. Art. 95 GG; they are referred to as ordinary jurisdiction (for the civil and criminal courts), administrative jurisdiction (for the administrative courts), fiscal, labour and social jurisdiction for the respective courts. This division is meant to guarantee competent legal protection by specialized courts and judges.[37] Contrary to common law systems, the administrative courts are an integral part of the judicial branch of the state and share the judicial power.[38] Besides the five branches of the judiciary, which are of equal status,[39] there is the Federal Constitutional Court which holds final jurisdiction over constitutional questions, including the annulment of primary legislation.

The jurisdictions of the different courts are defined by law. The allocation between ordinary and public litigation is to be elucidated. Section 40 para. 1 VwGO grants access to administrative courts 'in all public law disputes of a non-constitutional nature insofar as the disputes are not explicitly allocated to another court by a federal statute.' Such an explicit exemption is provided for in § 40 para. 2 VwGO, which assigns certain claims to the civil courts, for example, property claims from

35 Singh, *supra*, n. 4 at p. 121. However, a violation of legal requirements of form or procedure does not necessarily lead to the rescission of the administrative act by the court, cf. § 46 VwVfG.

36 The chart contains a simplified model, excluding the constitutional courts of the federal states and the military and disciplinary courts.

37 Schoch, *supra*, n. 12 at para. 65.

38 Singh, *supra*, n. 4 at p. 119.

39 Disputes are solved by a Joint Panel of the Supreme Courts of the Federation.

sacrifice for the public good or compensation claims from the violation of public-law obligations that are not based on a public-law contract. This provision has led to some jurisdictional disputes between the civil and the administrative courts, since their interpretation, especially if a claim is based on culpa in contrahendo, is highly controversial.[40]

The civil court's jurisdiction is defined in § 13 Judicial System Act (GVG) as follows: 'The civil courts shall have jurisdiction over civil disputes, family matters and non-contentious matters ... as well as criminal matters for which neither the competence of administrative authorities nor the jurisdiction of the administrative courts has been established and for which no special courts have been created or permitted by provisions of federal law.'

Thus, the German system of legal protection differentiates between civil and public law disputes. According to the Joint Senate of the Supreme Federal Courts the nature of the dispute depends on the nature of the legal relationship from which the claim derives.[41] More precisely, many authors refer to the nature of the legal basis for the plaintiff's claim.[42] From both perspectives the nature of the underlying law has to be determined.[43]

In order to determine the nature of a law, several theories have been developed: the interest theory, the subordination theory and the subject theory.[44]

- According to the interest theory, a legal norm is public, when it secures public or general interests, and it is private, when it secures private or individual interests. However, the public administration also uses private law for public purposes[45] and public and private interests are also not necessarily exclusive, as can be illustrated through human rights guarantees.[46] Guaranteeing various freedoms, human dignity and property rights in a society serves the realization of private interests, but is at the same time defined by the constitution as a predominantly public concern with the state acting as an instrument for its implementation.[47]
- According to the subordination theory a legal norm is to be qualified as public, when it consists of a relationship between a superior and a subordinate. However, the theory fails to explain the principle upon which this relationship of superior and subordinate is based.[48] In a modern legal system the relationship between the citizen and the state is characterized by individual rights and limited powers of the state for intervention with such rights, not as one of superiority and subordination.[49]
- The subject theory differentiates according to the subjects of allocation, i.e. the addressees to whom rights or duties are given. Public law norms authorize or exclusively oblige holders of sovereign authority, while private law norms may authorize or oblige everyone. Although this remains the leading theory at present, it does not answer the question of whether the

40 BGH, DVBl. 1986, p. 409, 410; Ferdinand O. Kopp/Wolf-Rüdiger Schenke, *Verwaltungsgerichtsordnung Kommentar*, 18th edn (München: Beck, 2012), § 40, para. 71.

41 GmS–OGB, BGHZ 97, 312, 131–132, also confirming BVerwGE 129, 9, 10.

42 Dirk Ehlers, in: Friedrich Schoch/Jens-Peter Schneider/Wolfgang Bier (eds), *Verwaltungsgerichtsordnung* (München: Beck, 2011), § 40, para. 205 et seq.

43 Dirk Ehlers, in: Dirk Ehlers/Friedrich Schoch, *Rechtsschutz im Öffentlichen Recht* (Berlin: De Gruyter, 2009), § 21, para. 77.

44 For details cf. Ehlers, *supra*, n. 43 at § 40 para. 221–225.

45 Singh, *supra*, n. 4 at p. 8.

46 Ehlers, *supra*, n. 16 at § 3 III 2, para. 17.

47 Arno Scherzberg, in: Ehlers/Schoch (eds), *supra*, n. 43 at § 13, para. 9.

48 Singh, *supra*, n. 4 at p. 9.

49 Hufen, *supra*, n. 2 at § 11, para. 16.

legal norm addresses a public authority (and not a private legal entity, which the state is as well) and in cases of doubt needs additional criteria. However, as a rule of thumb the subject theory helps to achieve satisfactory results, although the judiciary continues to use the subordination theory.[50]

Generally speaking, public law disputes relate to the use of administrative powers, for example, in the area of public order and security, building permits, revenue matters, environmental law issues, subsidies, access to public institutions like schools and universities, and public welfare and civil service matters, while private law disputes are those relating to commercial activities of the administration and private transactions for the performance of its functions.[51]

Between Social, Financial and Administrative Courts

Public law cases can fall within the jurisdiction either of the administrative courts or of the social and financial courts according to § 1 SGG, § 1 FGO. Typical cases within the jurisdiction of the social courts are disputes relating to social and unemployment insurance, cf. § 51 SGG. The financial courts usually deal with tax disputes as stated in § 33 FGO. All other claims and disputes have to be brought before the administrative courts.

Within the Administrative Courts

Within the three levels of the administrative courts, the (lower) administrative courts (comprising 52), the higher administrative courts (consisting of 16) and the Federal Administrative Court, the lower courts generally act as courts of the first instance, unless the original jurisdiction is assigned differently, cf. § 45 VwGO. As court of the second instance, the higher administrative courts adjudicate on the right of appeal on points of fact and law against judgments of the lower courts and on the rights of complaint against their other decisions, cf. § 46 VwGO. The Federal Administrative Court is primarily a court of revision against final decisions of the higher administrative courts and in some cases also against final decisions of the lower administrative courts, cf. § 49 VwGO. Revision (appeal on points of law) is, however, only admitted as far as federal law is involved.[52] In a limited number of cases, for instance disputes aside from those of a constitutional nature between the Federation and the federal states and actions against the prohibition on associations imposed by the Federal Home Minister for Internal Affairs, the Federal Administrative Court has original jurisdiction and acts as court of the first instance.

Remedies

With regard to the administrative courts there are two categories of available remedies: 'appeal' (appeal on points of fact and law) and 'revision' (appeal on points of law). Their admissibility is finally determined by the law, thus there is no room for discretion.[53] According to § 124 para. 2 VwGO an appeal is, inter alia, to be admitted if the accuracy of a judgment is in serious doubt, if the case has special legal or factual difficulties, or if the judgment derogates from a ruling of a

50 GmS–OGB BGHZ 102, 280 (283) = NJW 1988, 2295, 2296.

51 For further details see Singh, *supra*, n. 4 at pp. 197–198.

52 Rainer Pietzner/Joachim Buchheister, in: Schoch/Schneider/Bier (eds), *supra*, n. 42 at § 132, para. 43.

53 Michael Happ, in: Erich Eyermann, VwGO, 13th edn (München: Beck, 2010), § 124, para. 6; Ingo Kraft, in: Erich Eyermann, VwGO, 13th edn (München: Beck, 2010), § 132, para. 13.

higher administrative court, the Federal Administrative Court or the Federal Constitutional Court, and is based on this derogation.

Similar restrictions apply for the admittance of a 'revision' according to § 132 para. 2 VwGO. These restrictions are meant to protect the higher courts from claims that are unlikely to succeed.[54] 'Appeal' and 'revision' serve a double purpose: on the one hand they guarantee the protection of individual rights and on the other they secure uniformity in the application of the law and allow its further development.[55] There are no privileges afforded to the administration in the course of judicial proceedings.

This system of combining two lower instances, which determine the facts and apply the law, and only one instance of legal review, has proven successful.[56] However, the excessive length of legal proceedings through the use of three instances and the excessive workload of the courts that has resulted thereof has been subject to criticism.[57] Therefore some legislative changes were passed in 1978 and 1996, which included provisions to transfer some primary competencies from the administrative courts to the higher administrative courts and to predicate the appeal on the admission by the administrative court or the higher administrative court. However, the long duration of the court proceedings still presents itself as a dilemma within the German Litigation system.

With regard to the social courts, there is a three-stage system consisting of the Social Court, the Higher Social Court and the Federal Social Court. The financial courts form a two-tiered system with the 'revision' to the Federal Fiscal Court as the only remedy (appeal on points of law cf. § 105 FGO).

Structure and Composition of the Courts

The number of lower administrative courts varies according to the size and population of the federal state in question, but only one Higher Administrative Court in each federal state exists, which helps to guarantee the uniform application of the state law. In comparison, there are many Higher Regional Courts for civil law litigation, but civil law in general is considered federal law, whereas in the field of public law, federal states law like police law or communal law is often applied.[58] Thus, the administrative courts' structure reflects the federal structure of Germany.

The administrative courts consist, like all German courts, of a president, presiding judges and regular judges. The president serves on the one hand as a judge and on the other as an organ in administering justice, exercising administrative supervision of judges and employees of the courts.[59] The administrative courts function in panels, called chambers, consisting of three professional and two honorary judges, as stated in § 5 VwGO. Each panel has a specific jurisdiction in dealing with, for example, asylum, education, public services, building permits etc. In so doing, a qualified and equal treatment of all litigants in the same category is assured. Cases that do not pose complex legal or factual questions and are of no specific public importance can be assigned to one of the professional members of the court, who will single-handedly adjudicate the case.

The higher administrative courts also work in accordance with a panel system, referred to as 'senates'. They generally consist of three professional judges. However, the law of federal states may increase the size of the senates by adding two honorary judges.

---

54 Max-Jürgen Seibert, DVBl. 1997, pp. 932–940, at 932.

55 Hermann-Josef Blanke, in: Sodan/Ziekow, *supra*, n. 3 at § 124, para. 44.

56 Kronisch, *supra*, n. 3 at § 2, para. 8.

57 Carl Hermann Ule, DVBl. 1983, pp. 440–446, at 446.

58 Kronisch, *supra*, n. 3 at § 2, para. 17.

59 Kronisch, *supra*, n. 3 at § 5, para. 6.

The Federal Administrative Court works according to the 'senate' model also. At present, the Court consists of 10 senates for general review, two senates specialized in disciplinary matters relating to the armed forces, and one senate adjudicating on disciplinary matters of the federal civil service.[60] The senates of general review consist of five professional judges, one presiding judge and four associate judges. The disciplinary senates consist of three professional judges and two honorary judges. If two senates differ in their view on a specific aspect of law, the matter is settled by an enlarged panel, called 'the grand senate', according to § 11 para. 5 VwGO. Currently, there are 59 judges working at the Court.

The social courts of first instance consist of chambers, with one professional judge as chairman and two lay judges cf. §§ 9, 12 SGG. Specific types of disputes are assigned to each of these chambers, like disputes on matters of social insurance, labour support, basic security for jobseekers, matters of social assistance or assistance to asylum seekers, disputes between health insurances and contracted medical practitioners, as well as the social compensation law and the severe disability law, cf. § 10 para. 1, 2 SGG. The courts of the second and third instance are sub-divided into senates consisting of three professional judges, including the chairman, and two honorary judges, cf. § 33 SGG.

The financial courts of the first instance are also sub-divided into senates and – as the administrative courts of the first instance – consist of three professional and two honorary judges, as long as there is no derogating provision calling for a single judge, cf. § 5 FGO. In the two-stage system of the financial courts, the second instance is the Federal Fiscal Court. It is sub-divided into senates as well, which consist of five judges, except for oral procedures in which only three judges need to be present, cf. § 10 para. 2, 3 FGO.

Conditions for Judicial Relief

The Prerequisite of an Individual Right

As stated above, Art. 19 para. 4 (1) GG guarantees legal protection of individual rights. It does, however, grant only protection *through* judges, not *against* judges. Thus, the constitutional guarantee opens access only to courts of first instance. There is no constitutional guarantee of appeal or revision.

Implementing the constitutional rule, §§ 40 et seq. VwGO govern the access to the administrative courts. According to these provisions, the existence of an individual right is a prerequisite for court access. This requirement is meant to exclude 'actio popularis' (actions based on the violation of public interests) as well as actions by parties who do not claim their own legally protected interest.[61] It also excludes actions based on political, cultural, religious or economic interests not protected by the law.

The petitioner must establish that their rights have been infringed upon by an administrative act or by its refusal or omission to act. This is laid down explicitly in § 42 para. 2 VwGO, which regulates the locus standi in case of an action for rescission and an enforcement action (action for mandamus): 'Unless otherwise provided by law, the action shall only be admissible if the plaintiff claims that his/her rights have been violated by the administrative act or its refusal or omission.' In today's understanding this prerequisite is applicable to almost all types of action in public law.[62]

60 BVerwG, *supra*, n. 1.

61 Helge Sodan, in: Sodan/Ziekow, supra, n. 3 at § 42, para. 365.

62 Thus, it also applies to the reformatory action, the action for an affirmative relief and the declaratory action. Cf. overview given by Arno Scherzberg, in: Erichsen/Ehlers (eds), *supra*, n. 16, at § 12, para. 28.

It is meant to protect the judicial system from an opening of the floodgates to claims based on political interests or personal beliefs without sufficient legal grounds. There are a few exemptions to this, which will be discussed later.

In very few cases statutory law explicitly states the existence of an individual right. In all other cases statutes require interpretation as to whether they grant individual rights or not. If, for example, the applicable procedural rules and substantive principles of planning were violated, it has to be determined whether these rules and principles grant an individual right to the person that is negatively affected by the outcome of the planning. There are competing theories on which criteria to apply. The protective rule theory[63] is most prominent in this regard. According to this theory, public law grants an individual right if legal interpretation indicates the following factors: (a) that the applicable law states that a particular obligation of the authorities exists; (b) that this obligation serves not solely the public interest, but individual ones as well; and (c) that the addressees are granted the legal power to enforce these interests against the administration.

A solely public interest, however, which is not at the same time an interest of an individual, is difficult to imagine.[64] In practice it is most difficult to decide whether a statute serves private interests or not. Because of theoretical flaws and practical problems the protective rule theory requires some modification. A suggestion would be to assume that an individual right exists if: (a) the statute seeks to protect a legal interest – the question of whether private or public is insignificant; (b) the protective nature of the statute is not accidental; and (c) certain addressees are granted the legal power to enforce such interests against the administration.[65]

This wider conception would also be in conformity with EU law, which is more generous with regard to the recognition of enforceable legal positions.[66] Consequently, the problem of defining the group of beneficiaries would be resolved.[67] At present, however, the traditional protective rule theory remains the prevailing viewpoint.

To distinguish from individual rights is the right of public authorities to solve disputes about their legal competences by claiming these competences before the courts, though notably the structure is similar to that of the individual right. This is accepted with regard to specific conflicts only. If a legal competence is infringed upon by another public authority, the conflict has to be solved in principle within the administration and if necessary by the government. Judicial relief, however, is granted if the competence in question is conferred as a defendable legal position.[68] This is the case if the disputing administrative organs serve as polar opposites in a system of checks and balances, as exists between the president of the town council and other members of this council, or the president of a university and others organs of this university like the senate or one of its faculties.

Associational Claims

Exemptions from the requirements set out in § 42 para. 2 VwGO need to be provided by an Act of Parliament. Such exceptions can be seen in § 61 BNatSchG (Federal Nature Conservation Act) and § 2 UmwRG (Environmental Appeals Act), which establish associational claims in the area

63 BVerfGE 27, 297, 307.

64 Scherzberg, *supra*, n. 33 at p. 3.

65 Scherzberg, *supra*, n. 33 at p. 3.

66 ECJ judgment of 05.04.1979, Case C-148/78 (Ratti), ECR 1979, 1629.

67 Schoch, *supra*, n. 12 at para. 138 ff.

68 Hans-Uwe Erichsen, Der Innenrechtsstreit, in: Erichsen/Hoppe/von Mutius (eds), *supra*, n. 4 at pp. 211 ff.

of environmental law. The UmwRG was meant to implement an EU Directive,[69] which itself serves to fulfil the EU's obligations of the Aarhus Convention.[70] The aim of the EU Directive is 'to preserve, secure, and improve the quality of the environment, as well as safeguarding human health, by facilitating and further extending public participation – in particular that of associations – and legal protection.'[71] Associational claims in national law were supposed to give access to the courts without requiring an infringement of an individual right.[72] Thus, the UmwRG entitles environmental associations to take action against breaches of environmental law by means of appeal from a purely environmental perspective.[73] In order to be able to file an appeal under the UmwRG, the environmental associations need to be recognized by the Federal Environment Agency. In order to obtain such recognition, the environmental association inter alia has to predominantly and not just temporarily encourage the objectives of environmental protection, be in existence for at last three years, offer guaranties of full performance of its duties, and allow any person who supports the objectives of the association to become a member with full voting rights in its general meetings.

In order to uphold the German system of administrative litigation law, where all actions are meant to protect and enforce individual rights, § 2 para. 1 no. 1 UmwRG in its original version restricted judicial review to legal norms that, even if the environmental organization did not need to claim a violation of their own rights, did in general protect individual rights. Consequently, access to the courts depends on the existence of another person's individual rights, which leads to circumventing the meaning of the associational claim. The criticisms in legal literature surround the issue that § 2 UmwRG would not be compatible with the EU Directive and the Aarhus Convention;[74] this was recently confirmed by the ECJ in the Trianel judgment of 2011.[75] The ECJ concluded that, although the member states have discretion on how to transform the procedural modalities of the directive into national law, they are bound by the principle of effectiveness as mentioned above, and may not render the exercise of EU-given rights difficult or impossible.[76] Thus, a violation of certain environmental provisions that originate in EU law may be claimed by environmental organizations regardless of whether German law perceives them as a protection of individual rights.[77] Consequently, the respective provision of § 2 UmwRG violates the primacy of the application of EU law and has been forced to be revised in its entirety. Since 2013 a new version of § 2 UmwRG is in force which no longer refers to the protection of individual rights.

69 Directive 2003/35/EG of 26.05.2003 on providing for public participation in respect of the drawing up of certain plans and programs relating to the environment and amending with regard to public participation and access to justice Council Directives 85/337/EEC and 96/61/EC.

70 Aarhus Convention on access to information, public participation in decision-making and access to justice in environmental matters of 25.06.1998; cf., http://www.umweltbundesamt.de/umweltrecht-e/verbandsklage/index.htm, last visited 08.08.2012.

71 Federal Environmental Agency, Greater rights on the part of environmental associations to file collective legal actions, cf., http://www.umweltbundesamt.de/umweltrecht-e/verbandsklage/index.htm, last visited 08.08.2012.

72 Schoch, *supra*, n. 12 at para. 175.

73 Federal Environmental Agency, supra, n. 71.

74 Schoch, *supra*, n. 12 at para. 180.

75 ECJ judgment of 12.05 2011, Case. C-115/09 (BUND v. Bezirksregierung Arnsberg), ECR 2011, para. 46ff.

76 ECJ judgment, *supra*, n. 26 at para. 25.

77 ECJ judgment, *supra*, n. 106.

Choosing the Right Action

The appropriate court action to be brought forward is dependent on the disputed administration's legal activity and the legal remedy sought. If the wrong action is chosen, the plaintiff will be given the opportunity to correct his claim within a specified period of time. There are:

1. statutory orders, legal rules issued by a government or administrative body, subordinate to a law, which explicitly entitles the administrative body to issue the ordinance;
2. by-laws, legal rules issued by public bodies with the right of self-organization, for example by-laws of communes, universities or public broadcasting corporations;[78]
3. administrative acts;
4. public law contracts;
5. administrative acts of fact; and
6. internal administrative regulations.

No legal remedy is provided against internal administrative regulations as these are directives within the administration that guarantee the uniformity of the application of the law; for example, in cases concerning discretionary powers. These regulations in general lack direct binding force.

Administrative acts cf. § 35 VwVfG (Administrative Proceedings Act), public administrative acts of fact and public law contracts fall within the jurisdiction of the (lower) administrative courts as courts of first instance. Administrative acts can be brought before courts through an action for rescission as well as an enforcement action cf. § 42 para. 1 VwGO. For public administrative acts concerning facts and public contracts, the correct action to be brought forward would be an action of affirmative relief, an application for an injunction or a declaratory action, depending on the plaintiff's claim.

The review of secondary legislation (statutory orders and by-laws) falls within the jurisdiction of the higher administrative courts as courts of first instance; the legal remedy is referred to as the review of legal provisions, cf. § 47 VwGO. However, the access to this review is limited. It is permitted for by-laws and certain statutory orders, issued in accordance with the provisions of the Federal Building Code, and depends, for all other acts of secondary legislation, on a specific admission by the law of the federal states. Thus, in many cases by-laws and statutory orders are excluded from the legal remedy of § 47 VwGO.[79] There are two ways to avoid a gap in legal protection. If acts of secondary legislation are implemented by an administrative act or an administrative act of fact, judicial review of the implementing act will encompass the legality of the secondary norm as its legal basis. For cases in which no implementation is necessary, the Federal Administrative Court accepts the action of affirmative relief as an appropriate instrument to open access to an effective judicial review.[80]

Exhausting Administrative Remedies

Prior to lodging an action for rescission or an enforcement action, the lawfulness and expedience of the respective administrative act – or the rejection of the motion to adopt it – has to be regularly reviewed in preliminary administrative proceedings, cf. § 68 para. 1 (1) VwGO. According to § 68

78 Maurer, *supra*, n. 5 at § 4, para. 24.

79 Markus Möstl, Normative Handlungsformen, in: Erichsen/Ehlers, *supra*, n. 16 at § 19, para. 36.

80 BVerwGE 111, 276, 278.

para. 1 (2) VwGO such a review is not required, 'if a statute so determines, or if the administrative act has been handed down by a supreme federal authority or by a supreme *federal state* authority, unless a statute prescribes the review, or the remedial notice or the ruling on an objection contains a grievance for the first time'. In recent years, despite severe criticism by many academics,[81] several exemptions to this requirement have been made in the law of federal states in order to hasten the litigation process. Furthermore, an enforcement action is admissible in derogating from § 68 if an application to carry out an administrative act has without sufficient reason not been decided on merits within three months of the filing of the application, cf. § 75 VwGO.

If applicable, the administrative remedy is sought by filing an objection, which 'shall be lodged in writing within one month after the administrative act has been announced to the aggrieved party', cf. § 70 para. 1 (1) VwGO. If the time limit is not observed, the action is not admissible. Exceptions are only made if the plaintiff was unable to adhere to a statutory deadline without due fault.

In the preliminary proceedings, the administrative authority has the duty to review their decision in accordance with the lawfulness and the expedience as stated in § 68 para. 1 (1) VwGO. As a result, the administrative authority may remedy the objection or uphold its decision. In the latter case, the plaintiff is entitled to approach the court by filing an action in writing.

Deadline Period

Certain actions must be filed within certain time constraints. For an action for rescission and the enforcement action, the deadline period is one month from the date of notice of the contested decision. It will extend to one year if the decision does not correctly state the legal remedy, the court with which such remedy lies, or the deadline period. For other kinds of actions, the estoppel by laches doctrine applies.

If the time limit expires without filing an action, the administrative act is final and conclusive. The delay may, however, be condoned by the court if it occurred to no fault of the plaintiff. Furthermore, the aggrieved individual may apply for a reopening of the administrative proceedings, cf. § 51 VwVfG, or a revocation or withdrawal of the administrative act, cf. §§ 48, 49 VwVfG.

Legitimate Interest in Bringing Proceedings

All applicants require a legitimate interest in bringing proceedings before a court. This unwritten principle is intended to protect the courts against abusive actions. If the conditions for judicial relief (as mentioned above) are fulfilled, the plaintiff in principle has a sufficient legal interest in bringing proceedings. However, this does not apply in a few cases,[82] namely if the aim of the plaintiff can be achieved in an easier, quicker, more extensive or cheaper way,[83] or if suing the administration would not improve the plaintiff's situation. However, the uselessness of the respective action has to be demonstrated convincingly.[84] The administrative authorities have no legitimate interest in bringing proceedings in the role of a plaintiff, as long as they are able to achieve their aim through a unilateral measure, for example with an administrative act.[85]

81 Overview given by Klaus-Peter Dolde/Winfried Porsch, in: Schoch/Schneider/Bier (eds), *supra*, n. 42 at Vorbemerkung § 68, para. 16.

82 See further Ehlers, *supra*, n. 43 at § 21, para. 185 ff.

83 BGHZ 55, 201, 206.

84 BVerwGE 121, 1, 1.

85 OVG Hamburg NJW 1989, 605, 605.

Legal Assistance and the Associated Costs

An important aspect of effective legal protection is providing legal assistance, mostly by a lawyer who helps the plaintiff to understand the applicable law and takes the appropriate measures in the court procedure. If the plaintiff is unable to afford legal assistance, the state is – as a result of the guarantee of effective legal protection in Art. 19 para. 4 GG – under certain circumstances obliged to provide this legal aid.

In this respect, for administrative litigation law the same rules apply as in civil law litigation according to the Code of Civil procedure (ZPO). Legal aid in Germany comprises financial support for the costs of the trial, cf. §§ 115–127 ZPO, and for the assignment of a lawyer, cf. § 121 ZPO. In public law litigation, a lawyer is not mandatory in first instance claims. However, the applicant may choose to be represented by one and therefore may apply for legal aid. Legal assistance is granted if there is a sufficient prospect of success and the plaintiff is unable to pay the fees due to their economic situation.[86] Thus, the applicant's proposition must be reasonable and proof to a certain degree must seem possible.[87] Given the need to provide effective legal protection under Art. 19 para. 4 GG, the barriers for gaining legal aid for deprived citizens are not supposed to be high.[88]

Interim Relief

Timing is of paramount importance in achieving effective legal protection. Therefore legal protection has to be provided within an appropriate period of time[89] and needs to include interim relief measures in order to protect the plaintiff from 'fait accompli' before the final verdict of the court is given.[90] Interim relief is governed by § 80 VwGO in case of an action for rescission, by § 47 para. 6 VwGO for reviews of legal provisions and by § 123 VwGO in all other cases.

According to § 80 para. 1 VwGO, an objection or an action for rescission against an administrative act may potentially lead to the suspension of the act in question. Exceptions to this rule do apply, cf. § 80 para. 2 VwGO, if the administrative act demands the payment of public charges, refers to urgent police measures, or if the suspensive effect is abolished by federal law or the law of the federal states, in particular for objections and actions on the part of third parties against administrative acts relating to investments or the creation of jobs. Moreover, the administrative authority, which has issued the administrative act or has to decide on the objection, has the power to order the immediate execution of the administrative act in the public interest or in the overriding interest of a party concerned. In all of these cases addressed in § 80 para. 2 VwGO interim relief can be applied for at the administrative court dealing with the main case, and will be granted if – in short – the public interest to immediately enforce an administrative decision does not outweigh the interest of the plaintiff to avoid a 'fait accompli'.[91]

For all other types of action, apart from the reviews of legal provisions, § 123 VwGO applies and interim relief will be granted by the court if there is a danger that, through changes in the existing conditions, the realization of a right of the plaintiff would be prevented or considerably

---

86 Georg Herbert, Administrative Justice in Europe: Report for Germany, p. 9, URL: http://www.aca-europe.eu/seminars/Trier2005/Allemagne_en.pdf, last visited 23.01.2013.

87 BGH NJW 1994, 1160, 1161.

88 BVerfG, NJW 2000, 1936, 1937.

89 BVerfG, NJW 2001, 3770, 3770.

90 Overview given by Singh, *supra*, n. 4 at p. 237 ff.

91 BVerfGE 35, 263, 274.

impeded upon. The court will issue an interlocutory order if the interests of the plaintiff outweigh the public interest in question, as long as the interlocutory order would not forestall the decision with regard to the main dispute.

The Administrative Court Procedure

The court procedure begins with the filing of an action in writing, which requires the identification of the plaintiff, the defendant, the subject-matter of what is at stake in the action, the specific motion, the facts and evidence serving as reasoning, the original or a duplicate of the impugned order, and the ruling on an objection as stated in § 82 VwGO. In case the court lacks territorial or substantive jurisdiction, the onus would be on the petitioner to refer it to the appropriate court.

If the facts are undisputed and the case does not involve any intricate factual or legal question, the court may decide by a decree after hearing the parties. In most cases, however, the court conducts oral proceedings after the exchange of submissions of the plaintiff and the defendant. The oral proceedings are direct in the sense that they are generally conducted by the deciding court itself, and they are usually open to the public.[92] Both parties have the right to present their legal viewpoint and the supporting facts, and the evidence is discussed and recorded.

In three of the sixteen federal states (Thuringia, Bavaria and Rhineland-Palatinate) a representative of public interest is appointed for each administrative court and a representative of the interests of the Federation is appointed at the Federal Administrative Court. They have to be informed of all the cases pending before their respective court and may decide to be present in the proceedings. Their role is to foster the proceedings with factual and legal statements, protect the public interests involved and guarantee, as far as is possible, relief for all parties involved.[93]

The representative is not an independent institution, but subject to directives of the respective government. This is why their role is reviewed critically today.[94] The representatives may lack a neutral and objective position. Their competences, however, are limited and do not exceed the competences of other parties.[95] Since the inquisitorial principle applies, the responsibility to investigate the truth lies fully upon the court. It is not bound by the pleadings and evidence presented either by the parties[96] or the representatives and is obliged to clarify relevant facts even without offers of proof by the participants.[97] The proceedings, as such, stand at the disposal of the parties and can be terminated by a withdrawal of the action by the plaintiff at any time.

There is no statutory rule that gives one category of evidence superiority over another. Therefore the evaluation of evidence by the courts is unrestrained. The court decides according to its conviction, which is formed by the overall result of the proceedings.[98] However, the judgment must be based only on facts and evidence that were the subject-matter of the proceedings and on which the parties had the opportunity to express themselves; they must not deviate from this.

---

92 For an overview of the procedure see BVerwG, *supra*, n. 1; Singh, *supra*, n. 4 at p. 226.

93 Ferdinand Kopp, Der Vertreter des öffentlichen Interesses in der Verwaltungsgerichtsbarkeit, DVBl. 1982, 277, 282.

94 Sabine Schlacke, *Überindividueller Rechtsschutz* (Tübingen: Mohr Siebeck, 2008), p. 116 ff.

95 Michael Gerhardt/Susanne Olbertz, in: Schoch/Schneider/Bier (eds), *supra*, n. 42, § 35, para. 15.

96 Singh, *supra*, n. 4 at p. 223.

97 Eberhard Schmidt-Aßmann, *Das Allgemeine Verwaltungsrecht als Ordnungsidee*, 2nd edn (Berlin: Springer, 2004), chapter 4, para. 63; Herbert, *supra*, n. 86 at p. 9.

98 BVerwG, *supra*, n. 1.

Legal Review Criteria and Extent of Judicial Review

The administrative courts' authority to adjudicate is regulated in §§ 113–115 VwGO. According to these provisions a claim is successful if the administrative act was unlawful and the plaintiff's rights therefore were violated. Thus, the courts are empowered to examine the legality of administrative acts as far as the violation of an individual right is at stake. Matters of policy and their execution as well as the expedience of the administrative action, however, belong to the domain of the executive and remain outside of the scope of judicial review.[99]

In general, the courts have the last word in defining the relevant legal provisions, ascertaining the facts and applying the law to the respective case.[100] However, if the applicable law leaves a margin of discretion to the administrative authorities, or in certain cases where legal terms are left vague, the judicial review is limited.

In a legal order based on the rule of law, discretion cannot mean arbitrariness.[101] Discretion is legally bound and to be exercised only for the purpose for which it is granted.[102] Within these limits, however, it provides the administration with room for manoeuvre on how to assess, evaluate and balance the individual and public interests in question and decide accordingly. These elements of the decision are exempt from the court's review.

If the administration is authorized to act at its discretion, courts have to examine 'whether the administrative act or its refusal or omission is unlawful for the reason that the statutory limits of its discretion have been exceeded or the discretion has not been used in accordance with the purpose of authorization.' Despite this wording of § 114 VwGO, any illegality of a discretionary action falls under the review of the courts. This entails the following aspects.

Failure to Use Discretion

If discretion is granted by the law, exercising it is obligatory. The court will rescind an administrative act if the authorities failed to exercise discretion completely or partially, for example by deciding cases of a particular class in a fixed manner without regarding exceptional circumstances of the individual case.[103] This does not prevent the authorities from laying down administrative regulations for the exercise of discretion or observing a definite administrative practice as long as exceptional circumstances are considered.

Abuse of Discretion

An abuse is characterized by an intentional or mistaken lack of an observance of the internal legal limits set for the exercise of discretion.[104] For example, discretion may not be exercised for an illegal purpose, according to personal preferences of the deciding public official, or in an inconsistent way, so that the result is not justified by the considerations on which it is based.

---

99 Schoch, *supra*, n. 12 at para. 253; Singh, *supra*, n. 4, pp. 133–134.

100 Schmidt-Aßmann, *supra*, n. 97 at chapter 4, para. 62.

101 Singh, *supra*, n. 4 at p. 151; Schoch, *supra*, n. 12 at para. 270; Michael Gerhardt, in: Schoch/Schneider/Bier (eds), *supra*, n. 42, Vorbemerkung § 113, para. 20.

102 Schoch, *supra*, n. 12 at para. 270.

103 Singh, *supra*, n. 4 at p. 157.

104 Singh, *supra*, n. 4 at p. 155.

Excess Discretion

Here the limits of discretion are not respected, equivalent to an 'ultra vires' exercise of power in common law.[105] Limits of discretion are set not only by the law authorizing it, but can also derive from constitutional provisions, mainly fundamental human rights, including the right to equality, and the principle of proportionality as the overriding rule of all state activities towards its citizens. The right to equal treatment, for example, can be violated if an administrative action deviates without sufficient reasoning from a consistently observed and legal administrative practice or an administrative regulation anticipating such a practice. According to the principle of proportionality interferences in fundamental rights, for example individual freedoms and property rights, are only admissible if, (a) the authorities choose an effective means to achieve a certain purpose; (b) this purpose is legitimate, which means in accordance with the law; (c) out of several effective measures to achieve this end the least restrictive to individual rights is chosen; and (d) the impairment of the individual rights at stake is not disproportionate to the designated ends. In this respect, the courts interfere with the administrative decision only in clear cases of disproportionality.

The right to equality and the proportional principle can limit the discretionary power so that in the case in question only one course of action may be legal.[106] This is part of the court's review. Thus, it includes the question of whether a measure taken by the administration was effective, but not the question of whether alternatives would have been more appropriate.[107]

Closely related to the review of discretion is the review of vague or indefinite legal terms. These terms like 'public interest', 'public order', 'urgency', 'reliability' or 'reasonable likelihood' as well as a 'serious reason' or an 'artistic value' are commonly used in statutes conferring powers upon the administration. They are, however, formulated in an abstract way and need operationalization in order to be applied in a specific situation. The Federal Constitutional Court and the Federal Administrative Court stated that the interpretation and application of such terms, even though they may imply value judgments, generally fall within the jurisdiction of the courts.[108] A full legal review is obligatory.[109] Exemptions are made if vague legal terms are used to implicitly provide a margin of appreciation for the administrative authority.[110] In this case, the courts may examine only whether this line has been crossed. If such a margin is not expressed explicitly, the respective law has to be interpreted as to whether or not it is provided.[111] However, Art. 19 para. 4 GG limits the acceptability of administrative margins of judgment to exceptional cases in which an unlimited legal review appears unfeasible or unreasonable, because of the courts' lack of expertise. Examples are the evaluation of performances in exams or in the preparation of the promotion of a civil servant, and value judgments that are assigned to plurally composed and independent committees of experts.[112]

---

105 Singh, *supra*, n. 4 at p. 155.

106 Singh, *supra*, n. 4 at p. 158.

107 Gerhardt/Olbertz, *supra*, n. 95, § 114, para. 9.

108 BVerfGE 84, 34; BVerwGE 35, 69, 74.

109 BVerfGE 64, 261, 279.

110 BVerfGE 61, 82, 111.

111 BVerfG NVwZ 2011, 1062, 1065.

112 Andreas Decker, in: Herbert Posser/Heinrich Amadeus Wolff, *Beckscher Online Kommentar-VwGO*, 2012, § 114, para. 36.

Final Court Decisions

In cases of an action for rescission, the unlawful infringement of an individual right leads to the annulment of that administrative act. In cases of an enforcement action, the court announces the obligation incumbent on the administrative authority to take effect of the requested act if the case is mature for adjudication. It is not mature for adjudication if a margin of appreciation lies with the administration. In this case, the court announces the administration's obligation to notify the plaintiff, taking the legal view of the court into consideration.

The final judgment is binding and becomes res judicata if the appeal is not admitted or the time limit for appeal of one month after service of the complete judgment has expired.

In 2011, out of the 37,100 cases brought before the administrative courts (which were not declared settled or where the action was not withdrawn), 28,149 (76 per cent) were won by the public authorities, 6,189 (17 per cent) were won by private parties, and 2,762 (7 per cent) were divided. It may also be of interest to note that about 14 per cent of all disputes before the administrative courts concern the right of asylum, 13 per cent taxes and duties, 12 per cent questions of public security and environmental protection, 10 per cent civil service law, 9 per cent questions of foreign nationals, and 9 per cent social legislation.[113]

Mediation

Mediation as an alternative form of dispute settlement is a well-discussed issue in Germany, not least because it might relieve the overburdened judiciary. In a litigation system that focuses primarily on the realization of individual rights, mediation can find a rightful place because it may – as long as there is no pressure on the plaintiff to consent – provide a rapid way to satisfy the individual's interests. Further positive effects of mediation are a shorter duration of the litigation process and a more appropriate and sustainable result, based on a deeper interaction between the parties.[114] After years of discussion and different model projects on the level of the federal states, the Federal Mediation Law was passed in 2012.[115] The VwGO has been amended accordingly.[116]

The Mediation Law differentiates between judicial and extrajudicial mediation. Judicial mediation is performed by a judge, who is not in charge of the initiated court case, whereas external mediation is performed by a qualified mediator.[117] The new Mediation Law requires legal standards for the education and supervision of external mediators in order to guarantee the effectiveness of their work. These standards have to be developed by the Ministry of Justice.

Mediation in the new law is understood as a voluntary procedure initiated by the concerned parties and carried out by an independent third party (mediator or judge). According to § 1 para. 1

113 Statistisches Bundesamt URL: https://www.destatis.de/DE/Publikationen/Thematisch/Rechtspflege/GerichtePersonal/Verwaltungsgerichte2100240117004.pdf?__blob=publicationFile, last visit 05.01.2013.

114 Rainer Pitschas, Verwaltungsrechtsschutz durch Gerichtsmediatoren?, in: Rainer Pitschas/Harald Walther (eds), *Mediation in der Verwaltungsgerichtsbarkeit*, Speyerer Arbeitsheft Nr. 173, 2005, pp. 33–42, at 33.

115 Law published in German under URL: http://www.gesetze-im-internet.de/mediationsg/BJNR157710012.html, last visited 07.08.2012.

116 § 173 VwGO now refers to the new §§ 278, 278a Civil Court Procedure Act (ZPO).

117 Providing both options allowed the different model projects to be continued, using judges as mediators in court trials since 2004; Harald Walther, Mediation in der Verwaltungsgerichtsbarkeit – Eine Einführung in die Speyerer Mediationsinitiative, in: Pitschas/Walther (eds), *supra*, n. 114, pp. 1–18, at 13 ff.

of the Mediation Law, the aim of the procedure is to solve a conflict by mutual agreement. The mediator leads the parties through the procedure. He assists the parties in their communication, helps them to define existing problems and conflicting interests, and fixes the result of the mediation in cases where an agreement can be met.[118]

Difficulties may arise with regard to the legal quality of the agreement achieved. A court's judgment after regular proceedings would be legally binding. The same applies to a settlement of the case for the record of the court. Such a settlement is to be qualified as a public contract, legally binding for both parties, which pivotally makes its execution possible.

The agreement at the end of a judicial or extrajudicial mediation, however, will usually not be intended as a binding public contract.[119] In many cases the administration needs flexibility to implement the agreed solution, for example, for the routing of a road, in an appropriate legal form, and this may require preceding administrative procedures and will require full compliance with the relevant substantive law. Especially in planning matters an advance commitment of the administrative bodies, before the final assessment and balancing of all interests, can be illegal.[120] Thus, in most cases the binding nature on the parties, especially on the administration, is merely factual.[121]

Deficits and Challenges of the German System

Several difficulties and limitations of the present German system of administrative litigation law are discussed amongst lawyers and legal academics, and in court rulings.

The Requirement of the Infringement of an Individual Right

As noted above, for a legal action to be admitted the petitioner has to establish that his individual right has been infringed upon by the administrative decision or action in question. Thus, in many cases of objective infringements of the legal order by the executive, legal review cannot be successfully initiated.[122] Consequently, a violation of collective interests like the protection of the environment or other legal objectives cannot be brought before the courts and the adequate balance of conflicting public and individual interests cannot be fully guaranteed.[123] This problem is not completely solved by the proposed revision of the protective-rule theory and the revision of the provisions on associational claims in the area of environmental law, as required by the Trianel judgment of the ECJ. Thus, further considerations are needed in this regard.

The Predominance of Substantive Law over Procedural Law

Due to provisions in the procedural law (§ 44a VwGO and § 46 VwVfG), the judicial protection of individual rights is in principle confined to substantive rights and excludes procedural rights. This reflects the serving function of procedural law, but also limits the legal review as far as compliance

118 Hufen, *supra*, n. 2 at § 3, para. 13.

119 Hermann Pünder, in: Hans-Uwe Erichsen/Dirk Ehlers, Allgemeines Verwaltungsrecht, 14th edn, 2010, § 16 III 1, para. 14.

120 BVerwGE 45, 309, 321.

121 Pünder, *supra*, n. 119 at § 16 III 1, para. 15.

122 Schoch, *supra*, n. 12 at para. 6.

123 Schoch, *supra*, n. 12 at para. 7.

with procedural law is concerned. The Administrative Proceedings Act allows the rectification of certain procedural errors, even during the judicial proceedings. According to § 46 VwVfG, remaining procedural errors are irrelevant as long as they did not obviously influence the contested decision.

Thus, an action for rescission based on illegal administrative proceedings is only successful if the procedural mistake is not rectified and it appears possible in the respective case that, in line with the due process, the administrative act would have been more favourable towards the plaintiff. Although in theory the burden of proof for the latter lies with the authorities, the courts frequently conclude that the decision is not influenced by the procedural error so the authorities in practice rarely bear the risk of their procedural malpractice.[124]

Incompatibilities with EU Law

In certain cases EU law that protects collective interests requires the admission of claims even without appropriate standing if the petitioner is affected by the infringement. In the Wells case, the ECJ ruled that § 46 VwVfG may not be applied if the procedural error relates to the EU requirement of an environmental impact assessment.[125] This, in a similar way to the Trianel judgment, highlights the constant challenge of how to properly integrate the specific instruments and requirements of EU law into the German system of administrative litigation law.

In the area of interim measures, the same difficulties arise.[126] Interim measures are meant to provide effective legal protection by preventing the citizens from fait accompli. The ECJ required in its Factortame decision,[127] that the member states provide interim measures against national laws violating EU law, even if the respective national law, like the British law in question, does not provide interim measures against the state. In German administrative law, interim measures are permitted by §§ 80, 123 VwGO. According to § 80 VwGO, objections and actions for rescission against an administrative act have a suspensive effect. If this act served to implement EU law, the suspension, however, would hamper the effective realization and the uniformity of the implementation of EU law in the member states. In the Tafelwein decision the ECJ therefore demanded the member states to override the suspense effect by an order of immediate execution in the public interest by the authority that issued the administrative act, referring to the principle of effective implementation of EU law as the relevant public interest.[128]

Duration of Court Procedures

Furthermore, the extensive duration of German court procedures demands a specific mention.[129] A decision of a court of the first instance takes an average of 11 months, while in the second instance an average of 10 months.[130] This endangers the efficiency of the legal protection as guaranteed

124 Schoch, *supra*, n. 12 at para. 303.

125 ECJ judgment of 07.01.2004, Case C-201/02 (Wells), ECR 2004, I-723, para. 70.

126 Thorsten Finger, Der Zugang zur deutschen Verwaltungsgerichtsbarkeit unter gemeinschaftsrechtlichem Einfluss, JA 2005, pp. 228–232, at 231.

127 ECJ judgment of 19.06.1990, Case C-213/89 (Factortame I), ECR 1990, I-2433 et seq.

128 ECJ judgment of 10.07.1990, Case C-217/88 (Tafelwein), ECR 1990, I-2879 et seq.

129 Ehlers, *supra*, n. 18 at p. 1447; Eberhard Schmidt-Aßmann, in: Maunz/Dürig (eds), *supra*, n. 24 at Art. 19, Part. IV, para. 262.

130 Statistisches Bundesamt, Publikationen im Bereich Gerichte/Personal, URL: https://www.destatis.de/DE/Publikationen/Thematisch/Rechtspflege/GerichtePersonal/Verwaltungsgerichte2100240117004.pdf?__blob=publicationFile, last visit 03.01.2012.

in Art. 19 para. IV GG. The duration of the court procedures has been the subject-matter of many cases before the Federal Constitutional Court and the European Court of Human Rights (ECHR).[131] The European Court referred to Art. 6 ECHR, which guarantees a decision 'within a reasonable time'.[132] This provision, however, is difficult to apply. The adequate span of time for court procedures depends mainly on the special circumstances of each individual case, which includes the complexity of the matter, the strategies of the lawyers, and the availability of judicial personnel at the courts.

In a 2010 judgment the ECHR addressed the extensive duration of court procedures in Germany and required changes to be made before December 2011.[133] As a response the German Parliament passed a law in order to provide protection against the long duration of procedures.[134] As a first step, the plaintiff if unsatisfied by the delays, would need to inform the court by a reprimand of delay that in his/her opinion the court's work is too slow. If there is no acceleration of the procedure, in a second step the plaintiff can raise a claim for compensation. This compensation amounts to €1,200 per year for immaterial damage in case compensation in other ways is not possible. Besides this, compensation can also be demanded for material damages, as for example in cases involving insolvency, if the material damage is caused by the delay. A loss of profit cannot be claimed. However, claims arising from the liability of public authorities can be filed beside the claim for compensation.

Conclusion

From the last quarter of the nineteenth century, a separate administrative litigation system has evolved in Germany. This has followed the emergence of the rule of law in the state–citizen relationship and the growing demand to protect and legally enforce the rights of the individual against the power of the state.

Today's administrative litigation system is based on more than 50 years of practical experience and the judicial elaboration of the Code of Administrative Court Procedure (VwGO). It is governed by constitutional principles that guarantee an effective review of administrative activities towards the individual. It does not, however, secure a complete legal review of the administration's compliance with the law, leaving a gap as far as the violation of collective interests is concerned, for example in regard to the protection of the environment.

Despite this problem and other aforementioned limitations, in the last 50 years of operationalization in judicial practice the German administrative litigation system has reached a high standard of legal protection of the citizen from arbitrary or unlawful state actions. Thus it plays a decisive role in the realization of the rule of law in Germany.

131 ECHR decision of 10.03.1980, Case 6232/73 (König vs Germany), Series A Nr. 27; BVerfGE 46, 14, 17 f.; BVerfGK decision of 06.06.01 – 2 BvR 828/01.

132 Eberhard Schmidt-Aßmann, in: Schoch/Schneider/Bier (eds), *supra*, n. 42, Einleitung, para. 141.

133 ECHR decision of 02.09.2010, Case 46344/06 (Rumpf vs. Germany). EuGRZ 2010, 700 et seq.

134 Cf. BGBl. I Nr. 60 of 2/12/2011, p. 2302.

Chapter 8
Administrative Litigation in England and Wales

Andrew Le Sueur

Introduction

This chapter is a concise account of administrative litigation in England and Wales. It charts the historical development of legal challenges to government actions as well as considering current problems. It is written as a point of reference for comparison with other legal systems, so four contextual characteristics are needed from the outset.

A Common Law System in a European Context

Firstly, administrative law in England and Wales is shaped by different legal orders: it is simultaneously both a common law jurisdiction (sharing similarities with other common law systems such as Australia, Canada and New Zealand) and 'European' (influenced over the past 40 years by legal modes of thought and practice from the European Union and the European Convention on Human Rights).

In a common law system, judges, rather than the legislature, have led the development of principles of administrative legality and the remedies available. There is no codified statement of administrative law or judicial review. Instead, one must look to the voluminous reported case law that has emerged from the courts, numerous Acts of Parliament on particular aspects of administrative law, and academic analysis and commentary. Rules and principles emerge, as a by-product, from particular concrete disputes that are brought before the courts. We have the principle of *Wednesbury* unreasonableness (discussed below) because a cinema company challenged a particular decision of a local authority of a town near Birmingham.[1] We have a principle of substantive legitimate expectation because a severely disabled woman, Miss Coughlan, challenged a decision by a health authority to shut down her care home on grounds that it was too costly to run, despite having previously assured her that it would be her home for the rest of her life.[2] These grounds of review were not first designed from principles but evolved in the light of practical experience, the submissions of counsel, and the responses of the judges presiding over the cases. As in other common law jurisdictions, judges are typically appointed to the High Court (which includes the Queen's Bench Division, of which the Administrative Court is part) and to tribunals (see below) aged 40 to 50, having had successful careers as lawyers at the independent bar or in law firms. Few judges have any experience of working in public administration or in politics. Appointments are made on the basis of professional merit, not party political affiliation.

The common law system is one of the United Kingdom's most enduring 'exports'. In the first half of the twentieth century, other jurisdictions that acquired common law systems through colonisation took a very deferential, even obedient, approach to English judgments. There was little

1 *Associated Provincial Picture Houses Ltd v. Wednesbury Corporation* [1948] 1 KB 223 discussed below.
2 *R (on the application of Coughlan) v. North & East Devon Health Authority* [2001] QB 213 discussed below.

reciprocity: judgments of the highest courts in the Commonwealth[3] (the High Court of Australia, the Supreme Court of Canada, etc.) were rarely cited in English case law. The subsequent shift since the 1960s has been away from the idea of '*the* common law' (which implied applying the same rules, concepts and standards across the family of common law jurisdictions around the world) to one in which there is recognition that distinctive national approaches may be necessary or desirable to accommodate the social and economic conditions and societal values of different countries. Thus, the case law on the liability of local authorities for negligently performed regulatory activities (such as an inspection of a new building to ensure compliance with safety rules) is different in England, Australia and New Zealand – though in each jurisdiction, the common law has been developed with an awareness of developments in other common law jurisdictions. To take another example: in India, the English case law on judicial review – including *Anisminic* and *Padfield* (discussed below) – has had a deep impact. The bolder Indian courts have, however, gone much further than the hesitant English courts in adopting proportionality as a common law ground for review; it remains to be seen whether the English courts will follow suit.

Although common law traditions remain strong, the United Kingdom has also been involved in the processes of European integration since the 1950s and more intensively since the 1970s. Rules, concepts and practices from the European Union (EU), the European Convention on Human Rights (ECHR or 'Convention rights'), and from the national legal systems of other European states are increasingly influential in the English courts. The two European legal orders have required English judges to adopt new methods of review, notably proportionality, when EU rights or Convention rights are raised in a case.

Nowadays, an English administrative lawyer has less in common with an Australian administrative lawyer than they had a generation ago, thanks to the influence of the Human Rights Act 1998 in England (which incorporated rights from the ECHR into domestic law) and the continuing lack of a national charter of rights in Australia. South African administrative law now has as its focus the right to just administration,[4] a right absent from the ECHR and English law. But a shared language (English), the common law method, and similarities in basic legal doctrine continue to make case law and legislative developments of other Commonwealth jurisdictions more accessible to English lawyers than the judicial thinking in countries across continental Europe.

Multi-level Governance

The defendants in administrative litigation actions are determined by the structures of government. A second context is therefore the character of 'government'. Over the past 40 years, the United Kingdom has shifted from having a relatively centralised system of government to one in which public power is distributed (falling short of becoming a formal federation) at four main levels:

1. the European Union – responsible for law-making across a broad range of policy areas, though most executive action taken in consequence of EU legislation is by the governments of the Member States;
2. central government – principally through the public office of 'Secretary of State';
3. regional government – devolved legislative and executive power in three parts of the United Kingdom – Scotland, Northern Ireland and Wales; and

3 The modern Commonwealth is an intergovernmental organisation of 54 'freely and equally associated nations' – former British colonies and dominions along with the United Kingdom itself.

4 Constitution of the Republic of South Africa 1996 section 33.

4. local government – the 373 elected authorities with responsibility for matters including planning permission, social services and some aspects of schooling.

Another feature of modern public administration, as in other countries, has been brought about by the ideas of New Public Management, leading to the delivery of many public services by business enterprises and charities rather than directly through public bodies.

Parliamentary Sovereignty and the Rule of Law

Thirdly, there is the paradox that judicial control over public power in the United Kingdom is simultaneously both weak and strong. It is weak in the sense that the constitutional principle of parliamentary sovereignty precludes the courts from judicially reviewing Acts of Parliament (primary legislation). Moreover, the United Kingdom has no codified constitution that could provide standards against which to judge the constitutionality of primary legislation. One consequence of the absence of a codified constitution and administrative law code, often hotly debated in academic circles, centres upon the constitutional foundations of judicial review. In one view, the role of the independent judiciary is to give effect to the will of Parliament as explicitly expressed *or implied* in the legislation. An alternative view is that, in carrying out judicial review, judges are exercising inherent common law powers that do not stem from any abstract notion of parliamentary intent.[5] The principle of parliamentary sovereignty has been qualified in recent decades. The EU legal order requires national courts at all levels to 'disapply' any domestic law, including primary legislation, that is contrary to EU law. The Human Rights Act 1998 stops short of empowering the courts to set aside primary legislation held to be incompatible with Convention rights, but they may instead make 'declarations of incompatibility'. Approximately 30 such declarations have been made since the Human Rights Act 1998 came into force. They do not affect the validity of the legislation but instead signal a warning to the government and Parliament that amendments are needed in order to bring the law into line with the ECHR. In almost all cases, the government and Parliament have responded by legislating to rectify the incompatibility

Judicial control of legality may be described as 'strong' in the sense that there is a political and legal culture respecting the rule of law in which government bodies comply with orders of national courts. It is of course open to a government body to appeal against a court ruling, and central government may persuade Parliament to enact primary legislation to change the law, but aside from these constitutionally acceptable means of seeking to alter a court ruling, there is effectively complete compliance. As discussed below, however, this does not imply that the government is always respectful of the role of courts and significant tensions have emerged between politicians and judges in recent years.

Alternatives to the Courts

A fourth point of context is that 'litigation' is only one method of redress for grievances against public bodies. Indeed, in recent years the government has encouraged the use of non-judicial dispute resolution methods. This is partly because these are regarded as less costly to the public purse, but also because they are considered quicker, more convenient and more accessible to people.[6]

5 For a collection of essays related to this debate, see Christopher Forsyth (ed.), *Judicial Review and the Constitution* (Oxford, Hart Publishing, 2000).

6 See further A. Le Sueur, 'Administrative Justice and the Resolution of Disputes', chapter 10 in J. Jowell and D. Oliver (eds), *The Changing Constitution* (7th edn, Oxford, OUP, 2011).

An aggrieved individual is normally expected to seek to resolve a dispute by using the internal procedures of the public body in question. In many situations, primary legislation creates a right of appeal against an administrative decision to a tribunal (which are, in effect, specialist courts). Only if there is no right of appeal or any other adequate procedure available to resolve a dispute will a claim for judicial review to the Administrative Court (part of the High Court, the senior-level trial court) be deemed appropriate. The number of judicial review claims received by the Administrative Court has grown significantly over the past 15 years but is still much smaller than the caseload of tribunals. The constitutional importance of the Administrative Court is that, in the common law system, its judgments not only resolve the particular dispute in a case but articulate principles and rules that will be applicable in future cases.

In addition to litigation, ombudsmen have been created. The two main ombudsmen are the Parliamentary Commissioner for Administration (dealing with central government) and Local Government Ombudsman (dealing with local authorities). They investigate allegations of 'maladministration' leading to injustice. Maladministration is not defined in the legislation creating the ombudsmen. In 1993, the then Parliamentary Ombudsman (Sir William Reid, a former senior civil servant, responsible for investigating national government bodies) stated that it included,[7]

> rudeness (though that is a matter of degree); unwillingness to treat the complainant as a person with rights; refusal to answer reasonable questions; neglecting to inform a complainant on request of his or her rights or entitlement; knowingly giving advice which is misleading or inadequate; ignoring valid advice or overruling considerations which would produce an uncomfortable result for the over-ruler; offering no redress or manifestly disproportionate redress; showing bias whether because of colour, sex, or any other grounds; omission to notify those who thereby lose a right of appeal; refusal to inform adequately of the right of appeal; faulty procedures; failure by management to monitor compliance with adequate procedures; cavalier disregard of guidance which is intended to be followed in the interest of equitable treatment of those who use a service; partiality; and failure to mitigate the effects of rigid adherence to the letter of the law where that produces manifestly inequitable treatment.

The grounds of judicial review increasingly overlap with the concept of maladministration. As Lord Justice Henry puts it:[8]

> What may not have been recognized back in 1974 [when the Local Government Ombudsman was set up] was the emergence of judicial review to the point where most if not almost all matters which could form the basis for a complaint of maladministration are matters for which the elastic qualities of judicial review might provide a remedy.

For most people, ombudsmen provide a far more accessible procedure than court proceedings because complaints can be made without legal advice or representation and there is no charge to the complainant. A large proportion of complaints are rejected without a full investigation. Where possible, the ombudsmen attempt to achieve a 'local settlement' of a complaint. Where a formal investigation is made, the ombudsman issues a report with findings and recommendations. The recommendations may include the request for the public body to make an apology or pay

7 Annual Report of the Parliamentary Commissioner for Administration (1993).

8 *R v. Local Commissioner for Local Government for North and North East England, ex parte Liverpool City Council* [2001] 1 All ER 462.

compensation. Recommendations are not enforceable but there is in general a very high level of compliance by central and local government. As well as dealing with individual complaints, the ombudsmen promote general standards of good administration through publications. What the ombudsmen cannot provide is authoritative decisions on points of law; nor do they have powers to grant an interim remedy while the matter is investigated.

Another aspect of the swing away from judicial resolution of disputes is the debate over whether (and if so, how) aggrieved people should be encouraged to use alternative dispute resolution (ADR) techniques, such as mediation, rather than adjudication in the courts and tribunals. The impetus for this development is partly a belief that ADR is 'better' for claimants; for government, there is also a belief (largely untested) that providing access to ADR is less expensive than formal court and tribunal proceedings. Mediation has been enthusiastically promoted as the exemplary resolution-focused method, with the potential to replace any other dispute resolution mechanism. Since Lord Woolf's *Access to Justice* report (which made radical changes to the whole civil procedure system in England and Wales in 1999), mediation has been widely adopted in civil cases but not in administrative cases.

In a 2001 judicial review challenge to a local authority's decision to close a care home, the Court of Appeal (which included Lord Woolf) took the opportunity to issue guidance on the desirability of using mediation and other forms of ADR instead of a legal challenge in the courts.[9] The court stated:

> This case will have served some purpose if it makes it clear that the lawyers acting on both sides of a dispute of this sort are under a heavy obligation to resort to litigation only if it is really unavoidable. If they cannot resolve the whole of the dispute by the use of the complaints procedure they should resolve the dispute so far as is practicable without involving litigation. At least in this way some of the expense and delay will be avoided. We hope that the highly skilled and caring practitioners who practise in this area will learn from what we regard as the very unfortunate history of this case.

Mediation undoubtedly may lead to relatively quick and cost-effective outcomes in many situations, but in the context of disputes between citizens and public bodies it needs to be adopted, if at all, with caution so as to ensure that it is being utilised for the right reasons. The stated benefits (speed, economy, better outcomes) that the mediation process offers are often more readily applicable to disputes over compensation, where mediation presents a viable alternative to an otherwise lengthy and prohibitively expensive court process. However, in the context of public law disputes, mediation has so far proven thin on the ground. Research conducted by the Public Law Project published in 2009 shows that there is little room for mediation as an alternative to judicial review as over 90 per cent of judicial review claims initiated are settled before reaching their final hearing *in any event*. The study concluded that mediating judicial review claims is not necessarily cheap or quick, although good outcomes for claimants can be achieved in some cases.[10]

9 *Re Cowl (Practice Note); Cowl v. Plymouth City Council* [2001] EWCA Civ 1935, [2002] 1 WLR 803.

10 V. Bondy and M. Doyle, *Mediation and Judicial Review: A Practical Handbook for Lawyers* (London, Public Law Project, 2011), 61.

Historical Development of Administrative Litigation

One of the characteristics of the English administrative litigation system, and the alternative non-judicial processes for resolving disputes, is that it has grown incrementally over a considerable period of time. No single person or body was responsible for its design. There was no single constitutional moment at which 'the system' (if it can be called that) was created. A brief historical explanation is therefore helpful in understanding the rather complicated picture.

Development of Court Procedures and Mechanisms for Review

By the middle of the eighteenth century, the Court of the King's Bench[11] was regularly issuing remedies known as 'prerogative writs', which had evolved to enable judicial scrutiny of official decisions and the lower courts.[12] These writs included certiorari (a judicial order quashing a decision), mandamus (an order requiring a public body to do something), prohibition (an order stopping a public body from taking action) and habeas corpus (to provide judicial control over decisions to detain individuals in prison). The functions of the government at this time were limited. At a local level, Justices of the Peace regulated wages and prices, implemented the Poor Law (designed to provide basic subsistence to people without work), and heard minor criminal charges.

During the nineteenth century, these local government functions were transferred to new elected borough and county councils. The King's Bench Division of the High Court came to retain the role of ensuring that councils did not stray outside the powers conferred upon them by Acts of Parliament and that decisions were made according to basic principles of procedural fairness. However, challenges to central government ('ministers' or 'the Secretary of State') were rare.

Throughout the twentieth century, and particularly from 1945 onwards, the functions of local government, central government, and other public bodies expanded into new areas. The welfare state was created, with government taking on greater responsibility for providing pensions, social security payments, health care and education. Many areas of business and social activity became subject to government regulation. Naturally, the increasing breadth and intensity of government activity created demand for ways of challenging decisions that individuals and business enterprises regarded as wrong. Rather than leaving these disputes to be dealt with by the ordinary courts, different tribunals were set up (by the 1990s, over 70 separate bodies existed). These were 'judicial' in the sense that they adjudicated on appeals, but they included members who were not lawyers (for example, medical experts). By the 1960s, tribunals were dealing with hundreds of thousands of administrative appeals.

The 1960s were a time of considerable social and political change in England. Administrative law did not escape the forces of change. A campaign for an ombudsman system as an alternative to the courts led to the creation in 1967 of the Parliamentary Commissioner for Administration, an independent public office attached to Parliament with powers to investigate cases of alleged injustice caused by maladministration by central government. A local government ombudsman was created a few years later in 1974. The impetus for these innovations was the growing need for redress mechanisms that were more affordable and accessible to ordinary people than the courts.

Following a report by the Law Commission (the official body responsible for making recommendations to the government about law reform), a new procedure for bringing forward legal

11 In 1875 this court became part of the High Court, with the name 'King' or 'Queen' reflected in one of its divisions: now it takes the form of the Queen's Bench Division.

12 See further H. Woolf, J. Jowell, A. Le Sueur, et al., *de Smith's Judicial Review* (London, Sweet & Maxwell, 2013), chapter 15.

challenges in the High Court was created. 'Order 53', as the new application for judicial review was known, was a single procedure for obtaining the various prerogative writs with a common time limit ('promptly and in any event within three months') and standardised rules on standing (applicants had to have 'a sufficient interest in the matter to which the application relates'). With the new procedure in place, the courts began to require all legal disputes about the legality of government actions to use Order 53 rather than ordinary civil proceedings. Under the new streamlined procedure, the judicial review caseload grew from 4,250 claims brought forward in 2000 to 11,200 in 2011. Almost all of this increase can be attributed to the surge within the category of immigration and asylum decisions, which reflects the rise of mass migration to the United Kingdom.

In 2000, the 'Administrative Court' was officially created, recognising the importance of judicial review within the High Court's caseload.

The Changing Scope of Judicial Review

Since the 1960s, the power of judges in England and Wales to review the legality of government actions has grown. This phenomenon can, on the one hand, be seen as evidence of increasing respect for the constitutional principle of the rule of law and as contributing to improving the quality of administrative decision-making. On the other hand, the development has become controversial: it has sparked antagonism between politicians and judges and prompted government attempts to restrict the availability and extent of judicial review.

There are two main facets to the growth of judicial power. One is attributable to decisions made by the judiciary; the other the inevitable consequence of political decisions about integration with Europe.

Firstly, the judiciary has used common law methods to expand the scope of judicial review. Since 1968, the courts assert jurisdiction over all errors of law made by government bodies, thereby reducing the autonomy of administrative agencies to interpret and apply law (wrongly) in their day-to-day work. New grounds of judicial review have been developed, such as legitimate expectation (in which a public body is required to honour undertakings granted to people, unless there is a compelling public interest reason not to do so – and the court decides whether there is such a justification). Judicial review has also been extended to cover a wider range of bodies, including self-regulatory organisations. The judiciary has been at the forefront of these developments.

Secondly, the growth of judicial power is linked to European integration and political decisions taken by the government and enacted by the UK Parliament. The English government and legal structures have been adapted to meet the standards required by the European Union (the now 28-member organisation that the United Kingdom first joined in 1973) and the separate European Convention on Human Rights (first signed by the United Kingdom in 1951 but not incorporated into domestic law until the Human Rights Act 1998). European legal principles, in particular proportionality review, have intensified the control judges may exert over governmental decision-making. European Union law also requires judicial control over parliamentary legislation: national law, including Acts of Parliament that are contrary to European Union law, must be 'disapplied' by national courts. Under the Human Rights Act 1998, although the courts have no formal power to strike down parliamentary legislation as incompatible with Convention rights, the courts may make 'declarations of incompatibility'. These developments have undermined traditional ideas of the constitutional principle of parliamentary supremacy (under which the English courts had no powers to question the legality of primary legislation).

Changing Government Attitudes to Law and Legal Proceedings

The United Kingdom can generally be said to be a country where the rule of law is respected. At the conclusion of court hearings, there are no significant problems of wilful non-compliance with court orders by public bodies. One of the few reported cases of non-cooperation is *M v. Home Office*,[13] in which the House of Lords made a finding of contempt against the Home Secretary (a senior government minister) after an asylum seeker was returned to his home country in breach of an undertaking given to the court that he would remain in the United Kingdom pending the final outcome of legal proceedings. When the government disagrees with a ruling there are two constitutionally accepted responses. Firstly, the public body may appeal to a higher tribunal (the Upper Tribunal) or court (the Court of Appeal and then the UK Supreme Court). Secondly, where the case is against the national government, ministers may propose legislation in Parliament altering the law to mitigate the effect of a court's ruling. For example, there was a widespread view among politicians that the courts had given an overly restrictive interpretation of the phrase 'functions of a public nature' in the Human Rights Act 1998, with the effect that human rights obligations did not apply to businesses running residential care homes for elderly people (in which local authorities placed people for whom they had a statutory duty to arrange care). The Health and Social Care Act 2008 changed the law. In another example of legislative reversal of the effects of judgments, the UK Supreme Court held that delegated legislation made by ministers seeking to give effect to United Nations terrorist suspect asset-freezing orders was ultra vires;[14] the government acted quickly to persuade Parliament to enact new primary legislation enabling the UN orders to be implemented.[15] The option of legislating in response to a court ruling may be limited or non-existent where the grounds on which a decision was considered lawful were in relation to another European legal system. As previously noted, European Union law has primacy over national law and even Parliament is bound to avoid contravening it. In relation to the ECHR, while Parliament is not bound to respond to a 'declaration of incompatibility' of an English court, the United Kingdom is bound by the ECHR as a matter of international law. This may be unpalatable to government and other politicians: for example, in 2005 the European Court of Human Rights held that a total ban on all prisoners voting in elections breached a Convention right[16] and the Council of Europe enforcement mechanism urged the United Kingdom to comply with the ruling without further delay. To date, this has not happened.

As well as formal reactions to judicial review proceedings, government ministers may respond informally in interviews with journalists and in political speeches. Until the mid-1990s, government ministers rarely commented on court proceedings. Since then, it has become increasingly common for ministers to speak to journalists about particular judgments (in which the government has lost) and judges, leading to periods of tension between the senior judiciary and ministers. Tabloid newspapers often disparage judges.[17] There have been calls for a more mature approach in which ministers accept the constitutional role of judges.[18] As one senior lawyer/politician remarked, 'In a

13 *M v. Home Office* [1994] 1 AC 377 (HL).

14 *Ahmed and others v. HM Treasury (JUSTICE intervening) (Nos 1 and 2)* [2010] UKSC 2, [2010] 2 AC 544.

15 Terrorist Asset-Freezing (Temporary Provisions) Act 2010 and Terrorist Asset-Freezing etc. Act 2010.

16 *Hirst v. United Kingdom* Application 74025/01 (Grand Chamber, European Court of Human Rights).

17 See H. Woolf, J. Jowell and A. Le Sueur, *de Smith's Judicial Review* (6th edn, London, Sweet & Maxwell, 2007), para. 1-050.

18 See House of Lords Constitution Committee, *Relations between the Executive, the Judiciary and Parliament* (HL 2006-07, 151).

democracy under the rule of law, it is not mature to cheer the judges when a win is secured and boo them when a loss is suffered'.[19]

In December 2012, the Ministry of Justice published proposals to restrict judicial review.[20] The motivation for the initiative is unclear. It followed a speech made by the Prime Minister in November 2012, which described judicial review as 'a massive growth industry in Britain today', stating also that many claims 'are completely pointless', and blamed court proceedings for impeding economic growth, especially construction projects. Subsequently, legislation has reduced the time limit for bringing some categories of judicial review from three months to six weeks; court fees for making claims have increased; and the opportunities to appeal are more restricted than in the past. The proposals were widely criticised by lawyers and academics alike.

It is no exaggeration to say that views on the role of judges in carrying out judicial review have become a divisive issue in British politics. Critics, including ministers in the current government and one senior judge, argue that over the past two decades there has been an unwelcome shift in power away from elected politicians accountable to Parliament towards the courts.[21] As evidence of this, critics point to a series of cases in which high-profile government policies have been held to be unlawful, especially in the politically contentious fields of counter-terrorism policy and attempts by government to control immigration. Supporters of the growth in judicial control argue for its necessity in giving practical effect to the rule of law. Rather than subverting the will of Parliament, in almost all cases the courts are ensuring that the government acts in accordance with the legislative framework established by Parliament. Moreover, the British version of judicial review is quite weak: judges have no general power to strike down primary legislation.

Judicial Review and Decision-making

Within the national government, attempts have been made since the mid-1980s to provide better legal awareness training so that officials are able to pinpoint the risks of judicial review challenges before they arise. A pamphlet entitled *The Judge Over Your Shoulder* is widely distributed; this explains the grounds of judicial review in non-technical terms and suggests ways in which officials can reduce the risk of challenges.[22] Policy-makers are encouraged to seek legal advice at an early stage of planning. Generally it can be said that 'Law and lawyers were no longer seen as peripheral to the process of administration. Administrators became more aware of the legal implications of their decisions and departmental lawyers tended to become involved at earlier stages of the policy-making process'.[23]

Recent research into the impact of judicial review at the level of local government has concluded that[24]

19 Lord Irvine of Lairg, 'The Impact of the HRA: Parliament, the Courts and the Executive' [2003] Public Law 308, 323.

20 Ministry of Justice, *Judicial Review: proposals for reform* (CP25/2012).

21 For example, Jonathan Sumption, 'Judicial and Political Decision-making: The Uncertain Boundary' [2011] Judicial Review 301.

22 Treasury Solicitor, *The Judge Over Your Shoulder* (4th edn, London, Government Legal Service 2006), at http://www.tsol.gov.uk/Publications/Scheme_Publications/judge.pdf, accessed 5 September 2012.

23 M. Sunkin and A. Le Sueur, 'Can Government Control Judicial Review?' (1991) 44 Current Legal Problems 161, 171.

24 M. Sunkin et al., 'The Positive Effect of Judicial Review on the Quality of Local Government' [2010] Judicial Review 337.

> By contrast with much earlier research [there is] evidence that judicial review may have positive influences which may have been under-recognised or unrecognised. In particular, our findings indicate that judicial review litigation may drive improvements in the quality of local government as measured by official indicators of quality such as the Government's comprehensive performance assessment of local authorities.

This study found, firstly, that local authorities that were rated as performing more efficiently than others experienced lower levels of legal challenges. Secondly, there was a small but significant correlation between an increase in the level of legal challenges and improved performance.

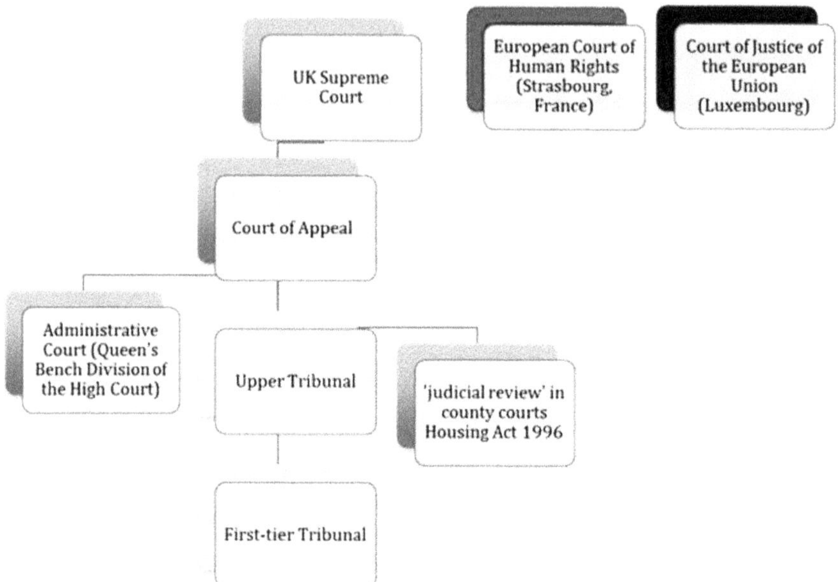

Figure 8.1 Institutional Arrangements for Administrative Litigation in England and Wales

Judicial Review and Appeals Contrasted

A sharp distinction is made between 'judicial review' and 'appeal'.

Judicial review operates where there is no express right of appeal or other suitable remedy for an aggrieved person. The grounds are those described below: (1) illegality; (2) procedural impropriety; and (3) irrationality, all of which were created by the courts using common law methods. The vast majority of judicial review claims are made to the Administrative Court, which is part of the Queen's Bench Division of the High Court, under Part 54 of the Civil Procedure Rules (which replaced the previous 'Order 53' procedure in 2000). There are also a variety of other specialist procedures, for example in planning and compulsory purchase cases, and for the ancient remedy of habeas corpus, which are also heard on the basis of common law grounds of judicial review by the Administrative Court. In 1996, power to hear judicial review claims relating to certain housing matters was transferred to local county courts.

Administrative appeals, in contrast, are created by Acts of Parliament. An appeal from an administrative decision may be made to a court but more usually to a tribunal. Since reforms in 2007, a single tribunal, the First-tier Tribunal, determines these appeals with a possibility of a further appeal to the Upper Tribunal. An example of a right of appeal is in the Health and Social Care Act 2012, which created a public body known as 'Monitor', responsible for ensuring that health service providers comply with licensing conditions. Section 92 creates an opportunity for appeal:

> (1) An appeal lies to the First-tier Tribunal against a decision of Monitor to – (a) refuse an application for a licence under section 87, or (b) revoke a licence under section 89(b).
> (2) The grounds for an appeal under this section are that the decision was – (a) based on an error of fact, (b) wrong in law, or (c) unreasonable.
> (3) On an appeal under this section, the First-tier Tribunal may – (a) confirm Monitor's decision, (b) direct that the decision is not to have effect, or (c) remit the decision to Monitor.

Efforts have been made in recent years to introduce a degree of flexibility as to which cases are heard by the tribunals and which by the Administrative Court. The benefit of tribunals is that tribunal judges will often have greater technical expertise and experience in handling some areas of law (for example, complex tax or social security questions) than the more generalist Administrative Court. The Administrative Court, however, may be more appropriate where the outcome of a case may set an important precedent to be followed in later cases. Under the Tribunals, Courts and Enforcement Act 2007 (which reformed the tribunal system), judicial review claims that are initiated in the Administrative Court may be transferred for determination by the Upper Tribunal, either because it falls into a category of cases announced by the Lord Chief Justice as more appropriate for the Upper Tribunal or where the Administrative Court decides that there is a particular reason for a case to be transferred.

A further aspect of the relationship between the Administrative Court and the tribunals is that an individual may challenge the lawfulness of a tribunal decision by making a judicial review claim to the Administrative Court. In other words, the Administrative Court has supervisory jurisdiction over the tribunals.[25]

Private Law Proceedings

In addition to judicial review and administrative appeals, there are also private law claims. Claims for damages resulting from torts (negligence, misfeasance in public office, trespass, etc.) alleged to have been committed by public bodies are not normally considered to be 'administrative law'; they are dealt with by the general civil courts (the county courts or the Queen's Bench Division of the High Court, depending on the size of the damages claim and the complexity of the issues of law and fact that arise). Administrative law questions may also arise collaterally in criminal proceedings, for example if a person prosecuted for breach of building development control argues that an enforcement notice issued by the planning authority is not legally valid. During the 1980s, the courts attempted to develop a concept of 'procedural exclusivity' under which claimants seeking to challenge the legality of administrative actions had to do so in judicial review proceedings in the Crown Office List rather than in ordinary civil proceedings.[26] This was criticised in academic

25 The relationship between the High Court and the new tribunal system was clarified by the UK Supreme Court in *R (on the application of Cart) v. The Upper Tribunal* [2011] UKSC 28, [2012] 1 AC 663.

26 *O'Reilly v. Mackman* [1983] 2 AC 273.

circles and it became clear that it was also not viable in practice unless made subject to large exceptions; courts now take a pragmatic approach and will permit questions of administrative law to be raised in most kinds of proceedings.

The Judicial Review Procedure

Claims for judicial review are made to the Administrative Court, part of the Queen's Bench Division of the High Court. Approximately forty of the 108 judges of the High Court have been nominated by the Lord Chief Justice to deal with judicial review. Few, if any, specialise only in administrative law; they also sit in on a variety of other civil cases. This is in keeping with the preference in common law jurisdictions for generalist rather than excessively specialist judges.

Several different procedures exist according to the subject matter. What is described below is the general procedure under Part 54 of the Civil Procedure Rules (CPR). CPR Part 54 judicial review proceedings occur in several phases.

Before commencing legal proceedings, a claimant is required to notify the public body of the potential claim in writing. Any suitable alternative remedies must also have been exhausted: if an Act of Parliament creates a specific right of appeal to a tribunal or court that must be used instead of judicial review.[27] As noted above, the parties are encouraged to consider whether some form of ADR should be used. During this period, the claimant and his lawyers will gather the relevant evidence. Many claimants do not have the financial resources to instruct lawyers; for the poorest there may be the possibility of obtaining legal aid funding from the Legal Services Commission.

If the claimant wishes to proceed with a claim, the next step is to apply to the Administrative Court for 'permission' (known as 'leave', before 2000).[28] This must be done 'promptly and in any event within three months' from when the grounds for judicial review arose.[29] The court has discretion, which it rarely uses, to extend the time limit. The primary requirement for promptness has occasionally led to permission being refused even before the end of the 3-month period. The lack of a firm limitation period has been criticised as undermining the principle of legal certainty.

The claim form must specify the decision challenged and provide details of the grounds of the legal challenge. In most cases, relatively specialised practitioners at the Bar will draft these. The claim form is filed in the Administrative Court and the claimant must serve it, along with any witness statements, on the defendant public body and any interested parties. The public body must respond in writing (an 'acknowledgment of service') within 21 days.

If the public body's response is to defend the decision, the claimant will request the court to determine the application for permission. This is a written procedure at which the judge considers whether the claimant has an arguable case, ensures that the claim is being made within the appropriate time constraints, and verifies that there is no alternative remedy that ought to be used. The vast majority of permission applications are refused:[30]

> There were 18,811 applications for permission to apply for judicial review in the Administrative Court, a 12 per cent increase on 2010. Of these, 11,200 were received, 6,391 applications were refused and 1,220 were granted. The majority of these applications, as in previous years, concerned asylum and immigration matters.

27 Pre-Action Protocol for Judicial Review, at http://www.justice.gov.uk/courts/procedure-rules/civil/protocol/prot_jrv, accessed 17 May 2014.

28 Senior Courts Act 1981 section 31.

29 Senior Courts Act 1981 section 31.

30 Ministry of Justice, *Judicial and Court Statistics 2011* (London, 2012), 65.

A claimant who is refused permission may appeal to the Court of Appeal. The purpose of the permission stage is for the court to satisfy itself, on a quick perusal of the documents, that the claimant has an arguable case. There has been academic criticism, following empirical studies, that different judges have significantly different grant/refusal rates.

If permission is granted, there may be further negotiation between the claimant and public body leading to the claim being withdrawn. The number of claims progressing to a full hearing is relatively small: there were 396 applications for judicial review in 2011 (a 14 per cent decrease from 2010). Of these, 174 were allowed, 213 dismissed and 9 were withdrawn.[31] Hearings take place several months after the permission stage; the Administrative Court has in the past had a backlog of cases. The judge hears oral submissions from counsel for the claimant and defendant. A hearing may last from two or three hours (if the claim is simple) to two or more days (for complex cases). It is possible for a person (or more usually a campaign or interest group) to seek the court's permission to 'intervene' by making oral or written submissions.

Until recently all judicial review hearings took place in London, but there is now a scheme to 'regionalise' hearings so that they may be heard in High Court centres in major cities outside of London, if this is more convenient for the parties. In a straightforward case, judgments may be given orally at the conclusion of the hearing; alternatively, the judge may reserve their judgment and issue a written judgment at a later date.

Several different remedies may be granted: a quashing order; an order prohibiting or requiring the public body to do something; and a declaration of the law.

The parties must pay court fees at various points during the course of the proceedings. The major costs associated with judicial review are, however, for legal advice and representation. The claimant's lawyer's fees for even a relatively short and simple case are likely to be GBP 10,000 (= RMB 101,000). Moreover, the normal rule is that an unsuccessful party must pay the winner's legal fees. Judicial review has become virtually unaffordable except for the very poor (who may be eligible for legal aid), the very rich, or claimants who are able to obtain free legal advice. Where a case involves a point of public importance, the court may grant a 'protective costs order' to set a reasonable cap on the amount that the claimant would have to contribute to the public body's legal costs if the claimant's challenge is unsuccessful.

Either side may appeal to the Court of Appeal and then to the UK Supreme Court. Permission to do so is required from either the appeal court or the court below. A relatively large proportion of the Supreme Court's caseload is judicial review appeals.[32]

Appeals and the Tribunal System

The Tribunals, Courts and Enforcement Act 2007 created a new tribunal system. There are now two principal tribunals: the First-tier Tribunal and the Upper Tribunal. These replaced a myriad of more than 70 separate tribunals that had developed haphazardly over the years. The First-tier Tribunal and Upper Tribunal are organised into subject-based 'chambers':

---

31 Ministry of Justice, *Judicial and Court Statistics 2001* (London, 2012), 65.

32 In 2011–12, 22 of the 58 judgments were public law cases; the comparable figure in 2010–11 was 22 of the 57 judgments: see C. Knight and T. Cross, 'Public Law in the Supreme Court 2011–2012' [2012] *Judicial Review* 330; A. Le Sueur, 'Panning for Gold: Choosing Cases for Top-level Courts', chapter 12 in A. Le Sueur (ed.), *Building the UK's New Supreme Court: National and Comparative Perspectives* (Oxford and New York, OUP, 2004); T. Poole and S. Shah, 'The Impact of the Human Rights Act on the House of Lords' [2009] *Public Law* 347.

Upper Tribunal

1. Administrative Appeals Chamber
2. Tax and Chancery Chamber
3. Immigration and Asylum Chamber
4. Lands Chamber

First-tier Tribunal

1. War Pensions and Armed Forces Compensation
2. Social Entitlement Chamber
3. Health, Education and Social Care Chamber
4. General Regulatory Chamber
5. Tax Chamber
6. Immigration and Asylum Chamber
7. Land, Property and Housing Chamber

The tribunals handle a vastly greater number of cases than the Administrative Court. In 2011 to 2012, in the First-tier Tribunal, the Social Entitlement Chamber received 370,800 appeals (the largest jurisdiction); the Immigration and Asylum Chamber, 112,500.[33]

The rationale for having a tribunal system is that they deliver justice that is more accessible, more informal, speedier and with greater subject-specific expertise than the Administrative Court can offer. Until the 1950s, there was some debate as to whether tribunals should be regarded as part of the administration or separate from it. Their status is now clear: they are judicial bodies, with an independent judiciary, fully independent from the government. The tribunal judiciary now forms part of a single judiciary with colleagues sitting in the mainstream courts. A single agency (Her Majesty's Court and Tribunal Service) provides administrative support to both tribunals and the mainstream courts of England and Wales.

Whereas the jurisdiction of the Administrative Court to hear judicial review claims is historic and finds its origins in the common law, tribunal jurisdiction is more recent and exclusively statutory. A right of appeal to a tribunal exists only if there is one expressly created by an Act of Parliament. Appeals may be on questions of fact as well as law.

The composition of the First-tier Tribunal varies according to the subject matter. It may consist of a single, legally qualified tribunal judge, or a panel of three members. Where panels are used, they typically consist of a legally qualified tribunal judge in the chair with two non-lawyers as the 'wing members' – for example, medically qualified members where entitlement to disability benefits or mental health detentions are under consideration, or accountants in tax cases. There are also differences, according to the subject matter, in whether appellants are represented by lawyers or appear in person; and whether the public body is legally represented or allows an official to present the case. The methods used also vary across different chambers and particular cases: in some, the proceedings are clearly adversarial in character; in others, the process is far more investigative or inquisitorial, with the tribunal judge taking a leading role in eliciting relevant information from the appellant.

In the great majority of cases, appellants are not legally represented when they appear before a tribunal. Legal aid (public funding for legal advice and representation) is available only where the liberty of the person or human rights is at stake (for example, in asylum and mental health appeals). Under the Legal Aid and Sentencing Powers Act 2013, legal aid has been abolished in most other

33 Ministry of Justice, *Annual Tribunals Statistics, 2011–12* (London, 2012).

tribunal proceedings (as part of government spending cuts following the world economic crisis). Some basic advice may be available from voluntary legal advice services such as Citizens Advice Bureaus and Law Centres.

The Upper Tribunal is an appellate body, a 'superior court of record'. Its judges are drawn from among the High Court justices and senior judges from the First-tier Tribunal. The Tribunals, Courts and Enforcement Act 2007 confers jurisdiction on the Upper Tribunal to carry out 'judicial review'. It has at its disposal almost all of the powers of the Administrative Court to determine appeals originating from the First-tier Tribunal using the general grounds of judicial review. An appeal may, if thought appropriate, be transferred from the Upper Tribunal to the Administrative Court, and vice versa. Judgments of the Upper Tribunal considered to include important points of law are published for guidance in other cases.

The Expansion of Judicial Review Grounds

Looking at the evolving scope of judicial review, four main themes can be identified. Firstly, how the English courts have used common law methods to create and develop legal principles for judicial control over the legality of administration. Secondly, how the English courts have approached the task of interpreting legislation in the context of administrative law. Thirdly, how the courts have expanded the scope of their jurisdiction: judicial review has become wider and more deeply set in recent years. Fourthly, there has been a search for alternatives to courts – through ombudsmen, tribunals and alternative dispute resolution (ADR).

The Creativity of the Common Law

Judges have developed the grounds of judicial review of administrative actions as part of the common law. The practice of 'precedent' is a central feature of this method of law-making: generally speaking, judges are strictly bound by statements of law contained in decisions of higher courts and in previous decisions of their own court. Since 1966, the highest court (now the UK Supreme Court; previously the Appellate Committee of the House of Lords) may depart from its own previous statements of law.[34] Precedent therefore has a constraining effect, as can be illustrated by reference to the question of whether proportionality should be a ground of judicial review under the common law (considered below).

Procedural fairness

The doctrine of precedent has not, however, generally hindered the remarkable development of principles of administrative legality through a series of landmark judgments. Judge-made law is particularly important in setting standards for procedural fairness, with courts insisting from the seventeenth century onwards that a person had a right to be heard (*audi alteram partem*) when decisions are made that affect him, in some circumstances. In the mid-nineteenth century, the courts explained their role as being to 'supply the omission of the legislature': legislation empowering a government body to take administrative action may not state expressly what, if any, procedural protections a person could benefit from, but it was the court's task to ensure that a fair decision-

34 See L. Blom-Cooper, '1966 and All That: The Story of the Practice Statement', chapter 9 in L. Blom-Cooper et al. (eds), *The Judicial House of Lords 1876–2009* (Oxford, OUP, 2009).

making process was used.[35] Judicial attitudes changed in 1915 and for a period of almost 50 years they retreated from insisting on procedural fairness, preferring to cultivate esoteric and inflexible distinctions between the characteristics of different types of decision-making ('administrative', 'executive', 'ministerial', 'quasi-judicial', 'judicial') and how a person was affected ('rights' and 'privileges'), with the result that procedural fairness applied only if a situation fell within a recognised category. These highly technical classifications were swept away in 1963 by *Ridge v. Baldwin*, in which the House of Lords repudiated the idea that principles of procedural fairness applied only to decisions of a judicial character.[36] They achieved this by reconceptualising the previous case law. A period of administrative law famously described by two commentators as 'a dreary catalogue of abdication and error' was brought to an end.[37] In subsequent years, the courts have used open-textured standard of a general duty of 'fairness'. The difficulty, of course, is that this may lead to uncertainty as to what precise requirements of procedural fairness are required in any particular context.

Irrationality

Another creation of the common law is the principle that, if a public body makes a decision that 'is so unreasonable that no reasonable authority could ever have come to it, then the courts can interfere ... but to prove a case of that kind would require something overwhelming'.[38] This concept and constitutional rationale for '*Wednesbury* unreasonableness' or 'irrationality' review may at first sight seem straightforward; it catches patently absurd decisions. One difficulty in applying it is that the broad standard of 'unreasonableness' provides little guidance to either public bodies or the courts. By what criteria do you assess whether a decision is reasonable or not? In *Council of Civil Service Unions v. Minister for the Civil Service*, Lord Diplock in the House of Lords stated:[39]

> It applies to a decision which is so outrageous in its defiance of logic or of accepted moral standards that no sensible person who had applied his mind to the question to be decided could have arrived at it. Whether a decision falls within this category is a question that judges by their training and experience should be well equipped to answer, or else there would be something badly wrong with our judicial system.

This is not entirely convincing. Public bodies are sometimes surprised when a carefully considered decision is overturned on the grounds of being 'unreasonable'.

A second problem with irrationality review is that it sets a very high threshold ('*so* unreasonable that *no* reasonable authority') that must be met by a claimant seeking to argue that a decision is

35 *Copper v. Wandsworth Board of Works* (1863) 14 CB (NS) 180.

36 [1964] AC 40 (HL). Ridge was a senior police officer, summarily dismissed by a police authority (chaired by Mr Baldwin) following Ridge's prosecution and acquittal for corruption. The police authority made its decision without inviting Ridge to attend a hearing or providing him with an opportunity to make representations.

37 B. Schwarz and H.W.R. Wade, *Legal Control of Government, Administrative Law in Britain and the United States* (Oxford, OUP, 1972), 320.

38 *Associated Provincial Picture Houses Ltd v. Wednesbury Corporation* [1948] 1 KB 223 (CA). APPH unsuccessfully challenged the legality of a local authority's decision to bar unaccompanied children from cinemas on a Sunday.

39 *Council of Civil Service Unions v. Minister for the Civil Service* [1985] AC 374 (often referred to as 'the GCHQ case'). The minister issued an instruction banning officials working at the Government Communication Headquarters (the signals intelligence agency) from membership of trade unions.

unlawful. The courts have responded to this criticism in two ways. One is that they tend now to rephrase the test as being the question of whether the decision is 'within the range of reasonable responses'.[40] Another response has been to recognise that there ought to be variable intensities of review according to the circumstances of the case. This approach was first developed in 1996, when the Court of Appeal held: 'The more substantial the interference with human rights, the more the court will require by way of justification before it is satisfied that the decision is reasonable'.[41] Where important individual rights are at stake, the courts adopt an 'anxious scrutiny' approach: this means that there is a more than usually rigorous examination of the case; the threshold of unreasonableness is lowered – it is no longer synonymous with 'absurdity'; and the burden of argument shifts from the claimant to the defendant public body. The claimant no longer has to demonstrate unreasonableness, but rather the public body needs to produce a justification for the decision that satisfies the court in proving that it was appropriately arrived at.[42]

Proportionality

English courts deciding questions of European Union law and adjudicating on 'qualified' rights[43] from the ECHR incorporated into domestic law by the Human Rights Act 1998 routinely use proportionality review as a technique of adjudication. But whereas the English courts have been keen to develop irrationality review, they have taken a far more cautious approach to developing proportionality as a common law ground of review. The leading case remains *R v. Secretary of State for the Home Department Ex parte Brind*.[44] The government issued executive orders banning the news media from broadcasting the direct speech of people in Northern Ireland who were declared to be apologists for paramilitary terrorist organisations; Brind was a television producer. The House of Lords rejected an argument that the court should use proportionality review. (This case was decided several years before the Human Rights Act 1998 had incorporated Convention rights.) The main qualm of the court was that, if proportionality standards were used, the court would cease to be concerned only with legality and would instead be interfering with the merits of the case. The question of whether proportionality should be a common law ground of review has come before the courts on several occasions since *Brind*,[45] but the Supreme Court has not addressed the question again.[46]

40 See H. Woolf, J. Jowell and A. Le Sueur et al., *de Smith's Judicial Review* (7th edn, London, Sweet & Maxwell, 2013), chapter 11.

41 *R v. Secretary of State for Defence, ex p Smith* [1996] QB 517. The applicants were dismissed from the armed forces solely because they were discovered to be homosexual. Their judicial review challenge was unsuccessful, but they succeeded in subsequent legal proceedings before the European Court of Human Rights.

42 See generally *R (on the application of YH) v. Secretary of State for the Home Department* [2010] EWCA Civ 116, [2010] 4 All ER 448.

43 Notably ECHR article 8 (right to private life and home), 9 (manifesting religion), 10 (freedom of expression) and 11 (freedom of assembly). These rights may be limited by the state 'in accordance with the law' to achieve a recognised 'legitimate aim' (such as national security or to protect the rights of others), so long as the limitation is 'necessary in a democratic society'. These are all issues for the court to decide.

44 [1991] 1 AC 696.

45 See *Association of British Civilian Internees (Far East Region) v. Secretary of State for Defence* [2003] EWCA Civ 473, [2003] QB 1397 at [34]–[35].

46 *Somerville v. Scottish Ministers* [2007] UKHL 44, [2007] 1 WLR 2734 at [56], Lord Hope: 'In my opinion it would not be appropriate for your Lordships to seek to reach a decision on this issue in the circumstances of this case'.

Legitimate expectation

The courts have, using common law methods, created and developed legitimate expectation as a ground of review over the past 20 years. The essence of the ground is that a public body that undertakes (in words or actions) to exercise its discretion in a particular way for the benefit of a person will be bound by that undertaking unless there is some strong countervailing public interest justifying a departure from it. Initially, the courts recognised 'procedural' legitimate expectations, compelling public bodies to adopt procedures that had been promised.

More recently, the courts have protected 'substantive' legitimate expectations, seeking to compel the public body to provide the benefit it had promised. In a leading case decided in 1999, the claimant was a severely disabled woman in need of institutional care. She was told by the public authority that if she moved from the hospital to a special care unit then that would be 'her home for life'. A few years later, the public authority proposed to close the special unit (which it said was too costly to run) and move the claimant elsewhere. The Court of Appeal held that the decision was unlawful.[47] In the ensuing years, the courts have sought to articulate and refine the circumstances in which a legitimate expectation arises (for example, it must be clear, unambiguous and devoid of qualification) and the standards against which the courts should judge a public authority's decision to disappoint a person. The case law suggests that what is required of a public body to ensure that a legitimate expectation is protected varies according to the context: (a) in some situations, it may be sufficient for the court to be satisfied that the public body was mindful and considered the position of the disappointed person before making the decision; (b) the court may apply unreasonableness review – the decision is unlawful if no reasonable public body would have made the decision; (c) most strongly, the court may apply proportionality review and consider whether a fair balance has been struck between the interests of the disappointed person and any other relevant public interest.

Statutory Interpretation

During the twentieth century, there was a huge increase in the amount of primary legislation created by Parliament (Acts of Parliament) and secondary legislation (regulations, orders, rules, etc.) made, under delegated powers, by ministers and other public bodies. Much administrative litigation is centred upon questions regarding the interpretation of legislation. In England and Wales, it is the judiciary that has the role of making binding rulings on the meaning of legislation made by Parliament and ministers. As Lord Diplock explained,[48]

> By 'illegality' as a ground for judicial review I mean that the decision-maker must understand correctly the law that regulates his decision-making power and must give effect to it. Whether he has or not is par excellence a justiciable question to be decided, in the event of dispute, by those persons, the judges, by whom the judicial power of the state is exercisable.

The main problem facing the courts is that legislation conferring executive powers on ministers and local authorities is often very broadly expressed. Traditionally, the role of the English courts is to give effect to the 'intention of Parliament':[49]

---

47 *R v. North and East Devon Health Authority Ex parte Coughlan* [2001] QB 213.

48 *Council of Civil Service Unions v. Minister for the Civil Service* [1985] AC 374 (HL).

49 *R (on the application of D) v. Secretary of State for Work and Pensions* [2010] EWCA Civ 18, [2010] 1 WLR 1782, [47].

> The object therefore is to find 'the intention expressed *by the words used*'. The various aids to construction are designed to assist that task, not to supplant it. In other words: 'If there is nothing to modify, alter or qualify the language which a statute contains, the words and sentences must be construed in their ordinary and natural meaning.' (*Halsbury's Laws Statutes Vol 44(1) Reissue* para 1487; cited by Bennion *Statutory Interpretation* 5th edition p 549, as a statement of the 'plain meaning' rule.) That remains the governing principle, at least in the context of domestic law, unless the natural meaning as so ascertained produces absurdity.

The court may face two kinds of questions when analysing legislation:

1. the *meaning* of words (which may be unclear or ambiguous); in relation to this task, the courts have since 1992 been willing to consider what was said by the minister during parliamentary debates as the legislation was made;[50]
2. the *purpose* for which a statutory power has been conferred on a public body; the courts may not refer to ministerial statements in carrying out this task;[51] they work out the purpose by considering factors such as the overall scheme set out in the Act and the reasoning behind the enactment of the legislation.

The idea of 'purpose' is often at the heart of a dispute. In *Padfield v. Minister of Agriculture, Fisheries and Food*, the House of Lords rejected the government's argument that there could be 'unfettered discretion': in exercising their powers, public bodies 'must act lawfully and that is a matter to be determined by looking at the Act and its scope and object in conferring a discretion'.[52] As Lord Bridge conveyed in *R v. Tower Hamlets LBC Ex p Chetnik*,

> before deciding whether a discretion has been exercised for good or bad reasons, the court must first construe the enactment by which the discretion is conferred. Some statutory discretions may be so wide that they can, for practical purposes, only be challenged if shown to have been exercised irrationally or in bad faith. But if the purpose which the discretion is intended to serve is clear, the discretion can only be validly exercised for reasons relevant to the achievement of that purpose.[53]

A related concept is that of whether the public body took into account an irrelevant consideration in making the decision, or failed to take account of a pertinent factor. One senior practitioner, recently appointed as a justice of the UK Supreme Court, has argued that the search for parliamentary intention 'is nominally an exercise in interpretation. But in reality it is an inherently legislative one'.[54] This was a criticism that judges have become too intrusive in governmental decision-making.

Two other developments relating to statutory interpretation should be noted. Firstly, in recent years the courts have developed the 'principle of legality'. Judges presume that Parliament does

50 *Pepper v. Hart* [1993] AC 593 (HL): where legislation is obscure or ambiguous, counsel may make reference to statements of the minister when the legislation was introduced, where such statements are sufficiently clear.

51 *R v. Secretary of State for the Environment, Transport and the Regions, ex parte Spath Holme Ltd* [2001] 2 AC 349.

52 [1968] AC 997.

53 [1988] AC 858.

54 Jonathan Sumption, 'Judicial and Political Decision-making: The Uncertain Boundary' [2011] Judicial Review 301.

not intend to interfere with basic rights recognised by the common law, such as access to the courts, unless a statute is absolutely clear that this was intended.[55]

Secondly, the Human Rights Act 1998 section 3 has placed a new interpretative duty on courts (in cases where Convention rights are in issue): 'So far as it is possible to do so, primary legislation and subordinate legislation must be read and given effect in a way which is compatible with the Convention rights'. If the court cannot reach an interpretation that is consistent with Convention rights using various interpretative techniques including if necessary 'reading in' qualifications to the legislation,[56] then it may make a 'declaration of incompatibility' under section 4. A declaration does not affect the validity of the primary legislation, but it does signal to ministers and Parliament that incompatibility exists.[57]

Expansion of the Judicial Review Jurisdiction

A third theme in this brief survey of administrative litigation is the expansion, by the courts, in the types of decisions and actions that come within the remit of potential judicial review. This has been achieved in a number of steps.

In *Anisminic Ltd v. Foreign Compensation Commission*, the House of Lords in 1969 asserted the principle that *all* 'errors of law' made by public bodies are amenable to judicial review.[58] Previously a category distinction had been drawn between 'jurisdictional' errors of law (about whether the body had the power to *embark* on the decision-making process) and 'non-jurisdictional' errors of law (those made *after* a public body had lawfully commenced a decision-making process); in individual cases, the distinction was often hard to draw, and the case law was inconsistent and somewhat incoherent. *Anisminic* simplified the law and in doing so enabled the courts to intervene in a much broader range of cases than they could previously.

Another expansion of the court's jurisdiction was made by the House of Lords in *Council of Civil Service Unions v. Minister for the Civil Service*.[59] Before 1983, it was generally thought that national government decisions granted under the legal authority of 'prerogative powers', were immune from judicial review.[60] The House of Lords held that the mere fact that the legal authority for a minister's decision was a prerogative power (rather than an Act of Parliament) did not preclude the court reviewing it so long as the subject matter was 'justiciable'. In subsequent cases, the courts have held an ever-wider range of decisions to be justiciable including, for example, the prerogative of mercy (a minister's discretion to release a prisoner early), discretionary payments to

55 *R v. Secretary of State for the Home Department Ex parte Pierson* [1998] AC 539; *R v. Secretary of State for the Home Department Ex parte Simms* [2000] 2 AC 115.

56 There is a large amount of literature on this issue.

57 Approximately 30 declarations have been made between 2000 and 2012. In all cases, the ministers have acted (or are planning to act) to legislate to address the problem identified by the court.

58 [1969] 2 AC 147. The FCC was set up to distribute compensation following the nationalisation of British assets by the Egyptian government. The FCC was held to have misinterpreted the rules applicable to Anisminic.

59 See above. The Constitutional Reform and Governance Act 2010, rather than prerogative powers, which now governs the management of the civil service.

60 Prerogative power is 'the residual power inherent in the Sovereign, and now exercised mostly on the advice of the Prime Minister and Ministers of the Crown': The Cabinet Office, *The Cabinet Manual: a guide to law, conventions and rules on the operation of government* (London, 2011), 2.

people wrongly convicted of crimes, the power to issue and withhold passports, or decisions over whether to give diplomatic assistance to British persons abroad.[61]

Another expansion took place in the Court of Appeal decision of *R v. Panel on Take-overs and Mergers, ex parte Datafin*.[62] Prior to 1987, courts assumed that only bodies exercising powers conferred by Act of Parliament (or after the *Council of Civil Service Unions* case, prerogative powers) were reviewable. In *Datafin* the court held that a non-statutory, non-state body was carrying out 'public functions' and was therefore subject to review. Other non-statutory bodies have subsequently been held to be reviewable, including the Press Complaints Commission (a self-regulatory body for newspapers) and the managers of a privately owned psychiatric hospital. Bodies regulating sports and religious communities, on the other hand, have not been regarded as carrying out public functions.

One further area of expansion has been the liberalisation of standing requirements. The Act of Parliament setting out the framework for the judicial review procedure stipulates that a claimant must have 'a sufficient interest in the matter to which the application relates'.[63] In the past the courts interpreted this narrowly: thus, a campaign group representing the interests of small businesses was held not to have standing to question the legality of how the tax authority dealt (too favourably, it was said) with workers in the newspaper industry who had failed to pay tax;[64] and a campaign group did not have standing to review a minister's decision not to protect the archaeological remains of a theatre where Shakespeare plays were performed.[65] From the mid-1990s onwards, the courts have taken a more relaxed approach and now pressure groups, campaign organisations and public-spirited individuals are able to bring judicial review claims even if they are not directly affected by the decision.[66]

Deficiencies in the Law and Obstacles to Implementation

The lack of coherence in the system as a whole is a major problem. As noted above, the administrative justice 'landscape' in England was not designed concurrently: it has evolved piecemeal over time. At a practical level, people aggrieved by government decisions are faced with what may seem to them like a complex array of different routes to redress, including internal complaints procedures, tribunal appeals, judicial review and the ombudsmen.[67] This is compounded by the dispersed responsibility for leading and managing the whole system: central government (through

61 H. Woolf, J. Jowell and A. Le Sueur et al., *de Smith's Judicial Review* (7th edn, London, Sweet & Maxwell, 2013), chapter 3.

62 [1987] QB 815. The Panel, set up in 1968, administers the City Code on Takeovers and Mergers; its central objective is to ensure equality of treatment and opportunity for all shareholders in takeover bids. Since *Datafin*, the Panel has been designated as a supervisory authority under the EC Directive on Takeover Bids (2004/25/EC) and has statutory functions under Part 28 of the Companies Act 2006.

63 Senior Courts Act 1981 section 31.

64 *R v. Inland Revenue Commissioners Ex parte National Federation of Self-Employed and Small Businesses Ltd* [1982] AC 617.

65 *R v. Secretary of State for the Environment Ex parte Rose Theatre Trust Company Ltd* [1990] 1 QB 504.

66 See for example *R v. Secretary of State for Foreign Affairs Ex parte World Development Movement* [1995] 1 WLR 386.

67 For further discussion, see V. Bondy and A. Le Sueur, *Designing Redress: A Study about Grievances against Public Bodies* (London, Public Law Project, 2012).

the Ministry of Justice, the Cabinet Office, and several other departments), the redress institutions themselves and the Law Commission all have roles to play. The Administrative Justice and Tribunal Council, an independent advisory body, had within its remit the aim to 'keep under review the administrative justice system as a whole with a view to making it accessible, fair and efficient', but it was abolished in 2013 by central government as part of a drive to cut public spending in the face of the global economic crisis. What is missing is a sustained strategic vision. Attempts have been made, from time to time, to suggest how different parts of the system could operate more effectively in unison, notably the idea of 'proportionate dispute resolution' set out by the government in 2004.[68] In the foreseeable future, thoughts of improving administrative justice will be heavily influenced by the austere cost-cutting culture now embedded across the government.

The accounts of reforming administrative compensation law illustrate the difficulties faced in attempting to bring about change at a political level. In English law, there is no general right to damages for unlawful administrative actions that cause financial loss. In judicial review proceedings, the Administrative Court may award damages only if, in addition to establishing that there has been a breach of the grounds of judicial review, the claimant can establish a private law tort claim (for example, negligence, misfeasance in public office, false imprisonment or trespass). For several years, the Law Commission attempted to develop ambitious proposals for a major reform of damages law, but this ended in failure when the national government indicated that it was firmly opposed to the idea.[69] The government's concern was that new powers for the Administrative Court to award damages would be costly for public bodies, diverting resources away from other public purposes. The reform initiative has therefore stalled and is unlikely to see a revival.

At the judicial level, several illustrations of how the dynamic common law system has developed and expanded judicial review were discussed above. Change is not always easily brought about – as we saw in relation to the continuing debate about whether proportionality should be adopted as a common law ground of review. Another example of the failure of the common law method to develop effective rules is that English common law has not developed in order to create a general duty on public bodies to give reasons for their decisions. There are, however, a growing number of 'exceptional' circumstances in which the Administrative Court quash decisions that have not been accompanied by an explanation. This includes where there is a judicialised process (such as a disciplinary hearing) and where a decision concerns personal liberty. In various situations, Acts of Parliament impose reason-giving duties. However, the overall picture is sporadic and lacks coherence.

The Future

Earlier in this chapter, the hostility of politicians to judicial review was described, along with government proposals to restrict the availability of judicial review. Although England and Wales is a jurisdiction in which, generally speaking, the rule of law is respected by the government and court rulings are implemented, it would be wrong to be complacent about the future of judicial review. Certainly, it seems likely that politicians and officials whose decisions are subject to legal challenge will continue to question the legitimacy of judicial review. Practising lawyers, judges and academics need to assert the value and importance of judicial review in a mature democracy as a way of achieving administration under the law. One of the problems that needs to be addressed is

68 Department for Constitutional Affairs, *Transforming Public Services: Complaints, Redress and Tribunals* (Cm 6243, London, 2004).

69 Law Commission, *Administrative Redress: Public Bodies and the Citizen* (HC 6, London, 2010).

the complexity of much of the case law that has developed in recent years, as rules have been made more sophisticated, exceptions carved out, and new principles articulated. At the very heart of it, the legal standards enforced through administrative litigation can be stated in a straightforward way:[70]

1. Public bodies must have legal authority for their actions and must act within the scope of that legal authority.
2. Executive powers must be exercised within the object and purpose of the legislation that confers the said power on them.
3. Where a statute gives a public body discretionary power, that power must be used to further the scope and object of the statute – not for an extraneous purpose.
4. Public bodies must take into account all legally relevant considerations and avoid taking into account those that are irrelevant.
5. Where a statute gives decision-making powers to a public body, that body (not another one) must exercise its discretion: except in some recognised circumstances, it is unlawful to delegate the power.
6. Fair procedures must be followed.
7. Where a statute gives a public body discretionary power, the public body acts unlawfully if it adopts a rigid policy, with no exceptions, as to how the discretion will be exercised.
8. Public bodies act unlawfully if they are biased. They also act unlawfully if a fair-minded and informed observer, having considered the facts, would conclude that there was a real possibility of bias.
9. A public body's decision is unlawful if it is 'unreasonable' or 'irrational'. This may involve: giving manifestly inappropriate weight to a factor; being illogical, arbitrary, inconsistent or uncertain: giving inadequate or incomprehensible reasons; or making a decision based on inadequate or mistaken facts.
10. A public body's decision is unlawful if it is disproportionate. (This is not yet accepted as a common law ground of review in English law.)
11. Unless Parliament stipulates clearly to the contrary in a statute, a decision-maker should act in compliance with the rule of law, including access to justice and the principle of equality.
12. A public body acts unlawfully if it creates a legitimate expectation (for example, by giving a clear and unambiguous assurance) that a particular procedure will be followed or a benefit conferred and later seeks to retreat from it without an adequate justification.

Without judicial review procedures, and appeals to tribunals, it would be impossible for people to enforce these fundamental principles of lawful and good administration.

---

70 See H. Woolf, J. Jowell, A. Le Sueur et al., *de Smith's Judicial Review* (7th edn, London, Sweet & Maxwell, 2013), chapter 1.

Appendix

Table 8.1 Administrative Litigation Timeline in England and Wales

1615	Grounds of review	Natural justice (procedural fairness) for officials deprived of their office: *Bagg's Case* (1615) 11 Co Rep 69b
By mid-17th century	Remedies	Courts had developed 'prerogative writs' (certiorari, mandamus, prohibition, habeas corpus) as discretionary remedies
Throughout 19th century to early 20th century	Grounds of review	Natural justice (procedural fairness): right to be heard applied in a variety of contexts. *Cooper v. Wandsworth Board of Works* (1863) 14 CB (NS) 180: the courts will 'supply the omission of the legislature'. *Board of Education v. Rice* [1911] AC 179: public bodies 'must act in good faith and fairly listen to both sides'
1852	Grounds of review	In *Dimes v. Grand Union Canal Company* (1852) 3 HLC 759 House of Lords develops grounds of apparent bias: any direct financial or other interest in the outcome of a case automatically disqualifies the decision-maker
1905	Grounds of review	*Mayor of Westminster v. London & North West Railway Company* [1905] AC 426 (HL): court may review the purpose for which a public body is exercising a statutory power
1915–1963	Grounds of review	Courts retreat from applying natural justice: *Arlidge* [1915] AC 120. Different categories of decisions are developed: only those 'judicial' in character benefit from procedural fairness: see for example *Nakkuda Ali v. Jayaratne* [1951] AC 66
1933	Legislation	Administration of Justice (Miscellaneous Provisions) Act 1933 introduces requirement that applicants for judicial review obtain 'leave' of the court (later renamed 'permission')
1948	Grounds of review	Court of Appeal in *Associated Provincial Picture Houses Ltd v. Wednesbury Corporation* [1948] 1 KB 223 develops ground that, if a public body makes a decision that 'is so unreasonable that no reasonable authority could ever have come to it, then the courts can interfere … but to prove a case of that kind would require something overwhelming' (Lord Greene)
1958	Legislation/ alternatives to court	Tribunals and Inquires Act 1958 attempts to reform tribunal system (but proliferation of tribunals continues, creating an ever more complex system)
1959	Academic	S.A. de Smith, *Judicial Review of Administrative Action* (1st edn, London, Stevens, 1959) published: the first detailed account of the principles underlying judicial review case law
1961	Academic	HWR (Sir William) Wade, *Administrative Law* (1st edn, Oxford, OUP, 1961) published
1963	Grounds of review	In *Ridge v. Baldwin* [1964] AC 40 House of Lords repudiated idea that only decisions of 'judicial' character imposed duty of procedural fairness (see 1915 above). This was a start of a new era of activism in which the courts subjected the government to ever-greater judicial scrutiny

1967	Alternatives to court	Parliamentary Commissioner Act 1967 creates 'parliamentary ombudsman' to investigate injustice caused by maladministration in central government departments
1968	Grounds of review	In *Padfield v. Minister of Agriculture, Fisheries and Food* [1968] AC 997 House of Lords rejects government argument that there could be 'unfettered discretion': in exercising their powers, public bodies 'must act lawfully and that is a matter to be determined by looking at the Act and its scope and object in conferring a discretion …'
1969	Grounds of review/ scope	In *Anisminic v. Foreign Compensation Commission* [1969] 2 AC 147 House of Lords assert that all errors of law made by public bodies are amenable to judicial review, not only those that were 'jurisdictional'
1971	Grounds of review	In *British Oxygen v. Board of Trade* [1971] AC 610 House of Lords develops principle that public body may not lawfully fetter its discretion by adopting a rigid policy; it may have a policy but must remain willing to depart from the policy in particular cases
1973	Legislation/grounds of review	United Kingdom becomes a member of the European Economic Community (later the European Union). Case law of the European Court of Justice incorporated into English law: see European Communities Act 1972
1974	Alternatives to court	Local Government Act 1974 creates 'local government ombudsman' to investigate injustices caused by maladministration by local authorities
1978	Court procedure	Rules of the Supreme Court, Order 53 creates new procedural framework for making an application for judicial review
1981	Court procedure/ remedies	Supreme Court Act (now renamed Senior Courts Act) 1981 creates statutory framework for judicial review procedure and remedies
1983	Grounds of review/ scope	In *Council of Civil Service Unions v. Minister for the Civil Service* [1985] AC 374 the House of Lords holds that a minister's decision authorised by a 'prerogative power' was not immune from judicial review. Lord Diplock restates the grounds of judicial review. Court develops ground of legitimate expectation. Idea of 'justiciability' developed
1983	Court procedure	In *O'Reilly v. Mackman* [1983] 2 AC 273 House of Lords adopts 'procedural exclusivity' rule requiring all challenges to legality of public body decision to be made by judicial review (not ordinary civil proceedings); this is greatly criticised and later the rule is relaxed
1987	Grounds of review	In *R v. Panel on Take-overs and Mergers, ex parte Datafin* [1987] QB 815 Court of Appeal expands scope of judicial review to include non-governmental bodies exercising 'public functions'
1990	Remedies	In *R v. Secretary of State for Transport, ex parte Factortame Ltd* House of Lords for the first time makes interim order 'disapplying' provisions of an Act of Parliament incompatible with European Community law (see 1973)

Throughout 1990s	Academic	Debate about the constitutional foundations of English judicial review: is it related to the intention of Parliament or to the inherent common law powers of the courts?
1991	Grounds of review	In *R v. Secretary of State for the Home Department, ex parte Brind* [1991] 1 AC 696 House of Lords rejects argument that proportionality is a ground of review in English common law
1992	Interpretation	In *Pepper v. Hart* [1993] AC 593 House of Lords decides that, where legislation is obscure or ambiguous, counsel may make reference to statements by the minister when introducing the legislation to Parliament (reported in *Hansard*) where such statements are sufficiently clear
1994	Grounds of review	In *R v. Secretary of State for the Home Department, ex parte Doody* [1994] 1 AC 531 House of Lords states there is no general duty on public bodies to give reasons for a decision, but particular circumstances may require reasons to be given
1994	Scope	In *R v. Secretary of State for Foreign Affairs, ex parte World Development Movement* [1995] 1 WLR 386 court affirms trend of liberalising 'standing' rules to enable wider range of people not directly affected by a decision to make judicial review challenges
1996	Grounds of review	In *R v. Secretary of State for Defence, ex p Smith* [1996] QB 517 Court of Appeal develops concept of variability in intensities of unreasonableness review: 'The more substantial the interference with human rights, the more the court will require by way of justification before it is satisfied that the decision is reasonable'
1997	Interpretation	In *R v. Secretary of State for the Home Department, ex parte Pierson* [1998] AC 539 House of Lords develops 'principle of legality': courts presume that legislation does not intend to deprive people of their common law rights unless clear and specific words are used; see also *R v. Secretary of State for the Home Department, ex parte Simms* [2000] 2 AC 115
1998	Legislation/grounds	Human Rights Act 1998 enacted (in force October 2000), incorporating rights from the European Convention on Human Rights into English law: section 3 alters way in which courts interpret legislation; section 4 permits courts to make 'declarations of incompatibility'; section 6 creates a new ground of judicial review; section 7 restricts standing to 'victims'
1998	Legislation	Data Protection Act 1998 creates statutory duty to request personal information held by public bodies
1999	Grounds of review	In *R v. North and East Devon Health Authority, ex parte Coughlan* [2001] QB 213 Court of Appeal develops ground of substantive legitimate expectation
2000	Court procedure	Civil Procedure Rules Part 54 replaces Rules of the Supreme Court Order 53 (see 1981 above) as main procedure for making a claim for judicial review; 'Administrative Court' created with the High Court
2000	Legislation	Freedom of Information Act 2000 creates statutory duty of access to official information

2001	Grounds of review	In *R (on the application of Daly) v. Secretary of State for the Home Department* [2001] 2 AC 532 House of Lords clarifies that proportionality must be used as a ground of review where the claim relates to a 'qualified' ECHR right (arts 8–11)
Early 21st century and continuing …	Grounds of review	In a series of cases (too numerous to list here), the courts develop and refine their approach to adjudicating judicial review claims made under Human Rights Act 1998 section 6: issues include proportionality review for 'qualified' Convention rights (mandated by the European Court of Human Rights) and the degree of 'deference' that courts should show to government
2001	Grounds of review	In *Porter v. Magill* [2002] 2 AC 357 House of Lords restates bias ground: 'Whether, having regard to all the relevant circumstances, as ascertained by the court, the fair-minded and informed observer, having considered the facts, would conclude that there was a real possibility that the tribunal was biased'
2004	Grounds of review	Court of Appeal in *E v. Secretary of State for the Home Department* [2004] QB 1044 creates new ground of judicial review based on the principle of fairness
2004	Reform plans	Department for Constitutional Affairs (now Ministry of Justice) publishes White Paper *Transforming Public Service*s (Cm 6243) outlining 'proportionate dispute resolution' and encouraging alternatives to judicial review (especially mediation)
2007	Alternatives to court	Tribunals, Courts and Enforcement Act 2007 creates new tribunal system: First-tier Tribunal and Upper Tribunal
2011	Legislation	Localism Act 2011 expands legal powers of local authorities by creating a 'general power of competence'

PART III
Administrative Litigation Systems in Transitional Eastern European States

Chapter 9
Administrative Litigation in Poland

Mateusz Błachucki

Introduction

During the last three decades Poland has re-established external control of public administration and placed it in the hands of the administrative courts. From 1980 onwards, one can discern a notable expansion in the scope of the jurisdiction of the administrative courts.[1] Although administrative litigation in Poland remains far from ideal, the crucial and indispensable role of the administrative courts in Poland is undeniable. Many factors have collectively brought about the overall success of administrative courts in Poland. Administrative courts are capable of providing the highest degree of impartiality in relation to public authorities, affording individuals effective judicial protection against legal infringements of public administration. Administrative courts greatly differ from the common courts. The role of the former is to adjudicate on the legality of activities undertaken by the public administration. Administrative courts do not replace public administration; instead, they ensure that it follows the principle of legality.

This chapter examines the historical context, the current reality alongside the possible future development of administrative courts in Poland. It first presents the roots of the contemporary model of administrative litigation. Following this, the existing model of administrative courts is examined. All of the key issues at the crux of administrative litigation in Poland will be subsequently analyzed in turn. First, an examination of institutional matters will be instigated, alongside a more overarching description of both competences and the internal organization of the administrative courts. Second, there will be a discussion of the jurisdiction of the courts and the relevant criterion upon which judicial scrutiny is applied. This will be followed by an exploration of the procedural issues. In the final sections of the chapter, the various difficult areas with regard to the present-day state of administrative litigation in Poland will be addressed, finally drawing upon the prospective developments that will hopefully ensue in the future, in order for this already remarkable system to be cultivated and to mature.

Historical Overview of Administrative Courts in Poland

A Promising Backdrop: Prior to 1945

During the nineteenth century Poland was not an independent nation, though various forms of administrative courts did exist in the Polish territories in both the Grand Duchy of Warsaw[2] and the Polish Kingdom.[3] However, these institutions had far more in common with the public

1 The Supreme Administrative Court was reintroduced in 1980.

2 Poland was a semi-independent country subordinated to Napoleonic France (1807–1815).

3 Despite its name, it was not an independent country but a part of the Russian empire with some form of local autonomy (1815–1832).

administration than with the independent courts at that time.[4] During this period the Polish territory was occupied by three empires, namely Austria, Russia and Prussia. Consequently, three disparate traditions were each influencing and moulding the Polish way of thinking with regard to the administrative courts.

After regaining its independence in 1918, the Supreme Administrative Tribunal was established. The promulgation of the Constitution of the Republic of Poland on 17 March 1921[5] merely confirmed that administrative courts were needed in order to exercise control over the public administration. The Constitution assumed the ambitious task of formulating a strong administrative court system in Poland. Unfortunately, hardly any of these endeavours were achieved.

The fundamental legislation regulating the Polish system of administrative courts was the Act established on 3 August 1922 concerning the Supreme Administrative Tribunal.[6] This vital piece of legislation afforded the administrative courts the jurisdiction to adjudicate all administrative decisions, with the exception of those that had been expressly exempted. Article 1 of the Act ordered the establishment of the Supreme Administrative Tribunal in order to review the legality of administrative rulings and decisions that had been issued by the general public authorities or the local government. Furthermore, it provided that the Supreme Administrative Tribunal would be the only competent administrative court until the latter lower-instance administrative courts were constructed. This provision limited the competence of the Supreme Administrative Tribunal and precluded it from reviewing the legality of legislative acts that had been the legal basis of previously challenged administrative decisions. This Act also guaranteed both the independence of the Supreme Administrative Tribunal from any other public authorities or courts, alongside the finality of their delivered judgments.

A Stagnant Beginning: 1945 to 1980

During German and Soviet Union occupation of the Polish territory through World War II, administrative courts did not function in Poland. The establishment of the People's Republic of Poland resulted in the termination of the administrative courts. Although their existence was highly disputed from the outset, opponents to the administrative courts were successful in convincing the governing party and parliament that they should refrain from reinstating the administrative courts after World War II. It was argued that, in the new socialist system of governance, in comparison to the more hostile capitalist regimes, there was in fact no opposition between the State and the people and therefore such a mechanism was unnecessary. In the new system, public administration was a true servant of the people and all conflicts would either dissolve or would be promptly resolved within the administrative hierarchal system.[7] Furthermore some argued that, following the end of World War II and the creation of the socialist regime, the administrative law system in its entirety was in need of an overhaul in order to rebuild and harmonize it with the new structure.[8] Opponents of the administrative courts criticized both the lengthy and convoluted court proceedings, which

4 H. Izdebski, *Sądownictwo administracyjne w Księstwie Warszawskim i w Królestwie Polskim do 1867 roku* [Administrative courts in the Grand Duchy of Warsaw and the Polish Kingdom before 1867], Czasopismo Prawno-Historyczne 1974, No 2, p. 126.

5 Journal of Laws No 44, item 267.

6 Journal of Laws No 67, item 600.

7 S. Widerszpil, *Teoretyczne problemy rozwiniętego społeczeństwa socjalistycznego* [Theoretical problems of developed socialistic society], Państwo i Prawo 1971, No 12, p. 10.

8 M. Wyrzykowski, *Sądownictwo administracyjne w Polskiej Rzeczpospolitej Ludowej* [Administrative courts in the People's Republic of Poland], Warsaw 1983, pp. 20–21.

ultimately led to the unjustifiably drawn-out final settlement of administrative cases.[9] Furthermore, the complexity of the administrative court proceedings was a barrier for the normal individuals to access justice. Last but not least, it was argued that the creation of the administrative courts might lead to an opening of the litigation floodgates to vast numbers of complaints, which would ultimately paralyze the functioning of the court. This would have an adverse effect on the effective execution of the administrative powers.[10]

A Reflective Change: 1980 to 1990

The abolition of the administrative courts proved to be an unwise decision. Three decades had passed without an independent administrative court system and this had adversely impacted the quality of the work of the Polish public administration. This was brought to an end when the Polish parliament adopted the *Supreme Administrative Court and amendment of the Administrative Procedural Code* on 31 January 1980.[11]

The Act of 1980 was to a large extent founded upon similar foundations to the 1922 Act. The single-instance Supreme Administrative Court ('SAC') was established on 1 September 1980. The SAC was a court of cassation that reviewed decisions from a legality viewpoint. Contrary to the pre-war Act of 1922, the new legislation based the jurisdiction of the court upon an exclusive list of administrative law matters in which the court was competent to adjudicate. Article 196(2) of the Administrative Procedural Code regulated that the SAC was competent to hear complaints from administrative decisions in specified matters. Furthermore, it anticipated the possibility of the widening of the scope of jurisdiction of the SAC through separate legislation. In the decade that followed, subsequent administrative laws augmented the competences of the SAC to hear complaints from decisions issued upon the basis of said legislation. Regulating the scope of the jurisdiction of the administrative courts was from the very outset the source of major difficulties. The list of decisions that would be subject to appeal was prepared on the basis of the subject matter – specific areas of administrative law were indicated. In practice, administrative courts soon discovered cases where it was unclear whether a challenged decision fell within the proscribed category or not.[12] Fundamentally, some important matters were left outside the scope of the jurisdiction of administrative courts.

The SAC consisted of its headquarters in Warsaw and several other regional offices. It should be noted that the legal statuses of the headquarters in Warsaw and the regional offices were the same; there was no hierarchical subordination of the regional offices to the headquarters. As such, the regional offices acted on behalf of the SAC and issued final judgments that were not subject to appeal proceedings. The number of regional offices created was adapted to societal needs and ultimately depended on the number of cases brought forward from the various areas of Poland. The first regional offices were established in 1981 in Cracow, Katowice, Gdańsk, Poznań and Wrocław. Until 1990 there were eight regional offices of the SAC.

Despite the limited jurisdiction of the administrative courts, they played a significant role in changing the legal culture in Poland. Though at the beginning many authorities struggled to adjust

9 J. Starościak, *Studia z teorii prawa administracyjnego* [Studies in the theory of administrative law], Ossolineum, Wrocław 1967, p. 66.

10 M. Wyrzykowski, *op. cit.*, p. 25.

11 Journal of Laws No 4, item 8.

12 Sprawozdanie z działalności Naczelnego Sądu Administracyjnego za okres od 1.IX do 31.XII [Report from the activities of the Supreme Administrative Court between 1 September and 31 December 1980], Warsaw 1980, p. 21.

to the new situation where their actions and decisions were scrutinized, administrative litigation as a whole gradually saw an improvement. Case law of the SAC began to clarify many complex legal issues of administrative law and administrative procedure.[13] Furthermore, it corrected misinterpretations of the Administrative Procedural Code and started improving administrative practice of public administration in Poland. Just seven years after the re-establishment of the administrative court system, academics observed that the case law of the SAC was so important that it was impossible to study administrative law without knowing the jurisprudence of the court.

Gaining Strength: 1990 to 2002

After the change of the political regime in 1989, the position of the SAC was bolstered. First of all, the scope of the jurisdiction of the court was widened and it became competent to hear complaints relating to all administrative decisions. The exhaustive list of the certain types of administrative matters subject to scrutiny was replaced by a general clause of competence for the administrative court. Second, the supervision of the Supreme Court was limited. Third, the SAC became competent to adopt resolutions in clarifying complex legal issues. However, the organization of the SAC itself remained unchanged, as a single instance court with ten regional offices. All offices continued to exercise equal authority and there were no ordinary legal procedures in place through which you could challenge their rulings.

In 1997 the present-day Constitution of Poland was adopted. The Constitution determined both the organization and jurisdiction of the administration courts in Poland. It further provided for the establishment of a two-instance system of administrative litigation. Moreover, the Constitution eliminated the supervision of the Supreme Court over the SAC.

Progress and Provisions: 2002 to the Present

While the 1997 Constitution provided a new organization of the administrative court system, one of the transitional provisions of the Constitution postponed its implementation for five years. During this time there was a lively and rather intense discussion among scholars, practitioners, judges and politicians on how to effectively organize the administrative court system. The judges of the SAC played a leading role in this dialogue. They eventually prepared the final drafts of the statutes regulating the organization, jurisdiction and procedures of the administrative courts. They also managed to convince the President and the parliamentary majority to accept their proposals. Finally, the Polish Parliament adopted three acts establishing the new system of administrative litigation: Act of 25 July 2002 – *Law on the Regime of Administrative Courts*,[14] hereinafter referred to as General Law on Administrative Courts; Act of 30 August 2002 – *Law on Proceedings before Administrative Courts*,[15] hereinafter referred to as Procedural Law of Administrative Courts; and Act of 30 August 2002 – *Provisions Implementing the Act – Law on the Regime of Administrative Courts and the Act – Law on Proceedings before Administrative Courts*.[16]

---

13 M. Kulesza (ed.), *Materiały do nauki prawa administracyjnego* [Materials for studying administrative law], Warsaw 1985, p. 7.

14 Journal of Laws 2002, No 153, item 1269, with further amendments.

15 Journal of Laws 2002, No 153, item 1270, with further amendments.

16 Journal of Laws 2002, No 153, item 1271.

Institutional Framework of Administrative Courts

Nowadays, there are two instances of the administrative courts in Poland: voivodeship (regional) administrative courts and the SAC. Sixteen voivodeship courts exist in Poland. This section aims firstly to present the competences of the voivodeship administrative courts and the SAC in turn. Following this, other institutional matters will be discussed, including the internal organization of the courts and the requirements of the judges. Lastly, two graphs will be provided, to outline the path of proceedings when the courts are adjudicating a case. This covers two possible scenarios. The first describes the ordinary course of proceedings and the second provides for the route where the central government authority issues a decision in the first instance. Differences are visible between those two paths, especially in relation to the second administrative instance, which exists only in the ordinary route. However, it is clear that differences in the administrative proceedings do not affect the course of proceedings in the court litigation phase.

Division of Competences and Tasks between the Administrative Courts

The basic rule regarding the division of competences between the voivodeship administrative courts and the SAC is provided for in Article 3 of the General Law on Administrative Courts. This provides for the general assumption that all cases falling within the jurisdiction of administrative courts shall be heard, in the first instance, by the voivodeship administrative courts. Article 3(1) states that the SAC supervises the activities of the voivodeship administrative courts within the limits specified by the Law. This supervision aims at preserving both the legality and uniformity of the jurisprudence of the voivodeship administrative courts.[17] In particular, the SAC has the authority to hear all appeals made against the rulings of the voivodeship courts, to adopt resolutions clarifying the legal issues at hand and to adjudicate on other matters falling within their ambit that have been specified in separate statutes.

Jurisdiction of Voivodeship Administrative Courts

Jurisdiction of the voivodeship administrative courts is determined by Article 13 of the Procedural Law of Administrative Courts. First, voivodeship administrative courts hear all administrative court matters, except for those exclusively reserved for the jurisdiction of the SAC. Second, voivodeship administrative courts are competent to hear complaints challenging the activities of the public administration authority that have a seat within the territory where the voivodeship of the court is located. The seats and territorial jurisdiction of the voivodeship administrative courts are determined by two regulations enacted by the President of Poland.[18]

---

17 A. Kabat, *Uchwały Naczelnego Sądu Administracyjnego podjęte w latach 2004–2007* [Resolutions of the Supreme Administrative Court 2004–2007], Zeszyty Naukowe NSA 2008, No 6, p. 11.

18 Regulation of 25 April 2003 on the establishment of the voivodeship administration courts and the determination of their seats and territorial jurisdiction, Journal of Laws No 72, item 652; regulation of 13 August 2004 on the transfer of competences regarding Lubuskie and Świętokrzyskie voivodeship from voivodeship courts in Poznań and Cracow to voivodeship courts in Gorzów Wielkopolski and Kielce, Journal of Laws No 187, item 1926.

Jurisdiction of the Supreme Administrative Court

Jurisdiction of the voivodeship courts is determined very broadly and is based on a general competence clause. Jurisdiction of the SAC is regulated in a wholly opposite way. According to Article 15(1) of the Procedural Law of Administrative Courts, the SAC is competent to:

1. hear appeals against the rulings of the voivodeship administrative courts;
2. adopt resolutions clarifying the law where its application has roused disparities in the jurisprudence of administrative courts;
3. adopt resolutions clarifying legal issues that raise considerable doubts in the context of a particular administrative court case;
4. resolve disputes between local government authorities and between local government appellate boards, as well as between local government authorities and central government administration authorities; and
5. hear other matters falling within the competence of the SAC by virtue of separate statutes.

Furthermore the SAC hears disciplinary cases against judges of the administrative courts. The list of competences of the SAC proves that it serves as a supervisory court for the voivodeship courts. This supervision may take the form of challenging the rulings of the voivodeship courts or adopting two kinds of resolutions in clarifying complex legal issues.

Legal Requirements for Judges

Adjudication in the administrative courts is entrusted to judges. Polish General Law on Administrative Courts does not allow for the participation of citizens in the decision-making process in administrative courts. Even during the fierce discussions that preceded the establishment of the two-instance administrative courts, there was no such call for an introduction of juries into the administrative litigation system. This view is in line with the general scepticism surrounding the participation of juries in courts and the tendency to limit this participation even in the common courts.

The distinct status of the administrative courts in comparison with the common courts is easily seen with respect to regulating the appointment of judges. In Poland, to become a judge in a common court one must take a special training programme lasting three years and then take the subsequent special exam for judges. The result of this is that the judges of the first instance common courts are relatively young and inexperienced. The opposite situation can be seen with regard to the judges in the administrative courts. While there is no special training for administrative court judges, the law requires that candidates should have up to ten years of experience in the practical application of the law. Judges of administrative courts are usually former judges from the common courts or public prosecutors, and some are former advocates. When the administrative courts were reintroduced in 1980, a significant number of judges came from the civil service. Such an interesting mixture of both knowledge and experience of the common court judges and the civil servants proved to be one of the main factors in bringing about the success of the administrative courts. Unfortunately, more recently there has been a tendency to prevent civil servants from entering into the administrative courts.[19]

The General Law on Administrative Courts establishes standards for the candidates who wish to become judges of the administrative courts. Though the standards are relatively high, they

19 This problem will be discussed in more detail in the last section.

are wholly rational, aiming to select the best possible candidates.[20] Candidates for the post of a judge of a SAC must meet the same standards as for the voivodeship courts, with some minor modifications.[21] Judges of the administrative courts are appointed by the President of Poland upon the request of the National Council of the Judiciary. The National Council of the Judiciary selects candidates among persons presented to this institution by the general assembly of the respective administrative court. Judges are appointed to a seat in a specified court for an indefinite period of time and are independent and subject only to the Constitution and statutes. In 2012, there were 90 judges of the SAC.

Internal Organization of Administrative Courts

Organization of the voivodeship administrative courts and the SAC is very similar. Therefore, in the subsequent discussions, most of the attention will be granted to the internal organization of the voivodeship courts, with references to the SAC when necessary.

There are currently 16 voivodeship courts, which corresponds to the number of voivodeships in Poland. The SAC is a single institution and is located in Warsaw. Within each of the voivodeship administrative courts, there are numerous divisions. These divisions are split according to chosen criteria, i.e. areas of law. The number of divisions depends on the particular needs of the particular court. They are both created and dissolved easily by the President of the SAC. However, the division of the SAC is far more complex. This Court comprises the Financial Chamber, the Commercial Chamber and the General Administrative Chamber. Chambers are divided in terms of the subject matter, but may be further divided still. Aside from the chambers, there are two additional bodies that function within the SAC: the Chancellery of the President of the Court and the Bureau of Court Jurisprudence. The first serves as the administration of the Court. The second is an analytical body authorized with the task of collecting and studying the jurisprudence of the administrative courts. Detailed rules of the internal organization of the administrative courts are determined separately for the voivodeship courts and for the SAC.[22]

20 According to Article 6(1) of the General Law on Administrative Courts, candidates for the post of a judge of a voivodeship court must: (1) be a Polish citizen and fully enjoy civil and citizens' rights; (2) have a flawless character; (3) have graduated from a law faculty at a university in Poland with a Master of Laws degree, or abroad with a degree recognized in Poland; (4) be physically capable of performing the functions of a judge; (5) have attained the age of 35 years; (6) show a high level of knowledge in the field of public administration and administrative law, as well as other legal disciplines connected with the functioning of public administration; (7) for at least eight years, have been employed or in service as judge or prosecutor, or have performed for at least eight years the profession of advocate, legal counsel or notary public, or have been employed for at least ten years in public institutions at positions connected with administrative law making or have served as judge associate in a voivodeship court for at least two years. This requirement does not apply to persons with the title of professor and habilitated doctors of law.

21 These modifications are as follows: (1) the candidate must have attained the age of 40 years. This requirement does not apply to the judges who have been serving as a judge of a voivodeship administrative court for at least three years; and (2) the candidate must have been employed or in service for at least ten years as judge or prosecutor, or have performed for at least ten years the profession of advocate, legal counsel or notary public. This requirement does not apply to persons with the title of professor and habilitated doctors of law.

22 Internal rules of the organization of the voivodeship administrative courts were established in the Resolution of the President of Poland on 18 September 2003, Journal of Laws No 169, item 1646. Rules of the internal procedure and organization of the Supreme Administrative Court were adopted by the General Assembly of Judges of the Supreme Administrative Court on 9 February 2004, Official Gazette of the Republic of Poland No 11, item 176.

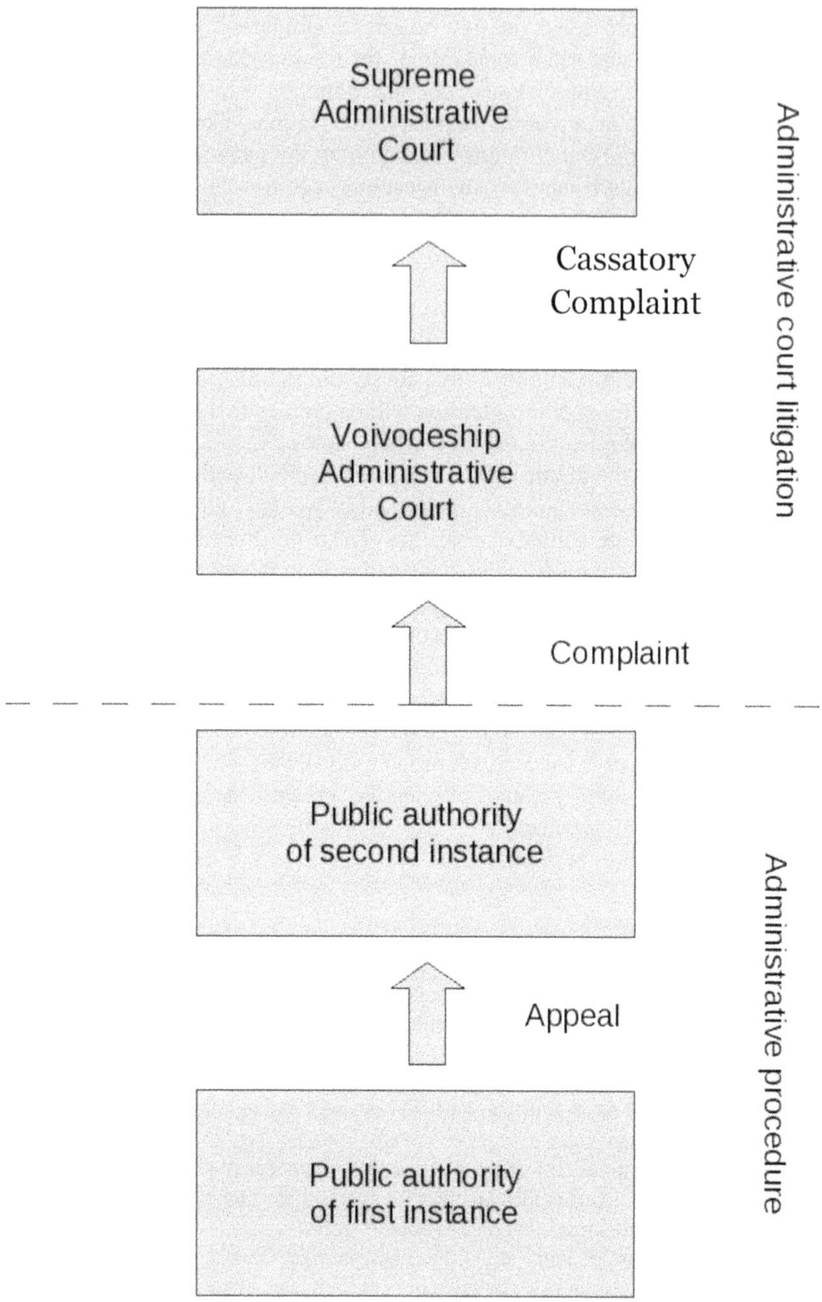

Figure 9.1 Proceedings in Cases against Non-central Governmental Decisions in Poland

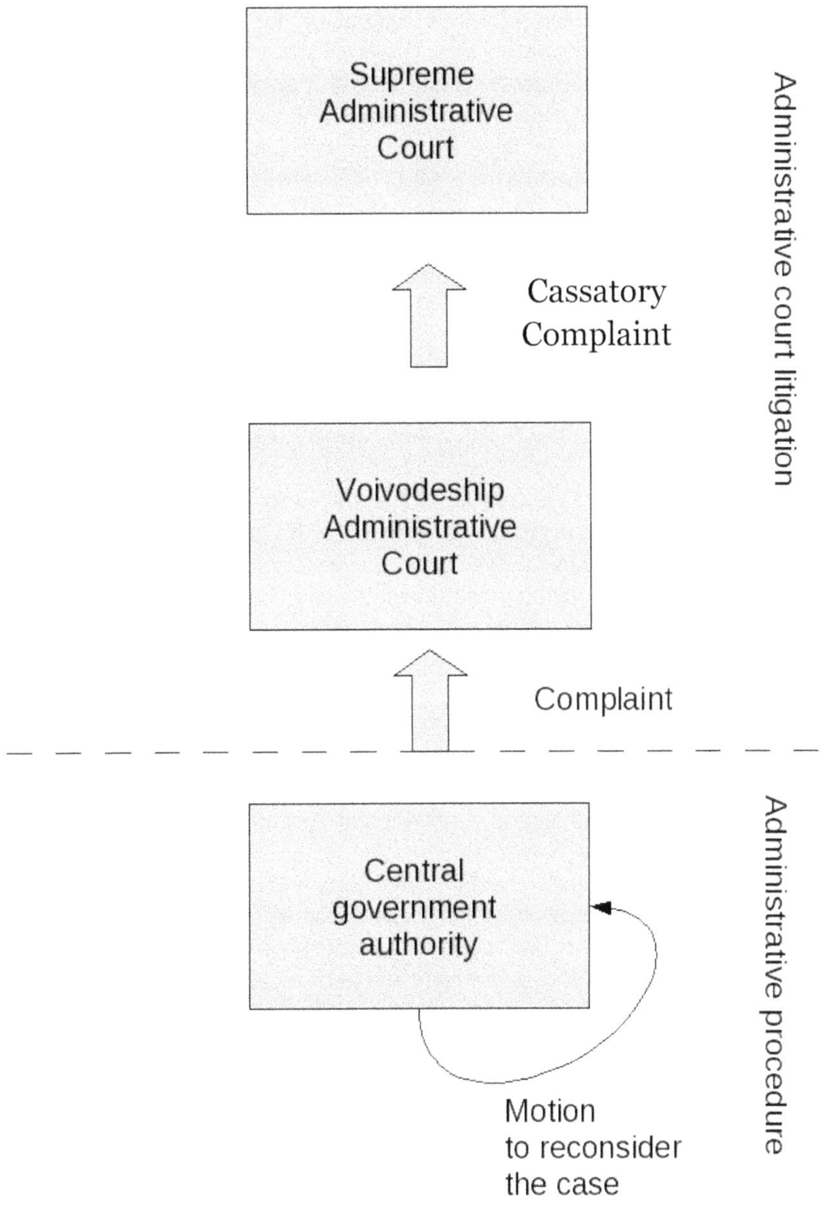

Figure 9.2 Proceedings in Cases against Central Governmental Decisions in Poland

Each of the administrative courts (both the voivodeships and the SAC) has three organs: the president of the court, the general assembly of judges of the administrative courts (general assembly) and the board of the administrative court (board of the court). The president of the court presides over the court and represents it in terms of external relations. The functions of the general assembly are both advisory and electoral (it elects candidates for the posts in the court). The board of the court serves a managerial purpose.

Lastly, a very important issue from the point of view of the organization of the administrative courts is their financial independence. To guarantee this independence, the budgets of the administrative courts are prepared by the SAC and are concluded without any interference with the general budget of the government. Article 14(1) of the General Law on Administrative Courts states clearly, 'the minister of finance includes the draft revenue and expenditure budget of administrative courts, in the wording established by the President of the Supreme Administrative Court, into the State budget.' Such a guarantee plays an important practical role, since it precludes the central government from putting any political pressure on the administrative courts through the financial instruments.

The Scope of Judicial Review of the Polish Administrative Courts

A detailed description of the jurisdiction of the administrative courts is established in Articles 3 to 5 of the Procedural Law of Administrative Courts. Articles 3 and 4 contain a positive list of the matters falling within the remit of the administrative courts, whereas Article 5 designates the five categories of the exemptions from this jurisdiction. According to Articles 3(2) and 4, the administrative courts control the activities of the public administration and adjudicate on complaints made against:

1. administrative decisions;
2. administrative orders issued in administrative proceedings, which are subject to interlocutory appeal or those concluding administrative proceedings, as well as orders resolving cases on their merits;
3. administrative orders issued in enforcement proceedings, which are subject to interlocutory appeal;
4. acts or actions, other than decisions and orders, made within the area of public administration affecting the rights or obligations of individuals ensuing from the provisions of law;
5. written interpretations of tax law issued in individual cases;
6. local law adopted by the local government and territorial government administration;
7. normative acts adopted by the local government and their associations, other than those specified in the previous subparagraph, in respect of matters falling within the scope of public administration;
8. acts of supervision over the local government;
9. failure to act as well as extensive and drawn-out administrative proceedings by the public authorities in matters referred in subparagraphs 1 to 5; and
10. motions to resolve jurisdictional disputes between local government authorities and between self-government appellate boards.

The widest and most important group of administrative acts that fall within the jurisdiction of the administrative courts are the administrative decisions. Decision-making is the most typical form of activity for the public authorities. A decision is an external act of the execution of public power that determines rights and/or obligations of an individual. Decisions are issued upon binding provisions in order to settle administrative cases and are directed toward specific individuals in specific cases.[23]

23 Resolution of Supreme Court of 5 February 1988, III AZP 1/88, OSPiKA 1989, No 3, item 59.

Many statutes use different names for administrative decisions, such as permission, authorization, approval or concession. Therefore it is not the formal description but the substance of the act that determines the legal character of the act.[24] When challenging a decision the complainant may contest the operative part of the decision, as well as the legal reasoning. The administrative courts are competent to solely set aside on the basis of the defective legal reasoning even though the essence of the decision is correct.[25] Furthermore the decision may be challenged in whole or in part.

The second and third categories of acts that are capable of being challenged before the administrative courts are orders. There are a variety of orders and they may be issued in either administrative or execution proceedings. Orders usually resolve any procedural problems that have arisen during the course of the proceedings. Contrary to decisions, not all of the orders may be subject to complaint.

The fourth category covers various acts that have a different legal character. Administrative courts reiterate that such an act must be addressed to an individual.[26] One set of acts falling within this category are acts concerning registration in public registries.[27] Such acts of registration are purely technical, but often one cannot execute one's rights without registration. Since the acts are neither decisions nor orders, one would not be able to challenge them before the court if they were not included in this category.

The fifth category is the newest one and it concerns individual written interpretations of tax law that have been issued in individual cases. Polish tax authorities are competent to issue, upon request, individual interpretations of tax law. Such interpretations are not a source of law, but, considering the complexity of tax law interpretations, they may be controlled by the administrative courts. It has been established in the case law that administrative courts are able to control the substance of the interpretation and verify whether the understanding of tax law presented by the tax authority is correct and in conformity with the binding rules.[28]

With regard to the sixth to eighth categories, acts adopted by the local government and territorial governmental administration may be challenged before the administrative courts provided that they either constitute local regulations or are other non-specified normative acts in respect of matters falling within the scope of the public administration. Local government plays an important role in Poland and is responsible for organizing the daily functioning of the local communities. Local government is independent from both the central and territorial government administration. Therefore, administrative courts are best placed to control the activities of local governments. Importantly, administrative courts do not merely control the activities of local governments but they may also secure its independence. Local authorities are entitled to make challenges before the administrative courts concerning acts relating to the supervision of central government over the local governments.

The ninth category concerns the activities of the public administration, which falls within the jurisdiction of administrative courts. This consists of the failure to act as well as complaints against extensive and drawn-out administrative proceedings by the public authorities in matters concerning issuing decisions, orders, written interpretations of tax law, and other acts or actions made within

24 Judgement of Supreme Court of 18 October 1985, II CR 320/85, OSNC 1986, No 10, item 158.

25 Judgement of Supreme Administrative Court of 30 June 1983, I SA 178/83, ONSA 1983, No 1, item 51.

26 Order of Supreme Administrative Court of 16 September 2004, OSK 247/04, ONSA WSA 2004, No 2, item 30.

27 3, ONSA 2004, No 1, item 5.

28 Resolution of Supreme Administrative Court of 8 January 2007, I FPS 1/06, ONSA WSA 2007, No 2, item 27.

the area of public administration affecting the rights or obligations of individuals ensuing from the provisions of the law. It is not possible to contest a failure to act by public authorities in relation to any other activities.[29] However, a parallel complaint can be lodged to challenge the extensive and long administrative proceedings by the public authorities. Failure to act takes place when the public authority in question does not observe the set time limits and takes no action regarding the proceedings. Extensive and drawn-out administrative proceedings take place when public authorities observe the time limits but they undertake actions that are purely formal and useless, with no intention of solving the case.

Last but not least, administrative courts resolve jurisdictional disputes between public authorities. There are two categories of jurisdictional disputes falling within the ambit of the administrative courts: (1) disputes between local government authorities and between local government appellate boards; and (2) disputes between local government authorities and central or territorial governmental administration.

Judicial Review: The Principle of Legality

Polish administrative courts both control the activities of the public administration and secure the protection of individual rights. The notion of 'control' is crucial in understanding the rationale behind the system and in analyzing the material scope of the jurisdiction of courts. There are two direct consequences of describing the competences of the administrative courts as controlling the public administration. First, administrative courts review challenged decisions or acts through the principle of legality. Second, they may issue only cassatory rulings, i.e. either uphold or set aside the contested act. Individuals may seek protection from administrative courts, but one cannot expect that administrative courts will replace the public administration. Such a narrow scope of the jurisdiction of administrative courts has a source in the constitutional principle of the separation and balancing of powers, where the executive branch is solely responsible for performing functions of public administration.[30] The Polish model of administrative litigation is based on adjudicating on the legality of challenged administrative acts. If we were to widen the scope of the administrative courts' jurisdiction, it would lead to a substitution of the public administration by courts in performing their duties.[31]

The role of the administrative courts is to control the public administration in Poland. This means that the role of the administrative court in settling administrative disputes is secondary. The court may annul a decision or force the public authority to execute its competences. However, the court cannot replace the public authority in settling administrative cases on their merits. Therefore it is the public authority that is ultimately responsible for the final resolution of disputes and not the administrative courts.[32] The administrative courts, when reviewing the challenged decision or other act, are obliged to judge whether the public authority violated binding law to such a degree that it affected the outcome of the case. Such a control must be undertaken in three parts in order to

29 Order of Supreme Administrative Court of 16 September 2004, OSK 247/04, ONSA WSA 2004, No 2, item 30.

30 L. Garlicki, *Konstytucja Rzeczypospolitej Polskiej. Komentarz* [Constitution of the Republic of Poland. Commentary], Vol. I, Warsaw 1999, p. 7.

31 T. Woś, *Reforma sądownictwa administracyjnego – projekty dalekie od ideału* [Reform of the administrative courts – projects far from ideal], Państwo i Prawo 2001, No 7, p. 31.

32 R. Hauser, *Założenia reformy sądownictwa administracyjnego* [The concepts underlying the reform of administrative litigation], Państwo i Prawo 1999, No 12, p. 23.

evaluate whether: (1) the challenged decision violates substantive binding provisions; (2) rules of procedure were observed during the whole proceedings; and (3) the public authority acted within its competences and jurisdiction.[33]

When deciding upon the legality of challenged administrative acts, the administrative court must take into consideration the hierarchy of binding legal norms in Poland. This hierarchy is set out in Article 87(1) of the Constitution. According to this provision there are four basic sources of domestic law: the Constitution, statutes (acts), ratified international agreements, and regulations. The most important is the Constitution, which is the highest source of binding law. It provides the limits and direction for all further normative acts. What is also very important is that administrative courts should not ignore norms of international law. Article 9 of the Constitution clearly states that the Republic of Poland fulfils obligations resulting from binding international law. Therefore the review of challenged administrative acts includes ensuring the conformity of those acts with binding international agreements.

Another interesting aspect of the principle of legality is with regard to its historical nature. During the twentieth century, Poland was an independent country for fewer than 20 years. During several decades, civil rights and liberties were limited or even abolished. Sometimes this was a result of administrative decisions taken by the public administration. Such decisions are contrary to the principles of the rule of law and are incompatible with the republican and liberal forms of government. However, administrative courts when adjudicating the cases are obliged to take into consideration solely the law and facts pertaining to the case in question, correlating to the date of the issued decision. As a result, it is irrelevant that the law of that date did not meet any commonly accepted criteria for decent and just regulation (a common situation with regard to the legislation of communist Poland). Therefore, unjust communist legislation that has served as a legal basis for the decision cannot be a ground for annulment of the decision, at present.[34]

The principle of legality is the only means through which the administrative courts can adjudicate, with one exception. This exception is generally stated in Article 1(2) of the General Law on Administrative Courts, which declares, 'the review [of administrative courts] shall be performed from the point of view of conformity with law, unless otherwise provided by statute.' The only statutory provision creating the legal possibility for the administrative courts to issue a substantive and not cassatory judgment is Article 154(2) of the Procedural Law of Administrative Courts. According to this provision, if the public authority fails to execute the judgment of an administrative court, the court may impose a fine on the authority and additionally adjudicate on whether there exists or not a right or obligation. This adjudication on the merits of the case is possible only if this is in line with the legal character of the case and the factual and legal background of the cases raises no doubts. This Article is rarely invoked in the case law of the administrative courts and raises some doubts over whether this provision is contrary to the general model of administrative litigation and whether the administrative courts have adequate legal instruments to execute this provision properly, i.e. administrative courts are precluded from conducting comprehensive evidence proceedings.[35] As result of these limitations, even if the courts issue judgments based on Article 154(2), they usually fine the authority and oblige it to issue a decision.

---

33 Judgment of Supreme Administrative Court of 26 January 2006, I GSK 1421/05, nyr.

34 Judgment of Voivodeship Administrative Court of 20 October 2005, IV SA/Wa 1187/05, nyr.

35 J. Zimmermann, *Polskie sądownictwo administracyjne (uwagi o projekcie ustawy o Naczelnym Sądzie Administracyjnym)* [Polish administrative litigation (remarks on the draft Act concerning the Supreme Administrative Court)], Krakowskie Studia Prawnicze 1993–1994, No XXVI–XXVII, p. 50, or J. Jendrośka, *Nowy model sądownictwa administracyjnego w Polsce* [New model of administrative litigation in Poland], Państwo i Prawo 1996, No 8–9, p. 28.

Proceedings before the Administrative Courts

This section examines the course of proceedings before the voivodeship courts and the SAC. In many respects, there are no differences in the course of the proceedings between the two. The differences result from the varying competences held by the courts.

Initiation of Proceedings

Proceedings before administrative courts may be instituted upon a complaint or motion from the party concerned, or in exceptional situations in *ex officio*. The most important method of instigating administrative litigation is related to the lodging of the complaint. It commences the proceedings and leads to the review of that challenged act or action of the relevant public authority. Motions of the parties begin the course of 'special administrative litigation',[36] resulting in resolving competence disputes between public authorities. Court proceedings may be exceptionally initiated *ex officio* in case of proceedings aimed to restore lost or damaged case files.[37] Despite this apparent plurality in the forms in which one can initiate court proceedings, the most prevalent is the former, which serves the fundamental goal of administrative litigation, i.e. the protection of individuals against any illegal acts of public authorities.

Court proceedings begin from the date upon which the complaint is lodged. The complaint must be lodged through the intermediary of the public authority whose act is to be challenged. Lodging the complaint directly to the court is legally ineffective, even if the time limit is observed. The court has no obligation to forward the complaint onto the relevant public authority.[38] When the complaint is lodged, the public authority may, if it is justified, change their decision or pass the complaint with the case files to the court.

The Concept of the Party to the Proceedings

Administrative courts aim to resolve whether the challenged act issued by the public authority is in conformity with binding law. Court proceedings are contradictory in nature and therefore two parties will be taking part in the process, i.e. the complainant and the public authority whose act or activity is being contested. There are four categories of entities able to lodge a complaint against an administrative decision or other act: (1) everyone who has a legal interest in the court proceedings, as well as public interest intervenients; (2) a public prosecutor; (3) the Ombudsman; or (4) a social organization, within the scope of its statutory activity and in matters affecting the legal interests of other persons, provided that it has taken part in administrative proceedings.

The first category is the most important and it comprises all individuals who claim that the outcome of the proceedings affects their legal interest or rights. The legal interest must be grounded upon the binding law.[39] A factual interest is not protected by the court proceedings; a legal interest is the objective criterion. Wrongly designating who is the addressee of the decision and in consequence issuing the decision to the individual who had never been a party to the

36 W. Chróścielewski, *Wszczęcie postępowania sądowoadministracyjnego* [Institution of proceedings before administrative court], Państwo i Prawo 2004, No 3, p. 63.

37 Such proceedings may also be initiated upon a motion from the party.

38 R. Hauser, J. Drachal, E. Mzyk, *Dwuinstancyjne sądownictwo administracyjne* [Two instances of administrative courts], Warsaw-Zielona Góra 2003, pp. 95–96.

39 Judgment of Supreme Administrative Court of 15 April 1993, I SA 1719/92, OSP 1994, No 10, item 199.

administrative proceedings enables that individual to lodge a complaint.[40] In this situation, the legal interest of the complainant rests within the setting of a defective and groundless decision. The analyzed provision uses a very broad clause of 'having a legal interest'. This leads to the conclusion that the complainant does not have to prove the infringement of his legal interest but only that the contested act affects his legal interest.[41]

What remains a characteristic trademark of Polish law is that it provides wide grounds for public intervention to challenge administrative decisions. This can predominantly be attributed to numerous historical reasons. Under the Communist regime, public prosecutors or social organizations were to play an important role in maintaining social and legal control over the public administration and counteracting the illegal actions of public authorities. A similar task was given to the Ombudsman, whose role is to intervene when citizens' rights are infringed by an illegal action of the public administration. However, in practice public interventions are relatively rare.[42]

The Procedural Law of Administrative Courts does not provide grounds for group complaints. However, if there is more than one entity wishing to bring forward a complaint, they are able to lodge a collective complaint acting as one complainant, provided that their complaints concern the same decision, order, act or action, or a failure to act, issued by the same authority. This provision is frequently used to challenge decisions of local governments that may be issued to more than one individual.

The Complaint: Concept and Legal Requirements

Each lodged complaint should meet certain basic requirements, both substantive and formal in nature. With regard to the formal aspects, each complaint should inform the court of the name and address of the complainant, the essential motion (i.e. description of the challenged action of the public authority), and the signature of the complainant. From the substantive position, before lodging the complaint, the party is obliged to use all available regular legal remedies to challenge the decision or other act in appellate administrative proceedings. If these proceedings prove to be ineffective, the party concerned may go to the court. The complaint must be lodged to the court within the specified statutory time limit. The length of the time limit depends on the type of act or action that is being challenged before the court. Usually it is 30 days from the date of the issuance of the decision or other act to the complainant. However, the public prosecutor or Ombudsman may lodge the complaint within six months from the date of the decision on the party of the challenged act.[43]

As mentioned before, the complaint is lodged through the intermediary of the public authority whose act or action is being challenged. The authority should within 30 days either find the complaint justified and change its decision or transfer the case files together with its response to the complaint directly to the court. The authority may not control the complaint or find it inadmissible. Its role is purely as an intermediary unless it finds the complaint justified. What is important is that

40 Judgment of Voivodeship Administrative Court of 27 January 2004, III SA 1617/02, OSP 2005, No 11, item. 128.

41 E. Bojanowski, Z. Cieślak, J. Lang, *Postępowanie administracyjne i postępowanie przed sądami administracyjnymi* [Administrative proceedings and proceedings before administrative courts], Warsaw 2004, p. 241.

42 There are some areas of administrative law where public intervention is especially active, such as that relating to environmental law or law on access to public information.

43 This time limit does not apply to lodging complaints against local regulations adopted by the local government or territorial government administration.

the authority whose act has been challenged, may decide that a complaint is warranted up until the date that the trial begins. In such a case, the authority issues a new decision that follows the motion of the complainant and court proceedings are discontinued.

To guarantee the effective cooperation of the relevant public authority in transferring the complaint with the case files, the Procedural Law of Administrative Courts provides certain sanctions for inactions. If the authority does not transfer the files within the time limit prescribed, the court may, upon request of the complainant, impose a fine on the authority. If the imposition of a fine fails to provoke action and the authority has not transferred the complaint to the court, the court may, at the request of the complainant, hear the case on the basis of the received copy of the complaint, provided that the facts and applicable law do not raise reasonable doubts. This is the most far-reaching consequence of the breach of the duty to transfer the files. Unfortunately, administrative courts hardly ever settle cases on the basis of this provision. Finally, the lack of cooperation of the public authority with the court empowers the president of the court to notify the supervisory authority about the illegal behaviour of the supervised authority. The basic defect of the described mechanism is that it may be initiated only by the party in question. The court may not discipline the public authority acting *ex officio*. In practice, it requires a lot of effort from the party involved and ultimately the end result may be far from satisfactory: for example, the fine may be paid by the authority and the files still not transferred, leaving the party to further pursue the complaint.

A successful transferral of the complaint and the files of the case does not necessarily determine a successful outcome in the court proceedings. This is especially true when the court finds legal barriers that preclude it from hearing the case. In such a situation the court ends the case on the basis of formal grounds and rejects the complaint. This may occur when:

1. the case does not fall within the jurisdiction of the administrative court;
2. the complaint was lodged after the expiration of the prescribed time limit;
3. formal deficiencies of the complaint have not been corrected within the prescribed time limit;
4. the matter subject to the complaint between the same parties is already pending or has already been validly decided;
5. one of the parties has no capacity to act as a party in court or if the complainant does not have procedural capacity and they have not been substituted by a statutory representative or there are defects in the composition of the authorities of an organizational unit being the complainant, which prevents it from operation; or
6. the lodging of a complaint is inadmissible for other reasons.

A complaint does not have a suspensive character. Therefore, lodging a complaint does not prevent the execution of a challenged act or action. However, such suspension may take place if it is so ordered by the authority whose act or action was challenged or by the court that is to hear the complaint. The suspension may be ordered *ex officio* or upon a motion. Suspension is a discretionary power of the authority concerned. The only limitation in this regard concerns those decisions that were issued under the premise of immediate enforcement. The suspension may regard the whole or a part of the contested act. Furthermore, the court may decide to suspend the execution of the contested act if there is a danger of serious damage or hardly reversible consequences. This may take place at the request of the complainant. Orders suspending the execution of challenged acts or actions may be modified or reversed at any time by the court if the circumstances have changed and they may in turn expire with the issuance of the judgment by the court.

Composition of the Courts

Administrative courts usually adjudicate their cases in a panel of three judges during an open trial. A public hearing of a case is the basic guarantee of transparency in court proceedings.[44] Within the panel, one of the judges acts as the presiding judge and another as judge rapporteur. Sometimes both functions may be assigned to the same individual. The presiding judge chairs the trial in both opening and closing proceedings. Between trials they may issue court orders. Judge rapporteurs report the facts of the case during the trial and prepare written statements as part of the overall judgment. Judges are designated to cases by the president of the division of the court. The designation of judges to an adjudicating panel hearing a case at trial or in a closed session, is regulated by the rules relating to the internal procedure of administrative courts that was previously mentioned.

Evidence Proceedings

Since the administrative courts control decisions through the use of the legality principle, there is no need to conduct evidence proceedings. The court takes into consideration the established facts and the state of the law that exists at the time when the decision was issued. Therefore, the court relies on evidence produced during the administrative proceedings. There is one exception to this general rule. Article 106(3) of the Procedural Law of Administrative Courts creates the possibility for conducting limited evidential proceedings. However, two requirements must be fulfilled in order to conduct such proceedings. These are as follows: (1) it is necessary to clarify substantial doubt; and (2) evidence proceedings will not extend excessively the proceedings on the case.

The substantial doubt should be of such a nature that it precludes the court from performing proper control of the challenged act. The second requirement eliminates the possibility of allowing the testimonies of experts during evidence proceedings, as well as hearing witnesses.[45] In practice, the only new evidence that is admissible relates to documents. Administrative courts point out that Article 106(3) does not allow for producing new evidence that existed during the administrative proceedings, which the party then refrained from submitting.[46] Furthermore, the analyzed provision may not be effectively invoked by the party to contest facts established by the public authority in the challenged decision.[47] The Procedural Law of Administrative Courts does not regulate evidence proceedings apart from the aforementioned provision. Therefore, when producing evidence the administrative court applies the relevant provisions of the Civil Procedural Code.

Mediation Procedures and Simplified Procedures

Introduction of the two-instance administrative litigation system was undertaken in conjunction with the creation of new mechanisms that aimed to streamline court proceedings. Therefore, two types of new proceedings were constructed: mediation and simplified procedures. Neither of them was used in administrative litigation prior to 2002, and from the outset their instigation resulted in intense discussions. These discussions may be summed up by saying that both the allies and

44 Exceptions to this rule are very rare and limited to situations where legally protected secrets may be disclosed and the clause of *ordre public* applies.

45 Judgment of Supreme Administrative Court of 25 February 2000, I SA 428/99, nyr.

46 Judgment of Supreme Administrative Court of 6 October 2009, II FSK 615/08, nyr.

47 Judgment of Supreme Administrative Court of 20 January 2010, II FSK 1306/08, nyr.

opponents of the new procedures were in favour of speeding up the court proceedings, but their stances differed with regard to the effectiveness of the new mechanisms in achieving that goal.

During the last two decades, mediation has increasingly gained more attention in Poland. The scope of the mediation procedures is widening over time and now caters to civil, criminal and administrative procedures. Regulation of mediation differs and depends on the individual character of the procedure in question and the type of the case referred to in this procedure. The Procedural Law of Administrative Courts regulates mediation in Articles 115 through to 118. The ultimate objective of mediation in the administrative litigation system is to settle cases between the relevant parties. Article 115(1) states that mediation is to be carried out in order to clarify and reconsider the facts and legal circumstances surrounding the cases and provide a settlement for the relevant parties, within the limits of the existing law. Mediation may be instituted by the parties themselves, i.e. complainant or an authority or *ex officio* and is conducted by the judge or the court clerk as designated by the president of the voivodeship court.

There are two different types of outcome that can result from the mediatory mechanism. First, on the basis of the arrangements made during the mediation proceedings, the authority may choose to set aside or modify the challenged act. Second, if the parties are unable to come to a resolution, the case is then referred back to the court in order to be adjudicated. However, even in situations where the parties reach an agreement through a settlement, one of these parties may later change their mind. If the party changes his mind, he may challenge this new decision or act within 30 days from the date of the delivery of the act. When this situation occurs, the court jointly hears both the new and old complaints. Conversely, in a scenario in which no complaint is lodged and the initial dispute is resolved through mediation, the court discontinues proceedings.

The essence of the simplified procedure is the possibility of adjudicating a case by a single judge sitting in a closed court. Cases are capable of being referred to the simplified procedure if they satisfy the following criteria: (1) the decision or order has been affected by an invalidity that is referred to in Article 156(1) of the Code of Administrative Procedural or to other rules or has been issued in violation of the law that provides a basis for the resumption of the proceedings;[48] (2) a party has requested that the case be referred for a hearing in accordance with the simplified procedure, and none of the other parties has demanded, within 14 days from the notification of the filing of the request, that a trial be conducted. Furthermore, the case may be referred to be heard under the simplified procedure in the event referred to in Article 55.2 of the Procedural Law of Administrative Courts.[49] Even if the case is referred to be heard under the simplified procedure, the court hearing the case in accordance with the simplified procedure may refer that case to be heard under the regular procedure at a trial.

Neither of the two prescribed proceedings has provided any real success in the streamlining of the administrative litigation system. Statistics have shown that the present regulation of mediation and the simplified procedure have in this way failed.[50] There are several reasons behind this outcome. First, mediation becomes ineffective because parties do not have any real incentive to commit wholeheartedly to the procedure. At the end of the proceedings, a complainant may disrespect the outcome of the negotiations and challenge this new decision. This in turn undermines the whole negotiation process. The final outcome is that using mediation only prolongs administrative litigation. Second, the simplified procedure is of no use to the parties themselves. Contrary to

48 These provisions describe the most significant and obvious violations of substantive and procedural law that may occur during administrative proceedings.

49 This provision concerns a sanction for the authorities for failing to transfer the files of the case and has already been analyzed in the previous sections.

50 Statistics included in the Appendix.

the intuitive approach, the simplified procedure is designed for the most severe infringements of the law. Such complicated cases demand full proceedings in which the rights of all parties are capable of being observed. It is of no surprise that hardly any party in fact decides to initiate these proceedings, as the public authorities are unlikely to give their approval.

Rulings of the Courts

The administrative courts may issue two categories of rulings, either as judgments or orders. The most important process action taken by the courts during the course of proceedings is through the delivery of judgments. In principle, all administrative court cases should be resolved through the use of judgments. In judgments, the courts discern whether the complaint is justified and consequently what the legal ramifications are for an identified infringement of the law for the challenged act or action. Furthermore, the principle of *res iudicata*[51] is applicable exclusively to judgments. With regard to orders, these are issued by the administrative courts when procedural issues arise during the course of court proceedings. Orders resolve any temporary issues or matters that do not relate to the subject of the court proceedings. Usually orders are capable of being changed easily by the court at any time, until the conclusion of the proceedings.

A court hears a case once the complaint has been lodged with the relevant public authority, within the limits determined by the Procedural Law of Administrative Courts. First, the challenged decision sets the limits concerning the established facts and the law. The court may take into consideration only those facts and the state of the law that existed at the time of the decision's delivery. Subsequent changes of facts or binding provisions that follow may not affect a court's decision. Therefore, the administrative courts are not bound by the charges and demands of the complaint as well as the legal basis referred to as a ground for the claims. This does not mean that the court may choose to disregard the complaint. On the contrary, the complaint plays a vital role in the whole process. It institutes the court proceedings and serves as an initial indicator of the potential defects in the challenged act or action. The role of the analyzed rule is to enable the administrative courts to conduct complex and comprehensive analysis and control of the challenged acts. As a result, the court is obliged to go beyond the claims raised by the complainant if this is justified by the outcome of the review undertaken. Administrative courts control the challenged administrative decisions as well as the administrative proceedings leading to the issuing of these decisions.

When adjudicating a case, the administrative courts have an obligation to 'apply measures prescribed by statute in order to remedy the violation of law in relation to acts or actions issued or taken in all the proceedings carried out within the limits of the case'.[52] This ensures that the courts control all administrative acts undertaken during the proceedings, not merely the final acts that are challenged before the courts. Furthermore, the courts review administrative proceedings of the first and the second instance that took place during the administrative phase that led to issuance of the challenged decision.

The Procedural Law of Administrative Courts has created an important guarantee for the complainant. Administrative courts may not issue a judgment that disfavours the complainant.[53] This limitation of the courts' power to adjudicate serves as a guarantee for the complainant that their

51 An expression depicting how a matter that has already been adjudicated cannot be subject to reappraisal.

52 Article 134 of the Procedural Law of Administrative Courts.

53 This general prohibition of *reformatio in peius* does not apply if the court finds that there has been a serious violation of law resulting in the declaration of invalidity of the challenged act or action.

position will not be worsened as a result of court proceedings. This is also treated as an incentive for the complainant to initiate judicial control over the act or actions that have raised doubts.

The outcome of the court proceedings inevitably depends on the findings. First, the court may dismiss the complaint. This is ordinarily the path chosen when the court finds: (1) no violation of either substantive or procedural law and therefore the act or action is correct and legal; (2) violations of substantive or procedural law of a minor character that did not affect the outcome of the administrative proceedings; or (3) that the complainant had no legal interest in challenging the act or action. In the above situations, the court upholds the contested act and terminates the court proceedings of the first instance.

Administrative courts may equally conclude that the complaint is justified and that the contested act or activity should be removed from the relevant law. When a close analysis of a case finds that a violation of the law took place and that the challenged act or activity infringed the law, the court decides that the complaint is well founded. Due to the fact that discovered infringements may differ in their gravity, character or substance, the administrative courts may issue three different types of judgments. According to Article 145(1) of the Procedural Law of Administrative Courts, the court, granting the complaint against a decision or order, shall:

1. set aside the decision or order in whole or in part, if it finds that there has been (a) a violation of substantive law that has affected the outcome of the case, (b) a violation of the law that provides the basis to reopen administrative proceedings, or (c) another breach of the procedural provisions, if it would have substantially affected the outcome of the case; or
2. find that the decision or order is invalid in whole or in part, if there exists grounds specified in Article 156 of the Code of Administrative Procedure or in other provisions; or
3. find the decision or order to be issued in violation of the law, if there exists grounds specified in the Code of Administrative Procedure or in other provisions.

Such judgments may be delivered when the courts hear complaints against a decision or order. However, as was previously explained, administrative courts are also competent to control other acts or actions undertaken by the public administration. Depending on the type of challenged act or action, the administrative courts issue different judgments. When administrative courts hear the complaint against:

1. acts or actions, except decisions and orders, made within the area of public administration affecting the rights or obligations of individuals ensuing from the provisions of law or the written interpretations of tax law issued in individual cases – the court may set aside the contested act or interpretation and declare that the action has no effect;
2. local law adopted by the local government and territorial government administration, or normative acts adopted by local governments and their associations, other than those specified in the previous subparagraph, in respect of matters falling within the scope of public administration – the court may declare such a resolution or act invalid in whole or in part, or may declare that they have been issued in violation of the law, if a special provision excludes the declaration of their invalidity;
3. acts of supervision over the local government – the court may set aside that act; or
4. a failure to act by the public authorities – the court may oblige authorities to issue an act within the specified time limit or to perform an action, or to declare or recognize the rights or obligations resulting from the provisions of the law.

The relevant public authority is ultimately bound by the final judgment of the administrative court. The judgment is both final and valid if no appellate measure was lodged and the time limit for lodging such a measure has elapsed. If only a part of the judgment has been challenged, its remainder becomes valid following the expiration of the time limit for review, unless the SAC may on its own authority hear the case in that part as well. Valid judgments issued by the administrative courts are binding not only upon the parties themselves and the courts that have issued them, but also other courts and State authorities, and other persons (in instances where this is provided for in a statute). *Res iudicata* must be interpreted strictly and therefore it applies only in relation to the complaint and the subject matter of the adjudication by the courts. There are both formal and substantive consequences stemming from the judgments: for example, if a challenged act or action is annulled, there are substantive consequences for the authority in question. This public authority would be obliged to follow the interpretation of the law presented by the court, as well as any recommendations as to how to conduct administrative proceedings expressed in a court's judgment. This limits the scope of the administrative discretion of public authorities in adjudicating cases.

The final court judgment should be implemented without any unwarranted delay. However, occasionally public authorities fail to execute the rulings given by the administrative courts. This may result in applying disciplinary measures by the courts in relation to the authority concerned. Such measures may be applied by the appropriate court. However, this may only be applied when this motion has been instigated by a complainant. Prior to lodging a complaint for non-execution of the court's judgment, the complainant must call upon the competent authority to comply with the judgment. In case of non-observance of the court's judgment, the administrative courts are entitled to: (1) fine the authority – a fine may be imposed up to a maximum of tenfold the average wage in the national economy, calculated for the last year, as pronounced by the President of the Central Statistical Office pursuant to separate provisions; or (2) adjudicate additionally on whether a right or obligation does exist, if this is permitted in accordance with the nature of the case and any non-litigious circumstances surrounding its factual and legal status.

The non-execution of a court's judgment may have further consequences. First, the relevant authority may be obliged to pay compensation if somebody has suffered injury that has resulted from a lack of compliance with the court's judgment. The compensation is to be paid by the authority that has failed to comply with the court's judgment. If the authority has not paid the compensation within three months from the filing of a claim for compensation, the entitled individual may bring an action to a common court. Second, the administrative court adjudicating the case may inform the appropriate public authority or their superior authority about the substantial infringement of the law that was discovered during the course of the proceedings. A public authority is obliged to verify this information and notify the relevant court within 30 days indicating whether rectification is underway or if they intend to act.

Legal Remedies to Challenge an Administrative Court's Ruling

The Polish Constitution guarantees the right of any individual to have their case heard twice by both a voivodeship administrative court and the SAC. The Procedural Law of Administrative courts regulates all the legal means through which a party can challenge an administrative court's ruling. The type of court ruling determines the applicable legal means through which one can challenge it. Judgments and one specific type of order, i.e. an order concluding proceedings, may be contested with a cassatory appeal. The other orders indicated in the statutes may be challenged through an interlocutory appeal. Regulation of both types of appeals are similar; therefore the cassatory appeal will be analyzed more closely and the interlocutory appeal described to a more limited extent to show the basic differences between the two.

A cassatory appeal is an ordinary legal means, but its availability is limited by a variety of legal requirements. First, a cassatory appeal must be made on one of the following grounds: (1) a violation of substantive law caused by its misinterpretation or improper application; or (2) a breach of procedural rules, if that infringement could have affected the outcome of the case.

Second, a cassatory appeal should be prepared by a professional legal representative, for example an advocate, legal adviser, tax adviser (only in tax law matters) or a patent agent (only in intellectual property). Third, a cassatory appeal should meet the requirements prescribed in the procedural document for court proceedings and include: (1) a statement of the challenged decision with an indication of whether it has been challenged in whole or in part; (2) a determination of the grounds for cassation with the reasoning for such; and (3) the request for the reversal or modification of the decision that indicates the scope of the reversal or modification sought.

A cassatory appeal should be lodged directly with the court that has issued the challenged judgment or order. It should be lodged within 30 days from the date upon which the party was served with a copy of the decision with the reasons given. What is important is that the time limit is binding for the public prosecutor and Ombudsman.[54]

These special requirements have been met with some intense opposition, questioning whether they are necessary, proportional and constitutional. The debate was concluded by the Constitutional Tribunal, which ruled on the constitutionality of the provisions on cassatory appeals.[55] However, many scholars believe that there is room for a change in the regulation of cassatory appeals in the administrative litigation system.[56]

Contrary to the various criticisms, cassatory appeals set out the limits of the adjudication of the SAC. The court is bound by the reasons of the appeal. There is only one exception. The SAC is obliged to review the challenged court ruling *ex officio* through the prism of the invalidity of the proceedings, which itself occurs when:

1. the administrative court was not competent to hear the case;
2. the party does not have the capacity to be a party in court or the procedural capacity to do so, they do not have an agency appointed to represent them or a statutory representative, or the agent of the party has not been adequately authorized;
3. the proceedings already instituted before an administrative court are pending in the same case or when a valid judgment has been issued in such case;
4. the composition of the adjudicating panel has not complied with the provisions of the law or a disqualified judge has taken part in the hearing of the case;
5. the party has been deprived of the possibility to defend their rights; or
6. the voivodeship administrative courts have adjudicated the case, which instead falls within the jurisdiction of the SAC.

---

54 The only exception is that, if the decision is not served on a party, a public prosecutor and the Ombudsman may apply within 30 days from the date upon which the decision has been issued for reasons to be given for the decision and may lodge a cassatory appeal within 30 days from the date of the issuing of a copy of the decision with the reasons given.

55 Judgment of the Constitutional Tribunal of 20 September 2009, SK 63/05, Journal of Laws No 170, item 1224.

56 Z. Kmieciak, *Konstytucyjność skargi kasacyjnej do Naczelnego Sądu Administracyjnego* [Constitutionality of cassatory appeal in administrative litigation], Glosa 2007, No 1, p. 131.

When reviewing a cassatory appeal, the administrative court has the authority to reject the case if it does not meet the necessary formal requirements stated or if the time limit was not observed. Furthermore, the SAC can dismiss a cassatory appeal if: (1) the indicated grounds are not justified; or (2) the challenged ruling complies with the law despite the wrong reasons being given.

The SAC may find a cassatory appeal justified and as a result may reverse the judgment subject to review in whole or in part and remand the case for re-examination to the court that has issued the judgment. The court is limited by the cassatory appeal and may not review the parts of the judgment that were not challenged. There is one exception. The court may reverse the judgment in its part not challenged, if the remaining part had a serious legal defect leading to nullity of the proceedings. Moreover, the SAC may also issue other types of judgments, including: (1) if the complaint was subject to a dismissal by a voivodeship administrative court and the court dismisses the complaint; (2) if there have been grounds for the discontinuance of the proceedings before a voivodeship administrative court, the court shall discontinue the proceedings; or (3) if there has been no breach of the procedural rules that may have considerably affected the outcome of the case, but only a violation of substantive law has occurred, the court may reverse the challenged decision and hear the complaint. The SAC relies in its judgment on the facts as they have been established in the challenged judgment.

Aside from a cassatory appeal, there is also a second legal means available for the parties and other entitled entities through an interlocutory appeal. An interlocutory appeal may be lodged to the SAC against the orders of a voivodeship administrative court in instances prescribed by statute, and also against some orders.[57]

In contrast to the use of a cassatory complaint, an interlocutory complaint may be lodged only if a statute provides for it. This limited availability of the interlocutory appeal is a result of the legal character of orders. Orders usually serve for settling minor procedural issues and there is no rationale for allowing parties to challenge each of them. An interlocutory appeal should be filed within seven days from the delivery of the order and meet the requirements prescribed for in the document of court proceedings and also include a statement of the challenged order and a motion for its modification or reversal, as well as a brief motivation for the interlocutory appeal.

Resolutions of the Supreme Administrative Court

Apart from adjudicating on complaints, the SAC may also adopt resolutions. Resolutions aim to safeguard the unity of administrative court jurisprudence. They provide legal certainty and legal safety for individuals. Resolutions guarantee the observance of the principle of equality. The equal treatment of individuals means that any individual will be treated the same if the facts and applicable rules are also the same.[58] As pointed out earlier, this is an exclusive competence held by the SAC. There are two categories of resolutions: (1) 'abstract' – clarifying legal provisions whose application has caused disparities in the jurisprudence of the administrative courts; (2) 'concrete' – clarifying the legal issues that raise considerable doubts in the context of administrative court cases.

57 These orders comprise: (1) the transfer of the case to another administrative court; (2) the staying or refusal of the execution of the challenged decision, order, other act or action; (3) the suspension of the proceedings and the refusal to resume the suspended proceedings; (4) the refusal to give reasons for a judgment; (5) the correction or interpretation of a decision or refusal thereof; (6) dismissal of a motion for disqualification of a judge; (7) rejection of a cassatory appeal; (8) rejection of an interlocutory appeal; (9) reimbursement of costs of the proceedings, if the party has not filed a cassatory appeal; (10) imposition of a fine.

58 Judgment of Supreme Administrative Court of 7 November 2008, II GSK 457/08, nyr.

'Abstract' resolutions are adopted in order to clarify those provisions that were interpreted differently by the administrative courts. The subject of such a resolution is the clarification of legal doubts that are not connected to any particular administrative court case.[59]

Resolutions are adopted by the SAC by a panel of seven judges, the entire Chamber or the full panel of the SAC.[60] The decision on which panel will be assigned to a particular case lies within the hands of the President of the SAC. However, each panel may refer a case to the next panel, i.e. the panel of seven judges may refer a question of law to be resolved by a panel of the entire Chamber and the Chamber is able to refer it to the full panel of the SAC. The court may not adopt a resolution *ex officio*, but they instead always act upon request. 'Abstract' resolutions may be adopted upon the request of the President of the SAC, the Public Prosecutor General or the Ombudsman. 'Concrete' resolutions may be adopted upon the request of the adjudicating panel of the administrative courts. The SAC is not bound by the request and may refuse to adopt a resolution if they find that there is no need to do so.

Resolutions of the SAC are binding upon all judges of the administrative courts. The binding force of resolutions means that all administrative courts are obliged to follow them until they are changed by the SAC.[61] Therefore, if any panel of the administrative courts hearing the cases does not share the position taken in the resolution by the seven judges, the panel of the entire Chamber or by the full panel of the SAC, they are obliged to submit the arising legal issue for resolution by an appropriate panel. Any panel of the administrative courts refers to any panel of the voivodeship courts or the SAC.[62] Resolutions are binding irrespective of their character. Academics[63] and administrative courts[64] share the opinion that both 'abstract' and 'concrete' resolutions have the same binding effect. Therefore, 'concrete' resolutions are binding in particular cases that give reasoning for adopting the resolution but also in any other administrative court cases. Each resolution should consist of an element and a statement of reasoning. It is important to remember that only the operative part is binding on the administrative courts. A statement of reasoning has purely an explanatory value and it does not limit the administrative courts during their adjudication of cases.[65] Resolutions are directly binding only upon the administrative courts. However, public administrations may not disregard the resolutions of the SAC. Therefore, the administrative courts indicate that resolutions are also indirectly binding upon all public authorities.[66]

---

59 Judgment of the Supreme Administrative Court of 9 June 2010, I FSK 993/09, nyr.

60 The full panel of the SAC consists of all (90) judges of the SAC. So far, there has been only one resolution of the full panel of the SAC – Resolution of 26 October 2009, I OPS 10/09, ONSAiWSA of 2010, No 1, item 1.

61 A. Kabat, *op. cit.*, p. 13.

62 R. Hauser, A. Kabat, R. Hauser, A. Kabat, *Uchwały Naczelnego Sądu Administracyjnego w nowych regulacjach procesowych* [Resolutions of the Supreme Administrative Court in procedural regulations], Państwo i Prawo 2004, No 2, p. 29.

63 P. Krawczyk, *Uchwały konkretne Naczelnego Sądu Administracyjnego jako instytucja ujednolicająca stosowanie prawa w sprawach sądowoadministracyjnych* [Resolutions of the Supreme Administrative Court as an institution of unification of law enforcement in administrative litigation], Studia Iuridica Lublinensia 2006, No 7, p. 109.

64 Judgment of voivodeship Administrative Court of 28 June 2006, IV SA/Wa 2143/05, nyr.

65 Judgment of Supreme Administrative Court of 16 February 2007, I FSK 639/06, nyr.

66 Judgment of Supreme Administrative Court of 31 May 2005, FSK 2283/04, nyr.

Deficiencies in the Law and Problems in Implementation

Several difficulties can be identified in relation to the Polish administrative litigation system. These differ in both substance and relevance. The seven most prevalent issues are discussed below (they are not hierarchical):

Principle of Legality and Cassatory Rulings

There is a growing debate over whether the courts should have the competence to adjudicate cases on their merits and as such go beyond the legality of a decision. In the present system many individuals do not have an adequate level of court protection since administrative courts have a limited competence. The principle of legality as an exclusive criterion of controlling public administration may have two adverse effects. First, in limiting the jurisdiction of the administrative courts to review only the legal aspects of the cases, this may create only an apparent court protection. In many administrative law cases the law is clear, whereas the facts are disputable. Under the present rules, administrative courts may not conduct evidence proceedings and hence may not change the administrative decision. A good example of this issue can be seen in situations where administrative courts control administrative decisions issued, having conducted an examination. This takes place during admittance to the bar of advocates or in obtaining a higher educational rank (like habilitation). In those two situations, the crucial element is the evidence proceedings during the administrative process. Based on the outcome of the evidence proceedings, interpreting and executing the law is not problematic. However, administrative courts may intervene only in this last stage of reaching the administrative decision. The courts may not control the examination itself and, for example, verify the answers. Another adverse aspect of this solution is that the individual might wait for the final decision for many years. Having gone through two instances of administrative proceedings and two instances of administrative court proceedings, one may arrive again at the starting point and take the same route through.

This problem touches the very heart of the administrative litigation system in Poland. To remedy the situation, an amendment of the Constitution itself is inevitable.

Civil Courts and their Competency to Hear Appeals/Complaints against Administrative Acts

From 1990 onwards, one may observe that Polish legislators began to alter the general rule that the activity of public administration was controlled by administrative courts and began to allocate certain administrative matters within the jurisdiction of civil courts. Ordinarily there were no special reasons given for such an alteration in jurisdiction. Therefore, most of the changes were accidental or they were a consequence of earlier changes. This applies to certain decisions taken within the areas of anti-monopoly law, energy and telecommunication law, access to public information, civil service, disputes arising from agreements among local governments, and the delimitation of boundaries of real estate.[67] The most controversial issue surrounding this situation is that rarely an alteration of jurisdiction would be completed and in the majority of matters it resulted in a judicial jurisdictional dualism, i.e. the common court became competent to review certain aspects of the

67 This category is very specific, since the common courts have exclusive jurisdiction over those cases. Furthermore, matters involving the delimitation of boundaries of real estates are civil in nature and the administrative phase may be treated as a conciliary pre-court stadium of reaching agreement between the owners of neighbouring estates. In practice, judicial review of this category of cases does not raise substantial problems. However, judicial review of other cases does raise such problems.

case, whereas in relation to other aspects the administrative courts remained competent as well. This dualism induces new problems for those individuals seeking judicial protection.

An alteration of judicial jurisdiction in relation to administrative law cases raises different theoretical and practical problems. From the constitutional point of view, it is controversial to transfer judicial jurisdiction in administrative cases to civil courts. According to the Polish Constitution, administrative courts should be responsible for controlling the public administration. Moreover, the role of the courts in the Polish system of administration control is to control and not to replace the public administration. As a consequence of this alteration in the jurisdiction, the civil courts step into the competences of the public administration and yet bear no political responsibility for their actions. Furthermore, an alteration in the judicial jurisdiction in administrative law cases raises various problems – ranging from disputes of character and competences of the civil courts to denial of judicial protection. From the point of view of individuals, the other problems are perhaps the most significant, i.e. proceedings in civil courts take much longer than administrative litigation, there are jurisdictional disputes between civil and administrative courts, civil courts do not control administrative proceedings but only decisions that have been challenged, and civil law judges are not always experienced and sufficiently qualified to hear administrative cases.

Duration of Proceedings Brought before the Supreme Administrative Court

The establishment of the two-instance court proceedings has prolonged the administrative litigation process. Proceedings before the voivodeship administrative courts usually take four to six months. They appear to be very fast and effective. Unfortunately, this is not the case for the proceedings brought before the SAC. At present, the SAC handles cases in approximately 12 to 16 months.[68] This is considered too long. Statistics show that the SAC settles around 50 to 60 per cent of its pending cases. This proves that the proceedings of the SAC are not effective. This is strange, since the SAC does not conduct any evidence proceedings, cassatory appeals are prepared by the professional representatives, and the court is in principle limited to the motions of the complainant. Taking into account these characteristics, the SAC should have the capacity to handle cases more promptly than it does. Unfortunately, the SAC is not willing to take any reasonable action to change this. From time to time, judges claim that the solution to this problem would be a limitation of the availability of cassatory complaints.[69] However, this would only be the case when the cure is worse than the disease.

Execution of the Rulings of the Administrative Courts

In the Polish system of administrative litigation, courts have no competence to directly monitor the execution of their judgments, nor can they take any action *ex officio* to discipline the public authority to implement their ruling. Initiative rests with the individual seeking court protection. What is strange is that the party cannot go directly to the court but is obliged to call upon the public authority to implement the judgment and wait 30 days for their reaction. This waiting period further delays the execution of the judgment. Furthermore, the most significant legal instrument that may rectify this situation is ignored by the courts. In case of a failure to implement the court's judgment,

---

68 There are no data available on the average duration of proceedings before the Supreme Administrative Court.

69 See T. Woś, *Dwuinstancyjne sądownictwo administracyjne a konstytucyjne prawo do rozpatrzenia sprawy 'bez nieuzasadnionej zwłoki'* [Two instances of administrative courts versus constitutional right to adjudicate on a case without undue delay], Państwo i Prawo 2003, No 9, pp. 32–33.

an administrative court may adjudicate the case on its merits and settle the case. However, the administrative court does not use this competence in practice. Instead, they limit themselves to fine the authority for the non-execution of the judgment. Such a fine hardly ever helps the party to have their case settled. Furthermore, the fine is paid by the public authority and not by the individual who is actually responsible for this negligence in implementing the judgment.

Inefficiency of Mediation and the Simplified Procedures

Both mediation and the simplified procedures serve a function in aiming to streamline the settlement of cases. However, as was explained earlier, due to poor provisions those specific procedures are hardly ever used by the parties during the court proceedings. Parties to mediation lack the legal certainty that the outcome of the negotiation will not be challenged immediately after the conclusion of the mediatory process. This results in an under-usage of mediation. Furthermore, mediation is usually led by the court clerk and not by the judge. This results in some parties having far less confidence in the final outcome. Simplified procedures are also rarely instigated. In the Polish system, the simplified procedure serves to adjudicate the very complex cases. It seems contrary to common sense that the simplified proceedings serve to adjudicate the most complex cases. It should be the opposite, since the simplified procedure should be designed for the simple cases in order to be solved promptly. It is not surprising that parties do not agree to initiate simplified proceedings when the case is complex and the challenged decision seems to infringe the law to a large extent. Such cases require normal procedures with the full participation of all parties. What is disheartening is that these defects were blatant from the very outset but the Polish legislators were not eager to take them into consideration. Therefore, there should be comprehensive statutory amendments implemented to rectify this situation, otherwise mediation and the simplified procedure will remain artificial and empty.

Composition of the Courts and the Lack of Special Training for Administrative Judges

The administrative courts are in principle composed of judges who come from the public administration and as previously practising lawyers (civil law judges, public prosecutors or advocates). When the administrative courts were re-established in the early 1980s, the proportion of civil servants to other lawyers was almost 50:50. However, during the last decade only a few judges were nominated from among the civil service. This has resulted in the decreasing quality of the case law of the administrative courts. Administrative law is different from civil and criminal law. Therefore, it is doubtful whether public prosecutors practising criminal law or civil law judges implementing civil law are more competent than civil servants who adjudicate over administrative law matters during their service. Furthermore, prosecutors, civil law judges or even advocates do not have to take any special training before they become judges. The result is that people with no experience in executing administrative law become judges of administrative law. Administrative courts are rather peculiar in comparison to the other courts. Despite the fact that civil and criminal law judges must take the obligatory three-year special training, there is no such training for judges of the administrative courts. This has an adverse effect on the quality of the work of the judges of administrative courts. This problem is increasingly apparent, but the administrative courts choose to ignore it; as such, there is no real prospect of any substantial change in the near future.

Lack of Regulation of Jurisdictional Disputes between the Courts

As described in the section concerning jurisdictional judicial dualism, this may in turn lead to a denial of justice, as no court is deemed competent to hear the complaint. Usually this is the result of transferring some matters to the civil courts and sometimes it is the result of imprecise provisions. In many instances, both reasons are true. The courts are usually very opportunistic when declaring that they are incompetent to hear a case and are more than willing to transfer it to another court. In some situations, this results in refusing court protection to the citizen. The source of the problem is that the individual may not initiate proceedings that lead to the resolution of the jurisdictional dispute. Such proceedings may not be instituted because there is no institution that may conduct such proceedings. Before the establishment of the two-instance administrative court system, the Competence College existed. The Competence College was an *ad hoc* body designated to resolving disputes between courts. It functioned under the auspices of the Supreme Court. This College consisted of the judges of the SAC and the Supreme Court. The majority of the judges came from the Supreme Court. However, when the two-instance administrative court system was designed, the representatives of the administrative courts and the civil courts were unable to decide how many judges would represent each court. Judges from the Supreme Court wanted to maintain the *status quo*, whereas judges from the SAC wanted an equal number of judges from both courts to be seated in the Competence College. As a result of the lack of agreement between the courts, the Competence College was abandoned and consequently there is no such institution competent to resolve competence disputes between the courts in Poland at the present time.

The Future

There are currently three drafts of changes of legal provisions relating to the Polish administrative courts. Two legislative proposals which have been prepared by the members of the Polish parliament recommend some minor changes of housekeeping character. However, the third prepared draft is of important character and contains proposals for the amendment of the Procedural Law of Administrative Courts. It addresses some of the aforementioned deficiencies in the system of administrative litigation. Intended goals of the amendment were presented by the President of the SAC during a debate organized by the President of Poland.[70] The new proposals focus on:

1. disciplining the public administrative authorities in complying with administrative court judgments. This will involve the creation of new forms of procedures enabling administrative courts to secure the proper and prompt execution of their judgments by enabling courts to act *ex officio*;
2. widening the scope of the reformatory adjudication of the SAC. The SAC would gain new competences in order to avoid delivering cassatory rulings and issuing substantive judgments, changing judgments of the voivodeship administrative courts. As a result, the party will receive the final judgment and there will be no need for the reconsideration of the case before the voivodeship administrative court;

70 R. Hauser, *Zakres i kierunki zmian ustawy – Prawo o postępowaniu przed sądami administracyjnymi* [The scope and patterns of changes of the act – Law on proceedings before administrative courts] [in:] *Obywatel wobec administracji – konieczne zmiany w postępowaniu administracyjnym* [Citizen versus public administration – necessary changes in administrative procedure], Biuletyn Forum Debaty Publicznej, 2011, No 7, p. 10.

3. limiting the situations when public administrative authorities may issue cassatory decisions after the abrogation of the earlier decision by the court. Furthermore, the proposal may include enabling the voivodeship administrative courts to oblige public authorities to issue decisions determined in substance by the court; and
4. the simplification of the appeal procedure. Voivodeship administrative courts would gain the competence to change their judgment if they found the appeal justified and to declare appeals inadmissible if they are manifestly groundless.

The proposals were prepared by the judges of the administrative courts and were transmitted to the President of Poland in the autumn of 2012 with the intention of persuading the President to use his legislative initiative in presenting the proposals to Parliament. In the spring of 2013, the President launched the public consultations. As a result the President has decided to present parliament with the draft amendment which follows almost entirely the initial proposal of the judges. The abovementioned proposals are difficult to evaluate. Some of them address several of the issues raised earlier, like the inefficiency of the enforcement procedures or the widening of the scope of reformatory adjudication by the administrative courts. However, the remainder of the proposals steer in the opposite direction. The so-called 'simplification of the appeal procedure' will limit the accessibility of the cassatory appeals and the chance to present a case before the SAC. This should result in a reduction of cases falling under the review of the SAC and a shortening of the duration of proceedings before the court. However, such an outcome may be beneficial only for the judges of the SAC. As a consequence of the adoption of the amendment, the right of individuals to challenge judgments of voivodeship administrative courts will be limited. Therefore this proposal may not be favourable to individuals. Moreover, proposals do not confront the problems surrounding mediation and the simplified procedures or the ineffective mechanism of dispute resolution between the civil and administrative courts. Furthermore, the proposals ignore the necessity of any institutional and organizational changes of the administrative courts. This can probably be attributed to the fact that the authors are the judges of the SAC and so they want to preserve the *status quo* in this respect.

Conclusions

In 2012, 10 years had passed since the establishment of the two-instance administrative court proceedings system. Based on what has come to light during the course of this decade, judges of the SAC prepared proposals to amend the existing regulations. Several of the identified deficiencies have in turn been addressed, but a handful remains untouched. Furthermore, some of the proposals have proven highly controversial and have roused both concern and debate. The proposals remain in the consultation phase under the auspices of the President of Poland and to date they have not been presented to Parliament. Therefore, the process of amending the regulation of administrative litigation in Poland is still ongoing and the final outcome remains unknown.

Despite various deficiencies, the overall consensus of the Polish administrative court system is on the whole positive. The impact of the jurisprudence of the administrative courts on the work of public authorities is undeniable. Nowadays, it is not possible to imagine the functioning of a modern republican State without independent judicial control of the public administration. Poland's history indicates that, without independence and external control, the quality of the work of the public administration deteriorates. Such control is indispensable in securing the protection of civil rights *vis-à-vis* public authorities. Despite the success of the administrative courts, the Polish example teaches us that systems of legal norms and institutions should be subject to periodical revision. In line with alterations in the political, economic and social landscapes of development, statutes should also evolve. The cassatory adjudication system served its function for almost a century, but it is now high time for some substantial changes. Therefore, the impetus for change should come from outside the system of the administrative courts. Proposals prepared by the judges of the SAC may be regarded as partial solutions that aim at some changes, but that in fact preserve the *status quo*.

Appendix: Polish Administrative Courts in Statistics[71]

Table 9.1 Mediation Proceedings 2004–2011 in Poland

Year	2004	2005	2006	2007	2008	2009	2010	2011
Number of instituted mediation proceedings	679	204	172	87	36	21	11	23
Number of cases closed	170	117	66	17	16	3	2	8

Table 9.2 Simplified Proceedings 2004–2011 in Poland

Year	2004	2005	2006	2007	2008	2009	2010	2011
Number of cases adjudicated in simplified proceedings	902	1390	683	358	155	36	154	440
% of cases adjudicated in simplified proceedings in relation to all settled cases	1.08	1.59	0.87	0.53	0.26	0.06	0.24	0.64
Number of cases adjudicated in simplified proceedings in favour of complainant	506	884	454	295	109	21	62	203
% of cases settled in favour of complainant in simplified proceedings	56.1	63.6	66.5	82.4	70.3	58.3	40.3	46.1
Number of cases adjudicated in simplified proceedings rejecting the complaint	333	506	229	63	46	15	84	237

Table 9.3 Intervention Ratio of Administrative Courts in Poland

Year	Cases pending	Cases settled	Complaint succeeded (%)
1981	5,432	2,041	41
1982	8,776	8,116	35.4
1991	15,212	10,918	35.8
2000	65,094	62,260	29.5
2010	67,830	60,879	21.5
2011	69,581	65,699	22.5

71 Statistics cover all cases falling within the jurisdiction of administrative courts without distinguishing between the subject matter of cases.

Table 9.4 Cassatory Appeals Lodged before the Supreme Administrative Court 2004–2011 in Poland

Year	Number of cassatory appeals (includes new and already pending cases from the previous years)	Cases solved	Cases pending
2004	6,167	2,918	3,249
2005	12,798	6,535	6,263
2006	16,700	8,788	7,912
2007	17,342	9,347	7,995
2008	18,114	9,389	8,725
2009	19,185	10,013	9,172
2010	20,848	10,922	9,926
2011	24,595	11,352	13,243

Chapter 10
Administrative Litigation Law and Practice in Romania

Petra Gyöngyi

Introduction

The administrative litigation system in Romania allows for the possibility for citizens to contest the decisions rendered by the administrative authorities before a court in cases involving a breach of their rights or legitimate interests. Administrative litigation has a long-standing history within the Romanian legal system; several stages of development have been undertaken that showcase the progress made, though stagnated by the hiatus experienced between 1948 and 1965, during a part of the Communist period.[1] Currently, the Law on Administrative Litigation,[2] containing both substantive and procedural rules, governs the present-day system of administrative litigation.

This chapter presents an overview of the evolution of administrative litigation in Romania from its initiation to its current state. It assesses the influential factors that have brought about the developments in the Romanian administrative litigation. In particular, the historical influence, influence from foreign legal systems and organizational influences that have shaped the development of the administrative litigation law and its practice are presented. In the assessment, the following structure is adopted. The analysis begins with a brief historical overview of administrative litigation within the context of Romanian law, drawing upon the most important stages in administrative litigation. This is followed by the presentation of the current institutional arrangements for the administrative litigation process. Particular attention is assigned to illustrating the position of administrative litigation in the broader setting of the Romanian court system, as well as presenting the alternatives to administrative litigation. Next, the scope of administrative litigation is stated. At this point, the particular focus is upon a historical overview of the evolution of the scope of the administrative litigation system, as it serves an important function in providing the backdrop against which we can assess the current administrative litigation law and practice.

With the setting established through a general overview, the application of the principles of both legality and proportionality is presented in more detail. Accordingly, this is followed by an analysis that focuses on the progression in the conceptualization and application of the principle of legality, a fundamental principle of administrative litigation. Next, the principle of proportionality, applicable in Romanian administrative litigation as a result of the recognition of European Union law and the case law of the European Court of Human Rights (ECtHR), is assessed. A presentation

1 For a detailed presentation of Romanian administrative law *see* C. Rarincescu, *Contenciosul Administrativ Roman* (*Romanian Administrative Litigation*), 'Universala' Alcalay & Co., Bucharest (1937); A. Iorgovan, *Tratat de Drept Administrativ* (*Administrative Law Treaty*), vol. II, 4th edition, All Beck, Bucharest (2005); R.N. Petrescu, *Drept Administrativ* (*Administrative Law*), Accent, Cluj-Napoca (2004); Dana Apostol Tofan, *Drept Administrativ* (*Administrative Law*), vols I–II, All Beck, Bucharest (2004, 2008).

2 Law no. 554 of 2004 on Administrative Litigation, published in the Official Gazette of Romania no. 1154 of 7.12.2004, with subsequent modifications in 2005, 2007, 2008, 2011.

of the relevant case law stemming from the European courts, alongside reports of the European Commission, which are utilized as direct points of reference for the Romanian courts, allows for an evaluation of the changes made in improving judicial organization in Romania.

Stemming from this overview of the relevant case law of the administrative divisions of the courts, the practical problems created by the deficiencies in the law as well as the possible problems with regard to the implementation of the legislative framework are outlined. In completing this picture, the subsequent section presents some major challenges affecting the functioning of the administrative litigation system. In this regard, emphasis is placed upon the problems relating to the organization of the judiciary as a whole in Romania. Finally, in returning to the grander picture of administrative litigation in Romania, some future perspectives and possible directions are presented for administrative litigation. These considerations are based upon the historical contextualization, the influences of supranational legal systems, the difficulties experienced in implementing the law, and organizational factors affecting administrative litigation. Taking into account the aforementioned elements and sources, enables an insightful understanding of the evolution of administrative litigation in Romania and its future course.

The Historical Development of Administrative Litigation in Romania

The historical development of administrative litigation in Romania has undergone several stages. The first stage covers the period between 1867 and 1948. This initial period of administrative litigation is later separated by a hiatus during the communist era. Between 1948 and 1965 the possibility for the courts to review administrative decisions was abolished.[3] Despite administrative litigation being reintroduced into the Romanian legal system in 1967,[4] this legislation failed to produce any significant effects. A more effective reinstatement and reconsideration of administrative litigation in Romania appeared in the third stage, which began in 1990,[5] following the democratic transition.

The Inception of the Romanian Administrative Law and its Original Influences, 1864–1905

The Romanian administrative legal culture has strong historical foundations. It has developed mainly in tune with the French influences, with an interesting addition from the common law system.[6] In 1864, the Council of State was created, under the French influence. Administrative litigation has its origins in Romania in 1867, when the first legislation on judicial overview of administrative acts was introduced into the legal system.[7]

However, between 1866 and 1905, this system was abandoned and local courts were instead designated the role of adjudicating administrative law cases, following the common-law example. During this period, there was no legal basis for delimiting the competence of administrative litigation. Therefore, these delimitations were developed through the case law of the courts.[8] Contemporary dilemmas included whether it would be possible to adjudicate a case on the

3 Decree no. 128 of 1948 for abolishing administrative litigation.

4 Law no. 1 of 1967 on adjudicating by courts the claims of persons aggrieved in their rights through unlawful administrative acts, Official Gazette of Romania no. 67 of 26.07.1967.

5 Law no. 29 of 1990 on Administrative Litigation, Official Gazette of Romania no. 122 of 8.11.1990.

6 A. Iorgovan, *Tratat de Drept Administrativ* (*Administrative Law Treaty*), vol. II, 4th edition, All Beck, Bucharest (2005), p. 488.

7 *Id.*

8 *Id.*, p. 510.

basis of administrative law for a breach of the legitimate interests of an individual through an administrative act, or whether administrative litigation would be solely based upon a breach of a right, pertaining to an administrative act. An additional problem that appeared was in delimiting the scope of administrative litigation depending upon the type of administrative act in question.[9]

The 1905 to 1948 Period

The subsequent stage was marked by legislative changes concerning administrative litigation. A distinguishing characteristic of this period was the promulgation of specific legislation within the scope of administrative litigation. Accordingly, it was possible to contest an administrative act as part of the appeal procedure. For the purposes of adjudicating the appeal in administrative cases, the special administrative chamber of the Court of Cassation was created.[10] In 1910, the system of administrative litigation was again subjected to alteration when the special chamber of the Court of Cassation was dismissed and their competence handed to the ordinary courts in adjudicating administrative cases.[11] In 1912, the possibility to review the legality of administrative acts was reintroduced. However, the option of annulling an administrative act was not granted to the courts.[12]

In line with the new provisions of the Constitution of 1923,[13] the administrative litigation law was adopted in 1925.[14] According to this legislation, it was possible to review the legality of administrative acts only in cases where a breach of a right was invoked, which excluded claims involving a legitimate interest. During this period, the Romanian court organization system comprised various courts, including: courts of general competence, courts of appeal, administrative tribunals, and administrative jurisdictions – consisting of State-related institutions with the competence of solving complaints relating to public administration.[15]

The 1948 to 1990 Period

This era represented a rupture in the Romanian administrative litigation. During the Communist regime there was virtually no room left for the judicial review of administrative acts. Between 1948 and 1965 no system of the judicial review of administrative acts existed; and correspondingly, the previous legislation governing the review of administrative decisions was abolished.[16]

In 1967, a new law brought about the possibility of claims for judicial review of administrative acts once more. Although this law constitutes the beginning of contemporary administrative litigation in Romania, it was at this time rarely implemented in practice.[17] For the purposes of this present analysis, I do not probe into the peculiarities of this period. Nevertheless, several stages of developments can be distinguished even within this stage.[18]

9 *Id.*
10 *Id.*
11 *Id.*, without the possibility to annul the contested administrative acts.
12 *Id.*, p. 511.
13 Administrative litigation was conferred through Article 107 of the 1923 Constitution.
14 Law on Administrative Litigation of 23 December 1925.
15 A. Iorgovan, *supra* note 6, p. 512.
16 A. Iorgovan, *supra* note 6, pp. 512–513.
17 D.C. Dragos, B. Neamtu, 'Europeanisation of Administrative Law in Romania: Current Developments in Jurisprudence and Legislation', 2 *Review of European Administrative Law* 1, 2009, p. 89.
18 For more details *see* A. Iorgovan, *supra* note 6, pp. 512, 513.

The Reinterpretation of Romanian Administrative Law in 1991

The year 1989 marked the beginning of the democratic transition of the country. In 1990, the Law on Administrative Litigation was one of the first laws adopted by Parliament. According to Article 4, 'Jurisdictional–administrative acts – with the exception of those foreseen by Article 3 and the ones belonging to the domain of contraventions – can be appealed, after exhausting jurisdictional–administrative procedures, within 15 days from the date of communication, at the administrative section of the Supreme Court of Justice. The decision of the Court is final.'[19] This legal provision created the necessity to define the meaning of 'jurisdictional–administrative acts' and 'jurisdictional–administrative procedures' respectively. In this regard, it has been affirmed that 'any remedy which obliges the administrative body or the administrative officer to hear at least one of the parties involved and deliver a reasoned judgment, evokes essentially an administrative jurisdiction'.[20]

The Constitution of Romania entered into force after the adoption of the law on administrative litigation, in 1991. The provisions of the new Constitution stated that: '(1) Justice is realized through the Supreme Court of Justice and other courts of law established by law; (2) It is forbidden to establish extraordinary courts; and (3) The judicial competence and procedure is established by law'. This Article of the Constitution roused controversy over who were the competent bodies in the administrative litigation system. Though the Article enlisted judicial authorities with this authority and guaranteed it through the law, arguments had been made that this had been superseded by the provisions of the law on administrative litigation. According to this interpretation, administrative litigation during that period would only be possible before the competent judicial authorities.

Thus, the main challenge in interpreting the legislation created within this period concerned the competency afforded to bodies for adjudicating administrative claims. Accordingly, the question of whether only courts have the competence to review administrative decisions or whether the tradition of other administrative jurisdictions being afforded responsibility would be maintained in the Romanian legal system, was a subject for debate. The prevailing view stated that in this period the concept of 'l'administrateur–juge', inspired by the French system, was to be retained. Therefore, granting State authorities the competence to handle administrative litigation cases was not a contravention of the access to justice.[21]

From 'L'administrateur–juge' to Specialized Administrative Litigation after 2003

This last period involves the contemporary conceptualization of administrative litigation in Romania. Since Romania's accession to the European Union, one can note the impact of European values in the nation's compliance with their human rights obligations, established through the case law of the ECtHR.

In 2003 the Constitution was revised, and in the process it delivered a new constitutional framework under which the administrative litigation system currently functions in Romania. The amendment of the Constitution in 2003 provided some novelties and clarifications for conceptualizing administrative litigation. It stipulates, among the specifications in accessing justice, the concept of administrative litigation as functioning under the competence of courts. Accordingly, it introduced the principle that access to the specialized administrative courts

19 Law no. 29 of 1990 on Administrative Litigation, Article 4 (not official translation).

20 A. Iorgovan, *supra* note 6, p. 499.

21 A. Iorgovan, *supra* note 6, pp. 500–504.

(jurisdiction) is facultative and free.[22] By proceeding in this way, the 2003 amendment of the Constitution settled the problem of administrative jurisdiction in Romania that had existed in the preceding periods.[23] From this point on, administrative litigation has taken place within the following courts: first-instance courts, specialized sections of tribunals at the second level, and specialized sections of courts of appeal at the third level, as well as the specialized section of the High Court of Cassation and Justice of Romania on Administrative Litigation.[24]

Aside from bringing these clarifications into force, the revised Constitution also introduced a new main article, which governs the administrative litigation system. It confers the right for an aggrieved party who has been wronged by a public authority to seek review proceedings. Accordingly,

> any person aggrieved by his/her legitimate rights or interest by a public authority, by means of an administrative act or by the failure of the public authority to solve his/her application within the lawful time limit, is entitled to the acknowledgement of his/her claimed right or legitimate interest, the annulment of the act and reparation for the damage. The conditions and limits on the exercise of this right shall be regulated by an organic law. The State shall bear patrimony liability for any prejudice caused as a result of judicial errors. The State liability shall be assessed according to the law and shall not eliminate the liability of the magistrates having exercised their mandate in ill will or grave negligence.[25]

With regard to the procedural aspect, the Constitution specifies that administrative procedures should be regulated through the organic law.[26] Further specifications relating to administrative litigation appear in two more articles of the Romanian Constitution (conferring the power to the Prefect to challenge administrative acts before the courts).[27]

According to Article 126 of the Constitution, 'judicial control of administrative acts of the public authorities, relating to matters of contention that fall within the competence of administrative courts, is guaranteed, except for matters that concern relations with Parliament, as well as the actions of the military. The administrative courts who judge these contentious matters have the jurisdiction to solve the applications filed by those individuals aggrieved by statutory orders or, as the case may be, by provisions in statutory orders that have been declared unconstitutional'.[28] In addition, Article 123(3) confers the competence to the Prefects to challenge administrative acts in the courts. Accordingly, 'the Prefect (representative of the Government at the county level – P.Gy.) may challenge, in the administrative court, an act of the County Council, of a Local Council, or of a Mayor, in case he deems it unlawful. The act thus challenged shall be suspended de jure'.[29]

---

22 Constitution of Romania, 2003. Available at http://www.cdep.ro/pls/dic/site.page?id=371 (accessed 8.4.2013) Article 21(4). The full Article stipulates the following: '(1) Every person is entitled to bring cases before the courts for the defence of his legitimate rights, liberties and interests. (2) The exercise of this right shall not be restricted by any law. (3) All parties shall be entitled to a fair trial and a solution of their cases within a reasonable term. (4) Administrative special jurisdiction is optional and free of charge.'

23 For an extensive overview of the debate over who has administrative litigation, just courts or other State organs, *see* A. Iorgovan, *supra* note 6, pp. 500–508.

24 A. Iorgovan, *supra* note 6, p. 502.

25 Article 52, Romanian Constitution.

26 Article 73(3, k), Romanian Constitution.

27 Articles 123(5) and 126(6). A. Iorgovan, *supra* note 6, p. 483.

28 Article 126(6) (not official translation).

29 Article 123(5) (not official translation).

In completing the constitutional framework for administrative litigation, in 2004 new legislation was adopted on administrative litigation, in order to comply with the requirements correlating with the accession to the European Union.[30] Subsequent amendments to this law followed in 2005 and 2007, 2008 and 2011. Article 2 of the Law on Administrative Litigation begins with providing a definition of what constitutes administrative litigation, in light of the Romanian legislation and context. Accordingly, administrative litigation is deemed to mean, the 'method of solving through the administrative courts who has the competence, conferred by the law, to deal with legal disputes where at least one of the parties concerned is an administrative authority, and the conflict occurred by issuing or signing an administrative act, within the meaning conferred by the present law, either through a failure to solve the matter within the designated time restrictions or by an unjustified refusal of a right or a legitimate interest'.[31]

Administrative litigation in Romania is currently governed according to the aforementioned legal framework. There has been no adoption of a procedural code for administrative law. However, there is both an initiative and a draft version of this code that is subject to public debate.[32] This has not been adopted to date. Therefore, the procedural rules applied are those foreseen by the general law governing administrative litigation.

Accession to the European Union

One of the most remarkable changes in the Romanian system of administration resulted from the accession to the European Union. Romania, similarly to other Central and Eastern European states, could become a Member State of the European Union upon fulfilling certain conditions established by the European Commission. The reorganization of the system of administration was one of the main areas where substantive reforms were needed. Enhancing the administrative capacity of the country was a crucial requirement for transposing and applying the whole body of European Union law.

The preparation period preceding the accession of Romania to the European Union in 2007 was served with reforming the Romanian administrative law system. In this period, the European Commission set specific requirements with which Romania had to comply. The reform of the administrative system was one of the main areas of focus, alongside economic consolidation, the reform of the judicial system at large, and the protection of human rights.[33]

After Romania's accession in 2007, another significant change occurred in the status and competences of judges in adjudicating administrative cases. Local judges in all Member States and also in Romania operate as decentralized European Union law judges, responsible for the direct application of EU law and its basic principles. A detailed presentation of these tasks and the subsequent changes falls outside the scope of the present study. However, it remains worth mentioning that this was an important new role, to which administrative law judges had to adjust. In fulfilling this new competence, judges are also required to introduce preliminary questions to the Court of Justice of the European Union (CJEU), if necessary.

30 *See also*, D.C. Dragos, B. Neamtu, *supra* note 17, p. 89. European Commission, Regular Reports on Romania. Enhancing the administrative capacity of the country was a recurring theme in the evaluation reports.

31 Article 2(1,e) of the Law no. 554 of 2004 (not official translation).

32 Proposal for the Administrative Code of Procedure. Available at: http://www.mira.gov.ro/Documente/Transparenta%20decizionala/Proiect%20COD%20procedura%20administrativa.pdf (accessed 12.3.2013).

33 Criteria established by the Copenhagen European Council in 1993, the Madrid European Council in 1995, currently laid down by Article 2 of the Treaty on European Union, which have to be respected by states willing to join the EU according to Article 49(1) of the Treaty on European Union. Available at: http://eur-lex.europa.eu/LexUriServ/LexUriServ.do?uri=OJ:C:2008:115:0013:0045:EN:PDF (accessed 8.4.2013).

Through the direct effect of European Union law, the general principles of the European Union and the case law need to be directly applied by national judges. Administrative litigation is one of the fields of law that contains the most specific tasks and where the impact of European Union is most visible.[34]

Recent initiatives deriving from Romanian judges have shown some positive developments in adjusting to this new role,[35] in being responsible for administrative litigation in a multi-level legal system. This concerns the introduction and application of European legal principles in Romanian administrative litigation and will be discussed below. However, in order to understand and analyze such substantial aspects of administrative litigation in Romania, first the general organizational framework in which the courts review administrative law cases is sketched.

The Institutional Aspects of Handling Administrative Cases

Under the legislative framework governing administrative litigation, the judicial review of the lawfulness of administrative decisions remains the main means of contestation. Aside from this means, individuals aggrieved by an administrative decision, can turn to two other institutions of review: either filing an administrative appeal to an administrative authority or filing a complaint with the Ombudsman. Apart from these two alternatives, this section presents a brief reflection on the possibility to use mediation as an alternative to administrative litigation.

The Place of Administrative Litigation in the Romanian Court System

In the Romanian court system there are no specialized courts for administrative law. The first instance courts have general jurisdiction. At the level of tribunals and courts of appeal – representing the second and third tiers in the court organization system – specialized sections for administrative law are organized.[36] When it comes to the functioning of the courts, it has been observed that the administrative law section might merge with the civil and commercial law sections of the respective courts.[37] Finally, the High Court of Cassation and Justice, representing the highest level in the court organization structure, also has a section specialized in administrative litigation and fiscal business matters.[38]

According to the Romanian legislation, there are three possibilities to contest the lawfulness of administrative acts: through administrative appeals, judicial review, or filing private law claims. Furthermore, judicial review of administrative acts is possible either by directly contesting the administrative act in front of the competent court or introducing an exception of illegality initiated

---

34 U. Jaremba, *National Judges as EU Law Judges: The Polish Civil Law System*, Martinus Nijhoff Publishers, Leiden (2014); Michal Bobek, 'Thou Shall Have Two Masters: The Application of European Law by National Authorities in the New Member States', 1 *Review of European Administrative Law (REAL)* 2008; Zdeněk Kühn, 'The Application of European Law in the New Member States: Several (Early) Predictions', 3 *German Law Journal* 2008, pp. 563–582; Michal Bobek, 'A New Legal Order, or a Non-existent One? Some (Early) Experiences in the Application of EU Law in Central Europe', 2 *Croatian Yearbook of European Law and Policy* (CYELP) 265 (2006).

35 D.C. Dragos, B. Neamtu, *supra* note 17, pp. 87–98.

36 Law no. 304 of 2004 on the organization of courts, Article 35(2).

37 *Id.* D.C. Dragos, B. Neamtu, *supra* note 17, p. 88.

38 Law no. 304 of 2004 on the Organization of Courts, Article 18.

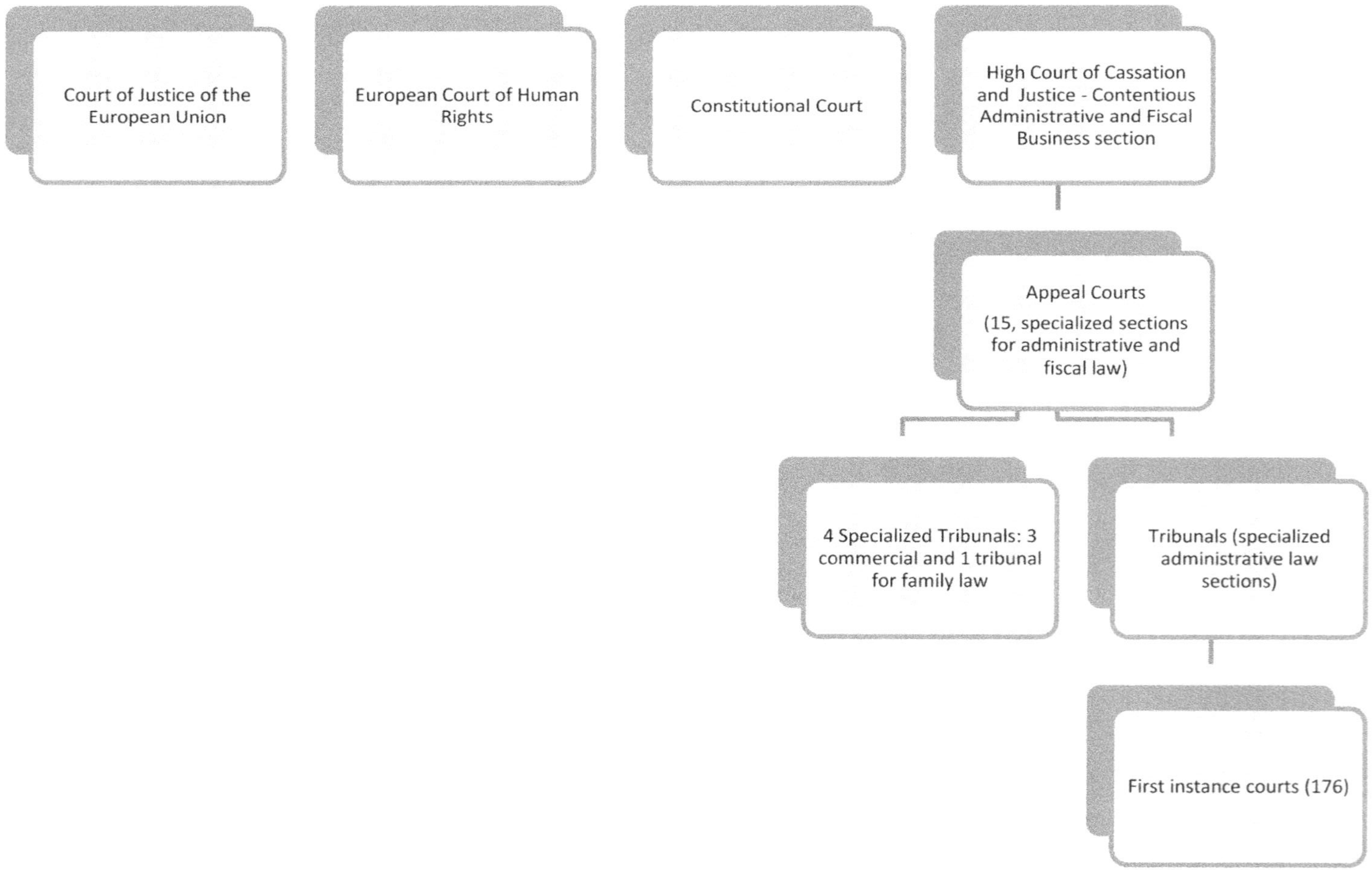

Figure 10.1 Institutional Arrangements for Administrative Litigation in Romania

during litigation proceedings of another nature.[39] The time limit for introducing a claim to the court is six months from the date of notification of the individual administrative decision. For general administrative decisions it is possible to request the judicial review without a certain time constraint.[40] The lawfulness of an administrative decision can be contested at any time, as part of a court action from another field of law.[41]

As regards the competence of the courts in administrative litigation, the specialized sections of the tribunals are competent to review the lawfulness of administrative decisions issued by the public authorities at the local or county level, as well as administrative decisions on taxes, contributions, customs debts and their accessories up to a certain monetary value. Courts of appeal are competent to review the lawfulness of administrative decisions, which are considered more important. Accordingly, the sphere of decisions reviewed by courts of appeal in administrative litigation includes decisions issued by central public authorities, in addition to those decisions on taxes, contributions, customs debts and their accessories with a high monetary value.[42]

The judicial review of administrative acts is naturally the main and most authoritative means through which one can contest the lawfulness of administrative acts. Nevertheless, aside from this possibility individuals can contest the lawfulness of an administrative act in other ways. In Romania at present, the main alternatives are administrative appeals and filing a complaint with the Ombudsman.

Administrative Appeals

An administrative appeal, according to the legislation in Romania, must precede the judicial review of an administrative act. Administrative appeals are 'request(s) addressed to a public authority by which the aggrieved person asks for administrative measures to be taken regarding the administrative decision: annulment, modification or even issuance of a decision – when this has been refused by the administration'.[43] The legal basis for administrative appeals can be found in the general law on judicial review of administrative acts. As mentioned in Article 7 of Law no. 554/2004 on Administrative Litigation, an administrative appeal is possible under an objection, hierarchical appeal or improper hierarchical appeal (the appeal is not addressed to the hierarchically superior body to the issuing authority). In the case of improper administrative appeals, the review can be executed for example by the prefects, or the Romanian Court of Auditors.[44]

Administrative appeals may be lodged within 30 days starting from the date when the administrative decision was issued. For the group of individual administrative decisions, it is compulsory to request an administrative appeal procedure before filing a complaint with the courts. The possibility to lodge an administrative appeal remains at the disposal of the individual within six months from the date when the decision was issued, provided that sufficiently 'reasoned grounds' are brought forward to support it. The public authority, through its discretionary power, decides the existence of sufficiently reasoned grounds.[45] As such, the exercise of this extensive discretionary

39 *Id.*

40 Article 11 of Law no. 554 of 2004 on Administrative Litigation.

41 *Id.*, Article 4.

42 *Id.*, Article 10.

43 D.C. Dragos, M. Swora, A. Skoczylas, 'Administrative Law Appeals in Romania and Poland: A Topical Comparative Analysis', *Transylvanian Review of Administrative Sciences*, No. 37E/2012, pp. 39, 40.

44 For more details, *see id.*, p. 41.

45 For more details, *see id.*, p. 42. *See also* A. Iorgovan, *supra* note 6.

power might be abused in practice.[46] The proposal for remedying this practical problem emerged from academic analysis and the case law of the Romanian High Court of Cassation and Justice is set to apply similar criteria that are used by the courts in civil law cases for 'reactivating the time-frames for filing procedural acts'.[47]

Furthermore, another shortcoming of the current procedure might be said that the decisions based on an administrative appeal need to be reasoned.[48] Such an input measure would be important for increasing the legitimacy of administrative appeals. Imposing such a requirement would also be in line with the Council of Europe's Committee of Minister's Recommendation stating that 'member states shall ensure that parties receive appropriate information about the possible use of alternative means'.[49]

Alternatives to Administrative Litigation

A relatively new institution in Romania for solving claims related to administrative decisions is the creation of the Ombudsman office.[50] The institution of the Ombudsman in Romania does not represent an alternative to courts in the real sense of the word. There is one Ombudsman in Romania, with no powers to investigate maladministration. However, upon the request of a citizen or acting upon their own initiative, the Ombudsman can request the administrative review of cases from the competent administrative authority. The Ombudsman can request an appeal to the hierarchical administrative authority (to that of the issuing authority) or appeals to other (controlling) public authorities. The recommendations made by the Ombudsman possess the power of persuasion. In addition, they are subject to neither parliamentary nor judicial review.[51] The Romanian national Ombudsman 'can decide upon administrative appeals lodged by individuals. In addition, the Ombudsman can lodge an administrative appeal to the issuing body or to its hierarchically superior authority'.[52] Accordingly, based on the review of the legislation, the institution of the Ombudsman appears as an intermediary between the individuals on the one hand and the courts or political actors on the other.

Nevertheless, some developments in practice may fundamentally hinder whether the role of the Ombudsman is capable of being fulfilled. Recently the appointment of the Ombudsman led to criticism; this was with regard to guaranteeing the independent status of the position from undue political influence. More specifically the appointee was supported only by the governing party, and did not receive support from the opposition.[53] In this context, the European Commission drew

46 See *id.*

47 *See id.*, p. 43. *See* for example Romanian High Court of Cassation and Justice, Administrative Law Section, Decision no. 3441/2002.

48 *Id.*, p. 43.

49 Council of Europe, Committee of Ministers, Recommendation Rec (2001) 9 on Alternatives to Litigation between Administrative Authorities and Private Parties, Article 3.2.a.ii.

50 Law no. 35 of 1997.

51 For more details *see* D.C. Dragos, B. Neamtu, D. Balica, 'The Romanian Ombudsman and its Interaction with Courts', *Transylvanian Review of Administrative Sciences*, No. 31E/2010, p. 61.

52 *Id.*, p. 41. The functioning of the Ombudsman institution is regulated through Law no. 35 of 1997 on the Organization and the Functioning of the Ombudsman Institution, Official Gazette of Romania no. 48 of 20.3.1997.

53 *See* European Commission, Cooperation and Verification Mechanism Regular Report, January 2013, available at: http://ec.europa.eu/cvm/docs/com_2013_47_en.pdf (accessed 8.4.2013).

the Romanian government's attention to the fact that citizens' rights can only be respected by an independent institution of the Ombudsman.[54]

In addition, there can be other practical barriers affecting the functioning and the efficiency of the Ombudsman institution. As a novel research in Romania,[55] the interaction of the Ombudsman with the courts has been explored by employing qualitative methods. The outcome of the research was based on documentary analysis and structured interviews conducted with judges. It shows that this interaction between these actors is rather limited. Furthermore, none of the actors is willing to develop this relationship. The underlying consideration identified by the research and referred to by the interviewed subjects was the independence of the judiciary.[56]

Mediation

Mediation was introduced into the Romanian legal system in 2006, with an eye on transposing the Directive of the European Union on mediation.[57] As can be noticed, mediation – but also alternative dispute resolution mechanisms in general – are relatively new devices in Romania. Mediation is not a traditional means of solving disputes; it is not embedded in the national judicial culture. In addition, mediation is not directly applicable to administrative litigation.

When it comes to the implementation of mediation into the Romanian legal system, problems – similar to other European states[58] – can be observed concerning the delimitation of the conciliatory powers conferred to judges and referring cases for mediation.[59] As mediation is not an alternative to administrative litigation under Romanian law, this alternative dispute resolution mechanism is not discussed in detail in the present study. Suffice to say that its implementation does indeed face practical problems.

As concerns its application as an alternative to administrative litigation, mediation can be applied in some specific cases in connection with administrative litigation in the field of administrative contracts. For example, it is applicable to public procurement procedures and contracts according to the legislation that governs mediation. Nevertheless, a general reluctance has been signalled in utilizing mediation as an alternative dispute resolution mechanism for disputes arising from public procurement cases.[60]

The proposed administrative procedural code, which could expand the procedural rules on administrative litigation, is suggested in Law no. 554 of 2004 on Administrative Litigation, which makes reference to mediation. When contesting the lawfulness of an administrative act issued by a public authority, mediation is not acceptable given the differences in the relative powers of the parties in the conflict. Nevertheless, when the private party in a conflict concerning an administrative act comprises multiple subjects with conflicting interests, these could be solved

54 *Id.*

55 *Id.*

56 *Id.*

57 Directive 2008/52/EC of the European Parliament and Council of 21 May 2008 on Certain Aspects of Mediation in Civil and Commercial Matters, OJ L 136 of 24 May 2008.

58 This matter was established in the former Code of Civil procedure of Romania by Article 131. As of February 2013 a new Code of Civil Procedure entered into force.

59 P.M. Gyongyi, 'Conquering New Terrain: The Implementation of Mediation Directive in Hungary and Romania', 15 *Nederlands–Vlaams tijdschrift voor Mediation en conflictmanagement* 2011, p. 2.

60 D.C. Dragos, 'Alternative Dispute Resolution Mechanisms in the Field of Public Procurement: Between Effectiveness and Constitutionality', *Transylvanian Review of Administrative Sciences*, No. 34E/2011.

through mediation.[61] Then, the mediation agreement must be taken into account by the public authority. Therefore, mediation could be applicable during the process of issuing an administrative act. As can be seen, mediation has a very limited field of application in administrative litigation, and it does not represent an alternative to solving individuals' claims for the breach of a right or a legitimate interest by a public authority.

The Scope of Judicial Review

Alongside the institutional settings of administrative litigation, the scope of review conferred by law to the courts is the other essential element in mapping administrative litigation. Emerging from the rights guaranteed by the Romanian Constitution, the judicial review of administrative acts is based on the procedure enshrined in the 2004 legislation, whereby individuals can contest an administrative act in front of the courts in case of a breach of a substantive right or that of a legitimate interest. The evolution of the scope of judicial review is marked by some internal debates rooted in the Romanian legal system. In this sense the historical overview of the scope of judicial review can be instructive for contextualizing some of the theoretical debates that ultimately may result in differences in the practice of the courts.

The Historical Development of the Scope of Judicial Review[62]

The contemporary expansion of the scope of judicial review has evolved through different phases of the main legislation. Each stage posed different problems of interpretation, leading to a contemporary system with issues of interpretation that can be traced back to a larger, historical setting. The 1967 law on administrative litigation represents the first stage.

Courts could review only individual administrative decisions whose lawfulness was challenged. In order to fall within the review competences of the courts, the administrative act must be of an individual character and it must be issued by a governmental body, with the exception of the Council of Ministers. A particular requirement was that courts could review only unlawful administrative decisions. Completing the preliminary administrative review procedure was mandatory before requesting a court to review the administrative act. Finally, the contested decision could not form part of the acts falling outside the scope of judicial review.[63]

Accordingly, the unlawfulness of an administrative act was a specific requirement in this period. This requirement has been shown as a very burdensome condition to prove by the individuals involved.[64] This condition was changed to a breach of right or that of a legitimate interest through the subsequent legislation in 1990.

1990 Legislation

The 1990 legislation introduced some changes with regard to the scope of judicial review. The conditions referring to the issuing body have been widened: the issuing authority could be any

61 Article 79, Proposal for an Administrative Procedural Code, available at: http://www.mira.gov.ro/Documente/Transparenta%20decizionala/Proiect%20COD%20procedura%20administrativa.pdf (accessed 12.3.2013).

62 *See also*, R.N. Petrescu, *supra* note 1, pp. 369–375.

63 A. Iorgovan, *supra* note 6, p. 519.

64 *Id.*

administrative authority. More importantly, on a conceptual level, the individual character of the administrative decision was not a requirement anymore. Consequently, a general administrative decision could be contested in front of the courts as well. Similarly, the strict conditions of the breach of a right were extended, as it was possible to contest the legality of an administrative decision also for breaching a legitimate interest of a person. However, these conceptual changes on the scope of judicial review of administrative decisions needed to be integrated into the practice of the courts and the functioning of administrative litigation in Romania.

What can be discerned from the academic analysis by scholars assessing this transition in practice, is that the scope of administrative litigation was not reconfigured in light of these conceptual changes, but rather, the new grounds for judicial review were seen as a simple 'variant' of the previous legislation without taking into account the fundamental changes.[65] This view originated from scholarly work and was followed by the case law as well.[66] These problems point to the need to match a conceptual change introduced by new legislation with a reconsideration of the scope of administrative litigation.

2004 Legislation

In 2004 modifications were made to the grounds of review of administrative decisions by courts, in adopting the new law governing administrative litigation.[67] The changes mostly concerned the definition of an administrative decision, conditions for standing, and the notion of legitimate interest.[68] Accordingly, the new legislation permitted the administrative review of both general and individual administrative acts.[69] For the former, judicial review is possible with no time limitations. For the latter, the judicial review should be requested within 6 months after the administrative act has been communicated to the individual.[70] In addition, the exception of illegality can be raised against any kind of administrative act without any time limit.[71]

Overall, the scope of judicial review can be summarized as follows: the contested decision must be an administrative act; the claim must refer to a breach of a right or that of a legitimate interest, the contested decision must be issued by a public authority; the prior administrative appeal procedure must be completed; the contestation must be introduced within the legal framework as foreseen by the law; and administrative acts issued before the current legislation cannot be reviewed.

What is Capable of being Reviewed by the Administrative Divisions of the Courts?

In expanding the actual scope of judicial review in administrative litigation, the definitions of the terms used in the legislation become relevant. The notion of administrative act is defined as a 'unilateral act(s) with individual or normative character, issued by a public authority for the purposes of executing the law or organizing the execution of laws, creating, modifying or discontinuing legal relations'.[72] Another relevant specification of the law is that administrative contracts are assimilated to administrative acts, and consequently can be reviewed by courts. Therefore, contracts concluded

65 For further discussion, *see* A. Iorgovan, *supra* note 6, p. 519.
66 *Id.*
67 Law no. 554 of 2004 on Administrative Litigation.
68 Article 1, Law, no. 554 of 2004. For an academic analysis *see* A. Iorgovan, *supra* note 6, p. 520, 521.
69 *Id.*
70 Law no. 554 of 2004, Article 11.
71 Law no. 554 of 2004, Article 4.
72 Law no. 554 of 2004, Article 2(1,c) (not official translation).

by public authorities for the purposes of 'for valuing public property, executing public works, providing public services, public procurements or any other contracts as foreseen by special laws'[73] fall within the ambit of the review of the administrative courts.

The notion of public authority refers to 'any state authority or those belonging to administrative–territorial units, conducting their activities with public power, to satisfy a legitimate public interest'.[74] In addition, 'private legal entities which by law have obtained the status of public authority or which are authorized to provide public service' are also considered as public authorities.[75] Consequently, any decision issued by such bodies can be reviewed by the competent administrative courts.

Whether the Courts apply the Principles of Legality or Proportionality

As has emerged from the overview above, the main grounds for judicial review of administrative decisions in Romania concerns questions pertaining to legality. The Romanian courts in administrative law cases review decisions issued by public authorities mainly based on the principle of legality. This principle has been embedded in the administrative litigation system.

The academic definitions given to the principle of legality vary in the two main schools of thought in Romanian administrative law. Accordingly, the school from *Cluj* considers legality as a condition for the validity of an administrative decision, together with the principle of opportunity. According to the *Bucharest* school, legality appears as a condition of validity for an administrative decision. However, the principle of opportunity is a condition of the legality of an administrative decision.[76] These differences in definitions also had an impact on the case law of the courts adjudicating administrative litigation.

The Application of the Principle of Legality by the Courts

In the application of the principle of legality, Romanian courts had to react to shifts in legislation determining the scope of judicial review. These shifts referred to the possibility to review both individual and general administrative decisions and as to whether an administrative decision could be contested for a breach of a right or also in the case of a breach of a legitimate interest. The possibility to review administrative acts both of an individual and general character by courts, has been conferred already under the 1990 legislation. The most notable judicial decisions came from the Constitutional Court.[77] The Constitutional Court pronounced the view according to which the scope of review was extended to administrative decisions of a general character in a decision from 1994.[78] However, what is notable is the recent case law of the High Court of Cassation and Justice on this matter. Accordingly, the courts developed the meaning and applicability of the principle of legality in order to solve this long-debated issue in the country's administrative law, which resurfaced in 2004 with a legislative alteration.

---

73 *Id.*

74 Law no. 554 of 2004, Article 11.

75 Law no. 554 of 2004, Article 2(1,b) (not official translation).

76 For more details *see* A. Iorgovan, *supra* note 6, pp. 41, 42.

77 R.N. Petrescu, *supra* note 1, p. 383.

78 Constitutional Court of Romania, Decision no. 33 of 19 April 1994 and Decision 34 of 27 April 1994. *See also* R.N. Petrescu, *supra* note 1, pp. 383, 384.

The 2004 legislation extended the applicability of the exception of illegality to individual administrative acts. The underlying logic was in strengthening and extending the principle of legality.[79] Accordingly, the exception of illegality could be introduced in cases of both individual and general administrative acts, without any time limits. As such, judicial review was made possible for controversies originating from the period before the 2004 legislation entered into force. Thus, the effects of the law were extended retrospectively.

The new legislative changes appeared to be contrary to the underlying logic governing the judicial review of administrative acts through an exception of illegality. Given the nature of the act, being individual, the admission of the exception of illegality produced the effects of the annulment of an act; whereas the legal effect of admitting an exception of illegality should be that of rendering the act unlawful for the contested situation, without annulling it.[80] This is why this procedure had been historically developed and applied to administrative decisions of a general character.[81]

As a response, the High Court of Cassation and Justice addressed this problem in a decision concerning the contestation of an individual administrative act: invoking the rules of occupying the functions of a rector at a public university. Here, the impossibility of retaining the position having already completed two consecutive terms was contested. The court rendered that, given the fact that the court decision contested in this case had been issued before the 2004 legislation had entered into force, the case could not be reviewed by the court.[82] As the court observed,

> Law no. 554 of 2004 is applicable to individual or normative administrative acts communicated or published as of 6 January 2005. The exception of illegality as described in the new regulation can be invoked only in the case of administrative acts issued after the new legislation entered into force. For administrative acts issued before that date, the general principles admitted through the case law of the courts become applicable. For these reasons the exception of illegality has to be rejected as inadmissible. Similarly to the decision of the appeal court in this matter, although it was given on different legal grounds, the Court rejected the appeal of the plaintiff, considering that the inadmissibility of the exception of illegality had not changed.[83]

After such a restrictive interpretation given by the High Court of Cassation and Justice in this matter, the legislator responded by amending the 2004 legislation. This time it was explicitly stated in the law governing administrative litigation that a restrictive interpretation was not possible.[84] This movement of the legislator was met with a ground-breaking judicial decision from the High Court of Cassation and Justice.

Accordingly, the courts found a solution to these problems created by the amendment of the legislation, by complying with their obligations to effectively apply European Union law and their role as decentralized European Union law judges.[85] In this case, they relied on the principle of legal

79 D.C. Dragos, B. Neamtu, *supra* note 17, p. 91.

80 *Id.*, p. 92.

81 This was also the solution accepted in French law, which formed the source of inspiration for the Romanian legislator.

82 High Court of Cassation and Justice, Decision no. 5455 of 2005.

83 *Id.* (not official translation).

84 Law no. 554 of 2004 Article 4, para. 1 as amended in 2007.

85 T. Nowak, F. Amtenbrink, M. Hertogh, M. Wissink, *National Judges as European Union Judges*, Eleven International Publishing, The Hague (2011); U. Jaremba, 'The Impact of EU Law on National Judiciaries: Polish Administrative Courts and their Participation in the Process of Legal Integration in the EU', 12 *German Law Journal* 3, 2011.

certainty as a principle of European Union law, directly applicable to administrative litigation in Romania and in line with the case law of the European Court of Human Rights.[86]

Through its 2008 decision on a case concerning the public domain, the High Court of Cassation and Justice rendered the request of the plaintiff inadmissible by relying on the case law of the European Court of Human Rights, in elaborating upon the principle of legal certainty. The cases on which the Romanian court relied were some landmark cases decided by the European Court against Romania.[87] On several occasions the European Court of Human Rights held that 'the decisions of a court should be challenged within a time limit and should not be open for review for an indefinite time'. This finding was corroborated by the court, with the requirement imposed on the judge to assure the pre-eminence of the Convention against national provisions.

In addition, the High Court of Cassation and Justice based its decision on a line of cases emerging from the Court of Justice of the European Union. In particular, this second line of cases refers to the role of national courts to guarantee the effective implementation of EU law.[88] Based on these main considerations, the Romanian court decided that definitive administrative acts should be assimilated to final court decisions.

As can be seen in the case at hand, the principle of legality was interpreted by relying on the principle of legal certainty. Although the exact application of the principle remains debatable – arguably exceeding the competences of the courts in applying and interpreting the law – the general trend of accepting European legal principles within national administrative litigation was praised.[89]

The Application of the Principle of Proportionality

The principle of proportionality does not feature among the fundamental principles governing the Romanian administrative litigation system. It is, however, a fundamental principle of European Union law,[90] which requires direct application by the national courts of Member States of the European Union, including Romania. Despite this fact, the principle of proportionality is not widely applied by Romanian courts in administrative litigation. The main and most developed principle remains that of legality. Nevertheless, the principle of proportionality might be used in deciding cases where a possible infringement of the European Convention of Human Rights or European Union law is invoked.

Accordingly, these two main European sources represent the influence over the conceptualization and application of the principle of proportionality by Romanian administrative courts. One is the principle of proportionality as developed in the legal system of the European Union. The other is the principle of proportionality emerging from the case law of the European Court of Human Rights. In these cases, concerning qualified rights guaranteed by Articles 8–11 and Article 14 of the European Convention of Human Rights, it is assessed whether there has been an interference with a right, whether State authorities had a legitimate interest for said interference, whether it was

86 For a detailed analysis *see* D.C. Dragos, B. Neamtu, *supra* note 17, pp. 93–95.

87 ECtHR, *Brumarescu v. Romania*, Appl. No. 28342/95; ECtHR, *Dumitru Popescu v. Romania*, Appl. No. 71525/01; ECtHR, *Beian v. Romania*, Appl. No. 30658/05.

88 CJEU, C-383/06 Netherlands – Vereniging Nationaal Overlegorgaan Sociale Werkvoorziening; C-384/06 Gemeente Rotterdam v. Minister van Sociale Zaken en Werkgelegenheid; C-385/06 Sociaal Economische Samenwerking West-Brabant v. Algemene Directie voor de Arbeidsvoorziening.

89 For more on this *see* D.C. Dragos, B. Neamtu, *supra* note 17, pp. 94, 95.

90 P. Craig, *EU Administrative Law*, chapter 19, 2nd edition, Oxford University Press, New York (2012).

necessary in a democratic society, and as a final step the court assesses whether the interference was proportional to the pursued aims.[91]

In several cases the administrative and fiscal section of the High Court of Cassation and Justice made reference to the principle of proportionality. Express reference is made to the case law of the European Court of Human Rights in most of the cases where the principle of proportionality is applied.

A notable number of cases where the principle of proportionality was applied concerned the legality of the reduction of public employees' salary by 25 per cent by law for the purposes of re-establishing the budgetary equilibrium of Romania. For example, in its relevant decision the High Court of Cassation and Justice made express reference to the principle of proportionality and the relevant case law of the European Court of Human Rights in this sense, when deciding on the legality of reducing the salaries of governmental employees by 25 per cent for guaranteeing the economic equilibrium of the State budget. In this case it was invoked that the right to salary constituted a property right guaranteed by Article 1, Protocol 1 of the European Convention of Human Rights and the above-mentioned reduction would be in breach of this right. The Romanian court observed that the measure interfered with the individuals' property rights. However, the measure was not disproportionate with the aims pursued by the State, namely that of re-establishing the equilibrium of the State budget. Accordingly, the High Court of Cassation and Justice considered that adopting such a measure falls within the margin of appreciation of a given State.[92] Several decisions following the same line of argumentation have been made by the High Court of Cassation and Justice.[93]

In other cases, the High Court of Cassation and Justice made reference to the principle of proportionality emerging from the EU legal order. For example, most recently, reference was made to the principle of proportionality in the case law of the Court of Justice of the European Union in decisions revoking financial grants,[94] or applied in tax law cases.[95] In both types of cases, the principle of proportionality is invoked as a general principle of European Union law, applicable in the case. The proportionality test was applicable for determining whether the interests of the individual justified the suspension of the decision to impose tax for the duration of the litigation, as opposed to the interest of the State to collect these taxes.

Although most often the principle of proportionality appears as a European principle directly applicable to the Romanian legal system, there are also cases where the courts applied this principle on their own initiative by finding a national legal basis for such. For instance, the principle is referred to in individualizing administrative sanctions or assessing lawyer's fees.[96] In addition, the

---

91 For a detailed presentation of the application of the principle of proportionality *see* A. Stone Sweet and J. Matthews, 'Proportionality Balancing and Global Constitutionalism', 47 *Colum. J. Transn't L.* 73, 2008–2009, pp. 145–152; D. Harris, M. O'Boyle, E. Bates, C. Buckley, *Law of the European Convention on Human Rights*, 2nd edition, Oxford University Press (2009), chapter 8.

92 High Court of Cassation and Justice, Decision no. 1202/2012.

93 For example, Decisions number 1952/2012 and 1953/2012 also concerned the reduction of salaries of public employees. The first case in this sense was decision number 20/2011, but also decisions 2593/2012 and 2635/2012.

94 The invoked cases of the Court of Justice of the European Union were: C 58/08 *The Queen, v. Ltd*; C 146/05 *Collee KG and Finanzanet*; C-45/2006 *Campina GmbH & Co v. Hauptzollamt Frankfurt*.

95 For example, High Court of Cassation and Justice, Decision no. 1988/2010, High Court of Cassation and Justice, Decision no. 2597/2011.

96 For example, High Court of Cassation and Justice, Decision no. 2556/2010.

principle of proportionality was applied in a case where the unlawfulness of the act could not be proven. This latter example represents an interesting reference to the principle of proportionality.

In this case, the Supreme Court of Cassation and Justice proceedings to the subsidiary analysis to that of opportunity gave some clarifications over the applicability of the principle of proportionality. The court stated:

> Although the competent court needs to assess the legality of the contested act, once notified, the court has the right to verify the existence of certain factual elements invoked by the public authority in motivating its decision. The judge has a discretionary power to assess the proportionality between the utility of a given administrative measure on one hand and its social and financial cost on the other. The existence of factual motives and their correct assessment constitute aspects related to the legality of the administrative act which need to be in line with its scope and its content.[97]

Taking these into account, the Supreme Court opined that the lower court did not exceed its competence by proceeding to a legitimacy analysis of the administrative decision; in fact, the analysis constitutes a minimum control in this case.[98] Although this last example remains an isolated one in the case law of the Supreme Court of Cassation and Justice, it exemplifies the openess of judges to apply other principles alongside that of legality.

Deficiencies in the Law and Issues of Implementation

As can be expected, the shifts in the laws governing administrative litigation and the task of implementing supranational legal orders into the national legal sphere do create some difficulties both at the legislative level and when it comes to implementing the basic principles of administrative litigation by the courts. Some of the main deficiencies and problems of implementation will be outlined below. Based on the timeline of administrative litigation in Romania, three deficiencies or controversies in the law are selected, all of which cause problems in implementation.

A Broad Scope of Reviewing both Individual and General Administrative Decisions

The most recent legislative changes concerning the admissibility and grounds of review of administrative cases created some practical problems in the Romanian system for administrative litigation. Accordingly, since 2004 the older dilemma of admissibility of general administrative decisions has been settled. Judicial review of the legality of decisions issued by public authorities was possible.

In the academic literature, the opinion has been expressed before the relevant legislative changes that a general administrative act cannot be in breach of an individual's right or legitimate interest. A breach is only possible in case of an administrative act of an individual character that was issued based on the general administrative act.[99]

These difficulties in interpreting the scope of administrative litigation point to the importance of an adequate legal framework. Introducing novel concepts in the framework of administrative litigation may lead to difficulties or inconsistencies in the judicial practice. This particular shift

97 High Court of Cassation and Justice, Decision no. 2438/2006 (not official translation).

98 *Id.*

99 A. Iorgovan, *supra* note 6, p. 525, reference to the opinion expressed by T. Draganu.

also resulted in the adjustment of the procedural rules establishing the time limits for introducing complaints in front of the relevant competent court. Ultimately, the results were not only more extensive time limits – such as admitting an exception of illegality of individual administrative decision with no time limit – but also the retrospective application of the new rules. Accordingly, the legislation conferred the possibility to file a complaint in case of administrative decisions issued before the legislative changes entered into force. Ultimately, the High Court of Cassation and Justice was forced to clarify these points in a number of decisions, by applying principles emerging from European law.[100]

The Interpretation of 'Legitimate Interest'

Another major change in the scope of administrative litigation was the extension of the possibility to claim not only an infringement of a right but also that of a legitimate interest. Accordingly, a private legitimate interest is defined by the Law as entitling the individual 'to claim a certain behaviour for realizing a future and foreseeable, subjective right'.[101] In contrast, public legitimate interest makes it possible to 'claim a certain behaviour as the basis for considering the realization of a fundamental right, exercised collectively or for defending a public interest'.[102]

In practice, disputes arise when interpreting the notion of legitimate interest in light of the concrete facts of the particular case. In particular, it appeared problematic to decide in which cases can or cannot an individual invoke the breach of a legitimate interest.[103] Consequently, the applicable law for the claim would be either administrative law or civil law.

No General Duty to Provide Reasoning in Administrative Appeals

Some practical problems can be signalled with regard to the effectiveness of alternatives to administrative litigation. When it comes to administrative appeals, the lack of a requirement on giving reasons represents a shortcoming in the legislative framework that causes practical problems.[104] By exercising their legal competence, administrative authorities have a discretionary power to reject appeals, with no obligation to give reasoned grounds for their decision to do so. This can ultimately affect the outcome of future administrative litigations, since the reason for rejecting an administrative appeal can be the inexistence of reasoned grounds on which the claim can be based without further explanation.

On the one hand, it must be mentioned that placing more emphasis on the duty to give reasons would be important since reasoning can constitute additional information for the individual on whether or not to file a complaint with a court.[105] On the other hand, it has been shown that administrative

100 D.C. Dragos, B. Neamtu, *supra* note 17, pp. 87–95.

101 Law no. 554 of 2004, Article 2(1,p) (not official translation).

102 Law no. 554/2004, Article 2(1,r) (not official translation).

103 For example, D.C. Dragos, 'Implicatiile revizuirii Constitutiei asupra contenciosului administrativ: Discutii privind semnificatia sintagmei "interes legitim"' (The Implications of the Constitutional Revision over Administrative Contentious: Discussions on the Significance of the Notion 'Legitimate Interest'), 2 *Revista Transilvana de Stiinte Administrative* 11, 2004. For a detailed analysis *see* A. Iorgovan, *supra* note 6, pp. 553–575.

104 D.C. Dragos, M. Swora, A. Skoczylas, *supra* note 43, p. 43.

105 F. Emmert, 'Rule of Law in Central and Eastern Europe', 32 *Fordham International Law Journal* 2, 2008, p. 584.

appeals contribute to the effective functioning of the administrative litigation system.[106] Combining these two elements shows the importance of this duty for the proper functioning of administrative appeals in a legal system. This is especially the case when it is compulsory to file an administrative appeal against individual administrative decisions before filing a complaint to the courts.[107]

Major Challenges and Problems in Judicial Practice Concerning the Handling of Administrative Cases

When it comes to significant obstacles affecting the functioning of the courts, the present overview identifies two main sources of interference, without the pretention of being inclusive of all factors affecting the handling of cases. The two main problems are related to the caseload of the courts and the expertise of judges in the field of administrative law. These two problems are identified as two organizational factors that can seriously hinder the activity of administrative units of general courts.

Caseload of the Courts

There are several practical problems with a potential negative effect over delivering judgments within a reasonable time or affecting the quality of the judgments given in administrative litigation. One of these challenges is the imbalanced workload of the courts. This is a difficulty for judicial organization in Romania in general,[108] but is also problematic in producing an effect on administrative litigation. For example, recently Romanian courts – mostly in regions close to the borders – have been swamped by a certain type of administrative case as a result of the ruling of the Court of Justice of the European Union on the environmental tax for cars.[109] For example, a significant increase in the number of cases concerning administrative litigation at courts of appeal was observed in the first semester of 2012 as opposed to the same period in 2011. The total number of registered cases increased from 49,459 to 99,308; most frequently, the cases concerned the annulment of administrative acts or contesting taxes.[110]

A particular case might have caused a surge in the number of cases. Accordingly, imposing a tax for the first registration of a used car was found to be contrary to EU law. As a result, all previous instances could be contested in front of administrative courts. The introduction of a simplified administrative procedure and the connected legislative change would relieve Romanian courts from approximately 10,000 cases.[111] In this case, introducing administrative procedures was a suggestion of the European Commission for dealing with the problem of an imbalanced workload,

106 D.C. Dragos, M. Swora, A. Skoczylas, *supra* note 43, p. 39.

107 Article 7 of Law no. 554 of 2004.

108 European Commission, European Commission, C(2006) 6569, 'Commission Decision of 13/XII/2006 establishing a mechanism for cooperation and verification of progress in Romania to address specific benchmarks in the areas of judicial reforms and the fight against corruption', Available at: http://ec.europa.eu/enlargement/pdf/romania/ro_accompanying_measures_1206_en.pdf (accessed 4.2.2013). *See* in general, F. Emmert, 'Administrative and Court Reform in Central and Eastern Europe', 9 *European Law Journal* 3 (2003), pp. 288–315.

109 Superior Council of Magistracy, Report on Activity of Court in the first semester of 2012. Available at: http://www.csm1909.ro/csm/index.php?cmd=2301 (accessed 4.2.2013).

110 *Id.*, pp. 10,11.

111 European Commission, CVM Report Romania, February 2013. Available at: http://ec.europa.eu/cvm/docs/com_2013_47_en.pdf (accessed 4.2.2013), p. 8.

currently overseeing judicial reforms in Romania. Thus, it is a suggestion emerging from the supranational level. In the particular case, the affected courts relied on the internal organizational flexibility to deal with a big group of very similar cases. For example, a special unit would decide upon this group of cases on a given day of the week.

Another group of cases that has been causing a steady caseload for administrative courts was the restitution of, and compensation for properties that were nationalized before 1989. This is an ongoing and significant problem, seriously affecting the caseload of the courts as well as the functioning of the Romanian legal system. For instance, the European Court of Human Rights considered it a systemic problem,[112] which could not be solved for an extended period of time, resulting in numerous applications before the European court. Recently the European Court of Human Rights delivered a pilot judgment,[113] against Romania.[114] The existence of a pilot judgment of the European Court of Human Rights shows that there is a 'structural or general deficiency in national law or practice' that resulted in the fact that 'a large number of applications to the Court concerning the same problem ("repetitive") cases were pending or likely to be lodged'.[115] In this situation the ECtHR accepted that,

> in the complex and socially sensitive context of Romania's transition to democracy and the reparation of past injustices, which entailed far-reaching economic consequences, the establishment of a legislative framework may have encountered some difficulties and delays (*see* mutatis mutandis Broniowski v Poland [GC], no. 31443/ 96, Para. 162 ECHR 2004-V). Nevertheless, the administrative authorities' failure to respond to the restitution claims lodged under Laws nos. 112/1995 and 10/2001, combined with the lack of a remedy during the above-mentioned period, imposed a disproportionate burden on Mrs Atanasiu and Mrs Poenaru and thus impaired the very essence of their right to access a court.[116]

Following the pilot judgments of the European Court of Human Rights, the Romanian High Court of Cassation and Justice sitting as a full court, rendered a judgment in the interest of the uniform application of the law, on the passive procedural quality of the State in certain cases. National courts interpreted this quality in an inconsistent manner, creating uncertainty in the application of the law. The High Court of Cassation and Justice addressed this problem and also took into account the judgments of the European Court in this sense.[117]

Thus, organizational problems ultimately also created problems as regards the uniform application of law in this case, also affecting administrative litigation. For example, the High Court of Cassation and Justice sitting as a full court rendered that, in cases where the administrative

---

112 Council of Europe, Committee of Ministers, Resolution Res(2004)3 on judgments revealing an underlying systemic problem, 12 May 2004. Available at: https://wcd.coe.int/ViewDoc.jsp?id=743257&Lang=fr (accessed 8.4.2013).

113 Council of Europe, Committee of Ministers, Recommendation Rec(2004)6 on the improvement of domestic remedies, 12 May 2004. Available at: https://wcd.coe.int/ViewDoc.jsp?id=743317 (accessed 8.4.2013).

114 *See* European Court of Human Rights, Atanasiu and others v. Romania, Appl. nos. 30767/05 and 33800/06.

115 Council of Europe, Committee of Ministers, Recommendation Rec(2004)6 on the improvement of domestic remedies, 12 May 2004, Appendix, para. 13.

116 European Court of Human Rights, Atanasiu and Poenaru v. Romania, Appl. nos. 30767/05 and 33800/06, paras. 122, 123.

117 High Court of Cassation and Justice, Decision no. 14 of November 2011.

authorities do not respond to the applicant's claim within the period prescribed by the law, administrative courts become competent in deciding the matter.[118] As can be seen, the High Court of Cassation and Justice had to decide on both issues of access to courts but also on inconsistent application and interpretation of the law by the courts.

Lack of Expertise

Another practical problem related to adjudicating administrative law cases is the specialized nature of the field and also the rapid changes to which judges need to adapt – this may be a result of frequent legislative changes or the specialization required by national judges to directly apply European Union law. For the former, the continuous training system was meant to assure the expertise of judges in a number of fields. However, for example in the fields of social securities or public procurement, no or very limited training has been offered.[119] Applying European Union law, points to a more general problem of national judges' expertise in this separate and specialized field of law.[120] A detailed analysis falls outside the scope of the present chapter. Nevertheless, it remains an important issue to address when assessing the expertise, which is required of judges in administrative litigation.

Currently problems emerge with a lack of specialization in the fields of disputes over social securities or public procurement. In these fields, given the rapid pace of developments and legislative changes, an up-to-date expertise is required. The continuous training system attempts to fill this gap, although guaranteeing a trainer specialized in these fields also seems to be a challenge in practice. Therefore, guaranteeing the expertise of the judges in certain sub-fields of administrative law and flexibility in dealing with the increased case law of the courts is discussed as a solution to this problem.

Finally, irrespective of problems with guaranteeing expertise in sub-fields of administrative law or European Union law, there are no discussions of having specialized administrative courts in Romania. Although specialized courts for family law and commercial law have been introduced into the Romanian legal system,[121] this initiative has been abandoned. The discussion on the specialization of judges adjudicating administrative law cases is limited to their sufficient expertise in both national law and European Union law.

Concluding Remarks: Continued Improvements are Necessary

The purpose of the present analysis has been to present an overview of some underlying factors influencing the contemporary stance and developments in Romanian administrative litigation. The analysis points out some challenges for administrative litigation law and practice in Romania that need to be addressed in the future. The first challenge appears to be coordinating administrative

118 High Court of Cassation and Justice, Decision of 19 March 2007.

119 Superior Council of Magistracy, Report on the Activity of the Superior Council of Magistracy 2012. For example, in 2011 specialized training has been offered on the newly introduced codes of civil and criminal procedure, but not in specialized fields of administrative law. In the training schedule for 2012 and 2013 offered by the National Institute of Magistracy, there is at least one specialized training offered per year in public procurement and fighting corruption and a more general one on administrative law. Available at: http://www.inm-lex.ro/index.php?MenuID=141 (accessed 4.2.2013).

120 *See* U. Jaremba, *supra* note 34, pp. 319–322.

121 Law no. 304/2004 on Judicial Organization, Article 37.

litigation with alternative means of solving administrative disputes. In the case of administrative appeals, the lack of legal specifications for providing reasoning hinders the effectiveness of this procedure. However, the alternative offered by the institute of the Ombudsman in practice is not used to its full potential. Moreover, guaranteeing the fundamental principles for fulfilling the Ombudsman's role, such as the principle of independence, should not be taken for granted.

At the same time, similar to other fields of law, solving disputes in a timely manner and simplifying procedures, becomes a relevant aspect also for administrative litigation. The recommendations pointing to the increased role of simplified procedures from the European Commission are instructive in this sense.[122] Improving the implementation of the existent alternatives, as well as addressing shortcomings in the current legislative framework appear as important elements towards an effectively functioning and well-designed system of alternatives to administrative litigation.

Second, further steps in the Europeanization of Romanian administrative law are needed. This new role needs to be embraced and further accommodated in the activity of administrative units of the courts, which require both expertise and willingness. The national and supranational systems are becoming increasingly interwoven. Although the application of European principles can still be considered a novelty in Romanian administrative litigation, the increasing consideration that the new principles are given certainly show a positive trend.[123]

Nevertheless, this process requires an increased level of expertise and 'fluency' of judges in at least two legal orders, with that of the European human rights as an interrelated third. Achieving the necessary level of expertise is a challenge in several Member States and represents an ongoing dilemma. Furthermore, the application of European law in legal systems might also pose some practical constraints.

However, the inclusion of the European legal order in the national one displays an important potential. As it has been seen with the application of the principle of legal certainty, applying these novel principles might solve historical controversies in administrative litigation. The key to this potential remains to be sufficient expertise in the scope of application of the principles.

Finally, it remains crucial to comply with fundamental principles necessary for the proper functioning of administrative litigation. In particular, guaranteeing the principles of independence and legal certainty did not appear well emphasized in the practice of amending the law on administrative litigation or appointing the Ombudsman. Recent events point to some tensions between the political branches of the government and the courts, especially when it came to delimiting the scope of administrative litigation. Guaranteeing and further reflecting upon the basic principles of administrative litigation becomes relevant. The Romanian administrative law system – although it has a long tradition – given its hiatus during the Communist period, needed to be reinvented again in 1990. As a relatively new system, the application and the acceptance of some of the basic principles of administrative litigation remains an important point of focus for administrative litigation.

Romania might also serve to be a useful example of how to integrate legal culture into a relatively newly reconsidered and recreated system of administrative litigation. It shows some interesting trends on how to comply with possible external influences given these circumstances. Along the way of finding solutions that are functional according to the local legal culture, basic principles underlying new measures must not be forgotten. Among the future perspectives, guaranteeing fundamental principles in a liberal–democratic society must also not lose any ground.

122 European Commission, Cooperation and Verification Mechanism Report, February 2013. Available at: http://ec.europa.eu/cvm/docs/com_2013_47_en.pdf (accessed 8.4.2013), p. 3, 7.

123 D.C. Dragos, B. Neamtu, *supra* note 17, p. 90.

Appendix

Table 10.1 Chronology of Laws and Institutions on Administrative Litigation in Romania

1864	Legislation	Council of State was created.
1866		New constitution. The Council of State was abolished.
1867	Legislation	Judicial review of administrative acts was introduced into the Romanian legal system.
1865–1905	Legislation	Under common-law influence, jurisdiction was given to ordinary courts.
1910	Legislation	The Administrative Law section of the Cassation Court was discontinued.
1923	Legislation	New constitution.
1925	Legislation	New legislation on administrative litigation. Judicial review of the legality of administrative acts is possible for a breach of a right, not that of a legitimate interest.
1948	Legislation	The judicial review of administrative acts was abolished through Decree no. 128 of 1948.
1965	Legislation	Administrative litigation reintroduced.
1967	Legislation/grounds of review	New legislation on administrative litigation was adopted, with limited implementation in practice. Judicial review is possible through a direct review or through a direct procedure started at the court. For introducing a direct complaint against an administrative decision to courts it was required that the administrative act have an individual character; the exception of illegality is applicable for administrative decisions of a normative character.
1989		Democratic transition.
1990	Legislation/grounds of review	New legislation on administrative litigation. The requirement of the individual character of the administrative act is not maintained for judicial review, the administrative act can be in breach of a right or a legitimate interest.
1991	Legislation	New constitution.
1993	Grounds of review	Constitutional court decision no. 37/7/1993. The judicial review is possible for both administrative acts of an individual character as well as administrative acts of a general/normative character.
1994	Grounds of review	Constitutional Court decisions – 33/1994 and 34/1994.
1997	Legislation	The Romanian national Ombudsman institution was created by adopting Law no. 35/1997 (amended in 1998, 2002 and 2004).
1997	Jurisdiction	Administrative review is possible against any act issued by a public authority, not only an administrative authority. Romanian Constitutional Court Decision 97/1997. Ordinary courts are competent to review the administrative acts.
2002	Grounds of review	High Court of Cassation and Justice 3441/2002.

2003	Legislation/grounds of review	The Constitution was amended. In Article 52 a new legal basis was introduced for administrative litigation. Accordingly, a claim can be introduced in case of a breach of right or legitimate interest of an individual by a public authority.
2004	Legislation/grounds of review	New legislation for administrative litigation was adopted. Administrative review is possible not only for individual acts but also for general administrative acts (the notion of administrative act is defined and limited). The exception of illegality is applicable for both individual and general administrative acts.
2005	Grounds of review	High Court of Cassation and Justice decision no. 5455 of 2005 tries to limit the applicability of the exception of illegality to general administrative acts.
2007	Legislation	Amendment of the Law of Administrative Litigation.
2007		Romania becomes member of the European Union.
2007	Grounds of review	The High Court of Cassation accepts and introduces general principles of EU law in the Romanian administrative law system (legal certainty).
2008	Grounds of review	High Court of Cassation and Justice, Decision no. 2547 of 2008: a restrictive interpretation to the exception of illegality of individual administrative acts is given, not being applicable to decisions issued before the new legislation introducing this measure entered into force, by relying on the principle of legal certainty. Decisions following the same line of argumentation were 2786/2008 and 2885/2008.

Index

Note: data in tables and figures is indicated by page numbers in **bold**.

For Product Safety Concerns and Information please contact our EU representative GPSR@taylorandfrancis.com
Taylor & Francis Verlag GmbH, Kaufingerstraße 24, 80331 München, Germany

www.ingramcontent.com/pod-product-compliance
Ingram Content Group UK Ltd.
Pitfield, Milton Keynes, MK11 3LW, UK
UKHW050051200926
475702UK00019B/2772
* 9 7 8 1 1 3 8 6 3 7 6 3 4 *